POWER

AND

RESTRAINT

Jeff,
I hope you
enjoy it!

★

POWER

AND

RESTRAINT

THE RISE OF THE UNITED STATES

1898-1941

JEFFREY W. MEISER

GEORGETOWN UNIVERSITY PRESS
WASHINGTON, DC

Library of Congress Cataloging-in-Publication Data

Meiser, Jeffrey W., author
  Power and restraint : the rise of the United States, 1898–1941 / Jeffrey W. Meiser
    pages cm
  Includes bibliographical references and index.
  Summary: American foreign policy between the late nineteenth century and the beginning of World War II is anomalous from the perspective of international relations (IR) theory. During this period, the US was a rising power par excellence, but it did relatively little to transform this newfound power into global influence. Despite the dramatic increase in its economic power, the US maintained its traditional distaste for European modes of diplomacy and imperialism, and it failed to capitalize on many opportunities to expand its political-military power. This behavior runs counter to most thinking in IR throry, which is that rising states tend to become revisionist powers seeking to expand their influence and challenge the existing order. Jeffrey Meiser concludes that American strategic restraint was caused by democratic domestic political institutions and norms. This work is important for understanding more about the history of America's international relations, and it is also important for understanding how regime type in today's rising powers, namely China and India, is likely to shape the character and impact of their ascent in the international system.
  ISBN 978-1-62616-177-1 (alk. paper) — ISBN 978-1-62616-179-5 — ISBN 978-1-62616-178-8 (alk. paper)
  1. United States—Foreign relations—20th century. I. Title.
E744.M425 2015
327.73009'04—dc23

                                                                    2014023304

Cover design by Faceout Studio. Cover image: Aerial view of USS Arizona on the East River in New York City, 1918 / Library of Congress Prints and Photographs Division

♾ This book is printed on acid-free paper meeting the requirements of the American National Standard for Permanence in Paper for Printed Library Materials.

16 15   9 8 7 6 5 4 3 2   First printing

Printed in the United States of America

For Dinah

CONTENTS

TABLES

PREFACE

In 1894 Sir Arthur Conan Doyle published the Sherlock Holmes story "Silver Blaze," which became famous for a rather unusual piece of evidence: a dog that didn't bark. In the story, a prize thoroughbred went missing from its stable days before the Wessex Cup horse race. One piece of evidence that Holmes used to identify the thief was the observation that the dog in the stable did not bark during the burglary. Holmes inferred that the dog did not bark because he knew the thief. This inference narrowed the pool of suspects considerably and led Holmes to drastically revise his theory of the crime from outside job to inside job. International relations scholars, and political scientists in general, have not followed the example set by Sherlock Holmes. Too often we have missed out on opportunities to accumulate important evidence by ignoring dogs that didn't bark, or to use political science terminology, "negative cases." The reason for the exclusion of negative cases is probably due to the difficulty of proving why something did not happen. Identifying nonevents and then finding evidence to explain why they didn't happen is challenging, and in some cases quixotic. What is the evidentiary burden for establishing an expectation? How do you determine which factors caused a nonevent to not occur? There are no easy answers to these questions, but that does not excuse the lack of effort.

This book is a study of one particularly important nonbarking dog: the United States as a rising power. The United States, like other modern rising powers, should have implemented an aggressive, revisionist, expansionist grand strategy, but instead it implemented a grand strategy of restraint. This book documents my struggle to conceptualize and explain this puzzle in a relentlessly empirical, theoretically progressive, and practically relevant manner. I hope that my argument that the domestic structure—institutions and culture—is the most important cause of American restraint encourages others to take domestic structure more seriously in foreign policy analysis. While international relations scholarship is well known for its attention to the structure of the international system, I believe that scholars and practitioners would benefit more from a clear understanding of the various forms of domestic structure and a systematic investigation of how these different structures shape foreign policy and grand strategy.

Many generous individuals contributed to this project. I owe a lot to my thesis advisors at Johns Hopkins University: Steven David, Daniel Deudney, and Adam Sheingate. They were the perfect team, giving me enough feedback to keep me going in the right direction without imposing themselves on the project. I continue to benefit from their wisdom and friendship.

I would also like to thank the following people for reading and commenting on various versions or parts of the argument presented in this book: Hassan Abbas, Rameez Abbas, Thomaz Costa, Jason Davidson, Geoffrey Gresh, David Hendrickson, John Mearsheimer, Henry Nau, Barry Posen, Ariel Roth, Scott Silverstone, Brock Tessman, and Patrick Thaddeus Jackson. Ari Roth also provided moral support and gave me an opportunity to hone some of my ideas while teaching at the Global Security Studies MA Program at Johns Hopkins. Two anonymous reviewers provided many thoughtful suggestions and challenging questions that significantly improved the book. Don Jacobs, the international affairs editor at Georgetown University Press, made a variety of suggestions that have increased the clarity of my ideas and has been a pleasure to work with throughout the publication process. Despite all this help, flaws remain, which are my responsibility. The ideas communicated in this book do not represent the views of any employer, past or present.

The achievement that this book represents would be meaningless if I didn't have a loving and supportive family to share it with. Dinah has been more patient with my slow process as a graduate student and junior professor than I had any right to expect. I could not have made it to this point without her support. Henry is too young to read this book, but I hope someday he will read it and be proud of his father.

INTRODUCTION

Of all manifestations of power, restraint impresses men most.
—COLIN POWELL quoting Thucydides

IN 1898 THE UNITED STATES OF AMERICA stood on the cusp of world empire. It was a country on the rise and everybody knew it. The United States had the largest economy on the planet and US economic growth was outpacing all other great powers.[1] On the domestic political front, the North and South had established a modus vivendi and the continental frontier was officially closed, causing many Americans to look abroad for new strategic and economic opportunities. The proexpansionist Republican Party dominated the executive branch, which meant that American leaders were open to ideas about new uses of American power abroad. Regionally, the United States was surrounded by weak and failing states and empires, which provided the opportunity and justification for expansion. Internationally, the dynamics of interstate competition and international norms favored expansion: the imperatives of realpolitik and ideological tenets of social Darwinism and the white man's burden formed a heady mixture of self-interested and idealistic motives for imperialism. A particularly American form of expansionist ideas, referred to as "large policy," was justified for strategic, economic, and cultural reasons, drawing on the traditional American goals of keeping Europeans out of the Western Hemisphere, maintaining economic expansion by gaining access to new markets, and the newfound desire to promote American values and institutions abroad.

In other words, the United States exhibited all the characteristics we have come to associate with rising powers: increasing relative power, growing external interests, the emergence of domestic rationales for expansion, and an expanded concept of security. The question is whether the American experience after 1898 is consistent with the expectations of international relations theories of

Colin Powell famously had this quote prominently displayed in his office when he was Chairman of the Joint Chiefs of Staff. However, it is not a direct quotation from Thucydides, but instead the quote "faithfully paraphrases Nicias' speech in Book Six (chap. 11) of The Peloponnesian War" (Hornblower and Stewart 2005, 269.)

rising power grand strategy. International relations theory predicts that rising powers will become revisionist states seeking to expand their influence, conquer new territory, and challenge the existing international order. This expectation is largely confirmed by the historical record of other rising powers of the modern era, including Great Britain, Japan, Germany, and the USSR. These countries went to war to conquer large swaths of territory, both at the periphery and at the center of the international system. Randall Schweller provides the best summary of our expectations for the behavior of rising powers:

> As states grow wealthier and more powerful, they not only seek greater world-wide political influence (control over territory, the behavior of other states, and the world economy) commensurate with their new capabilities; they are also more capable of expanding their interests and, if necessary, of waging large-scale, hegemonic wars to revise drastically or overthrow entirely the established order. Simply put, the stronger and richer a state becomes, the more influence it wants and the more willing and able it will be to fight to further its interests.[2]

Did the American experience in the early twentieth century follow the predictions of theory and the pattern of history? Does US behavior in the late nineteenth and early twentieth centuries match the description in Schweller's quote? Conventional wisdom and the weight of scholarly opinion say yes.[3] In 1898, the United States became embroiled in a foreign war and emerged victorious with spoils that included several new colonies: the Philippines, Puerto Rico, and Guam. Subsequent foreign policy decisions seem to reinforce this expansionist trend. Under Theodore Roosevelt the United States proclaimed its authority to exercise police power in the Western Hemisphere. President Taft's "dollar diplomacy" is synonymous with the American drive for regional hegemony. Woodrow Wilson infamously proclaimed that it was the duty of the United States to show Latin America how to elect good men, by force if necessary.[4] However, a closer look reveals that American grand strategy was more restrained than commonly believed, particularly relative to other great powers of this era. One simple measure of US restraint is the level of colonial territory it accrued compared to other great powers: by 1913, the United States claimed 310,000 square km of colonial territory, compared to 350,000 for Spain, 2,360,000 for Belgium, 2,940,000 for Germany, and 32,860,000 for the United Kingdom (see Table I.1). This disparity only increased over time, especially compared to other rising powers. While the United States was systematically liquidating its protectorates in the 1920s and 1930s, Japan was conquering most of East and Southeast Asia, and Germany was establishing its European Empire.

The purpose of this book is to take a closer look at the puzzle of American underexpansion—or why the United States expanded so little during its rise. In an examination of 34 cases of potential or actual expansion between 1898 and

TABLE i.1
Selected Economic Statistics, 1900–1950

	1880		1900		1913		1938		GDP Growth Rates (1870–1913)	GDP Growth Rates (1913–1950)	Area of Colonies in 1913
	GDP	% of World Manufacturing Output	GDP	% of World Manufacturing Output	GDP	% of World Manufacturing Output	GDP	% of World Manufacturing Output			
USA	161,095	14.7	312,866	23.5	517,990	32.0	800,295	31.4	3.94	2.84	310
Japan	—	2.4	50,045	2.4	68,933	—	169,367	3.8	2.44	2.21	290
Germany	52,950	8.5	99,227	13.2	145,068	14.8	220,359	12.7	2.83	0.30	2,940
Italy	45,669	2.5	58,799	2.5	93,399	2.4	140,833	2.8	1.94	1.49	1,530
Russia/ USSR	—	7.6	154,049	8.8	232,351	8.2	405,220	9.0	2.40	2.15	—
France	82,011	7.8	115,645	6.8	143,125	6.1	185,633	4.4	1.63	1.15	10,590
UK	114,953	22.9	176,504	18.5	214,464	13.6	284,165	10.7	1.90	1.19	32,860

GDP: in million 1990 Geary-Khamis Dollars (Maddison 1995, 180–183, 186–187).
Percent of World Manufacturing Output (Kennedy 1987, 149, 202); except for Japan in 1938 (Schweller 1998, 205).
GDP Growth Rates (Maddison 2001, 187, 217) (the Russia/USSR entry includes all the territory of the USSR).
Area of Colonies in 1,000 sq. km. (Bairoch 1993, 83).

1941, the main finding is that in almost every case US expansion was either delayed, rejected, or more limited in scope and duration than one would expect given the interests and power advantage of the United States. In addition, many of the cases of expansion resulted in significant backlash and eventually retrenchment (i.e., reversal of territorial expansion). The cumulative effect of this delay, limitation, prevention, backlash, and retrenchment was an American policy of strategic restraint.

The United States exhibited a grand strategy of restraint between 1898 and 1941 because the political structure of the United States prevented the mobilization of resources and the centralization of state power necessary for the successful implementation of an expansionist and revisionist grand strategy. In case after case, large-policy advocates attempted to use prominent positions in the executive branch, Congress, and the private sector to transform the traditional US foreign policy from strategic restraint to strategic expansionism characterized by increased political–military control of foreign territory (or more simply territorial expansion). But the strategic culture and political institutions of the United States consistently acted as a restraint on new ideas about the strategic direction of the United States. Separation of powers, anti-imperialist norms, and a geographically decentralized electoral system restrained American expansion during the initial drive for imperialism and fostered rollback of the limited expansion that did occur. More specifically, Congress frequently opposed executive branch expansionist attempts through its treaty, appropriations, and investigative powers, as well as their informal power to shape press coverage and public opinion through public statements, nonbinding resolutions, and by simply introducing legislation. Congressional action sometimes led public opinion, but more often was a response to an American public that was skeptical of territorial expansion. The anti-imperialist elements of American strategic culture ensured that a significant portion of the American public would oppose expansionist policies and that an even larger portion of the American public would only support expansion that was cheap, easy, and could be construed as somehow consistent with anti-imperialism. Because it was believed that Americans would express their concerns over imperialism at the ballot box, anti-imperialist norms provided rhetorical weapons to leaders and advocacy groups that opposed American expansionism. From their base in New England (and sometimes the South and Midwest), anti-imperialists maintained constant pressure on the executive branch. Restraint also originated from the executive branch through presidents' perception of American interests and values and the presidents' own self-interest and values. Presidents like Wilson, Harding, Hoover, and Franklin Delano Roosevelt were personally opposed to imperialism and therefore, at times, exercised self-restraint. Others, like Theodore Roosevelt and Taft, were forced to suppress their imperial instincts in order to win elections.

The relative importance of separation of powers, anti-imperialist norms, and electoral federalism changed over time. From 1898 to 1913, anti-imperialist norms and checks and balances played the most important roles in causing restraint through the mechanisms of anti-imperialist public opinion and opposition in Congress to the policies of the executive branch. The anti-imperialist sentiment of at least a large minority of the US citizenry found a voice among Democrats and a few prominent Republicans, who maintained their influence on American foreign policy through Congress. The divided foreign policy powers of the American system, especially the advise and consent treaty power of the Senate, created a check on the expansionist policies of the executive branch. Anti-imperialist sentiment also influenced foreign policy through presidential elections. It was dangerous for any national political leader to embrace territorial expansionism, because of the dissonance it created with most Americans. Anti-imperialism and nonintervention never became the primary issue of concern for a majority of Americans, but at critical junctures public opinion was mobilized to restrain American foreign policy. The charge of imperialism was consistently viewed as a powerful rhetorical weapon to use against presidents who presided over increased control over foreign territory.

After 1913, a shift in the dynamics of restraint occurred. The incentives for Congress to oppose expansionist policies of Democratic president Woodrow Wilson were weaker than under Republican presidents for two reasons. First, Democrats in Congress had a political incentive to support the policies of their copartisan in the executive branch. Second, most Republicans in Congress were torn over supporting expansionist policies they favored and taking the opportunity to criticize military interventions as imperialistic. Thus from 1913 to 1920 institutional restraints were relatively weak, which meant that normative restraints played a more important role. The central mechanisms of restraint during this period were public opinion, President Wilson's perception of American norms (i.e., what kind of foreign policy was appropriate for the United States), and Wilson's own personal commitment to anti-imperialism.

Beginning in the 1920s, the drive for American expansionism had been almost totally dissipated by the constant counterpressure of domestic restraint. The return of the Republican Party to power in 1921 did not auger a return to the expansionist drive of the Roosevelt and Taft era, because it had become conventional wisdom that the American people did not support imperial adventures. With the emergence of Franklin D. Roosevelt's Good Neighbor policy in the 1930s, political–military expansionism was officially repudiated. During the 1920s and 1930s some influential individuals and groups still argued for political–military expansionism—and some presidents were tempted by these arguments—but public opinion, electoral calculations, and separation of powers effectively restrained the executive.

Concepts and Definitions

This section defines, discusses, and defends the central concepts used throughout this book.[5] My aim is to use commonsense, straightforward language where possible. However, in some cases the political science literature is a bit obtuse, and some jargon must be discussed and utilized in order to fully engage with the existing literature. In other cases the lack of clear definitions requires me to provide my own definitions for some key terms.

Rising Powers

Rising powers can be conceptualized in a variety of ways. In much of the international relations literature, the term "rising power" is used without being clearly defined, even when it is a central to the main argument of a book or essay.[6] One of the better definitions of rising power is given by Woosang Kim and James Morrow in their widely cited article "When Do Power Shifts Lead to War?" They define rising powers as states going through a "power shift," defined as "predictable, long-run changes in relative capabilities as opposed to transitions, the moment when one nation's capabilities surpass another's."[7] This basic definition captures the key characteristic of a rising power: the long-run increase in relative capabilities. I build on this definition by adding a second foundational element that allows us to identify nation-states that are most likely to significantly affect world politics. A long-run change in relative capabilities only matters when the rising state changes the hierarchy of world power. For example, we don't care much if Peru becomes more powerful than Qatar or if Fiji becomes more powerful than Togo. But we care a lot if China passes the United States. With these factors in mind, I define a rising power as a nation-state on a long-term growth trajectory that is moving up in the hierarchy of states from secondary power to great power or from great power to hegemon. In other words, by definition, rising powers have a significant effect on the hierarchy of power in the international system. This definition suggests two subtypes. The first subtype of rising power is emerging power, and the second subtype is potential hegemon (see Table I.2). States transitioning from secondary to great power are emerging powers, and great powers that are transitioning to hegemon are potential hegemons. Emerging powers seek to dominate their neighborhoods and gain the recognition as a great power. Potential hegemons seek to go beyond their neighborhoods to dominate the core of the international system and achieve recognition as hegemon.[8] Using these definitions, in the 1850s and 1860s the United States is an emerging power (it passed Germany in the early 1850s), and after the 1870s the United States is a potential hegemon as it passes Great Britain, the leading power in the international system.

TABLE I.2
Definitions of Rising Powers

Type of Rising Power	Defining Characteristics	Predicted Behavior
Emerging powers	States that are moving from secondary to great powers	Regionally focused territorial expansion and a demand for great power status
Potential hegemons	States that are moving from great powers to hegemons	Attempt to dominate the international system by replacing the existing hegemon and transform the international order

Relative economic power—measured in relative GDP—is the best way to designate a rising power because it reflects a long-term increase in the capacity of a nation-state relative to other great powers.[9] Other potential measures either produce results very similar to relative GDP, or measure something other than long-term power shifts.[10] For example, the size of a country's military seems to be a less important measure of whether a nation-state is rising or falling. First, changes in military spending can occur rapidly, and therefore this does not seem to be very useful for determining long-run changes in relative power. Second, military spending is likely to correlate with GDP over the long run and therefore does not add much to our understanding of which states are rising and falling. The same is true of energy consumption, the output of steel, and so on. Third, military spending is a policy output rather than a policy input. In other words, military spending is the result of a policy decision rather than an independent measure of the overall material power of a nation-state.

Expansion and Restraint

A second set of concepts helps to distinguish between two general grand strategy orientations: expansion and restraint.[11] Expansion in the context of grand strategy is simply an increase in influence. From this simple definition it is possible to increase specificity by adding modifiers to form types of expansion such as economic, cultural, and political expansion. One could also label expansion in terms of motivation—that is, revisionist, opportunistic, or stabilizing expansion. For the purposes of this book we are most interested in political–military expansion or territorial expansion. Political–military expansion is an increase in the degree of control over foreign territory and accretion of powers that undermine the sovereignty of foreign states.[12] Robert Gilpin argues that a rising power will tend "to demand a larger bundle of welfare and security objectives" and that the two primary objectives of a rising power are "the conquest of territory in order to advance economic, security, and other interests" and "to increase their influence over the behavior of other states."[13] Both of these objectives are encapsulated by the term political–military expansion.

I have chosen the level of expansion and restraint as the focus of this book instead of the equally common but significantly more complicated term "revisionism." Drawing on the work of classical realists, Jason Davidson provides a useful definition of revisionism. Revisionists are defined as "states that seek to change the distribution of goods (territory, status, markets, expansion of ideology, and the creation or change of international law and institutions)" in the international system.[14] While any of the goods listed in the definition could be used to measure revisionism, the type of revisionism that matters most is the territorial kind—political–military expansion. Political–military expansion is the key signifier for revisionism because it demonstrates a willingness to mobilize vast resources and risk war to change the status quo. There is a widespread agreement that territorial conflicts are "more prone to militarized conflict behavior," "more escalatory," and "more difficult to resolve" than other conflicts.[15] Furthermore, "territorial disputes are the most prevalent issue that leads to war and can also be a leading cause of state death."[16] In short, territorial disputes make states more war-prone, and since territorial expansion inherently involves territorial disputes, all things being equal, expansionist states will tend to be more war-prone. Political–military expansion is therefore the most risky type of expansion and demonstrates a high level of commitment to changing the status quo. Furthermore, even among industrialized countries, conquest can deliver benefits to the conquering state and is therefore a component of a power maximization strategy that, according to realists, should trigger balancing by other nation-states.[17]

While most international relations scholarship on rising powers emphasizes the importance of revisionism, the focus of this text is on the element of revisionism that is most important from the perspective of international security and the national security of status quo states: political–military expansion. In fact, it is the territorial expansionism (and the concomitant war-proneness) of rising powers that is the real concern of international relations scholars and national security practitioners, not revisionism in the abstract. With these arguments in mind, the remainder of this book will refer to territorial or political–military expansionism as the main threat that arises from rising powers.

The opposite of expansion is restraint. Generally the term "restraint" refers to some form of limitation on behavior. Often restraint is used to specify a situation where inaction occurs despite a context favorable to action or the opportunity to act.[18] In its clearest form, restraint is inaction despite a strong incentive to act. In world politics, restraint is measured in terms of an unwillingness to use a material power advantage to make gains at the expense of other states. It is a relative rather than an absolute measure of a state's grand strategy. Thus the analyst has to compare the opportunities for expansion to the state's actual foreign policy to measure the level of restraint. Restraint is determined by the overall pattern of behavior by a country, and is judged relative to other similar countries. Restraint should be conceptualized along a spectrum that ranges from lack of expansion to limited expansion, to delayed expansion to backlash against expansion (which makes future expansion less likely), to retrenchment of previous expansion. Restraint cannot be measured without first identifying opportunities for expansion, which requires a theory of expansion (described in the next chapter). For the purposes of this book, the two strongest forms of restraint are the absence of territorial expansion despite clear opportunities and incentives for expansion, and the reversal of territorial gains from previous episodes of expansion (also referred to as retrenchment). Delayed expansion is the coding for a case where restraints prevent the expansionist effort from being implemented long enough to force expansionists to expend additional resources to achieve their goal. Limited expansion is the coding for cases where restraints cause expansionists to achieve significantly less political–military expansion than they intended. Backlash is operationalized as occurring in cases where negative reaction to an expansionist effort decreases the probability of subsequent expansion.

Backlash typically occurs when the public changes its view of US government policy. Changes in perception occur when policies that were formerly viewed as benign become viewed as imperialistic or in some other way improper. Changes in perception also occur when policy is seen as a failure. In other words, incompetent expansionism can cause backlash, as can expansionism that rules a people despite their dissent.[19] The importance of limited expansion and backlash should be clear. Limited expansion means that expansion is partially prevented. Any case coded as limited expansion must exhibit a significant difference between what expansionists hope to achieve and what they actually achieve. Backlash imposes political costs on expansionists as public opinion turns against expansionist actions, which discourages future acts of expansionism. The importance of delayed expansion may be less clear. Delayed expansion provides anti-imperialists time to mobilize opposition to expansion, allows the press and public to become informed about the proposed expansion, may diffuse interest in a given expansionist policy (especially if expansionist preferences are weakly held and the delay is long), and may allow for new elections to change the balance of power within the legislative and execute branches. The general importance of all three outcomes is that they send a message to expansionists that their goals cannot be easily achieved, and that the achievement of their goals is going to be costly.

Grand Strategy and Foreign Policy

Both grand strategy and foreign policy are ways to refer to the behavior of nation-states. Foreign policy is the behavior of a nation-state in the international realm. Grand strategy is often defined as the long-term plan political leaders and their advisors develop to guide foreign policy. The term is used differently in this book. Here, grand strategy is defined as the long-term pattern of behavior of a nation-state.[20] It can be the result of a well thought out plan, or it can simply be the pattern that emerges from the day-to-day practice of foreign policymaking. At first thought it may seem that this definition goes against the fundamental meaning of grand strategy; however, in practice, we refer to the grand strategy of containment having been effective (using the term as synonymous for an overall foreign policy plan) and to the evolution of the grand strategy of containment as the actual shift in the behavior of the United States (using the term as synonymous with the long-term pattern of foreign policy). This definition of grand strategy allows for the possibility that the long-term pattern of a state's foreign policy may be unplanned or even contrary to the stated national doctrine of a country. Grand strategy is an outcome; no assumption is made about whether it is an intended or unintended outcome. Therefore, strategic restraint is restraint at the strategic level and not necessarily the result of a well thought out plan.

Research Design

Two questions drive my research: What theory best explains American strategic restraint from the 1890s to World War II? Why do some rising powers implement territorially expansionist grand strategies and some implement grand strategies of strategic restraint? Answering these questions requires the use of several complementary methodological tools. Before describing these tools, it is important to specify the main assumption underlying my methodology: the best way to answer the research questions above is to identify the causal mechanisms that produced American strategic restraint. The focus on causal mechanisms is an epistemological position supported by a large body of philosophy of science scholarship.[21] This approach is based on the "historian's method of causal imputation . . . [which] differs from the mode of causal inference in statistical-correlational studies."[22] Causal analysis is less concerned with issues like degrees of freedom and significance tests, and more concerned with establishing what actually happened in a particular relevant case. Thus it is more important to establish a causal chain linking the independent and dependent variables than to seek to multiply the number of cases to create a large number of data points. The methodological tools I used in this project are summarized below.

Methodology

Process tracing is the primary form of analysis used in this study because it is the best method for following a chain of causation and identifying causal mechanisms.[23] Once causal mechanisms are identified it is possible to determine which theory offers the best explanation for a given event—that is, the best accounts for the causal mechanisms and outcomes. This process begins with the identification of hypotheses (predicted outcomes) and causal mechanisms (predicted processes) derived from the theory or theories being tested or developed.[24] Not only should the observed behavior in question be consistent with the theoretically derived hypotheses, but the reasons for that behavior and the mechanisms that cause that behavior should also be consistent with the causal mechanism specified by the theory. Furthermore, the number and size of the predicted processes and outcomes should be congruent with the number and size of the causal phenomena. For example, if theory predicts that a rising power will implement grand strategies of political–military expansionism because of capability-status mismatches, then a very large increase in power should lead to a high level of territorial expansion with evidence that political leaders are pursuing expansion to increase the status of their country.

The research design for this project is also reliant on the comparative method and counterfactual analysis. A comparison between the United States and other modern rising powers is necessary to show that American grand strategy during the period of study is anomalous, and helps identify the causal mechanisms that explain the variance in the dependent variable (grand strategy). First, the set of modern rising powers must be established. According to the definition given above, modern rising powers must exhibit the following: long-run economic growth, upward movement in the ranks of great powers, and industrialized economy. Following these criteria, modern rising powers include: (1) Great Britain, 1830s–early 1900s; (2) Japan, 1868–1945; (3) Germany, 1870–1944 (primarily the mid-1800s–1918 and 1930s–1945); (4) USSR, early 1930s–early 1940s; and (5) the United States, 1853–1941.[25] In Table I.1, descriptive statistics are used to compare the changing relative position of great powers in the international system (the distribution of power) and to show their level of territorial expansion. Since most cases of rising powers grand strategy appear to be adequately explained by existing theory, these cases are used to establish the normal or average behavior of a rising power, characterized as highly expansionist and revisionist.[26] This analysis sets the stage for comparing the US case with the average situation of modern rising powers.[27] The US case is subject to a detailed analysis that allows me to identify why it did not behave as a normal rising power.

Counterfactual analysis is crucial to the overall conceptualization of the research design for this project. First, the logic of counterfactual analysis provides the basis for the argument of this book. I seek to explain why something didn't happen. To do this I must shift attention from the factual (what did actually happen) to the counterfactual (what should have happened, according to the predictions of theory and pattern of history).[28] Second, each of the thirty-four cases covered in this book follows the same logic, only on a smaller scale. In the case studies, counterfactual analysis allows for the identification of critical

junctures and helps to evaluate the casual importance of the independent variables.[29] By using detailed knowledge of the cases, it is possible to identify critical
decisions or events that could have plausibly created a different history from
what actually occurred. Counterfactuals are most useful when historical actors
actually debated different courses of action and the decision was a close call. In
my analysis, counterfactual analysis cannot be used to determine what might
have been if the United States had a completely different set of institutions. This
would violate the "minimal rewrite of history" rule of counterfactual analysis.[30]
However, counterfactuals can be used to determine what might have been if
Congress did not veto specific presidential proposals for increased expansionism
or if US public opinion (rooted in strategic culture) had shifted to decisively
favor expansionism.

The above methods are strengthened by choosing to focus on a case that is
"deviant" and "crucial."[31] The United States as a rising power is deviant because
international relations theorists generally predict that rising powers will be revisionist. It is a crucial case for the domestic structure approach because the
United States has a particularly high level of institutional and normative
restraint; if US institutions and norms did not restrain its grand strategy, then a
theory based on domestic restraints suffers considerable damage. It is also a crucial case for theories that predict that an increase in material power will lead to
revisionism and expansionism (e.g., power transition theory, neoclassical realism) because the United States grew the most and the fastest during the modern
era and therefore should have been the most revisionist and expansionist great
power in modern history.

Case Selection

Most of this book is devoted to a combination of comparative analysis and
within-case process tracing of the United States, covering 34 cases of potential
American political-territorial expansion (see Table I.3). These 34 cases were
chosen to represent virtually the entire population of cases.[32] In selecting the
cases I follow the "possibility principle" as defined by Mahoney and Goertz:
"Only cases where the outcome of interest is possible should be included in the
set of negative cases; cases where the outcome is impossible should be relegated
to a set of uninformative and hence irrelevant observations."[33] Applying this
principle, I identified each case where territorial expansion was reasonably likely
by applying the criteria that (1) policymakers had to actually consider implementing expansionist policies and (2) we have a theoretical rationale for believing expansion is likely. The main types of evidence used are public and private
statements of policymakers and the judgment of experts on the history of American foreign policy. To the extent that cases are excluded, the missing cases would
likely favor nonexpansion. It is easy to identify cases of expansion, but difficult

TABLE I.3
Summary of Cases and Outcomes

Case	Outcome[1]	Explanation	Causes of Restraint
1. Teller Amendment (1898)	Restraint	Law passes prohibiting the annexation of Cuba	Congressional opposition
2. Annexation of Hawaii (1898)	Delayed expansion	Territorial gain after decades of interest and several failed attempts at annexation	Congressional opposition
3. Annexation of the Philippines, Puerto Rico, and Guam (1898)	Delayed expansion	Territorial gain after intense, conflictive domestic debate	Congressional opposition and public opinion
4. The Philippine-American War: extending control over the Philippines (1899–1902)	Delayed expansion and backlash	War for control of Philippines that marks the founding of the American anti-imperialist movement	Congressional opposition, public opinion, electoral concerns
5. Boxer War and occupation of Beijing (1900–1901)	Limited expansion	Multinational intervention to reestablish stability; US passed on opportunities to establish bases or concession in China	Fear of public and congressional opposition, security concerns, electoral concerns
6. American occupation of Cuba and the Platt Amendment (1899–1901)	Delayed and limited expansion	Establishment of Cuban protectorate, but annexation rejected	Public opinion, electoral concerns, and congressional opposition
7. Acquisition of the Panama Canal Zone (1901–1903)	Delayed expansion and backlash	US gained rights to the Canal Zone after decades of debate; Roosevelt subsequently accused of imperialism	Congressional opposition and public opinion
8. Customs receivership and rejected protectorate in the Dominican Republic (1904–1907)	Delayed and limited expansion	After three years of debate a formal customs receivership was established, but protectorate status was rejected	Congressional opposition and public opinion

TABLE I.3 (Continued)

Case	Outcome[1]	Explanation	Causes of Restraint
9. Intervention in Cuba (1906–1909)	Limited expansion	Limited military occupation to establish political stability, although some called for a long-term occupation	Fear of congressional and public opposition, electoral costs, and international opposition
10. Attempts to strengthen US position in the Philippines (1907)	Restraint	Roosevelt's attempt to invest in the economy and security of the Philippines rejected by Congress	Congressional and public opposition
11. Informal customs receivership in Liberia (1910)	Delayed and limited expansion	Informal customs receivership through US banking consortium established because of Senate rejection of formal control	Congressional opposition
12. Failed customs receivership in Honduras (1911–1912)	Restraint	Customs receivership rejected by legislatures in both countries	Congressional opposition
13. Nicaragua intervention (1910)	Limited expansion	Limited intervention in Nicaraguan civil war to protect foreign lives and property and somewhat inadvertently aided the rebels	Fear of congressional opposition
14. Rejected customs receivership and rejected protectorate in Nicaragua (1910–1911)	Restraint	Short-term, informal customs receivership established after Senate rejected formal control	Congressional opposition
15. Intervention in Nicaragua (1912)	Expansion and backlash	American marines deployed to protect lives and property and defeat rebellion; subsequent Senate investigation undermined the popularity of "dollar diplomacy"	Congressional opposition caused backlash

TABLE I.3 (Continued)

Case	Outcome[1]	Explanation	Causes of Restraint
16. Occupation of Veracruz (1914)	Limited expansion	Short-term occupation of Veracruz, Mexico; goals reduced after public opposition emerges in US and Mexico	Public opinion, world opinion, and leader values
17. Intervention and occupation of Haiti (1915–1916)	Expansion	Chronic political instability triggered military intervention and occupation	N/A
18. Occupation of the Dominican Republic (1916–1924)	Expansion	Chronic political instability triggered military intervention and occupation	N/A
19. Nicaragua customs receivership and rejected protectorate (1916–1917)	Delayed and limited expansion	The Senate rejected two attempts to establish a protectorate over Nicaragua, but did agree to a de facto American customs receivership	Congressional opposition
20. Invasion of Northern Mexico (1916–1917)	Limited expansion	Temporary military incursion carefully limited by Wilson	Leader values and public opinion
21. Political intervention in Cuba (1917–1921)	Limited expansion	Attempt to establish political and economic stability through presidential envoy	Leader values and public opinion
22. Push to intervene in Mexico (1919)	Restraint	Wilson rejected push for intervention by Congress and State Department	Leader values and presidential opposition
23. Attempted increase in financial oversight in Liberia (1922)	Restraint	Senate rejected proposed customs receivership and loan	Congressional opposition
24. The "moral readjustment" of Cuba (1923)	Limited expansion	Attempt to reform Cuban politics ends after loan approved	Public opinion and electoral incentives

TABLE I.3 (Continued)

Case	Outcome[1]	Explanation	Causes of Restraint
25. Withdrawal from Dominican Republic (1924)	Retrenchment	Public opinion and personal belief in nonintervention led Harding to end US military occupation	Public opinion, congressional support, and leader values
26. Withdrawal from Nicaragua (1925)	Retrenchment	The US withdrew its remaining marines when political stability was established	Public opinion and electoral incentives, US national interests
27. Nonintervention in Mexico (1925)	Restraint	A push for intervention by interest groups and the executive branch restrained by Congress	Congressional and public opposition
28. Occupation of Nicaragua (1926–1927)	Limited expansion	A new series of rebellions led to another US intervention, but opposition led to quick search for exit strategy	Congressional, public, and world opposition
29. Nonintervention in the Dominican Republic (1930–1931)	Restraint	US failed to intervene when Trujillo used unconstitutional means to gain power	US and Latin American public opinion and leader values
30. Withdrawal from Nicaragua (1933)	Retrenchment	A grueling guerilla war and public opposition led the US to withdraw its military forces	Congressional, public and world opposition, leader values
31. Withdrawal from Haiti (1934)	Retrenchment	After an 18-year occupation, increased congressional and public opposition after 1929 led to the US withdrawal	Public opinion, congressional opposition, world opinion, leader values
32. Nonintervention in Cuba (1933)	Restraint	Roosevelt resisted calls for a military intervention after a series of coups in Cuba	Public opinion, congressional opposition, world opinion, US national interests

TABLE I.3 (Continued)

Case	Outcome[1]	Explanation	Causes of Restraint
33. Nonintervention in Mexico (1938–1940)	Restraint	Mexico nationalized oil industry, but public, Congress, high-ranking officials, and President Roosevelt sought compromise not confrontation	Leader values, public opinion, congressional opposition, world opinion
34. Nonintervention in Central America (1936)	Restraint	US failed to act after dictators took power in Nicaragua and El Salvador	Leader values, public opinion, congressional opposition, world opinion

to identify cases of nonexpansion. Nonevents can be very useful, but are often ignored and thus are less likely to be the subject of historical analysis.[34]

Scope of the Project: Selection Bias?

For some, the narrative of this book will seem truncated. It seems quite convenient that this project begins after the era of Manifest Destiny and before the American Century. What about American grand strategy before 1898? What about American grand strategy after World War II? This section addresses both questions.

American Grand Strategy before 1898

American grand strategy between its founding and the Spanish-American War should be divided into two distinct periods: a period of unabashed continental expansion (1787–1865) and a period of unambiguous external restraint (1865–1898). Taking the latter first, Fareed Zakaria demonstrates that American grand strategy between the US Civil War and 1898 is marked by high levels of strategic restraint.[35] Zakaria does an excellent job of summarizing the political dynamics of this period, and therefore it seems unnecessary to repeat this analysis. The period from 1787 to 1865 is a bit trickier. This was the golden age of American territorial expansionism, but the United States does not become a rising power until after around 1853, the point at which the country enters the great power club (at least in terms of relative economic power).[36] Since expansion prior to the beginning of the international rise of the United States is not relevant to a study of rising powers, the pre-1853 period of US diplomatic history is irrelevant.

This book only addresses the causes of and restraints on rising power expansionism and its arguments and findings are not necessarily relevant to expansion by other kinds of powers, including the antebellum United States.[37]

The only clear example of American expansion at the expense of a foreign country during the antebellum period is the Mexican-American War (1846–1848). This is the exception that proves the rule. The war was started through the duplicity of President Polk and ended up being a major subject of controversy, with many members of Congress opposing the war from the outset or disavowing their initial support, especially members of the Whig Party.[38] The war took longer and was much more costly than President Polk and most Americans expected. As the initial war-inspired nationalism wore off, many Americans turned against the conflict.[39] Even after its successful conclusion and accompanying territorial gains, the war remained controversial and was a central underlying cause of the Civil War that came close to tearing the country apart.[40] The Mexican-American War was a war of imperialism, presidential aggrandizement, and factionalism, which is why it was "the most reviled [war] in American history—at least until the Vietnam war of the 1960s."[41]

American Grand Strategy after 1941

The start of World War II was chosen as the cutoff point for the narrative, because by the 1940s the United States was no longer a rising power. This project is a study of rising power grand strategy, with a special interest in the behavior of rising powers when a clear, intense security threat is absent. In other words, the objective is to control for external threat as a determinate of grand strategy as much as possible in order to isolate the effect of an increase in material power on grand strategy. These conditions are not met for the United States after World War II. The post–World War II era is dominated by the Cold War, characterized by intense security competition between two peer competitors. Therefore after World War II, our questions and theoretical lenses must change.[42]

The purpose of this study is to determine what factors best explain the grand strategies of rising powers, with an emphasis on the question of whether an increase in power alone is enough to cause a state to become aggressively expansionist and revisionist. With respect to the American case, this purpose sets the potential temporal parameters of this study as approximately the 1850s to the 1940s. The specific interval of 1898 to 1941 is appropriate because of previous work on the period between the Civil War and the Spanish-American War.

Organization of the Book

The remainder of the book is organized as follows. Chapter 1 develops a theory of expansion and a theory of restraint. The theory of expansion brings together various strands of international relations scholarship to construct a set of propositions that tell us when expansion is likely. The domestic structural theory of restraint identified above is described in greater detail in chapter 1. Alternative theories of restraint are also discussed.

Chapter 2 provides an in-depth analysis of the nonannexation of Cuba, annexation of Hawaii, and annexation of the Philippines, Puerto Rico, and Guam. This chapter is crucial for describing the sources of American incentives for expansion and for showing that even during the period with the highest level of territorial expansion by the United States, the institutional restraints of separation of powers and normative restraints of anti-imperialism exercised a powerful influence on American grand strategy. Chapter 3 covers five cases ranging from the causes and dynamics of the Philippine-American War to the acquisition of the Panama Canal Zone. If the previous chapter was the story of an expansionist wave being slowed by the institutional and normative friction of the American political structure, this chapter is a story of the further dissipation of the wave's energy as it bowed to the realities of domestic structural restraint. Chapter 4 explains why American control of foreign territory actually declined between 1904 and 1912, despite the numerous factors that favored further expansion (e.g., plenty of easily conquerable territory when a popular, proexpansion president was in power). The United States intervened in the Dominican Republic and Cuba under Roosevelt, and in Liberia, Nicaragua, and Honduras under President Taft, but annexation was not seriously considered in any of these cases primarily because of institutional and normative restraints. In addition, the most important American colony—the Philippines—was set on a path to independence.

Chapter 5 provides the first cases of a Democratic presidency and of unified government. During Woodrow Wilson's term in office (1913–1921) the United States embarked on its most expansionist policies since 1898, with the occupation of Haiti and the Dominican Republic, major military interventions in Mexico and Cuba, and the use of gunboats and a significant military presence to maintain influence in Nicaragua. Nevertheless, expansionist acts by the United States were limited (and in one case prevented) by separation and balance of powers, electoral incentives, public opinion, and the personal principles of Woodrow Wilson.

Chapter 6 covers the transitional period between the Wilson era when mainstream American leaders still advocated for expanding political-military intervention and the ultimate total disavowal of intervention by the Franklin Roosevelt administration (1921–1933). The general goal of presidents Harding, Coolidge, and Hoover was to reduce the level and amount of American political-military control over foreign territory. As demonstrated by the nine cases in this chapter, the normative and institutional restraints of the American political system limited American expansion and caused much of it to be reversed, including withdrawals from the Dominican Republic and Nicaragua.

Chapter 7 argues that Franklin Roosevelt's foreign policy toward the Western Hemisphere was not a fundamental shift in American grand strategy, but instead was the resolution of an ongoing contradiction between the restraint of the political structure of the United States and the expansionist ambitions of individuals and organizations in the executive branch (and for a time in the Republic Party). This chapter focuses on the reasons for the emergence of the Good Neighbor policy and its implementation in the Caribbean Basin and examines the cases of nonintervention in Cuba, withdrawal from Haiti, and nonintervention in Mexico. The chapter concludes with an overview of several episodes of American foreign policy between 1936 and the attack on Pearl Harbor to demonstrate the consistent application of nonintervention and noninterference even as threats emerged in Europe, East Asia, and to a lesser degree Latin America.

The book concludes with a discussion of the broader relevance of key findings, a brief analysis of the normative and institutional restraints on Chinese grand strategy, and a discussion of implications for the future of American grand strategy.

Notes

1. US economic dominance spanned all measures of industrial might. In the 1870s the United States surpassed Great Britain as the largest economy in the world. By 1900 the United States was the dominant industrial power, producing twice as much iron and steel and consuming almost twice the energy of its nearest competitor. The United States also had the largest share of world manufacturing output and the largest industrial potential of any great power, an advantage that only continued to grow up through World War II. For a comparison of industrial output see Kennedy, 1987, 199–202. For GDP data see Angus Maddison's reconstruction of historical economic data at www.ggdc.net/maddison/oriindex.htm.

2. Schweller 1999, 3.

3. For a recent historical survey see Bender 2006, chapter 4; for the political science perspective see Trubowitz, Goldman, and Rhodes, 1999.

4. Munro 1964, 271.

5. Clearly defined concepts are crucial for successful social science analysis; see Goertz 2006.

6. Several recent studies use the term rising powers as a key concept, but do not define it. See for example Schweller 1999; Davidson 2006; Edelstein 2002.

7. Kim and Morrow 1992.

8. This construction is similar to Mearsheimer's (2001, 40–42) definition of regional and global hegemons.

9. Relative economic power is calculated by dividing the GDP of one great power by the sum of the GPD for all great powers. This is a systemic definition of rising powers similar to the approach taken by power transition theorists like Charles F. Doran (1991; with Parson, 1980).

10. Graphs of the Correlates of War (COW) index are very similar to the graphs of relative GDP.

11. My conceptualization collapses Johnston's (1998, 111–113) accommodationist and defensive strategies into the category of restraint and maintains the expansionist category.

12. Cf. Zakaria, 1999, 18.

13. Gilpin 1983, 23–24. The third objective Gilpin mentions is influence over the world economy.

14. Davidson, 2006, 14.

15. Hensel 2000, 60; Huth 2000, 87–94; Vasquez 2000, 338.

16. Valeriano and Van Benthuysen 2012.

17. On the benefits of conquest see Mearsheimer 2001, 148–152; Liberman 1993. On power maximization see Mearsheimer 2001, 2–3, 29–54. On recent developments that could encourage neoimperialism, see McDonald 2009.

18. See Ikenberry 1998/99; Gholz, Press, and Sapolsky 1997; Posen 2007.

19. Whether or not the United States has consent to rule a foreign people is part of the contested nature of expansionist policy. When the debate shifts toward a public perception that the policy is one of pure imperialism, opposition to that policy is likely to rise.

20. For definitions of strategy and grand strategy that view it as a plan see Biddle 2007; Owens 2007. For definitions of strategy and grand strategy as state behavior see Hart 1991, 321; Howard 2001. Henry Mintzberg (1994, 23–29) makes a similar distinction in the realm of corporate strategy.

21. For an overview see George and Bennett 2005, chapter 7; Manicas 2006.

22. George and Bennett 2005, 91.

23. On process tracing see George and Bennett 2005, 205–232; Van Evera 1997, 64–67.

24. This procedure is derived from Van Evera 1999 and 1997.

25. These findings are based on the author's analysis of Angus Maddison's reconstruction of historical economic data. For access to Maddison's data see www.ggdc.net/maddison/oriindex.htm.

26. For example, the Japanese, German, and Italian cases have been recently studied by international relations scholars: Snyder 1991; Kupchan 1994; Davidson 2006.

27. The phrase is from Van Evera 1997, 46.

28. Fearon (1991) suggests using existing theory to establish what should have happened.

29. Capoccia and Kelemen 2007.

30. Tetlock and Belkin 1996, 18, 23–25.

31. Deviant cases are important for identifying "new concepts or variables"; George and Bennett 2005, 114–115. The importance of crucial cases is self-evident, but see George and Bennett 2005, 120–123.

32. I have attempted to include all relevant cases.

33. Mahoney and Goertz 2004, 653.

34. For a discussion of this issue see Straus 2011, 343–362.

35. Zakaria 1999, 44–127.

36. The periodization of the rise of the United States is based on the author's analysis of Angus Maddison's reconstruction of historical economic data. For access to Maddison's data see www.ggdc.net/maddison/oriindex.htm.

37. Work by Silverstone (2004) and Friedberg (2000) suggests a broad applicability for a domestic structural approach to American foreign policy, but further study is needed to confirm this suggestion.

38. Polk declared that Mexican troops had crossed into US territory to attack American soldiers. However, the battle took place in the area between the Nueces and Rio Grande Rivers, a strip of land claimed by both countries. Mexico's claim was considered to be stronger at the time and by subsequent analysis by historians; see Howe 2007, 738. Many Whigs viewed the war as unconstitutional and unjust and consistently opposed the war. See Holt 1999, 233, 248–251.

39. Howe 2007, 762–770.

40. See Woodworth 2010.

41. Graebner 1980, 405.

42. For an analysis of the Cold War from a domestic structure perspective see Friedberg 2000.

1

---- ★ ----

THEORIES OF RISING
POWER EXPANSION
AND RESTRAINT

W HY ARE MOST RISING POWERS EXPANSIONIST? Why did the United States not follow this pattern? Answering these questions requires a theory of expansion and a theory of restraint. It is the purpose of this chapter to articulate these theories. The first part of this chapter focuses on rising power expansion. Explaining expansion is not a central goal of this book, but a theory of expansion is necessary to enable us to identify when we expect expansion to occur. Only after we set the baseline for expansion is it possible to identify cases of restraint. In other words, without a theory of expansion it is impossible to differentiate between cases where domestic structure actually causes restraint and cases where expansion is not likely. The second part of this chapter explains how domestic structure causes restraint, and then contrasts this theory with competing theories of restraint.

A Theory of Expansion

International relations theories of rising power grand strategy consistently argue that rising powers are war-prone, revisionist powers intent on implementing highly expansionist foreign policies meant to reshape the international order.[1] But why? International relations theory provides several explanations. While different theories of expansion are sometimes portrayed as rival explanations, I instead integrate them into a holistic approach to explaining expansion.[2] I assume that rising powers expand for a variety of reasons, but that all of these reasons are derived from the basic characteristic that defines a rising power: the long-term relative balance of power is shifting in their favor. This increase in relative power provides a rising power with new opportunities for expansion.[3] As a state's relative power increases, it gains an advantage in material power or increases its advantage over other states, thereby making expansion easier. Increased power provides the opportunity for expansion and a straightforward cost-benefit calculation provides the logic of expansion. According to Randall Schweller, "states expand when they can; that is, when they perceive relative increases in state power and when changes in the relative costs and benefits of expansion make it profitable to do so."[4] States also expand at a level and pace "commensurate with their new capabilities."[5] The new opportunities hypothesis is the foundational reason for political–military expansion by rising powers, and is best thought of as a necessary but not sufficient cause of expansion. The following two sections describe the types of opportunities that encourage a rising power to expand and the more proximate mechanisms that actually cause the expansion to occur.

New Opportunities for Expansion

The three main reasons for rising power expansion are opportunities to increase profit, security, and prestige. Profit comes mainly from expropriation of property and other assets. The clearest example of the profit motive is territorial conquest either for capturing industrial capacity or for obtaining the ever-increasing amount of resources required to maintain domestic economic growth.[6] Pushed to an extreme, this logic forms the basis of the offensive realist argument that states maximize power in order to ensure their own survival in an anarchic international system. Territorial conquest is a vital component of a power maximization strategy because it conveys clear economic and strategic benefits.[7] However, great powers will not simply attempt to conquer any and every piece of foreign territory they have access to. The expectation is that they will rationally choose specific territories that either increase their economic capacity or provide some other strategic benefit. And they will only act if they have a reasonable chance of success. In short, rising powers gain new opportunities for expansion and tend to take them when decision makers perceive the benefits to be higher than the costs.

Opportunities for expansion are not defined only by profit potential; the logic of security through expansion is also very strong among rising powers. Security goals that were previously out of reach become attainable as states increase in power. Or, put another way, rising powers are able to acquire more security because their new resources and capabilities allow them to do so. They have the newfound ability to fill up power vacuums to prevent other states from gaining a foothold in the neighborhood or gain a geographical advantage through the occupation of geostrategically important territory.[8] Drawing on balance of threat theory, Sean Lynn-Jones concisely and cogently communicates the logic of security through expansion:

States attempt to expand *when* expansion increases their security. In general terms, threats might cause a state to expand when three conditions are satisfied: (1) a threat exists; (2) expansion is an effective strategy for reducing the threat; (3) the state has the capability to adopt an expansionist strategy.[9]

When decision makers in rising powers perceive a situation of high vulnerability, they are especially apt to view aggressive expansionism as a viable—and even necessary—strategy.[10]

Finally, increased power creates the opportunity and desire to gain intangible qualities like influence, status, and prestige.[11] The status of nation-states is largely a function of their material power, but not entirely. There is no clear threshold that distinguishes a secondary power from a great power or great power from superpower. Therefore, rising powers often require some form of recognition from other states in order to gain higher status.[12] The problem for rising powers is that their status typically lags behind their material power, creating a power–status imbalance. Rising powers can prove they deserve a higher status "by challenging the existing order" and competing with status quo states.[13] Territorial expansion is one of the main ways that modern rising powers have attempted to demonstrate to other states that they are deserving of higher status.[14]

Agents of Expansion

Opportunities matter, but only if there are agents that act on those opportunities. The types of agents mentioned most often in the literature on expansion are interest groups, politicians, and government officials. Interest group theory posits that state action is best explained by understanding the goals of the dominant interest group coalition—usually united by economic interests.[15] In a historically nuanced account of imperialism, Abernethy argues that European expansionism in the nineteenth and twentieth centuries was driven by a conjunction of capitalist pursuit of profit and missionary pursuit of converts. These efforts destabilized traditional societies, and the ultimate failure of these efforts led business and religious leaders to request state intervention. Thus a coalition between public, private, and religious groups made expansionism possible.[16] This explanation is consistent with the classic interpretation and critique of British imperialism offered by John Hobson and revised by Vladimir Ilyich Lenin: imperialist economic interest groups (or financial capital) captured the policymaking process and turned it toward their own economic benefit. That the "superprofits" hypothesized by Lenin never materialized is not as important as the belief at the time that colonialism was profitable.[17]

More recent formulations of the interest-group explanation for expansionism build on this classic approach, but broaden our understanding of which interest groups will tend to support expansionism and how exactly they "capture" the state. Jack Snyder provides a particularly sophisticated application of the interest group approach, arguing that expansionist interest groups can gain control of the policymaking apparatus because they have inherent advantages over other interest groups in terms of "concentrated interests," "propaganda advantages," and "ties to the state."[18] In other words, expansionist or imperialist groups usually have much to gain, while the costs of expansion are diffused throughout society. Expansionist groups also have considerable influence in society and are usually strongly represented in state bureaucracies that have much to gain from expansion (e.g., the military, colonial agencies). From this perspective, expansion is explained by the logrolling power of expansionist interests and their ability to promote strategic myths about the necessity of expansion.[19]

Politicians and intellectuals provide the public justifications for expansion—sometimes as part of an expansionist coalition, sometimes in response to domestic problems or opportunities.[20] Regardless of the specific motivations of these individuals, their justifications for territorial expansion are typically stated in terms of grand ideas rather than in terms of narrow national self-interest or the claim that might makes right.[21] The promotion of grand ideas, like taking up the "white man's burden," can cause politicians and their broader coalition to become "politically entrapped by its own rhetoric."[22] Expansionist politicians, therefore, have vested interests in continuing expansion, because changing course would undermine their credibility and force them to admit they supported misguided policies.[23] Over time, the original ideological justifications for expansion can become taken-for-granted beliefs that crystalize into a national identity, or strategic culture that promotes and reinforces efforts to mobilize power to pursue ever more expansionist policies.[24]

The actions of colonial officials, diplomats, and entrepreneurs on the ground also push the boundaries of expansion. These agents of empire have vested interests in continued expansion, and their actions create a dynamic of positive reinforcement whereby each increment of expansion must be protected by additional increments of expansion. Abernethy uses the phrase "imperial inertia" to describe the process whereby unauthorized actions by colonial officials, diplomats, military officers, or private sector entrepreneurs can lead to control of new territory, presenting the home country with a fait accompli.[25] Actions on the ground by colonial officials, entrepreneurs, or indigenous leaders and groups can also trigger a crisis that compels increased intervention. The creation of vested interests and the internalization of expansionist justifications entrench initial experiments in territorial expansion and encourages future expansion.[26]

The success of expansionist endeavors can also initiate positive reinforcement. In his analysis of the expansion of war aims, Eric Labs argues that the achievement of initial goals fosters the sense that an expanded set of goals is also achievable.[27] This is positive reinforcement in is simplest form. From this perspective, expansion can begin as a rational response to international threats and opportunities, but then morph into an impossible search for absolute security or unrestrained ambition where each territorial gain must be protected through ever-increasing increments of expansion. In other words, expansion tends to beget more expansion—as the security perimeter expands, there is often not a clear point where a state has attained sufficient security and resources that it can safely stop expanding.[28]

In sum, rising powers expand because their increase in relative material power provides opportunities for profitable and security-enhancing expansion, they use expansion to align their status and prestige with their newfound material power, the dominant domestic political coalition favors expansionist foreign policies, and because expansion creates positive feedback.

The above discussion suggests that expansion is likely under the following background conditions:

1. If decision makers within rising powers perceive a relative increase in state power.
2. If decision makers within a rising power perceive that the gains from expansion outweigh the costs.
3. If decision makers within a rising power believe they have gained the capacity to occupy territory that can alleviate a strategic vulnerability.
4. If decision makers within a rising power perceive a power-status imbalance and expansion is perceived to be a solution to the imbalance.
5. If expansion is in the economic interests of the dominant domestic political coalition.
6. If the national identity, ideology, or strategic culture of the rising power portrays expansionism as appropriate or necessary.
7. If decision makers perceive that additional expansion will protect previous expansion.
8. If previous expansion fosters the perception that additional expansion will be easy and profitable.

Expansion is likely when these proximate causes are present:

1. The expansion of war aims provides specific opportunities to take and hold territory during the course of engaging in the use of military force.
2. Agents of expansion on the ground in foreign territory create fait accompli propitious for territorial expansion.
3. Crises that create focal points for any of the background conditions above (e.g., the failure of a neighboring state reveals the extent of the security vacuum, actions by other states that impugn status or prestige).

For any given rising power, the more reasons there are for expansion (i.e., the more "if" statements that are true), we should expect the probability and magnitude of expansion to increase.[29] We should also expect that one or more proximate causes are necessary for expansion to occur.

Many of the background conditions for expansion are present for the United States during the period of study. First, the United States was experiencing a relative increase in power and had recently passed all other great powers in terms of economic output. The United States therefore was recently an emerging power and rapidly moving into position as a potential hegemon. Decision makers in the United States were aware of the growing relative power of their country, and increasingly saw this power as usable. Second, the Republican Party was the majority party and Republican presidents were actively looking for opportunities to expand American influence. By 1896 "the Republican platform set forth a full-fledged expansionist agenda: European withdrawal from the hemisphere; a voluntary union of English-speaking peoples in North America, meaning Canada; construction of a US controlled isthmian canal; acquisition of the Virgin Islands; annexation of Hawaii; and independence for Cuba."[30] McKinley was elected on this platform—though admittedly, the main issues of the election of 1896 were domestic.[31] From McKinley's election until 1911 the Republican Party had unified control over the instruments of foreign policy decision making in the US government (see Table 1.1).

Third, many perceived economic expansion to be necessary for the continued prosperity of the United States, which weighted the cost-benefit analysis toward expansion. Overproduction was a key economic worry and external markets were seen as a solution. The increase in production following the Civil War, coupled with the closing of the frontier, popularized the "glut thesis"—the worry that overproduction would undermine economic health. The obvious response to the glut thesis was a foreign policy focused on obtaining new markets for American goods.[32] The importance of finding new foreign markets was brought into focus by an economic depression beginning in 1893.[33] Americans were also concerned about losing markets abroad as European countries raised tariffs and moved to partition China.[34] Advocates of opening new markets varied on the form of expansion that was needed, but their arguments could easily be drawn upon to justify territorial expansion.

Fourth, the rising power of the United States interacted with elements of national identity and social instability in a manner to produce a powerful justification for expansion. During the postbellum period the United States was undergoing a "psychic crisis" of social instability, which led some politicians and publicists to promote jingoism as a means to unite the country.[35] In the 1890s the national identity of the United States was under stress from the continuing reintegration of the South, the assimilation of Central and Southern European immigrants, and the myriad changes associated with industrialization, urbanization, and the closing of the frontier. Increasingly, the everyday life experiences

TABLE 1.1
Balance of Power in the US Government, 1897–1941

Year	Majority Party–House	Minority Party–House	Majority Party–Senate	Minority Party–Senate	President*	Balance of Power
Mar. 4, 1897–Mar. 3, 1899	R-204	D-113	R-47	D-34	R (McKinley)	Unified
Dec. 4, 1899–Mar. 3, 1901	R-185	D-163	R-53	D-26	R (McKinley)	Unified
Mar. 4, 1901–Mar. 3, 1903	R-197	D-151	R-55	D-31	R (McKinley)/ (T. Roosevelt)	Unified
Mar. 5, 1903–Mar. 3, 1905	R-208	D-178	R-57	D-33	R (T. Roosevelt)	Unified
Mar. 4, 1905–Mar. 3, 1907	R-250	D-136	R-57	D-33	R (T. Roosevelt)	Unified
Dec. 2, 1907–Mar. 3, 1909	R-222	D-164	R-61	D-31	R (T. Roosevelt)	Unified
Mar. 4, 1909–Mar. 3, 1911	R-219	D-172	R-61	D-32	R (Taft)	Unified
Apr. 4, 1911–Mar. 3, 1913	D-228	R-161	R-51	D-41	R (Taft)	Partially Divided
Mar. 4, 1913–Mar. 3, 1915	D-291	R-127	D-51	R-44	D (Wilson)	Unified
Dec. 6, 1915–Mar. 3, 1917	D-230	R-196	D-56	R-40	D (Wilson)	Unified
Mar. 5, 1917–Mar. 3, 1919	D-216	R-210	D-53	R-42	D (Wilson)	Unified
May 19, 1919–Mar. 3, 1921	R-240	D-190	R-49	D-47	D (Wilson)	Divided
Mar. 4, 1921–Mar. 3, 1923	R-301	D-131	R-59	D-37	R (Harding)	Unified
Dec. 3, 1923–Mar. 3, 1925	R-225	D-205	R-51	D-43	R (Coolidge)	Unified
Mar. 3, 1925–Mar. 4, 1927	R-247	D-183	R-56	D-39	R (Coolidge)	Unified
Dec. 5, 1927–Mar. 3, 1929	R-237	D-195	R-49	D-46	R (Coolidge)	Unified
Mar. 4, 1929–Mar. 3, 1931	R-267	D-167	R-56	D-39	R (Hoover)	Unified
Dec. 7, 1931–Mar. 3, 1933	D-220	R-214	R-48	D-47	R (Hoover)	Partially Divided
Mar. 4, 1933–Jun. 18, 1934	D-310	R-117	D-60	R-35	D (F. Roosevelt)	Unified
Jan. 3, 1935–Jun. 20, 1936	D-319	R-103	D-69	R-25	D (F. Roosevelt)	Unified
Jan. 5, 1937–Jun. 16, 1938	D-331	R-89	D-76	R-16	D (F. Roosevelt)	Unified
Jan. 3, 1939–Jan. 3, 1941	D-261	R-164	D-69	R-23	D (F. Roosevelt)	Unified

*Prior to 1934 presidents were inaugurated on March 4.

Data Source: Congressional Quarterly's Guide to Congress, Fourth Edition (Washington, DC: Congressional Quarterly, 1991).

of most Americans were inconsistent with the traditional understanding of American identity. The traditional view of the United States as an isolated, agrarian, Anglo-American society governed by an unobtrusive state contrasted with the new interdependent, industrial, multicultural society governed by an increasingly energetic state. The result of this cognitive dissonance was a search for a new understanding of national identity. Out of the American psychic crisis emerged a new outward-looking identity where an empowered state would pursue national goals abroad, spreading American civilization around the world. The nexus of growing material power and the emergence of the ideology of Progressivism fostered a new expansionist outlook and belief in the efficacy of state action. Political scientist Jonathan Monten calls this a shift in American national identity a shift from an "exemplarist" to "vindicationist" form of nationalist ideology.[36] Thus, from this perspective, American policy in the 1890s was the result of an increase in material power and a change in how Americans viewed themselves and their role in the world. Naval policy, war, and imperialism reflected and reinforced the emerging national identity.[37] Like economic anxiety, worries about the meaning and future of the "American experiment" were present in the discourse of American foreign policy in the 1890s.

Fifth, some influential Americans viewed expansion as strategically beneficial. The shift in American identity, combined with concerns over the future of economic prosperity and emerging ideas about American national interests, led prominent intellectuals and political leaders to favor what became known as "large policy." Beginning in the 1880s, a central aspect of American national interests was the search for foreign markets for American goods and naval bases to protect American international trade—in other words, more expansive economic and strategic interests.[38] Advocates of an expansive foreign policy combined arguments about America's mission to spread its institutions and values abroad with its new interests as a rising power. Americans were increasingly cognizant that economic growth and advances in technology were changing the position of the United States in the international system and making isolationism increasingly untenable.[39] Americans had an "increased self-awareness in the dynamic power that was growing at so violent a rate"; the dream of a world-class navy supported by colonies and coaling stations merged with the idea of the United States as a new great power destined to play a more active role in world politics.[40] Some also invoked the doctrine of Social Darwinism and the superiority of the Anglo-Saxon race in support of a more energetic and militaristic foreign policy that would spread American virtues to the rest of the world.[41]

Historian George Herring argues that Americans were aware of their increasing power and looked for opportunities to use it: "National pride, a resurgent sense of destiny, and a conviction that the United States as a rising world power must take responsibility for world events in its area of influence gave an increasing urgency to the Cuban crisis."[42] From this perspective, the War of 1898 is the culmination of American moves toward expansionism during the 1890s, a victory for large-policy advocates, and a sign of America's emerging great power status.[43]

The impact of these societal changes would not necessarily be confined to 1898; the factors are referenced by diplomatic historians throughout the early 1900s. Most of the conditions listed above influenced US foreign policy up through the 1940s. Some conditions become less important over time, others become more important over time. Overall, these background conditions fulfill many of the theoretical conditions for rising power expansion and consequently establish a presumption of US expansionism in the early twentieth century. Proximate causes of expansion vary on a case-by-case basis, and are discussed in later chapters. The remainder of this chapter explains how elements of domestic structure can restrain rising powers from pursuing expansionist grand strategies.

A Domestic-Structural Theory of Restraint

One of the central findings of political science is that there are some elements of political life that are highly durable and tend to shape political behavior over the long term by providing incentives and imposing restraints. These structural factors rarely determine action or provide the proximate cause of action; instead they shape behavior over time, often through small changes in the costs and benefits of action. These structural factors are the fundamental, deep causal elements of social science analysis. Structure is important because "the notion of structure does denominate, however problematically, something very important about social relations: the tendency of patterns of relations to be reproduced, even when actors engaging in the relations are unaware of the patterns or do not desire their reproduction."[44] There can be many forms of structure including international structure, political structure, social structure, and economic structure. For this book domestic political structure is the key concept and the independent variable. I define political structure as the fundamental institutions and norms of a polity.[45] Institutions are the basic rules of the game in political systems that specify the roles, powers, and duties of political actors.[46] The institutions most relevant for this study are those that govern the use of force abroad, the power of the purse, and the making of treaties. Societal norms, or beliefs and values, make up the culture of society. The cultural elements that are relevant for this study are categorized under the term "strategic culture," which is defined as that subset of beliefs and values of a society that relate to grand strategy, especially the "appropriate ends and means for achieving security objectives."[47]

Cultural approaches can be rivals to institutional approaches, but can also be complementary or even mutually reinforcing. Domestic-level constructivist theories have successfully been used in combination with institutional theories to explain the foreign policies of states across many issue areas.[48] In fact, among historical institutionalists it is common to include ideational factors in the definition of "institution."[49] Typically institutionalists refer to "norms" as the ideational or informal counterpart to codified, formal rules because both factors are viewed as having stable, enduring effects on political behavior. Because norms and institutions have similar effects on political action, they can go beyond complementarity to have a more powerful effect due to redundancy, which causes reliability and robustness.[50] As the case studies in this book demonstrate, redundant restraint produces reliability because when one element of restraint fails another is there to delay, limit, or prevent expansion. Robustness is the result of a multiplicative effect of redundant institutions and norms. Not only are there multiple restraints on any potential state action, but the different norms and institutions of restraint also reinforce each other so that simply adding up the restraints does not reveal their strength. For example, Woodrow Wilson ordered the occupation of Vera Cruz in 1914, but decided against implementing the full plan to blockade Mexico's coast because public outcry against the military operation reinforced and multiplied his own aversion to imperialism, which had been relatively dormant. Many other interactive effects between norms and institutions are seen throughout the cases.

How do institutions and norms work? Institutions and norms both restrict and empower. Institutions put limits on action by defining the types of behavior that are allowed and the penalties for deviance. Institutions also designate authority, foster collective action by providing predictability in interactions, assign duties and responsibilities, and distribute resources. By establishing formal rules and procedures, defining roles, and enumerating the relative authority of organizations and positions in the policymaking process, institutions set parameters for political action within which individuals and groups attempt to achieve their goals. Institutions foster stability and regularity by shaping what types of political action will be effective, which often privileges some groups over others. Institutions are also durable: it may be in an individual's or group's self-interest to violate an institution in the short run, but defection will be rare because of the overall value of maintaining the institution and the uncertainty over the benefits of a new institutional reality. More importantly, people obey rules when they believe them to be legitimate.[51] Over time institutions tend to become taken for granted and attempts to create significant change are rare, regardless of whether institutions have maintained their original functionality.[52]

Norms govern what is appropriate rather than what is allowed. Norms are "shared expectation[s] about behavior, a standard of right or wrong."[53] Norms create and shape the preferences, interests, expectations, goals, and beliefs of agents.[54] Norms come in two major forms. First, norms can be regulative/constraining, in that they impose costs on behavior and thereby shape interests. Costs of norm violation include a loss of status or prestige or moral standing.

Second, norms can be constitutive, in that they shape identity and become taken for granted. When norms become taken for granted, transgressing the norms is not even considered.[55] Norms empower actors that are seen to uphold and promote appropriate beliefs and behaviors and provide weapons that can be used to attack those attempting to promote normative change.[56] Patrick Thaddeus Jackson and Ronald Krebs demonstrate that political actors do not need to actually believe in norms in order to use them effectively, because the power of norms comes from their resonance with society at large.[57]

The importance of political structure is best understood through the concept of path dependence. Revisionism and expansionism of rising powers is a path-dependent phenomenon characterized by positive feedback in the form of increasing returns, the creation of vested interests, and self-reinforcing dynamics.[58] Rising powers tend to follow a path toward revisionism that can begin with relatively minor episodes of territorial expansion that, once successful in the initial stages, provide positive reinforcement and become locked in over time.[59] The basic insight that emerges from an understanding of path dependence is that the creation or emergence of institutions and norms shapes subsequent outcomes such that we can identify a specific path of development that begins with the foundational moment and carries forward through time. In other words, the initial decision or the spontaneous development of institutions and norms fundamentally shapes what comes after. Even when institutions or norms change, the new institutions and norms are layered upon the previous ones, making it extremely difficult to do away with the accumulated weight of past decisions and events.[60]

Path analysis requires the identification of critical junctures or branching events where a single decision or set of decisions highly constrains future choices.[61] Critical junctures are periods of uncertainty where major change is possible, but not always actualized.[62] Critical junctures may result in change or maintenance of the existing path.[63] A crucial mechanism for maintenance of the existing path is negative feedback.[64] When change is attempted, costs are imposed on advocates of change by supporters of the status quo (if the political structure gives them opportunities to do so) and the inertia of the existing structure. If the structural restraints are strong enough, advocates of change will eventually end their pursuit of change, or at least become quiescent while looking for a new opportunity. This is a learning process conceptualized as "learning by doing," a process summarized by economist Kenneth Arrow: "Learning is the product of experience. Learning can only take place through the attempt to solve a problem and therefore only takes place during activity."[65] Thus, advocates of change experience negative feedback in the form of costs and the inability to catalyze change, and over time learn from the experience that change is improbable regardless of continued efforts.

For some rising powers critical junctures may trigger a shift toward revisionism, while for other rising powers critical junctures may reinforce the existing path (e.g., restraint). For example, the United States avoided the path to revisionism because its domestic institutions and norms fostered negative feedback to expansion rather than the positive feedback required for a new path to be established.[66] American expansionists learned that it was politically costly to promote territorial expansion and very difficult to effectively implement expansionist projects because of the high level of structural restraint in the United States. In other words, the United States maintained its path of strategic restraint rather than switching to a new path of revisionism. To the extent that US institutions and norms prevented the consolidation of early expansionist moves, these institutions and norms eliminated a necessary condition for revisionism. In sum, more extensive expansionism and revisionism was a possible outcome for American grand strategy at various times between 1898 and 1941, but at critical junctures institutional and normative restraints prevented the positive reinforcement required to institutionalize a new path.

Scholars have produced a vast amount of scholarship in American and comparative politics using path dependence, but the same cannot be said of international relations. There are almost no applications of path dependence to foreign policy or grand strategy.[67] Thus a major theoretical contribution of this work is the application of the insights of historical institutionalism and path dependence to the area of foreign policy and grand strategy. This book also contributes to our understanding of path dependence by emphasizing how structural redundancy causes reliable and robust restraint, which generates negative feedback, which in turn affects behavior through learning. The next two sections describe in more detail how institutions and norms affect foreign policy by preventing change.

Sources of Institutional Restraint

For the purpose of this book we are most interested in how institutions and norms delay, limit, restrict, and prevent policy change because of our focus on explaining why some rising powers pursue strategic restraint and some pursue strategic expansion. The basic idea is that the transition from a grand strategy of restraint to a grand strategy of expansion requires a rising power to implement new, expansionist foreign policies. The implementation of new foreign policies requires advocates of expansionism to submit their preferred policies to the policymaking process. Their success at implementing these new policies is strongly affected by the institutions that govern the policymaking process. Expansionist foreign policies are less likely to be successfully implemented in countries with political institutions that make policy change difficult. There are three main institutional sources of restraint identified in the literature on the domestic sources of foreign policy: separation of powers, elections/public opinion, and federalism. The first two factors are important for a very simple reason: the more independent actors that can influence a policy before it is implemented, the more difficult it is to implement that policy. More specifically, separation of powers causes restraint because when policymaking authority is separated, different organizations within the government must agree before the state can take action. In democracies, the people have influence over policy through elections and by voicing their opinions. Elections cause restraint because elected officials can be removed from office if the citizenry disapproves of the policy decisions they have made. Public opinion restrains because it signals the possibility of future electoral retribution, but perhaps more importantly, public opinion can undermine the moral authority of political leaders who support unpopular policy. In a democracy unpopular policies are perceived to be illegitimate, and therefore subject to scrutiny by the public and press and criticism by rival politicians. The third factor, federalism, is important because it fragments interests geographically, making it difficult to create a coalition strong enough to overcome the barriers thrown up by separation of powers and by creating electoral incentives for parochialism. These three sets of restraints create a powerful incentive structure in the United States described concisely by Stephen Krasner: "The system makes obstruction easy, positive action difficult."[68]

Separation of Powers

The most important domestic institutional restraint on state action is separation of powers. Since at least Montesquieu, political theorists and practitioners have realized that dividing up the powers of the state among different branches of government and balancing these branches by giving them the authority to check the actions of each other is the central means of preventing the arbitrary use of power.[69] Theory holds that separation of powers forces policy advocates to obtain wide backing before a proposed policy can become law, and laws that have broad support are more likely to benefit society as a whole and less likely to favor one specific faction of society or cabal of officeholders.[70] Separation of powers also allows a minority to veto the will of the majority, and may allow a relatively small percentage of a society to hold hostage policy that would benefit the majority.

The logic of separation of powers is best captured by the veto point or veto player framework developed by Ellen Immergut and expanded and formalized by George Tsebelis.[71] A veto player is "an individual or collective actor whose agreement (by majority rule for collective actors) is required for a change in policy."[72] In other words, a veto player is an actor that must agree to a policy proposal before it can become law. The decisions of veto players determine the outcome of any policy debate because "for a particular change of the status quo to occur, a number of veto players must agree on it."[73] The more veto players there are, the more stable a political system and the more difficult it is to change policy. Tseblis argues that the number, cohesion, and congruence of veto players determine the relative amount of policy change that occurs. Veto players are most effective when they are numerous and cohesive, with divergent ideologies and interests.[74] Also, more veto players fosters a more transparent and open process. The more visibility interest groups have in the policy process and the more access they have, the more likely they are to be able to intervene in the process, which also increases the probability that an interest group that is negatively affected by a given policy is able to influence the policymaking process.[75]

Veto players are more or less important depending upon contextual factors. For example, if one political party controls all branches of government, the ideological distance between veto players is greatly reduced and the restraining effect of separation of powers is reduced. Also, if one of the veto players is highly fragmented, it may be susceptible to manipulation by another veto player, which would lead to separation of powers being less effective. In the American context we would expect divided government (when the opposition party controls at least one of the houses of Congress) and strong ideological differences between the parties to strengthen the effect of separation of powers. These expectations have been tested by scholars without coming to a consensus regarding the effect of divided government and polarization on policymaking, though the weight of evidence suggests that most scholars view divided government and high polarization as less auspicious for policy change.[76]

The concept of veto points or veto players has been especially influential in comparative politics and international political economy, and continues to produce scholarship on a wide range of issues. This scholarship has consistently shown that the greater the number of veto points, the more barriers there are to policy change and the greater the policy stability.[77] In other words, the institutional restraint of separation of powers makes policy change more difficult and political decision making more transparent. The veto points/players framework provides the means for comparing political systems both within and across regime types, and therefore allows us to compare democracies with authoritarian governments.[78]

The US political system usually has three institutional veto players: the Senate, the House of Representatives, and the president. However, due to changes in the rules governing the Senate and House over time, there have been additional veto players at different points in history. Currently, the filibuster/cloture rule in the Senate makes the minority party in the Senate a veto player if it controls one-third of the seats. Prior to 1890 the "disappearing quorum" rule allowed the minority in the House a veto by preventing a quorum by simply refusing to speak.[79] In some issue areas it is also possible for there to be additional veto players, such as committee chairs in Congress. Other actors, like interest groups and government agencies, may also act as informal or quasi-veto players if their cooperation is necessary for policy to be implemented.[80] In this study the main veto players are the president and Congress. In cases where expansion required a treaty, the president and the Senate were veto players. In cases where funds had to be appropriated, war had to be declared, trade agreements had to be passed, and other areas where laws had to passed, the House and Senate were both veto players along with the president.

Public Opinion and Elections

The second main check on state power is generated by the institutions of regular free and fair elections and freedom of speech. These two institutions are related in that they both allow for the citizenry of a country to express their opinion about public policy. Various mechanisms link public opinion and policy outcomes. First, in democracies with protected speech, the side with the most public support gains a certain moral authority, which translates to policy influence. For example, numerous studies have shown that public support for the president (measured by approval ratings) has an effect on what a president can accomplish: high ratings provide political capital and increase a president's influence with Congress.[81] Low approval ratings diminish the president and make legislative achievements more difficult. Second, the future also casts a shadow on these interactions, as all elected officials must consider the electoral effects of their foreign policy decisions and positions.[82] Elected leaders must be cognizant of possible electoral retribution for unpopular foreign policy actions. Therefore, democratic leaders are aware of the political effects of risky foreign policy actions, especially the use of force, and will have a strong incentive to avoid policy failure.[83] In sum, the opinion of the public matters because every national election is an opportunity to change policy by changing the individuals in charge of creating policy.

A second-order effect of free speech is an independent news media. If the news media's right to communicate to the public is protected, it is an independent source of information for the public and therefore can prevent the government or private actors from dominating public discourse. To the extent that the news media shapes public opinion and the views of policymakers, it becomes a potential force of restraint. The news media can have a direct effect on the perceptions of policymakers or an indirect effect on policymakers through its effect on public opinion. A rough consensus seems to hold that the news media is most influential when elite opinion is divided and when public demand for information is highest. Disputes among elites provide an opportunity for the media to be critical and still remain within the bounds of elite discourse while public demand for information pushes the media to go beyond the favorable narrative purveyed by the ruling party.[84] Thus the media does have an independent effect on public opinion and foreign policy, but that causal effect is through its provision of and framing of information rather than from staking out an independent position in policy debates.

In sum, the institutions of free speech and regular free and fair elections empower the public and news media to affect foreign policy decision making. Favorable public opinion (or at least quiescence) is a necessary condition for major foreign policies to be initiated; therefore the public acts as a quasi-veto player. Unlike Congress and the presidency, the media and public cannot authoritatively block policy, but public opinion can empower the opposition and, come election time, the citizenry can remove leaders from power. Furthermore, open debate and policy transparency allow a large cross-section of society to have an opportunity to shape the policymaking process and help prevent any one set of interests from determining policy. The argument here is about influence, not the substance of that influence. No assumption is made about whether the public or the media support or oppose aggressive foreign policy actions; the potential for influence is what matters, because gaining and maintaining public support is another barrier that advocates of new foreign policies must overcome. And the larger the change in policy and the more resource intensive it is, the higher the chance of elite dissensus, media scrutiny, and public attention.

Federalism and Elections

Two elements of federalism have the potential to restrain policy.[85] First, federalism empowers local and regional actors by reserving certain powers for state and provincial governments. As two prominent political scientists argue, federalism "somewhat restricts the ability to mobilize economic and political resources rapidly in the event of a serious international dispute. It also provides an institutionalized base from which regional political leaders can challenge government policy."[86] Second, and more importantly, electoral federalism creates a system where every elected official, except for the president, is beholden to a constituency at the subnational level (state/provincial or district level). Because public officials are elected by different geographical constituencies, each is compelled by the reelection imperative to promote different interests; the more diverse and divisive the interests are, the less likely that officials will agree on the definition of national interest and what policy the country should pursue.[87]

In the American system, the geographical diversity of the United States and the decentralized system of federalism foster the fragmentation of interests that has historically been expressed as sectionalism.[88] Because senators, representatives, and the president are elected by different geographical constituencies, each is compelled by the reelection imperative to promote different interests, and in the case of the president, balance among them. There is an incentive for members of Congress to look after the interests of their own state and district rather than the interests of the nation as a whole. There is therefore a considerable collective action problem to build a broad coalition that agrees on the overall grand strategy and even specific foreign policies that should be pursued by the United States.[89] The only officeholder that truly represents the nation as a whole is the president. But to get elected, the incumbent president must cobble together a coalition of state electorates to accumulate the necessary Electoral College votes. And to pass any legislation, the president needs to build a coalition of senators and members of Congress from across the country. Therefore the president needs broad society support to be able to undertake major foreign policy change.[90] Under these conditions it is extremely difficult for any one interest group or even coalition of interest groups to truly dominate national policy. Federalism itself does not present a check on state power; instead, it reinforces the checks provided by separation of powers and public opinion. Federalism helps decentralize Congress and empower minority interests while also heightening the importance of sectional public opinion.

Normative Restraint

Normative restraint is inherently different from institutional restraint. A given institutional structure makes restraint more or less likely depending upon the number of veto players and other obstacles to policy change. The simple logic is that the more chances there are for someone to block, delay, or limit a policy, the less likely it is to be fully implemented as planned. Norms affect behavior by shaping an individual's beliefs about appropriate action. Thus, it is the content of those beliefs that matter. Unlike institutions, norms do not inherently make positive action by the government more difficult; in fact, if the strategic culture of a country views aggressive expansion as appropriate, then the norms of that country actually facilitate the implementation of expansionist foreign policy. Norms are expressed through two central mechanisms: public opinion and the personal values of leaders.[91]

Public opinion is the aggregate expression of values and beliefs of some given population. Depending on the issue involved, public opinion can be a snapshot of what people think on a given day (i.e., short-term, weakly held beliefs), or can reflect deeply held norms of a society. When beliefs or values are consistent over time and do not contradict one another, they are stable and coherent and are described as "political attitudes" or "core values" or simply as "culture."[92] Clearly there is never full consensus in any society, but scholars have found country-specific, "reasonably enduring cross-cultural differences" that suggest (1) there is some level of uniformity of belief within countries and therefore a social phenomenon that we can call culture; and (2) it is possible to distinguish one culture from another in terms of differences in norms.[93]

Of course it is difficult to determine the specific content of culture. Political ideas are always contested, and even the most deeply held values can change over time. In fact, it is only through contestation over values that we can know how widely and deeply certain beliefs and values are held. Norms are highly durable, but are subject to change at certain points in time. Exogenous shocks or crises are often viewed as creating formative moments when norms are malleable.[94] Change is often catalyzed by "failures and surprises"—that is, events that undermine the fundamental elements of identity and ideas within a society.[95] But even in crisis situations change is not automatic; old identities and ideas must be "deconstructed" through challenges by political actors.[96] In other words, norms are created and recreated through political contestation.[97] It is in these moments of contestation that the impact of culture is most directly discernible.[98] Proponents of existing norms will attempt to convince fellow citizens that fundamental beliefs are under threat and need to be maintained, while proponents of change will argue that old values are irrelevant or in some way unsuited for current realities. The norms that resonate most strongly with the broader public win this contest.[99]

Norm contestation can have a direct effect on policymaking. When a policy is proposed that violates existing norms, we expect to see public displays of opposition. In other words, norm violation should be met with discontent from significant segments of the public. Public opposition to expansionist policy may occur before or after a policy is implemented. Opposition that emerges before a policy is implemented can cause restraint, limited expansion, or delayed expansion. Opposition that emerged after a policy is implemented can cause backlash. As noted above in the discussion of public opinion and elections, we expect more opposition when public attention, media scrutiny, and elite disagreement are high. Public discontent should be felt in constituent communications with elected officials and reflected at the ballot box. Modern politicians also feel the pressure of public displeasure through public opinion polls. Politicians of an earlier era experienced similar pressure through newspaper editorials, which are believed to have reflected public opinion.[100] We would also expect advocacy groups to emerge to combat the offending policy proposals. In sum, institutions of free speech and elections allow the public to influence foreign policy; the direction of that influence is shaped by the norms that make up the strategic culture of a society. Public discourse is the main conveyer of norms and therefore the central battleground for competing norms. When norms of restraint are articulated in the political discourse and are perceived to resonate with a significant portion of the public, these norms significantly impact policymaking.

The second mechanism through which norms influence policy is the personal values of political leaders, which is conceptualized here as the relevant beliefs of individuals in a position to independently affect foreign policy (of which veto players are the most important). The relevant beliefs are not only individual understanding of right and wrong, but also what individuals believe is consistent or inconsistent with the broader national values and what they see as the appropriate behavior of their country.[101] In a sense, then, political decision makers can exercise self-restraint if they forego an opportunity to act due to their own understanding of whether an action is consistent with their understanding of national strategic culture. Private and public statements by political leaders provide evidence of how their individual values affect their foreign policy decisions.

If we accept that public opinion and personal values of political leaders are mechanisms through which strategic culture affects policy, the type of effect still must be specified. For American strategic culture to act as a restraint on American foreign policy there must be antiexpansionist elements in American strategic culture. The main normative restraints in the American context during the period of study are antistatism and anti-imperialism. As many political observers have noted, the American people have a strong aversion to a strong centralized state and the use of state power and a long history of anti-imperialist beliefs, which hold that the governing of any people without their consent is immoral.[102] A corollary is the view that it is illegitimate to intervene to protect and support nondemocratic regimes. In his classic book on the subject, E. Berkeley Tomkins summarizes the central beliefs of anti-imperialists:

> The anti-imperialists contended not only that the problems of administering a colonial empire were myriad, complicated, and often highly distasteful, but also that imperialism, per se, represented a flagrant violation of the fundamental principles upon which the government of the United States was based. They emphasized that the United States had stood as the champion of liberty, democracy, equality, and self-government throughout the world and that imperialism, by its very nature, was a denial of the universal validity of these tenets.[103]

Thus, individuals and collectives that have internalized anti-imperialist and antistatist beliefs will tend to view the use of state power with suspicion—especially in the context of imposing American control over foreign territory and people—and favor political leaders and policies that minimize the use of state power.

In sum, a grand strategy of restraint for a rising power is likely under the following conditions:

1. If the foreign policy powers are separated and balanced between multiple branches of government, especially if the relevant branches of government are controlled by opposing political parties.
2. If regular, free, and fair elections occur.
3. If freedom of speech is protected.
4. If electoral federalism is present.

5. If the norm of anti-imperialism (antiexpansionism) is part of the strategic culture.
6. If the primary political decision maker is personally committed to anti-imperialism.
7. If the primary political decision maker believes expansion is inconsistent with the nation's strategic culture.

Conditions one through five are present for the United States throughout the period of study, and conditions six and seven vary according to who holds the presidency. These conditions clearly illustrate the presence of redundancy and the robustness and reliability that it brings. The conditions are necessary and sufficient for explaining American strategic restraint between 1898 and 1941. The argument in brief is that new expansionist ideas emerged in the 1890s and took root in some parts of the US government, but because these ideas did not change the strategic culture or institutional structure of the United States, these changes were shallow and temporary. The enduring anti-imperialist strategic culture and fragmented and decentralized institutions of the United States consistently acted as a restraint on new, expansionist ideas about the strategic direction of the United States and the new missions developed within organizations like the US Navy and State Department, because large numbers of Americans remained committed to the belief that the United States should not rule over foreign peoples and instead foreign nations should rule themselves.[104] Americans also tended to view the use of state power with suspicion and favor political leaders and policies that minimized the use of state power at home and abroad.[105] American institutions gave "voice opportunities" to these ideas, and created capacities and incentives for the opposition (usually in Congress) to impose costs on expansionists (usually in the executive branch).[106] Expansionist ideas and policies suffered from backlash and retrenchment over time as structural incentives produced negative feedback. Expansionists learned that the American system was hostile to their chosen grand strategy. Therefore the overall orientation of American grand strategy between 1898 and 1941 is one of strategic restraint caused primarily by domestic norms and institutions.

Haven't We Heard This All Before?

International relations scholarship that emphasizes the role of domestic factors is often referred to by the German word *Innenpolitik*. There are many laundry lists of domestic variables that have been found to have a causal effect on the foreign policies of states, but scholarship within this tradition has not been cumulative.[107] Andrew Moravcsik took a major step forward by identifying and

describing an approach that encompasses institutions, ideas, and interests, conceptualized as formulating the preferences of a state, but he does not make a
strong argument for why these factors should be aggregated as a single theory or
tradition.[108] As Brian Rathbun observes, domestic factors are not all alike, and
simply throwing them together does not make a cohesive theory.[109] Most scholars that have written on the domestic sources of foreign policy or grand strategy
had implicitly agreed with Rathbun, as demonstrated in their typical monocausal
arguments. There is a wide range of established international relations, comparative politics, and American politics scholarship that examines how domestic
institutional and normative structure shapes national policymaking and foreign
policy, but it is typically focused on one of three factors—institutions, ideas,
or interests. (This scholarship is useful, and can be found listed in the notes
throughout this chapter.) However, none of the scholars provides an explanation for how these factors work together (or against one another), and no
existing work known to this author seeks to apply the logic of (domestic)
structure to the task of understanding foreign policy and grand strategy.[110] As
many international relations publications have shown, structure at the international level has a powerful homogenizing effect on the behavior of states.
The distribution of relative power creates incentives that shape the actions of
states; for example, weak states have an incentive to become stronger or to ally
themselves with other states. The same basic logic of structure, incentives, and
behavior applies at the domestic level, as scholars of comparative and American politics know quite well.[111] Domestic structure concepts like path dependence, negative feedback, learning, inertia, institutional and normative
restraint, and redundancy can be applied to better understand continuity and
change in the behavior of states. One hesitates to make too strong an argument
about what is missing from a body of scholarship as thoroughly studied as international relations, and there are certainly some relevant publications not represented in notes of this book due to unfortunate oversights of the author;
however, a recent article on historical institutionalism in international relations provides some support for the idea that scholars have not paid sufficient
attention to domestic structure. Nowhere in the review article does the author
mention any publications that use a domestic structural approach to explain
foreign policy or grand strategy.[112]

By focusing on domestic structure it is possible to develop a more comprehensive and cohesive *Innenpolitik* theory. The domestic structural approach emphasizes the causal effect of political institutions and culture by demonstrating how
institutions and norms shape interests, policy ideas, and behavior. Thus the true
theoretical contribution of this work is one of creative recombination and application, and it should be judged in terms of the new insights it generates rather
than in terms of its originality.

Alternative Explanations

Domestic structure is not the only plausible explanation for American restraint. Defensive realism and economic interest group theory suggest alternative explanations for American strategic restraint. Both approaches are discussed below; the discussion is followed by a statement of hypotheses for each alternative explanation.

Defensive realism is synonymous with the neorealism of Kenneth Waltz.[113] Its central prediction is that states will tend to balance against international concentrations of power. This proposition has two main foreign policy implications. First, states will tend to expand their power by mobilizing resources internally (internal balancing) and by establishing alliances with other states (external balancing) in order to prevent any one state or alliance of states from dominating the international system. Second, states will moderate their aims to prevent the rise of balancing coalitions. These hypotheses have been elaborated, revised, and tested in a variety of publications.[114] The most well-known and widely utilized modification and elaboration of defensive realism is Stephen Walt's "balance of threat" theory.[115] Walt argues that states balance against threats rather than against power. Therefore, it would be consistent with defensive realism for states to expand when expansion is seen as an effective response to a threat and to retrench when expansion is not needed or when retrenchment is seen as an effective response to a threat.

Defensive realism can explain both expansion and restraint: states are generally not expansionist or revisionist, but may become so in response to specific types of threats.

Defensive realism provides a plausible explanation for the American case: American strategic restraint was the result of a perception that the threat environment required only limited expansion. More specifically, since the United States was relatively secure in the Western Hemisphere, it had no reason to implement a grand strategy of expansionism. However, in specific instances where European powers threatened to increase their influence in the Caribbean Basin and South America, the United States had to expand to meet those threats. Thus in a very parsimonious manner defensive realism can explain both the overall strategy of restraint and the specific instances of expansion.

Despite the plausibility of the argument, it does have a few problems. First, while American leaders did at times seek to expand American control of foreign territory because of perceived threats, this was generally a weak factor.[116] Second, the historical record shows that an optimistic threat assessment was not the primary cause of American restraint. Third, defensive realism fails to explain American reluctance to balance against rising powers in Europe and Asia, especially during the 1930s and perhaps as early as the 1910s.[117] In other words, in cases where defensive realism predicts expansion, the United States was restrained. Despite these problems, the value of balance of threat theory can only be determined through empirical analysis.

Balance of threat theory predicts restraint under the following conditions:

1. If the political leaders of the rising power do not perceive a threat.
2. If the political leaders of a rising power believe that the threat cannot be alleviated through expansion or is best alleviated through retrenchment.
3. If political leaders believe that expansion will trigger balancing.

The economic interests approach is the second main alternative hypothesis for restraint. Like threat perception, economic interests can explain variation in the level of expansion. The most recent and nuanced proponent is Kevin Narizny. He builds on the scholarship of many others, including Peter Trubowitz and Benjamin Fordham and reaching back to William Appleman Williams. While the particulars vary among these theorists, the main argument is that when economic interests that favor foreign trade and investment are the coalition in power, rising powers will tend to have more expansionist grand strategies. When these interests are weak or are not represented in the ruling coalition, then expansion is unlikely. Narizny's analysis differentiates between groups that were oriented toward the core of the international system and those oriented toward the periphery. Externally oriented interests that focus on the core of the system favor cooperation with other great powers. Externally oriented interests that focus on the periphery favor expansion in the periphery.

Economic interest group theory predicts restraint under the following conditions:

1. If expansion will not provide economic benefits to powerful interest groups within a rising power.
2. If the dominant political coalition of a rising power believes it will not benefit economically from expansion.

Moving Forward

The metaphor of a tidal wave is useful for explaining the broad outlines of the argument. In the 1890s, individuals and groups within the United States developed strong ambitions for the extension of US influence in world politics, especially in the Western Hemisphere and East and Southeast Asia. Like an earthquake triggering a tsunami, the expansionist outcome of the Spanish-American War unleashed a surging demand for political–military expansionism, creating a tidal wave of expansionist advocacy in the United States. But even as this wave gathered momentum, it was limited and undermined by the friction of domestic norms and institutions. The wave gradually receded, unable to dislodge US grand strategy from its foundation in institutional structure and strategic culture. Unlike other rising powers, expansionist advocates in the United States were unable to maintain their momentum long enough to create a fundamental shift away from the traditional American strategy of restraint.

The rest of this book is devoted to elaborating the argument that the United States exhibited a grand strategy of restraint during its rise to the status of potential hegemon because the domestic political structure of the United States delayed, limited, undermined, and prevented the implementation of an expansionist grand strategy. The argument is made through the construction of causal narratives for 34 case studies of expansion and potential expansion between 1898 and 1941. The purpose of analyzing 34 cases is not to keep score between rival theories; instead the purpose is to document the overall trajectory of American grand strategy over time and demonstrate that the constant counterpressure of domestic structural restraint significantly reduced the possibilities for expansion, and eventually ended the drive for expansion completely. The next chapter begins the empirical narrative by analyzing the causes of American expansion and restraint in 1898.

Notes

1. See for example Schweller 1999; Davidson 2006, 1, 19, 21–24; Edelstein 2002, 15; Johnston 2003, 6; Organski 1968, 361.
2. See Zakaria 1999 and Lynn-Jones 1998.
3. Gilpin 1983, 54; Zakaria 1999, 20; Mearsheimer 2001, 2–3, 37–40; Davidson 2006 27–28.
4. Schweller 1999, 2, and 1998, 75–76; Zakaria 1999, 38.
5. Schweller 1999, 3.
6. Liberman 1993, 125–153; Mearsheimer 2001, 147–152; Menon and Oneal 1986, 185–191; Choucri and North 1975; Choucri, North, and Yamakage 1992; North 1977, 569–591.
7. North 1977, 148–152; Liberman 1993, 125–153.
8. Schweller 1999, 3–6. See Desch 1993 for a definition of geostrategically important territory.
9. Lynn-Jones 1998, 170.
10. A high sense of vulnerability is caused by the perception that status quo powers are trying to block their rise. This perception can lead rising powers to use new capabilities to adopt increasingly expansionist and competitive policies to breakout of this encirclement (Kupchan 1994).
11. Wohlforth 2009, 28–57; Lebow 2010; Gilpin 1983, 30–34. For a general discussion of prestige as a motivation for state behavior see Markey 1999, 126–173.
12. As states rise, they tend to develop new "role conceptions" that require recognition from existing great powers in order to be validated; see Rynning and Ringsmose 2008, 32–33; Doran and Parson 1980; Tessman 2009.

13. Kupchan 1994, 78. From the perspective of social identity theory, all states want a positive self-image and will compete with other states to demonstrate their superiority; see Larson and Shevchenko 2010, 68–76.

14. For an example, see Wohlforth's (2009, 44–47) description of the causes of the Crimean War. According to Wohlforth, the conflict was caused by disagreement over the relative status of the protagonists (Russia, Britain, and France).

15. Trubowitz 1998; Narizny 2003, 2007.

16. Abernethy 2000, 238–241.

17. See Menon and Oneal 1986, 170–178; Hobson 1965.

18. Snyder 1991, 32–39.

19. On expansionism in general see Snyder 1991; on imperialism see Abernethy 2000, 238–241. Jason Davidson's (2006, 29–45) neoclassical realist theory goes beyond Snyder's theory to explore how internal pressures from expansionist interest groups combine with international pressures (or a permissive international environment) to foster revisionism.

20. The internal development and social dislocation inherent in a rising power create a favorable environment for the strengthening of nationalism and expansionism. Mansfield and Snyder (2005, chapter 7) discuss the tribulations of democratization, but several of their case studies also demonstrate how the socioeconomic dislocations of rising powers foster nationalism, expansionism, and war.

21. As Carr (1964, 145) notes, "human beings do in the long run reject the doctrine of might makes right."

22. Snyder 1991, 41–42.

23. See Kupchan 1994, 74–87.

24. See Snyder 1991, 92–95; Schweller 2009.

25. Abernethy 2000, 249.

26. Menon and Oneal 1986, 189; Snyder 1991; Kupchan 1994.

27. Labs 1997. For a thoughtful analysis of the incentives for expanding and contracting war aims see Clausewitz 1976, 75–99.

28. See Wohlfers 1965, 154; Desch 1993, 11–12, 179–180; Layne 2002/2003, 128–132; Kupchan 1994. This logic of expansion is the basis for Robinson and Gallagher's (1968, chapter 15) explanation for the enlargement of the British Empire. For an application of this principle to US diplomatic history see Weinberg 1963.

29. Van Evera 1997, 64–67.

30. Van Evera 1997, 308–309. For the text of the 1895 Republican platform see Commager 1949, 173–174.

31. LaFeber 1993a, 126–128; Hamilton 2006, 8; Offner 2004, 53.

32. LaFeber 1993a, chapter 2; Small, 1995, 29; Herring 2008, 270.

33. LaFeber 1963, chapters 4–6; Beisner 1986, 76–77.

34. Beisner 1986, 77; McCormick 1990.

35. The argument was originally stated in Hofstadter 1965, 145–187; for an elaboration of the social instability argument see LaFeber 1993a, 30–31, 39–44, 49–59, 103–113.

36. Monten 2005, 123–126, 132–140.

37. Rhodes 1999, 61–70; Beisner 1986, 80–91. See also LaFeber 1993a. On immigration see LaFeber 1993a, 46–49. On the creation of an imperial culture in the United States see Goldenberg 2000, 171–181.

38. LaFeber 1963, chapter 3.

39. Beisner 1986, 78–79; Trask 1996, 59.

40. Rystad 1975, 11, 38–42, 56–58.

41. LaFeber 1963, chapter 2; Brands 1995, chapter 8; Rystad 1975, 42–52. On ideas about racial hierarchy and Anglo-Saxon superiority see Hunt 1987, chapter 3.

42. Herring 2008, 311.

43. LaFeber emphasizes the emergence of a consensus between political and economic elites that US interests required a more expansionist policy in Latin America, LaFeber 1963, 150–283.

44. Sewell 1992.

45. According to one classic definition political structure is "a collection of institutions, rules of behavior, norms, roles, physical arrangements, buildings, and archives that are relatively invariant in the face of turnover of individuals and relatively resilient to the idiosyncratic preferences and expectations of individuals"; March and Olsen 1984, 734–749.

46. See North 1990; Lieberman 2002, 699; Steinmo, Thelen, and Longstreth 1992.

47. Quoted in Lantis 2006, 16.

48. See for example Owen 1997; Berger 1998; Duffield 1998.

49. North 1990.

50. See Walker 1992; Naeem 1998; Nowak et al. 1997.

51. See Tyler 2006.

52. Hall and Taylor 1996, 936–946; Elman 1995, 181–182, 185–187; Thelen 1999.

53. Tannenwald 1999, 436; see also Legro 1996, 120–121.

54. The relevant literature is vast, but see the essays in part 2 of Katzenstein 1996; Steele 2007, 904; Abdelal et al. 2006, 698.

55. Katzenstein 1998, 18–19; Tannenwald, 1999, 437. For the classic discussion of the taken-for-grantedness of norms see Swidler 1986, 273–286.

56. See Blyth 2002.

57. Krebs and Jackson 2007, 35–66.

58. On path dependence see Thelen 1999; Mahoney 2000; Pierson 2004; Page 2006.

59. See Schweller 1998, 77, 1999, 3.

60. The insight that institutions and norms can be layered on top of one another is developed in Mann 1984; Orren and Skowronek 1994; Thelen 2004.

61. See Bennett and Elman 2006.

62. Capoccia and Kelemen 2007, 354.

63. Capoccia and Kelemen 2007, 354; Legro 2000, 2005, 2007; Page 2006.

64. The seed of this argument can be found in Bennett and Elman 2006, 258; Dickson, Farris, and Verbeke 2001. As noted by Bennett and Elman, negative feedback is usually seen as a factor that works against path dependence, but it can just as easily work in favor of the maintenance of an existing path if it prevents the lock-in of a new path.

65. See Arrow 1962; Dickson, Farris, and Verbeke 2001.

66. For a comparison of positive and negative feedback effects see Dickson, Farris, and Verbeke 2001.

67. The only example I am aware of is Elman 1995. There are compelling reasons to believe that foreign policy, like other forms of public policy, is path-dependent. On the path dependence of public policy see Pierson 2006.

68. Krasner 1978, 70.

69. Montesquieu 1989; Rossiter 1961; Deudney 2004.

70. See Madison 1788.

71. Immergut 1990; Tsebelis 1995, 2002; Choi 2010.

72. Tsebelis 1995, 301.

73. Tsebelis 1995, 315.

74. Tsebelis 1995, 292–293, 301–302, 315.

75. See Mansfield, Milner, and Pevehouse, 2008, 72.

76. The literature on divided government in the United States is vast. A good place to start is the debate between and Mayhew and Kelly: Mayhew 1991, 1993; Kelly 1993a, 1993b. On polarization see Jones 2001; Fiorina and Abrams 2008; Layman, Carsey, and Horowitz 2006.

77. Immergut 1990; Tsebelis 2002.

78. See Mansfield, Milner, and Pevehouse 2007; Henisz 2000.

79. Congressional Quarterly 1991, 48.

80. Tsebelis 1995, 306–310. For example, if Congress and the president have highly congruent policy preferences.

81. See Sobel 2001; Baum 2004.

82. Aldrich et al. 2006, 478; Holsti 1992, 446–455; Baum 2004; Sobel 2001, 23–24.

83. Owen 1997, 43–47; Baum 2004; Bueno de Mesquita et al. 1999; Fearon 1994; Schultz 1998; Schweller 1992; Snyder 1991, 39.

84. Baum and Potter 2008, 40. Research on the effect of the media on foreign policy parallel research on the effect of public opinion on foreign policy, including using the same pluralist and elitist models. See Risse-Kappen 1991, 480–484.

85. The simple definition for federalism is a political structure that has two semiautonomous, overlapping levels of government; see Riker 1964.

86. Maoz and Russett 1993, 629.

87. Maoz and Russett 1993, 16–17, 27–28. The classic discussion of the restraining effect of an extended republic written by either Alexander Hamilton or James Madison remains relevant; see "Federalist No. 51," http://avalon.law.yale.edu/18th_century/fed51.asp.

88. Trubowitz 1998; Silverstone 2004, 42–48.

89. The classic work is Trubowitz 1998.

90. Trubowitz 1998, chapters 1 and 2.

91. See Tannenwald 1999, 462.

92. See Inglehard 1988; Feldman 1988; Schwartz, Caprara, and Vecchione 2010, 421–452.

93. Inglehard 1988, 1205. See also Inglehard 1990.

94. Legro 2000, 419–432; Legro 2005, 253; Blyth 2002, 284.

95. Berger 1996, 326.

96. Hattam and Lowndes 2013; Finnemore and Sikkink 1998, 887–91.

97. Herman 1996, 271–316; Berger 1996; Abdelal, et al. 2006; Finnemore and Sikkink 1998.

98. Swidler 1986, 273–286.

99. Old norms die hard; even when they lose appeal and are subsumed by new norms, they typically remain part of the public discourse for some time.

100. Eisinger 2000, 656.

101. This discussion draws on Tannenwald 1999, 462. This approach has some similarities with the work on the operational codes of leaders that was initiated by the groundbreaking work of George (1969).

102. Friedberg 2000; Lipset 1997. The roots of this belief system go back to the republican origins of the American Founding; see Deudney 2007, 161–189.

103. Tompkins 1970.

104. On the importance of organizational missions see Wilson 1991, 95–101. For an example of the new forms of missions developed in the armed forces see Shulman 1999. Precisely how many Americans were committed anti-imperialists and how many were sympathetic to anti-imperialist arguments is impossible to determine, but throughout this book evidence is presented to suggest that anti-imperialist critiques were consistently considered to be politically effective by politicians on both sides of the issue.

105. Friedberg 2000, 9–33.

106. The term "voice opportunities" is from Grieco 1996. The term was originally used by Hirschman 1970. See Howell and Pevehouse 2007b.

107. See the contributions in Rosecrance and Stein 1993.

108. Moravcsik 1997.

109. Rathbun 2010.

110. Aaron Friedberg's (2000) work comes closest to providing a comprehensive account of domestic factors.

111. Of course the defining features of international structure are quite different from the defining features of domestic structure, see Waltz 1979.

112. Fioretos 2011, 367–399.

113. Waltz 1979.

114. For recent elaborations see Glaser 1997; Taliaferro 2000/2001.

115. Walt 1987, x.

116. This point is supported in subsequent chapters.

117. The United States was roundly criticized by realists for its idealist and isolationist foreign policy during the interwar period. See Morgenthau 1950, 850–854; Kaufman 1992; Dueck 2001, 186; Mearsheimer 2009, 248–249.

2

★

ORIGINS OF
EXPANSIONISM

1898–1900

EGINNING IN THE LATE 1890s, the United States appeared to behave like a normal rising power by implementing an expansionist grand strategy. Since the 1870s the United States had been at the top of the international hierarchy in terms of economic power, but had eschewed turning this latent power into state power and passed up many opportunities to make territorial gains at the expense of weaker neighbors.[1] But 1898 was a major turning point: the United States joined the great power club through its military defeat of Spain and acquisition of colonies in the Caribbean and Asia-Pacific regions. However a close look at the events surrounding the Spanish-American War and its aftermath shows that even in this quintessential imperialist moment, the employment of state power was restrained by American domestic institutions and norms. The analysis below covers three foundational events during the emergence of the United States as a great power: the War of 1898 and nonannexation of Cuba, the annexation of Hawaii, and the annexation of the Philippines.

The War of 1898 and the Nonannexation of Cuba
(March–April 1898)

In 1898 political, economic, and social conditions favored an expansionist foreign policy, giving us a high expectation of expansion, given the right opportunity. The events surrounding the War of 1898 provided just that opportunity. However, that opportunity was only partially realized. In the same moment that the US Congress authorized the use of force to end the violence in Cuba, it also voted to renounce any territorial claims to Cuba, a potentially economically and strategically valuable piece of territory. Absent this congressional limitation made possible by separation of powers there would have been no restraint placed on American behavior toward Cuba subsequent to the US victory in its war with Spain. In other words, despite the clear incentives for expansion, Congress forced President McKinley to renounce territorial aspirations toward Cuba, significantly restraining American territorial expansion. As described below, Congress preemptively prohibited the annexation of Cuba in its authorization to use force to end the violence in Cuba, making this a clear case of restraint caused by the separation of powers supported by fragmented interests and anti-imperialist norms.

Authorization of Force and the Teller Amendment

On April 11, 1898, President McKinley asked Congress to pass a resolution authorizing the president to intervene in the Cuban-Spanish conflict, using force if necessary, to bring about peace and long-term stability in Cuba.[2] The House quickly complied with McKinley's request, but the Senate was more intransigent.[3] The final Senate bill contained two amendments limiting McKinley's freedom of action, the Turpie-Foraker and Teller Amendments. The former would recognize the Cuban rebels as the legitimate government of Cuba and the later would prohibit American annexation of Cuba in the event of US intervention.

The Turpie-Foraker and Teller Amendments emerged during debate over Chairman of the Senate Foreign Relations Committee Cushman K. Davis's three-part resolution that pronounced Cuban independence, ordered Spain out of Cuba, and instructed the president of the United States to ensure Spain's compliance. The Committee resolution was acceptable to McKinley. However, several members of the Foreign Relations Committee supported an amendment offered by Democratic Senator David Turpie (but written by Republican Senator Joseph Foraker) to formally recognize the Republic of Cuba. The amendment read: "The Government of the United States hereby recognizes the Republic of Cuba as the true and lawful government of that Island."[4] All but five Democrats supported the Turpie-Foraker Amendment and were joined by 24 Republicans. It passed 51 to 37 in the Senate. The winning coalition included 29 Democrats, eleven Silver Republicans and Populists, and eleven other Republicans.[5] These senators asserted the right of the Senate to recognize a foreign country and directly undermine the policy set forth by President McKinley. According to one McKinley biographer, the passage of the amendment demonstrated McKinley's "shattered influence over his party."[6] McKinley promised to veto any resolution recognizing Cuba, which set the stage for a major conflict between the Senate and the president.[7]

The revolt against McKinley continued. During the debate over the Turpie-Foraker Amendment, Silver Republican Senator Henry Teller of Colorado introduced his amendment. The text of the Teller Amendment reads: "Resolved . . . That the United States hereby disclaims any disposition or intention to exercise sovereignty, jurisdiction, or control over said Island except for the pacification thereof, and asserts its determination, when that is accomplished, to leave the government and control of the Island to its people."[8] Senator Teller purposely did not include any other Spanish possessions in his resolution against Cuban annexation, though he wouldn't necessarily have known that the conflict would extend beyond Cuba.[9] According to one recent interpretation, the impetus behind this resolution was "derived from various forces, those who opposed annexing territory containing large numbers of blacks and Catholics, those who sincerely supported Cuban independence, and representatives of the domestic sugar business, including sponsor Henry Teller of Colorado, who feared Cuban competition."[10] In other words, a coalition of racists, bigots, humanitarians, and US sugar producers combined to oppose annexation of Cuba. Support for Teller's amendment was so high that no roll call vote was required.[11]

Because the Teller Amendment was an important impediment to American expansion, it is worthwhile to focus on the reasons why it became law. First, the consensus among historians is that Senator Teller was influenced primarily by the sugar beet interests in the western states and by his anti-imperialist principles.[12] Henry Teller was a reformed imperialist who had once favored annexing Hawaii, Canada, and Cuba. After 1898 he consistently opposed the annexation of (and trade preferences for) sugar-producing territories.[13] Historian Lars Schoultz argues that it would be an exaggeration to claim that Teller was simply a tool of the nascent American sugar beet industry. He notes that Teller was unpredictable—he switched political party affiliation three times—and "it is equally possible that he and other anti-imperialists had heard enough from the jingos to fear that they would seize any opportunity to annex the island."[14] The influence of the Cuban lobby may have also had an effect. A member of the Cuban lobby claimed to have written the amendment and persuaded Teller to offer it as part of the congressional war resolution.[15] The important point is that various ideological and economic interest groups were able to work through Congress to push back against imperialists in the executive branch.

The final Senate resolution contained both the Turpie-Foraker and Teller amendments, and passed 67 to 21. It seemed that the Senate resolution would be approved by the House, until McKinley intervened. Through his cabinet and supporters on the Hill, McKinley made it known that the Senate resolution was unacceptable and that he was prepared to veto it.[16] Pressure from McKinley's allies began to bring dissident Republicans over to McKinley's side, especially the ones who favored a more aggressive policy. But a compromise was necessary to get the bill passed: the Turpie-Foraker Amendment was deleted, a clause declaring Cuba independent was included, and the Teller Amendment was retained.[17] Thus the resolution referred to Cuba as independent and prohibited annexation, but did not officially recognize an independent government of the Republic of Cuba. The resolution was approved in Congress on April 19 and was signed by the president on April 20, along with a final ultimatum for Spain to leave Cuba in 48 hours.[18]

Spain viewed the congressional resolution authorizing President McKinley to use force to resolve the Cuban-Spanish conflict as a virtual declaration of war.[19] Spain broke off diplomatic relations with the United States on April 21—the day after McKinley signed the authorization of force—and then declared war on the United States on April 23.[20] The United States declared war on April 25 (though Congress backdated their declaration of war to April 21) to widespread public approval. The Spanish-American War lasted only a few months, and by the time it was over, the United States was an imperial power. The victory in the War of 1898 strengthened the public appetite for expansion and reinforced the notion that the United States was a rising force in world politics, but the action of Congress through the Teller Amendment prevented the acquisition of Cuba.[21]

A Case of Restraint?

There can be no doubt that the United States significantly expanded its political and military control over foreign territory as a result of the treaty that ended the War of 1898. The war marked the emergence of the belief among many American leaders and significant segments of the public that the United States should involve itself in the affairs of a European country and its colony to the extent of going to war. This belief and the war that followed mark a major expansion in American political–military interests and ambitions abroad. A variety of permissive and proximate factors combined to produce this expansive attitude at this particular moment in American history: the long-term growth in American material power, jingoistic agitation by the so-called yellow press, outrage at Spanish atrocities, lobbying by Cuban-American groups, narrow economic interests, the increasing expansionism of the Republican Party, the belief that the United States needed an outlet for its economic overproduction, the emergence of strategic concepts such as large policy and navalism, and a growing unease among Americans about instability so close to their shore.[22] All of these factors combined to produce a more outward-looking national identity, specific anxieties about the violence in Cuba in 1898, and the national capacity to challenge Spain. As David Abernethy insightfully observes, "Power has two components: capacity to act and will to act."[23] In 1898 both components were in place for the use of American military power.

The multitude of incentives for expansion contrasts with the outcome of non-annexation of Cuba and a clear case of restraint. Two subsidiary points are important. First, the effect of the Teller Amendment is straightforward. The actions of Congress "guaranteed that the United States would pass over an opportunity to acquire Cuba."[24] It is highly suggestive that all the Spanish colonies not protected by the Teller Amendment—Puerto Rico, the Philippines, and Guam—were annexed by the United States (excluding the Carolines and remaining Marianas that were sold to Germany by Spain in 1899).[25] The amendment also formalized the moral purpose behind the popular support for American intervention. And despite future difficulties, McKinley abided by it.[26] Second, the Teller Amendment was foisted on the McKinley administration by Congress, and is therefore a case of one branch restraining another through the institutional mechanisms created by a separation of powers and checks and balances. Most historians see the Teller Amendment as a compromise between Congress and President McKinley. On the one hand, the amendment was seen as a victory for the anti-McKinley coalition and Cuban lobbyists, who had to give in on the question of recognition of Cuba. McKinley accepted the Teller Amendment, but he was not pleased.[27] On the other hand, McKinley had no intention of annexing Cuba, and therefore viewed the amendment as consistent with his goals.[28] Whatever the feeling at the time, the Teller Amendment was highly problematic for McKinley in the long run and certainly shaped the final settlement with Spain. Both points strongly support the hypotheses of domestic structural theory regarding the outcome of the case and the causal mechanisms at work. First, because both Congress and the president had to agree on war for it to occur, war was delayed by President McKinley's reluctance to commence hostilities. Second, the Teller Amendment was clearly an important restraint on American expansion that was due entirely to the separation of powers in the American political system and public norms and private beliefs against imperialism. The public and the press were also players, but recent research suggests that their role is much less prominent than previously portrayed.[29]

Alternative explanations for restraint find little support. While it is true that there was no major threat that could be alleviated by annexing Cuba, security concerns were simply not a significant part of the discourse. To the extent that security issues were relevant, they favored expansion based on the logic of navalism and large policy. Similarly, background economic conditions mainly favored expansionism. Domestic sugar producers did play a role in opposing annexation of Cuba, but they were part of a larger coalition that were "intervening in Cuba to help the Cuban people and not to annex the island," and believed that "removing Spain from the island would ultimately lead to full Cuban sovereignty."[30]

Annexation of Hawaii (July 7, 1898)

The United States annexed Hawaii less than three months after the declaration of war with Spain. On the surface this is an example of unfettered political–

military expansion, but annexation was delayed and only accomplished by relying on a legislative–executive agreement rather than a treaty. Annexation of
Hawaii was only the last step in a difficult, costly process that took decades to
achieve, but this case focuses on events during the McKinley administration.
Because the annexation of Hawaii occurred during the War of 1898, all of the
expansionist conditions identified in the previous case are also applicable in this
case. Three conditions deserve special attention: the popular belief that Hawaii
would facilitate access to the mythical China market, the wartime argument that
Hawaii was necessary to ensure the security of the West Coast of the American
homeland, and the actions of American-Hawaiians and the actions of agents of
expansionism on the ground in Hawaii that created conditions highly favorable
for annexation. These factors highlight the strategic and economic causes of
expansion while also refuting the explanations for restraint based on economic
and security interests. In this case, economic and security-based arguments were
important, but they were made mainly in favor of expansion. American sugar
producers did oppose annexation, but did not seem to have much influence on
policymakers. Anti-imperialists suggested that Hawaii would become a strategic
vulnerability, but in the wake of the impressive American victory against Spain,
this warning carried little weight. The outcome of this case is delayed expansion
caused by separation of powers through the mechanism of congressional opposition caused by anti-imperialist sentiment and divided economic interests. Not
only did congressional opposition cause delay, it also forced McKinley to use less
legitimate mechanisms for annexation.

Failure to Annex: The Triumph of the Anti-Imperialists

For four tumultuous years after the removal of Queen Liliuokalani in 1892 by an
American-Hawaiian coup d'état, Hawaii remained an independent republic.
Great efforts were made by the new leaders to make Hawaii part of the United
States, but anti-imperialism, racism, and conflicting economic interests in the
United States prevented annexation.[31] Throughout most of this period, the government of Hawaii continued to favor annexation as a means to deal with economic and security problems—the unstable market for sugar and growing
Japanese power in the Pacific. The election of 1896 brought William McKinley
and the Republican Party to power with an expansionist platform asserting that
the "Hawaiian Islands should be controlled by the United States and no foreign
power should be permitted to interfere with them."[32] Annexationists sought to
take advantage of this newly conducive political context. In April of 1897 the
Hawaiian minister sent the State Department a memorandum asking for the US
government to consider annexing Hawaii. The proximate cause of the treaty
seems to have been a dispute that emerged in February of 1897 between Japan
and Hawaii over Japanese immigration to Hawaii. The McKinley administration

viewed the proposal favorably and quickly negotiated an annexation treaty that then passed the Committee on Foreign Relations in July. The annexation treaty was approved by the Hawaiian Senate in September, but in the United States there was insufficient support in the Senate and the session expired without a vote being taken on the treaty.[33]

Opposition was led by American sugar producers, organized labor, and anti-imperialists. Sugar interests were relatively united and active in their opposition to annexation due to increased fear of competition from Hawaiian sugar, but still had relatively little influence on the annexation debate. Organized labor also worked against the treaty due to a feared influx of contract labor and Asian workers to the mainland. Again, the strongest force working against annexation was the normative argument made by anti-imperialists. They argued that annexation was inconsistent with the American republican tradition, historical commitments to an independent Hawaii, and the US Constitution. Anti-imperialists also emphasized that annexation would mean the incorporation of more non-whites into American society, and argued that Hawaii would be a strategic vulnerability and economically unimportant.[34] According to Thomas Osborne, the unifying thread among the antiannexationists was anti-imperialist beliefs: "The basic fact is simply that the anti-imperialists carried the day by appealing to hallowed American doctrines decrying territorial expansion overseas."[35] Widely held norms about the appropriateness of territorial aggrandizement was therefore the central factor that prevented the passage of the Hawaii annexation treaty.

Successful Annexation: The Triumph of the Strategists

In 1898, as the confrontation with Spain over Cuba intensified, debate over annexing Hawaii was again heard in the Senate. The importance of Hawaii was highlighted during the Spanish-American War when its ports were used to help support US troops in the Philippines.[36] Opponents held to the well-rehearsed antiannexation arguments; their message was amplified by the beet sugar lobby, led by sugar magnate Claus Spreckels.[37] It seemed that the antiannexationist coalition would again prevent territorial aggrandizement.

The blocking maneuvers of antiannexationists made ratification of the treaty untenable. Despite the advantage of a wartime presidency, McKinley could not count on a supermajority in the Senate and had to resort to a legislative-executive agreement rather than a treaty.[38] This maneuver would lower the vote threshold in the Senate, but force annexationists to gain majorities in both the Senate and the House. The resolution was reported by the Senate Committee on Foreign Relations on March 16, 1898, but soon stalled. A similar measure was reported by the House Committee on Foreign Relations on May 17. Gaining approval in the House would be no simple matter because of the control exercised by antiannexationist Thomas B. Reed, the powerful Speaker of the House.

Reed opposed annexation and successfully prevented debate on McKinley's proposal for three weeks, until pressure from his fellow Republican members of Congress and the McKinley administration proved too great. Pratt argues that "there was a limit beyond which even he [Reed] would not go in opposing the wishes of his party."[39] Once Reed's opposition was overcome, the outcome was not in doubt. On June 15, the resolution passed the House 209 to 91 with 55 abstentions and absences. Most of the opposition came from Democrats in the South and West, reflecting partisanship, anti-imperialist sentiment as well as sectional interests regarding race and the domestic sugar industry.[40]

In the Senate annexationists were confident they could pass the bill; the main issue was whether or not they could maintain a quorum throughout the debate. If they failed to do so, the opposition could force an adjournment delaying the issue until the next session.[41] The opposition apparently chose to forego a filibuster and, according to contemporary reporting by the *New York Times*, decided to allow a vote because "they had no desire to keep the Senate in session by purely dilatory tactics."[42] The resolution passed the Senate on July 6 by a vote of 42 to 21 with 26 abstentions (less than 50 percent voted in favor of annexation). Again the split was partisan and sectional: opponents included two Republicans, one Populist, and 18 Democrats; supporters included six Democrats (all from southern states except one from Maryland), one Independent, and 35 Republicans.[43]

The annexation of Hawaii was opposed for a variety of reasons, ranging from political, philosophic, and moralistic arguments to explicitly racist and self-interested arguments. Southern states contributed strongly to the antiannexationist vote. They opposed annexation 57 to 18 in the House and 12 to 7 in the Senate. Historian Joseph Fry argues that southern opposition to expansion was based on "racial concerns, potential economic competition, fear of enhanced federal power, and partisan politics."[44] Southern senators were also powerful spokesmen for anti-imperialism. One of the strongest advocates of anti-imperialism, Democratic Senator Augustus Octavius Bacon of Georgia, railed against the dangers of "Executive usurpation."[45] Other anti-imperialists argued that annexation would require more naval spending and "would be the first step toward colonialism and the destruction of the Constitution (which, they believed, could not easily extend across large expanses of water and over multiracial populations)."[46] They also argued that the United States already had informal control of Hawaii, and therefore annexation was unnecessary. Parochial components of the antiannexationist coalition included "antiimmigrant groups in California, sugar-beet interests, and organized labor that feared an influx of cheap Asian workers."[47]

Annexationists had an advantage in 1898 in that they could argue annexation was a military necessity: "The most important new argument for annexation declared Hawaii a way station and naval base vital for communication with the Philippines."[48] They reiterated the arguments about Hawaii serving as a "vital Western outpost" that would be used to protect American interests in East Asia and a future Nicaraguan canal.[49] Proponents stressed the strategic and commercial value of Hawaii and the threat of another power like Japan gaining control of the island nation.[50] Sugar interests were divided over whether and how strongly to oppose annexation.[51]

Why was annexation defeated in 1897, but successful in 1898? Three factors are important. First, pressure to increase influence in East Asia became especially intense in 1898 due to the increase in exports and the increased efforts by European powers to colonize the Asia-Pacific region.[52] Annexationists believed that the Asia-Pacific region was becoming increasingly important to the United States for economic and strategic reasons at the same time that the United States was losing influence in the region. Second, the Spanish-American War led directly to the annexation of Hawaii.[53] From this perspective, Dewey's victory over the Spanish at Manila Bay in the Philippines gave Hawaii added value as a base connecting the Philippines with the United States, and the Asia-Pacific component of the Spanish-American War suggested that Hawaii might help defend the West Coast. Whether or not these arguments were true, they gained traction in the press and were generally influential.

A third factor was necessary for the success of annexation in 1898: the political strategy of using a joint resolution rather than a treaty to annex Hawaii.[54] Annexationists switched from an institutional strategy of treaty ratification by a Senate supermajority to a joint resolution requiring majorities in the Senate and House of Representatives. It would seem to be a critical issue, because the final Senate vote on the resolution did not receive anywhere near the two-thirds majority required for treaty ratification. This change in strategy was successful, but not without triggering an outpouring of anti-imperialist outrage. For example, according to the contemporaneous reporting of the *New York Times*, Georgia Democratic Senator Bacon argued on the floor of the Senate that "the only proper method of annexing foreign territory was by means of a treaty." Furthermore, "Mr. Bacon contended that a statute of one country could not be made obligatory upon another country; hence the necessity of a treaty of annexation proceedings, as a treaty only can bind both countries." Bacon also argued that if the joint resolution were passed, the Senate "would surrender its treaty-making power."[55]

Senator Caffery, a Democrat from Louisiana, echoed the arguments of Bacon: annexation of territory by congressional resolution (or "purely legislative act") was unconstitutional.[56] In response, proannexationist Senator Stewart replied that Great Britain had taken parts of India by an act of Parliament, and similarly, the US Congress had full power to annex territory. Caffery replied that Stewart's argument "would constitute Congress as an absolute despotism."[57] In the House, Representative Dinsmore, a Democrat from Arkansas, echoed the constitutional arguments made by Senator Bacon.[58] This snapshot of the debate shows that the use of a joint resolution was controversial, while also highlighting the importance of norms and the connection between anti-imperialism abroad and worries about despotism at home.

Delayed Expansion

Hawaiian annexation is a particularly rich case that illustrates the multidimensional character of the collision between power and restraint. The main causes of expansion were an outgrowth of the conditions brought about by the War of 1898. Ongoing hostilities with Spain increased the strategic justification for expansion, and Dewey's victory in the Philippines provided extra incentive for the United States to establish a political and military presence in the Pacific Ocean. Hawaii was attractive strategically both as a means of increasing the reach of American power and to prevent Japan or a European power from gaining control of the islands. Economic explanations for the annexation of Hawaii seem weak. Commercial arguments had been around for decades, and there is little reason to believe they suddenly became more salient in July of 1898. Also, sugar interests in the United States were either opposed to annexation or neutral.[59] The specific path to annexation demonstrates the importance of individuals acting from within the annexed territory (American-Hawaiians) creating the facts on the ground (taking control of the government of Hawaii) favorable to American intervention and expansion.

Like the War of 1898, the annexation of Hawaii is not a straightforward case of expansion and instead is best categorized as delayed expansion. The annexation of Hawaii was defeated twice before finally being approved through a dubious and highly controversial executive–legislative agreement. A variety of groups opposed annexation for a variety of reasons, including racism and anti-immigrant sentiment (i.e., fear of the incorporation of more nonwhites into the United States); fear of economic competition from Hawaiian sugar producers and labor; partisanship; and hostility toward executive aggrandizement and fear that imperialism would undermine the Constitution. These interests found Congress to be a powerful means of opposing expansion and strength in the enduring anti-imperialist norms in American strategic culture. Absent the fragmented nature of American institutional structure and the resonance of anti-imperialist arguments, annexation would have occurred much sooner and would have been less costly to expansionists. Furthermore, the debate over the annexation of Hawaii became a dress rehearsal for the coming political conflict over the annexation of the Philippines, Guam, and Puerto Rico. Alternative explanations for delayed expansion find little support. Security-based arguments and economic interests did much more to foster expansion than restraint.

Annexation of the Philippines, Guam, and Puerto Rico (December 1898)

The fruits of victory in the Spanish-American War were the Philippines, Puerto Rico, and Guam. However, the debate over the first completely submerged the other two.[60] There were few objections to annexing Puerto Rico—its value lay mainly in totally eliminating Spain from the Caribbean and providing a strategic position for the United States.[61] Guam was taken as a base to facilitate the resupply of American forces in the Philippines.[62] But both are insignificant in comparison to the Philippines, the largest, most important colonial possession of the United States. It is vital to understand why and how the United States came to hold such a significant piece of territory so far from American shores. The reasons are many. The conditions favorable to expansion highlighted in the other cases in this chapter also apply to this case. The Philippines were seen as the key to the markets of East Asia, necessary for American power projection across the Pacific Ocean, the just deserts of a rising power that had just won a war, a symbol of prestige, and an opportunity for the United States to show the world that Americans were better than Europeans at spreading Western civilization. As with Hawaii, action by individuals in the foreign territory (in this case American sailors and soldiers) created facts on the ground that encouraged expansion. Having boots on the ground in territory considered to be ungoverned creates a powerful incentive for territorial expansion consistent with the logic of expanding war aims and David Abernethy's concept of "imperial inertia."[63] Finally, annexation seemed to be the least bad option from a strategic and (ethnocentric) humanitarian perspective. An independent Philippines would be annexed by Japan or Germany if the United States didn't do it, and the only other option was to allow Spain to retain it, which likely would have led it to be transferred to another great power.

The multitude of reasons why the United States annexed the Philippines brings to light a puzzle about how it occurred: in a disjointed, drawn-out, unplanned, and reluctant manner. The reason for the difficult drawn-out process was due to delays caused by domestic structure. The first delay occurred between May and October 1898, as McKinley deliberated over how much—if any—of the Philippines to ask for in the treaty negotiations with Spain. A central reason for this delay was McKinley's fear of public backlash over the long term. The second delay was created by anti-imperialists in the Senate. The first step toward gaining a better understanding of how the United States acquired the Philippines is an analysis of the war aims of the McKinley administration in the Pacific during the Spanish-American War and the decision by McKinley to take and hold the city of Manila. These two events occurred as part of the US warfighting strategy, but had the unintended consequence of handing the Philippines to the

United States. The third step of the analysis is the decision by President McKinley to seek the entire archipelago in negotiations with Spain. Analysis of these steps shows that the United States did not originally consider the possibility of annexation because of anti-imperialist norms and the simple fact that decision makers had not considered what to do with the Philippines until after the end of the war. The final step is the Senate ratification of the peace treaty that included annexation of the Philippines, Puerto Rico, and Guam. The last step shows the influence of domestic structure most clearly, but requires an explanation for why antiannexationists in the Senate were unable to prevent the annexation of the Philippines.[64]

War Aims and the American Asiatic Fleet

The Battle of Manila Harbor commenced on May 1, 1898. After six hours of combat the outmatched Spanish forces surrendered, suffering the destruction of ten ships and hundreds of Spanish sailors dead. Dewey's forces emerged relatively unscathed.[65] Following his victory at sea, Dewey ordered the Spanish artillery batteries in Manila to remain silent or he would destroy the city. He viewed their acquiescence as a de facto surrender.[66] News of the victory reached Washington via London and Madrid on May 2 or 3, and was confirmed on May 7 by a telegram from Dewey.[67] Secretary of the Navy John Davis Long notified Dewey on May 13 that two ships were being readied to resupply his forces. Ground forces were also to be dispatched, and Long asked how many Dewey required; the reply was five thousand. Spain also sent an expedition to reinforce its garrison at Manila, causing much concern in Washington and Manila Harbor. American naval strategists feared that if Spanish reinforcements reached Manila before American forces, Dewey would have to cede the harbor or risk destruction. The United States was fortunate that the Spanish expedition was ordered to return to Spain after the Battle of Santiago, and US reinforcements reached Dewey on June 30 (ground forces) and August 5 (armored monitor *Monterey*).[68] The city of Manila was taken by American forces on August 14, two days after the war ended—the time lag was caused by slow communications—and marks the first instance where actions outside the control of Washington made annexation more likely.[69] A ceasefire or Protocol of Agreement was signed on August 12, 1898, that settled the status of Spanish possessions in the Caribbean and Guam, but left the status of the Philippines to be determined at the peace conference, which would last from September 29 to December 10.[70]

The first issue that must be settled is why Dewey was sent to the Philippines in the days after the United States declared war on Spain. The preponderance of evidence suggests that the attack on the Spanish fleet at Manila was the result of a war plan to defeat Spain drafted by the navy in 1896 and revised in 1897.[71] Dewey's mission was developed by experts in the US Navy for the purposes of defeating Spain and was carried out with this goal in mind. The basis of the strategy was "the destruction of the enemy's power and will to fight" by "attacking the enemy's weakest positions at the periphery of its empire with the strongest available forces."[72] The plan called for attacking the city of Manila in cooperation with Filipino insurgents, and noted that reinforcements would probably be necessary to complete the task.[73] According to historian H. W. Brands, taking control of Manila "would serve the triple objective of preventing the Spanish vessels from joining the fight in the American theater, of depriving Spain of the revenue of the islands and of gaining a bargaining chip, at least, for subsequent peace negotiations."[74] Some historians have emphasized the role of Theodore Roosevelt in the taking of the Philippines. It is true that as assistant navy secretary Roosevelt was an active advocate of attacking Manila, but he had no influence on the original war plan.[75] Roosevelt also ordered the commander of the American Asiatic fleet, Commodore George Dewey, to stand by for offensive operations when Secretary of the Navy John Long was out of office; Long himself, however, after consultation with McKinley, gave the order to Dewey to attack the Spanish fleet stationed at the Philippines on April 25, 1898.[76] This evidence suggests that Manila was taken to achieve the political objective of the war, not the other way around.

Further evidence is supplied by McKinley's statements about Dewey's mission. McKinley sent Dewey to Manila to force Spain to capitulate, but was unsure what to do with the Philippines once the Spanish fleet was defeated. McKinley argued that Dewey went to the Philippines because he had to engage the Spanish fleet and that is where they were stationed:

> But as this had taken place at Manilla [sic] and not on the high seas [,] Manilla became a question from which we could not escape. It was necessary to attack Spain on that side of the world to protect our commerce and embarrass them at home, and having destroyed their fleet Dewey found that to be the safest and indeed the only harbor open to him as by laws of neutrality he was excluded from all other countries [sic] ports.[77]

The Spanish navy was defeated, but Spanish troops continued to occupy Manila and they could threaten Dewey's ships with their land-based bombardment. Reinforcements were therefore needed to consolidate the naval victory by occupying Manila. Sending reinforcements and ordering the occupation of Manila were triggered by Dewey's victory and were meant to further the goal of ending the war quickly and decisively, with the side benefit of giving the United States more leverage at the negotiating table, and again were consistent with the 1896 war plan.[78] McKinley himself stated that Dewey's victory at Manila Harbor and the actions taken to occupy Manila "greatly shortened" the war.[79] Historian Paolo Coletta argues that occupation of Manila was an unnecessary escalation of war aims, but as other historians have made clear and the McKinley quote suggests, part of the warfighting strategy was to hold Manila as a bargaining piece in the negotiations that would follow.[80] Furthermore, as noted above, even after Dewey's initial victory control of Manila was contested by Spanish forces. There was no guarantee that Dewey could hold his position in Manila Harbor without supplemental sea and ground forces. Spanish relief forces were on their way to relieve Manila soon after Dewey's victory.

After American forces occupied Manila, guidance from Washington was intermittent and ambiguous. As Grania Bolton argues, "Although there was some guidance from Washington in the form of orders and instructions, these did not constitute a coherent policy defining America's relationship with the insurgents."[81] The result was a "policy of drift" marked by a series of errors in judgment by the military commanders on the ground and lack of attention from Washington that eventually led to the outbreak of the Philippine-American War (covered in more detail in the next chapter).[82] Delays among decision makers in Washington over the composition of the treaty and its ratification prevented the communication of a clear strategy to American military commanders in the Philippines. Without a clear strategy from Washington, military officers could do little but try to implement American policy to the extent that they could understand it. However, the presence of US soldiers in the Philippines without the articulation of a clear American policy caused tensions with nationalists without allowing for American military commanders to take authoritative actions in dealing with nationalist leaders.

Thus, the initial presence of American sailors and soldiers on Philippine territory was simply a result of the American warfighting strategy, which highlights the importance of war as a proximate cause for territorial expansion. It is difficult to get troops out of foreign territory once they are in it. Furthermore, establishing a presence in foreign territory creates the possibility for officers or diplomats to take actions that increase US involvement in a manner unintended by political leaders. In the context of an ongoing war, expansion of military control of territory is typically advantageous, but has the unintended consequence of entangling the occupying power ever more deeply in the affairs of foreign peoples.

McKinley's Decision to Annex the Philippines

The decisive step toward annexation was McKinley's order to his peace commissioners to demand control of the Philippines during the peace negotiations with Spain. McKinley's position developed over several months' time. Between May and October of 1898 McKinley slowly increased his territorial demands toward the Philippines, illustrating "the endemic temptation to victorious nations to expand their demands beyond the stated objectives of a war."[83] In May of 1898, the official US position was to allow Spain to keep the Philippines except for a coaling station for the United States there or on the Caroline Islands. By July, the McKinley administration's plan was to claim only a Philippine harbor (Manila) for a naval base and leave the rest to Spain. By September McKinley modified his position to claim all of Luzon Island (where Manila was located). However, this position did not last long. The majority opinion among McKinley's advisors was that (1) it would be difficult and strategically unwise to attempt to occupy only Manila or Luzon due to the interdependence of the island chain, and that (2) the Philippine people could not govern themselves and would rapidly be swallowed up by Germany or Japan. Major General Francis V. Greene is thought to have been particularly influential in shifting McKinley toward total annexation. After returning from the Philippines, where he led the attack on Manila, he gave a report to McKinley favoring annexing the entire archipelago for the two reasons mentioned above.[84] By October, McKinley decided to annex the entire archipelago.[85]

Most historians argue that McKinley saw annexation as the least bad option strategically and the one most in line with his religious and moral beliefs. The most authoritative and authentic statement given by McKinley himself was recorded on November 19, 1898—a month after McKinley instructed his peace negotiators to gain the entire archipelago—by Chandler Parsons Anderson in a private discussion with President McKinley and Thomas Jefferson Coolidge in McKinley's office. According to Anderson's written record of the conversation, McKinley stated that the United States had to maintain control of all the Philippines Islands because (1) they could not be returned to Spain "for the very reasons which justified the war" (i.e., humanitarian reasons); (2) they could not be transferred to another European power because this would cause a war and would go against American interests; (3) it was the "responsibility" and "duty and destiny" of the American people to accept control of the islands; and (4) the "strategic interdependence of the islands" was such that the United States had to keep all of them or none of them.[86] In his own words, McKinley comes away as a "reluctant imperialist."[87]

The most convincing explanation is that to McKinley and his advisors, annexation seemed to be the only viable option for strategic and moral reasons. If the United States maintained control, the Philippines would be freed from the tyranny of European rule while being groomed for eventual independence.[88] After a careful review of the evidence, Richard Hamilton comes to two main conclusions about McKinley's decision to annex the Philippines. First, the decision was made only after a long and difficult process; there was no predetermined goal of annexing the Philippines. Second, the main factors influencing McKinley's decision were strategic and moral, and not the influence of big business seeking access to the China market or world markets, as LaFeber argues.[89] Hamilton does an especially thorough job of demolishing the argument that McKinley was convinced to annex the Philippines by business leaders interested in trade with China.[90]

A secondary but also important question is why President McKinley took so long to make his decision. First, he was unprepared. He did not consider the possibility of annexing the Philippines until after the War of 1898 began. McKinley famously proclaimed after Dewey's victory that he "could not have told where those darned islands were within 2,000 miles!"[91] Second, McKinley delayed because he believed that American norms would lead to widespread public opposition to annexing the Philippines over the long run. McKinley reportedly stated that "to give up the Philippines now would mean a great storm of criticism this winter but that to retain them would be to mean permanent criticism thereafter."[92] Even when McKinley overcame his fears of public opposition, he was well aware that strident anti-imperialist opposition would emerge once he publicly favored taking possession of the Philippines.[93]

In sum, the United States seemed to have three main options with regard to the Philippines: the United States could turn the archipelago over to another great power, keep it, or allow it to become an independent state. However, there was a fourth viable option promoted by anti-imperialists that was potentially consistent with American strategic and moral imperatives: making the Philippines an American protectorate. Anti-imperialists Carl Schurz and Senator George F. Hoar developed a plan that "sought to 'protect' a truly independent Philippine republic both by granting temporary American assistance and by securing an international guarantee of Philippine sovereignty and neutrality."[94] In classic republican fashion, this plan would secure the Philippines from the dual threats of internal anarchy and external conquest and would avoid the danger posed to both the Philippine and American people by direct US control (i.e., imperialism corrupts the oppressor and degrades the oppressed). At the same time, Hoar understood that it was necessary to appease the "strong feeling [among the American people] that it would be alike humiliating and dishonorable to give them back to Spain, or to let them become the prey of European Powers."[95] The Hoar-Schurz proposal failed to gain political traction for two reasons. First, there was a tactical error by Hoar in assuming that the Senate would reject the Treaty of Paris and the anti-imperialist proposal could then be added as an amendment to a new bill. Second, the anti-imperialist alliance fragmented. Senators Hoar and Schurz apparently developed their proposal too late to influence the development of McKinley's thinking and the treaty, and then focused their energy on defeating the treaty.[96] McKinley considered establishing a protectorate, but disliked the "more complex and ambiguous obligation"—he saw protectorates as having all the costs of annexation, but without the benefit of control.[97] McKinley reluctantly took the country to war, but once the United States was committed, the president worked to obtain as much benefit from the conflict as possible.[98]

McKinley's decision to include annexation of the Philippines in the US peace terms demonstrates the powerful incentive to maximize territorial gains in the context of a military victory and the influence of new strategic ideas about the role of the United States in the world, especially the beliefs that uncivilized peoples needed the aid and tutelage of the United States and that the United States must embrace its destiny as a great power. Despite the powerful incentives for territorial expansion, McKinley delayed the decision for expansion while he navigated the cultural and institutional restraints.

The Senate Debate over Annexation of the Philippines

Once McKinley decided to annex the Philippines, his administration and supporters devoted themselves to the task of convincing Congress and the American people of the wisdom of the decision. After gaining Spanish agreement on the disposition of the Philippines, the Treaty of Paris was signed on December 10, 1898, officially ending the war with Spain and establishing the United States as a global, colonial power. Soon after, on December 21, McKinley presented the Senate with a fait accompli by issuing an executive order for the US forces in the Philippines to establish American sovereignty over the archipelago. One historian pithily captures the logic of McKinley's action: "If the Senate were now to refuse to confirm the Treaty of Paris, it would be repudiating the declaration of the nation's commander in chief as well as the achievement of his peace commissioners."[99]

The debate over the treaty was contentious. The annexation question pitted Republicans, businessmen, and religious leaders against Democrats, intellectuals, and labor leaders (though there were many exceptions to these generalities).[100] Antiannexationists generally favored the acquisition of a naval base or coaling stations in the Philippines to protect American commercial interests in the Far East, but opposed annexing large inhabited areas of the islands.[101] Antiannexationists worried about the cost of administering the Philippines, the economic competition from Filipino labor, racial mixing, and constitutional issues of taking control of a territory that would never become a state. Anti-imperialists feared that the United States would come to resemble corrupt, centralized European imperial powers, losing its democratic, republican institutions and identity while imposing its rule on foreign peoples. They also foresaw the coming war with the Philippines, and argued that increased American involvement in Asia could lead to war with European powers. Antiannexationists also appealed to economic interests, noting that annexation would allow Philippine goods to enter the United States without being subject to tariffs, and therefore undercut American farmers.[102]

The most ardent expansionists felt drawn by duty and national interests to advocate for the United States to take on its share of the white man's burden to uplift and civilize the more barbarous regions of the globe. These men advocated opportunistic colonial expansion and saw the control of foreign territory and

peoples as the right and duty of the United States as a powerful, civilized country.[103] Supporters of annexation identified potential strategic and economic benefits, as well as the altruistic mission to civilize and modernize the Filipino people
and protect them from occupation by a less generous great power. An American
base in the Philippines would allow the United States to assert its interests in
the Far East and would help defend the West Coast of the United States in case
of an attack from the Pacific. It was argued that the United States would gain
economically through trade with the Philippines: the United States would
import agricultural goods and natural resources and export manufactured goods
and capital. Another major economic argument was that the Philippines would
give the United States an opening to the Asian trade. American entrepreneurs
dreamed of exporting everything from manufactured goods to cotton to the
fabled China market. The United States needed Manila as a distribution point
and naval outpost to protect American shipping. Annexationists had certain
advantages in the debate. They benefited from postwar euphoria of victory and
the fact that the United States possessed the Philippines, and therefore the decision was whether to give them up or not rather than whether to take them.
Annexationists could argue that the United States had won the Philippines
through war and possession was legitimated by treaty, and, therefore, it would be
humiliating to give them up.[104]

Public opinion was probably behind the annexationists. As H. W. Brands
notes, Congress was not overwhelmed by anti-imperialists petitions.[105] Analyses
of newspapers in 1898 suggest that at least a plurality of editorial pages were in
favor of annexation. Support for annexation seemed to be strongest on the West
Coast and weaker to the East and South. The business press was divided, but
most chambers of commerce and the National Association of Manufacturers
favored annexation. However, anti-imperialist sentiment was significant. The
most important antiannexationist group was the Anti-Imperialist League,
formed in November of 1898. It showed significant public support through a
rapid expansion to dozens of US cities.[106]

In January of 1899 the debate shifted to the floor of the US Senate, where it
was no foregone conclusion that the Treaty of Paris would be received favorably.
One historian notes that "after the treaty was in the hands of the Senate its
survival appeared improbable to contemporary observers both in and out of the
Senate."[107] The Senate debate was held in a secret or "executive" session
between January 4, 1899 and February 6, 1899. The problem for proponents—
generally Republicans—was the need for support from a significant number of
Democratic and Populist votes to gain the necessary two-thirds majority. Up
until early February, it seemed unlikely that annexationists could gain enough
support from the opposition without an amendment promising independence to
the Philippines. Even on the day of the vote, four of the senators needed for
ratification were seen as "doubtful."[108] According to proannexationist Senator

Henry Cabot Lodge, the vote of the second of the four senators on the fence was not secured until five minutes before the vote. After the vote he said that it had been "the closest, hardest fight I have ever known."[109] The final vote was 57 to 27 in favor of ratifying the Treaty of Paris: 40 Republicans, 10 Democrats, 4 Populists, 1 Silver Republican, 1 Silverite, and 1 Independent voted yea; 22 Democrats, 2 Republicans, 1 Silverite, and 2 Populists voted nay.[110] The two-thirds majority requirement was met with one vote to spare.

From the perspective of the historical development of president–Senate relations, passage of the treaty is surprising: "It came at a moment when no important treaty had been approved by the Senate for more than 25 years. It contained a radical departure from the traditional policy of the United States which the President requested the senators, of whom more than a third were political opponents, to approve."[111] Under these circumstances, it is important to ask why the Treaty of Paris was ratified by the Senate. Six factors are identified in the historical literature as crucial for gaining that narrow margin. First, partisanship was clearly a factor. Since the Republicans had an overall majority, it was easier for them to build the necessary two-thirds majority for treaty ratification.[112] Second, in a clever early decision to gain support for his policy, McKinley appointed the president pro tempore and the two most powerful senators in the Committee on Foreign Affairs—one Democrat and one Republican—to the peace commission.[113] Third, the McKinley administration and his supporters in Congress used public pressure and patronage to gain the votes of crucial wavering Democrats and Populists. McKinley put pressure on senators by going on a tour of the South promoting annexation and encouraging state legislatures to pass resolutions supporting annexation.[114] Republican leaders offered federal judgeships, cash bribes, patronage and funding for their states, and powerful committee positions for Democratic and Populist votes.[115]

Fourth, fighting between Filipino and American forces began on February 4, perhaps generating something of a rally-around-the-flag effect. Some analysts view this point as decisive. For example, Theodore Roosevelt thanked the Filipinos for "pull[ing] the treaty through for us," and McKinley voiced similar sentiments.[116] However, at most the start of hostilities could have affected only four votes, since the rest of the senators voted as they had promised prior to hostilities; Senator Lodge also commented on how little the skirmish seemed to affect the vote.[117] Nevertheless, the heightened sense of nationalism at the time was certainly favorable to passage of the treaty. Historians argue that winning the Spanish-American War in such a convincing fashion strengthened the imperialist sentiment in American society and the imperialist faction of the Republican Party politically.[118]

The final two factors reflect the ineffective and counterproductive strategies of anti-imperialists. The fifth factor was the decision by Senator Gorman, the Democratic leader in the Senate, to not filibuster the treaty, which seemingly went against the anti-imperialist strategy of delay.[119] Sixth, and most importantly, the decision of erstwhile anti-imperialist William Jennings Bryan to instruct his followers to vote in favor of the peace treaty and annexation was probably decisive. According to Pratt, "William Jennings Bryan came to Washington and urged ratification of the treaty on the ground that it was necessary to end the war and the Philippine independence might be more readily secured through action by the United States than through a renewal of negotiations with Spain."[120] Bryan also wanted the Spanish-American War settled so that the election campaign could focus on domestic issues; some argue that he had a more cynical motive of saddling the Republican Party with an unpopular war in the Philippines.[121] Bryan not only gave a public statement in favor of ratification, but also made personal appeals to Democratic allies to vote for the treaty.[122] A swing of two votes would have killed the treaty, and even a conservative estimate suggests that William Jennings Bryan was responsible for three votes.[123] It is simplistic to say that Bryan was responsible for the passage of the treaty, but it is also true that if he had thrown his weight behind the opposition, the treaty would not have passed.[124]

It must be noted that even if the vote had gone against McKinley he could have resubmitted the treaty to the next Senate, which would have had seven fewer opponents due to the results of the 1898 congressional election.[125] Anti-imperialist Andrew Carnegie wrote that defeat of the treaty would give "the Country time to reflect—I am certain that only time & discussion is needed to save us"; Carnegie's statement was in line with the strategy of delay implemented by the Anti-Imperialist League.[126] They hoped to delay the vote until the next session to buy time to build up public opposition to annexation.[127]

Gorman and Bryan's actions are illustrative of the overall lack of cohesiveness among the anti-imperialists that prevented agreement on a strategy to defeat the ratification of the treaty.[128] Historian Richard Welch views this factor as decisive: "Anti-imperialist divisions quite as much as master plans, economic ambitions, and the force of destiny helped assure the success of the Expansionists of 1898 and allowed President McKinley the right to determine for himself the number of alternatives a divine revelation might properly contain."[129]

On February 14, antiannexationists gained a small victory with the passage of the McEnery Resolution in which the US Senate declared that Filipinos were not citizens of the United States, disavowed permanent annexation, and promised to make the Philippines independent as soon as its people were ready for self-government. The resolution passed 26 to 22, but did not have the power of law because it was merely a resolution by the Senate not passed by Congress or signed by the president.[130] Most anti-imperialists actually opposed the resolution because it was so weak.[131]

Like the war itself, the Treaty of Paris created crosscutting cleavages in American domestic politics and has ambiguous implications. The intensity of the vote left a bitter taste in the mouths of many, and partisanship increased following the vote.[132] The treaty both ended the war with Spain and made the United States a colonial power. Because it was not simply a vote for imperialism, the implications of the treaty are difficult to discern.[133] One historian argues that "on the clear-cut issue of the annexation of the Philippines alone the expansionists would quite certainly have failed to muster a two-thirds majority."[134] It is also unclear whether the American people supported extended occupation and governance of foreign territory. Some historians argue that as McKinley toured the United States in 1898 he determined that Americans would support imperialism.[135] Another interpretation drawing on McKinley's own writings is that the president was worried about American public opinion turning against an extended occupation of the Philippines. His October speaking tour in the Midwest did not put McKinley's mind at ease about public support for annexation; McKinley predicted, "I can foresee for myself and for the people nothing but anxiety for the next two years."[136] McKinley biographer Morgan argues that the president viewed the public as supportive of annexation in the short term but saw this support as shallow, and that difficulties in the future could change this support.[137] Two recent surveys of the available public opinion indicators suggest that the public was fairly evenly divided on the issue of Philippine annexation in 1898 and 1899.[138]

Power or Restraint?

When the United States went to war against Spain the political objective was not the acquisition of territory. The annexation of the Philippines was the result of the war and not a goal of the war. Dewey's victory and subsequent occupation of Manila were part of a strategy for defeating Spain. Once territory was gained the McKinley administration was reluctant to give up the spoils of war, especially since there appeared to be strong strategic and moral reasons to maintain political–military control of the Philippines. Approval of annexation by the Senate was a close call, very contentious, and facilitated by poor strategizing by antiannexationists and the commencement of fighting between US and Philippine forces. Due to the long process involved in implementing annexation, this case is labeled one of delayed expansion.

The delay in annexation is best explained by domestic political structure. Despite the strong incentives for expansion, the decision to annex the Philippines was delayed for eight months as McKinley maneuvered through the barriers thrown up by separation of powers and the need for public acquiescence. McKinley took several months to carefully consider the level of support for territorial expansion and the long-term political ramifications of expansion. Once the president decided to pursue annexation, he had to seek approval by the Senate and therefore had to spend considerable time conciliating, bribing, and threatening opponents in order to secure passage of the Treaty of Paris. Antiannexationists criticized the cost of political–military control of the Philippines, the potential economic competition with Filipino labor and agricultural production, the potential for racial mixing, the increased likelihood of the United States going to war in East Asia, and the deleterious effects that imperialism has on republican government.

The historical record shows conditions very favorable to expansion, the most important of which was the establishment of military control over Manila during the course of the War of 1898. The contextual factors of a more assertive national ideology being promoted by large-policy advocates and perceptions about the strategic and economic importance of East Asia also played an important role in McKinley's thinking.[139] Despite these strong incentives for expansion annexation was delayed while McKinley was slowly convinced of the need for expansion, support for the annexation was constructed among the American public and in the Senate, and antiannexationists sought to delay a Senate vote. The delay occurred because of separation of powers (the need to gain the support of the Senate), strategic culture (the influence of anti-imperialism on public opinion), and the difficulty in building support in a highly fragmented political system. Security-based and economic explanations are not well supported by the evidence. As with the other cases, economic and security concerns tended to be offered more often in favor of expansion than in opposition, and so cannot explain restraint.

Conclusion

Without the decentralized state structure and anti-imperialist norms of the United States, territorial gains from the War of 1898 would have been more extensive and would have not engendered so much opposition and delay. The reinforcing interaction between these two factors prevented the annexation of Cuba and delayed the annexation of Hawaii and the Philippines. The uncertainty of public opinion and significant Senate opposition to expansion provided redundant incentives for the McKinley administration to be cautious in its advocacy for expansion. Both public opinion and separation of powers provided negative feedback to expansionist politicians when they seemed poised to embrace full-throated imperialism. Explanations for restraint resting on narrow economic interests or security concerns are not supported by the evidence. The business sector was divided on the issue of expansion.[140] Security was not often invoked as a reason for restraint and delay.

The causes of expansion between 1898 and 1899 are highly congruent with the predictions of realist and interest group theories of expansion. With respect to Philippine annexation, American leaders were driven to expand mainly

because of their understanding of American strategic interests and moral responsibilities toward the Philippines. Offensive and defensive realism also highlight
important causal factors, including the likelihood of the expansion of political
objectives during war and the logic of security through expansion.[141] A necessary
condition for US intervention in Cuba was the widespread belief that the US
sphere of interest now included Cuba, and that military force was a viable solution to instability in that sphere of interest. Americans elected representatives
of a party that advocated expansion in their platform and looked favorably on a
war with Spain. In the past, American ambitions toward Cuba had been limited
to offers to purchase the island from Spain. By the 1890s American leaders
seemed to have a sense that both capability and will were united behind a more
expansionist foreign policy.

Zakaria's neoclassical realist argument—that centralization of power in the
executive branch was a necessary condition for expansion—finds less support.
Zakaria does not convincingly demonstrate a causal connection between
changes in American institutional structure and the foreign policy of President
McKinley. He asserts that Congress was "relatively compliant," which is a
strange statement to make when Congress was consistently more belligerent
toward Spain than McKinley was, and the policy outcome seems closer to the
one favored by the majority of Congress.[142] Furthermore, Zakaria argues that
Congress "backed down" to McKinley on the negotiations over the Turpie-
Foraker and Teller amendments, and more generally over the issue of who would
control foreign policymaking.[143] But as the analysis above demonstrates, the final
deal was a compromise, and McKinley was saddled with the unwanted Teller
Amendment.

The security focus of defensive realism can provide a possible explanation for
both expansion and restraint in 1898. From this perspective, the United States
went to war to remove an unstable European power from the Western Hemisphere and then acquired territory that was useful for the defense of the United
States. In this narrative possession of Cuba would not have enhanced American
security, while the Philippines, Puerto Rico, and the Philippines were necessary
for national security reasons. The central problem with this explanation is that
few participants in these debates made these arguments. The main security-
related arguments all went in favor of expansion. Those arguing that American
security did not require expansion were anti-imperialists using the security argument to bolster their normative argument against expansion. Furthermore, the
mechanisms of restraint were shown to be separation of powers and concern
about whether the public would accept territorial expansion.

Interest group theory contributes to our understanding of this case by highlighting the importance of economic and ethnic (Cuban) interest groups in
fostering the military conflict over Cuba and the subsequent territorial expansion.[144] The narrow economic interest argument is not well supported by the

evidence, but the broader economic approach of scholars like Peter Trubowitz and Kevin Narizny find better support.[145] Narizny argues that the Democratic and Republic coalitions each had dominant economic interests and nominated candidates that supported these interests. The Republican coalition generally favored intervention in the periphery and therefore nominated a candidate that was at least sympathetic to these interests. What Narizny's argument brings to light is that it certainly mattered that the Republican Party held the presidency and a majority in Congress. A Democratic president and Congress would have approached the policy differently, though it is difficult to predict exactly how policy would have differed given that Democrats were the most belligerent party in 1898. It is possible that Republican control of government was a permissive cause of the War of 1898.

One caveat is necessary: Narizny focuses on the grand strategies of presidents and under his approach, and from the interest group perspective, McKinley should have strongly favored intervention in Cuba. But as the analysis above demonstrates, McKinley took a cautious approach to intervention. A relatively belligerent public and Congress would have allowed President McKinley to take the nation to war much sooner if that had been his preference. Therefore McKinley's actions belie the claim that his grand strategy was in favor of expansion into the periphery.[146]

In terms of the historiographical debates, the analysis in this book takes a position close to the "accidental empire" interpretation of American diplomatic history of the 1890s, and contrary to the Open Door school of historiography.[147] LaFeber, Herring, and others argue that American expansion was a result of the United States "pursuing its destiny deliberately and purposefully."[148] According to Louis Pérez Jr., the Cleveland and McKinley administrations, like most presidents before them, believed that Cuba either had to be controlled by the weak Spanish empire or had to be transferred to American control. From this perspective, all of the actions taken by McKinley between 1896 and 1898 were in pursuit of an unambiguous understanding of American national interest: Cuba could not be allowed to become an independent country or come under the control of a more vigorous European empire. As the Spanish position in Cuba became untenable, the American intervention in Cuba became inevitable in order to prevent Cuba from becoming independent.[149] However, most historians view Cleveland as a noninterventionist and document a high degree of indecision by McKinley—he seems to have been open to Cuban independence and repeatedly asked Spain to grant Cuba full independence.[150] The best historiography of McKinley's foreign policy reveals the details of the political negotiations involved in the debate over war and annexation, focusing on the complex decision making process, and develops a nuanced understanding of individual actions in the context of American norms and institutions.[151]

At this point in the narrative it is instructive to note the perfect storm of factors that led to the first and only colonial acquisitions by the United States.

First, the United States was mobilized for war with a declining great power. During war the centralization of policymaking and resource mobilization would be maximized, allowing for a much greater expansion of foreign policy aims than during peacetime. Second, the Cuban War of Independence was occurring extremely close to the coast of the United States and affected a fairly large number of Americans living in Cuba. Third, the Cuban Junta was skilled in highlighting the ineffective and brutal character of Spanish policy in Cuba. It is the humanitarian aspect that divided anti-imperialists and made the war at least somewhat consistent with anti-imperialist norms; it was a war to end Spanish imperialism in Cuba. Fourth, the annexation of Hawaii occurred through an unorthodox institutional strategy in Congress and was made possible by the American-Hawaiian coup d'état in Hawaii. Fifth, the annexation of the Philippines required an alignment of six factors, several of which were unusual or historically contingent, including the sudden onset of the Philippine-American War and the counterproductive political strategy of William Jennings Bryan. As the next chapter demonstrates, this perfect storm soon abated, and with it the wave of American expansionism began to recede.

Notes

1. These opportunities are documented in Zakaria 1999, 44–154.
2. For the text of McKinley's message see Commager 1949, 182–185.
3. Gould 1980, 87; Offner 1992, 187–191.
4. Quoted in Holbo 1967, 1327–1328.
5. Silver Republicans were a faction within the Republican Party that dissented from the platform position on the gold standard–bimetallism debate. Most of the Silver Republicans hailed from western states, where silver mining was an important industry. See Wellborn 1928; Ellis 1932.
6. Leech 1959, 187.
7. Leech 1959, 187–188; Gould 1980, 87.
8. Commager 1949, 186.
9. Pratt 1950, 54.
10. Herring 2008, 314.
11. Trask 1996, 55–56.
12. LaFeber 1993a, 144.
13. Schoultz 1998, 139.
14. Schoultz 1998, 140.
15. Schoultz 1998, 139–140 and 419 note 48; Auxier 1939, 304. See also Offner 1992, 189.
16. Holbo 1967 1331; Gould 1980, 87.
17. Holbo 1967, 1330–1333; Offner 1992, 190; Leech 1959, 187–188.
18. *New York Times* 1898a. American Minister to Spain Woodford failed to present McKinley's ultimatum to the Spanish government before he was deported by Spanish authority, much to the disappointment of McKinley; *New York Times* 1898b.

19. *New York Times* 1898b.

20. Loveman 2010, 165.

21. Herring 2008, 316.

22. On the causes of American expansionism in the 1890s see LaFeber 1963, chapters 2–6; Beisner 1986, 76–91; Hofstadter 1965 [1952], 145–187; Goldenberg 2000, 171–181; Shulman 1999.

23. Abernethy 2000, 30.

24. Schoultz 1998, 140.

25. This line of reasoning is suggested by Pratt 1950, 54.

26. Leech 1959, 188–189.

27. Offner 1992, 188–190.

28. LaFeber 1993a, 144; Hamilton 2006, 135. Offner (1992, 130) documents that McKinley rejected annexation of Cuba a little over a month before war was declared. Leech (1959, 189) also suggests that McKinley supported the Teller Amendment.

29. For older studies focusing on the importance of the press and public opinion see, Wilkerson 1967 [1932]; Auxier, 1939, 299–303. For more recent perspectives that see public opinion and the press as having a relatively minor role, see Hamilton 2006, chapters 5–6; Offner 2004, 52; Gould, 1980, chapter 4; Hilderbrand 1981, 8–51; Morgan 2003, 252.

30. Offner 2004, 60; Pérez 1998, 20–21.

31. See Loomis 1976, 96–224; Tate 1965, 258–268; Osborne 1981, 3–9, 81–84, chapter 7; Stevens 1945, 234–267; McWilliams 1988, 39–41; Brands 1995, 298.

32. Tate 1965, 264.

33. Stevens 1945, 270–293; Osborne 1981, 85–86; Pletcher 2001, 248–253.

34. Osborne 1981, 85–103. For additional discussion of the debates over annexation see Tate 1965, chapter 8.

35. Osborne 1981, 107; cf. Pletcher 2001, 253.

36. Hawaii was officially annexed on July 7, 1898, after most of the fighting ended, but before the official end of the war. For example, the Battle of Manila Bay occurred on May 1, 1898, and the Battle of San Juan Hill occurred on July 1, 1898. The War of 1898 lasted from April 25 to December 10, 1898.

37. Tate 1968, 252–254.

38. Herring 2008, 317–318. The annexation of Texas was seen as a precedent for this maneuver; Tate 1968, 254.

39. Pratt 1951, 321; Remini 2006, 264.

40. Pletcher 2001, 271–272; Tate 1965, 294–295, 300–301.

41. Pratt 1951, 322; Tate 1965, 302; *New York Times* 1898f; *New York Times* 1898c; *New York Times* 1898e; *New York Times* 1898d.

42. *New York Times* 1898g.

43. Pletcher 2001, 272–275; Tate 1965, 301–306.

44. Fry 2002, 118–119.

45. *New York Times* 1898c, 4.

46. LaFeber 1993a, 147. See also Osborne 1981, 110–120.

47. LaFeber 1993a, 148. For further discussion of antiannexation arguments see Osborne 1981, chapter 9.

48. Pletcher 2001, 270; Pratt 1951, chapter 9; *New York Times* 1898h.

49. LaFeber 1963, 409–410; Pletcher 2001, 251.

50. Stevens 1945, 293–294; Tate 1965, 293–294.

51. Pletcher 2001, 273–274. To a large extent Pletcher is endorsing the interpretation offered in Pratt 1951, chapter 9.

52. Osborne 1981, 125–135. For an extended discussion of the territorial concession issue see Tate 1965, 302–303.

53. Bailey 1969 [1931], 89–103; Tate 1965, 315; Pletcher 2001, 273–274. The *New York Times* (1898h) also emphasizes the role of the Spanish American War.

54. For a partial exception see Osborne 1981, 112–113.

55. *New York Times* 1898c.

56. *New York Times* 1898e.

57. *New York Times* 1898e.

58. *New York Times* 1898i.

59. Pletcher 2001, 270–274; Pratt 1951, chapter 9.

60. Pletcher 2001, 283.

61. Hamilton 2007, 65; Ninkovich 2001, 124.

62. Trask 1996, 382.

63. Abernethy 2000, 249

64. Coletta 1961.

65. Brands 1992, 23–24; Trask 1996, 96–105.

66. Trask 1996, 105.

67. After the Spanish forces at Manila refused Dewey's request to use their telegraph, Dewey cut the wire from Manila to Hong Kong. Until the cable was restored in August his communications with Washington had to be transmitted by ship to Hong Kong and then telegraphed to Washington. Trask 1996, 105, 369.

68. Trask 1996, 373–377; Pletcher 2001, 275.

69. Coletta 1961, 343; Brands 1992, 24; Pletcher 2001, 276, 284.

70. Hamilton 2007, 63–64.

71. Grenville 1968, 34; Coletta 1961, 342–343; Pletcher 2001, 284; Hamilton 2007, 66–67; Grenville and Young 1966, 267–276; Linn 2000, 7–8; The antecedents of the plan stretch back to 1894. Trask 1996, 73–78; Golay 1998, 22.

72. *Halle 1985, 7; Trask 1996, 423.*

73. *Hamilton 2007, 66; Golay 1998, 22.*

74. *Brands 1992, 22. See also Golay 1998, 18.*

75. *Grenville and Young 1966, 269–270; Brands 1992, 22–23; Trask 1996, 73–80.*

76. *Brands 1992, 23–24; Trask 1996, 96–105; Halle 1985, 9.*

77. *Smith 1985, 369–370.*

78. *Grenville 1968, 35; Hamilton 2007, 66; Trask 1996, 382–383.*

79. *Smith 1985, 370.*

80. *Coletta 1961, 343. For a presentation of both perspectives see Smith 1993.*

81. *Coletta 1961, 104.*

82. *Coletta 1961, 104, passim.*

83. *Coletta 1961, 341. For a theoretical discussion of expanding war aims see Labs 1997.*

84. *Smith 1985, 371–372; Hamilton 2007, 75, 82; Gould 1980, 134–135; Morgan 2003, 308. Hamilton notes that Greene's position was reinforced by Chief of the Navy's Bureau of Equipment Commander Royal B. Bradford, who had been to Manila to look for potential sites for naval and coaling stations. McKinley's own analysis mirrors the one he received from Greene; see Smith 1985, 271–272.*

85. *For a discussion of the evolution of McKinley's position on annexation see Pratt 1951,*
329–338; Gould 1980, 133–142; Brands 1992, 25–26; Coletta 1961, 344–347; Pletcher
2001, 275–276, 283–285; Hamilton 2007, 69–82; Morgan 2003, 304–322; Welch 1979,
6–10. During this period McKinley sought advice from a large number of government officials
and private individuals with various positions on the annexation issue; Hamilton 2007, 70–79.

86. *Quoted in Smith 1985, 369. The phrase "strategic interdependence" is Smith's (1985,*
372). Coletta's (1961, 345–347) analysis of McKinley's logic is similar, but puts more empha-
sis on commercial advantages gained from annexation and favorable public opinion.

87. *Smith 1985, 373–374; Smith 1993, 230–237. Other historians also view McKinley*
in this manner; Pratt 1951, 326.

88. *Brands 1992, 24–26.*

89. *See LaFeber 1993a, 156; LaFeber 1963, 411; cf. Pletcher 2001, 285.*

90. *Hamilton 2007, 84–94.*

91. *Quoted in May 1961, 244.*

92. *Smith 1993, 230; see also 224, 226–227.*

93. *Gould 1982, 102.*

94. *Welch 1964, 363.*

95. *Quoted in Welch 1964, 365.*

96. *Welch 1964, 367–380.*

97. *Gould 1980, 133; LaFeber 1963, 414; Brands 1992, 25; Morgan 2003, 313.*

98. *Healy 1988, 44.*

99. *Welch 1979, 18.*

100. Pletcher 2001, 277.

101. An anti-antiannexationist is anyone opposed to annexation for any reason; anti-
imperialists opposed annexation for normative reasons. See Osborne 1981, xv. Rystad
1975, 26.

102. Brands 1992, 26–30; Pletcher 2001, 281–283; Tompkins 1970, 161–213.

103. Beveridge 1907; Rystad 1975, 29–32.

104. Small 1995, 31; Herring 2008, 323; Brands 1992, 30–33; Pletcher 2001, 277–281;
Welch 1979, 18–19. See also Pratt 1951, 352–357.

105. Brands 1992, 30–33; cf. Smith 1985, 373.

106. Pletcher 2001, 277; Schirmer 1972, 111. See also Hamilton 2007, 72. An important caveat to keep in mind is that newspaper editorial pages were a highly imperfect
measure of public opinion; Golay 1998, 33.

107. Holt 1933, 166.

108. Holt 1933, 167. See also Gould 1980, 144–145, 149–150.

109. Quoted in Holt 1933, 168. See also Schirmer 1972, 121.

110. Coletta 1957, 139, note 23. Pratt and Holt categorize the Senators in a slightly
different manner—a few of the independents are difficult to categorize. See Pratt 1951,
358, note 139; Holt 1933, 169.

111. Holt 1933, 165.

112. Holt 1933, 169–170; LaFeber 1993a, 163; Hamilton 2007, 83.

113. Coletta 1961. Three out of the four were known expansionists who supported
keeping some portion of the Philippines, but only one advocated annexing the entire
archipelago; see Pratt 1951, 331–332.

114. Gould 1980, 143–144; Schirmer 1972, 110; Golay 1998, 34.

115. Coletta 1957, 139, 143; Coletta 1961, 349; Herring 2008, 320; Pratt 1951, 357;
Holt 1933, 171–173; Gould 1980, 144; Morgan 2003, 320; Schirmer 1972, 122–124.

116. Freidel 1969, 176–177; Coletta 1961, 348; Holt 1933, 170; Morgan 2003, 321. Roosevelt is quoted in Holt 1933 and Coletta 1961. One author argues that fighting was triggered purposely by American commanders on the ground in the Philippines; Schirmer 1972, 125–132.

117. Holt 1933, 171.

118. Brands 1992, 24; Pratt 1951, 327; LaFeber 1993a, 163–164; Welch 1979, 19.

119. Schirmer 1972, 118–120, 122.

120. Pratt 1951, 357. See also Coletta 1957, 131–146; Welch 1964, 377; Morgan 2003, 318–319.

121. Schirmer 1972, 109–110.

122. Holt 1933, 174–176; Schirmer 1972, 108.

123. Coletta 1957, 139–140; Pletcher 2001, 286. Holt argues that Bryan's position and actions explain most of the 17 non-Republican votes for the treaty; Holt 1933, 176.

124. Coletta 1957, 145; Gould 1980, 150; Harrington 1935, 222, esp. note 40. Holt (1933, 176) and Brands (1992, 34) hold Bryan responsible for the passage of the treaty. Several prominent anti-imperialists also blamed Bryan in the aftermath of the vote; see Holt 1933, 173–177.

125. Coletta 1957, 143; Freidel 1969, 176; Gould 1980, 142–143; Pletcher 2001, 286; Golay 1998, 41.

126. Holt 1933, 175.

127. Schirmer 1972, 114–115.

128. Welch 1964, 362–380; Pletcher 2001, 286; Gould 1980, 144–145; Schirmer 1972, chapter 8; Harrington 1935, 220–222.

129. Welch 1964.

130. Pratt 1951, 359–360; Pletcher 2001, 287; Hamilton 2007, 83; Golay 1998, 42–43. Senator McEnery may have been promised passage of his resolution in return for his yea vote on treaty ratification; Gould 1980, 149–150.

131. Golay 1998, 43.

132. Golay 1998, 43; Leech 1959, 358–361; Morgan 2003, 317–322.

133. Hamilton 2007, 82.

134. Coletta 1957, 142.

135. May 1961, 258–259; Freidel 1969, 174; Coletta 1961, 345–347; Pletcher 2001, 284–285.

136. McKinley quoted in Smith 1985, 370, 373. He had two more years left in his first term. One author views McKinley as an expert facilitator of public opinion, leading the people to the position he wanted them to take on the Philippines issue; Hilderbrand 1981, chapter 2. This argument runs counter to every major biography of William McKinley (see citations throughout this chapter).

137. Morgan 2003, 307. Over time McKinley became surer of the public support. Morgan 2003, 310, 314.

138. Pletcher 2001, 286; Hamilton 2007, 72.

139. Smith 1993, 215–219.

140. LaFeber argues that an important cause of McKinley's decision for war was the change in business sentiment from antiwar to prowar, but also acknowledges that the American business community was fragmented. LaFeber 1963, 384–393, 403–406; LaFeber 1993a, 141–142; Offner 2004, 51–52. Kirshner (2007, 44–57) makes a strong argument that the financial sector opposed the war. Hamilton argues persuasively that

business leaders opposed going to war (2006, 119–136). On the nonexistent threat of European intervention see LaFeber 1963, 405; Offner 1992, chapter 10; Trask 1996, 45–51.

141. Eric Labs's (1997) offensive realist argument that states will expand their war aims to maximize their postwar gains is most applicable.

142. Zakaria 1999, 154.

143. Zakaria 1999, 158.

144. On the role of the Cuban lobby see Hamilton 2006, 105, 112–113, 209; Auxier 1939, 286–305. Economic motivations should not be overstated. Business leaders did not play a major role in influencing the decision for war, and one would assume they would have the best idea of what policy was in their interests. Cuba in the 1890s is illustrative of the limited importance of the periphery to the US economy. Americans already had between $30 million and $50 million invested in Cuba, which amounted to 4–7 percent of total US foreign investment. See Pratt 1951; Hamilton 2006, 107, 119–138 (note 9); Rystad 1975, 14–18; Herring 2008, 309–311; Knight 1990, 235. Kirshner (2007, chapter 2) argues that the financial sector in particular was against going to war with Spain. Williams (1962), LaFeber (1963), and McCormick (1967) all emphasize the importance of business advocacy for expansion.

145. Narizny 2001, 151–217; Narizny 2003; Narizny 2007; Trubowitz 1998.

146. Narizny 2003 1–25. On Narizny's theoretical approach see Narizny 2007, chapter 1. On Narizny's analysis of McKinley's grand strategy see Narizny 2007, 93–99. All modern interpretations of McKinley's strategy during the Cuban crisis note his reluctance to go to war; see, for example, Trask 1982; Gould 1982; Offner 1992.

147. For example see May 1961; Pratt 1967; Pratt 1950.

148. Herring 2008, 309; LaFeber 1963, vii, passim; Pérez 1998, chapter 1.

149. Pérez 1998, 12–18; see also Pérez 1989, 320–322.

150. Hamilton 2006. For example, Offner shows that McKinley considered buying Cuba's independence from Spain as late as March 10, 1898; Offner 1992, 130, 144–145.

151. On McKinley's preference for a peaceful resolution see LaFeber 1963, 336–337, 400; Gould 1980, chapter 4; Offner 1992, 192–193, passim; Brands 1995, 309–314; Offner 2004, 50–61; Morgan 2003, 252, 257, 274, 280; Leech 1959, 190; Trask 1996, 56–58.

3
★

CONSOLIDATION
AND BACKLASH

1899–1903

B Y THE END OF THE War of 1898 the United States had acquired foreign colonies for the first time in its history. On the surface it seemed that 1899 inaugurated the emergence of the United States as a great power no longer subject to the isolationist ways of a young and vulnerable republic. This was supposedly the emergence of the United States as a great power and the inception of a new era of expansionism in American foreign policy. However, under the surface, the American domestic political structure exerted counterpressure on the expansionist impulses inherent in a rising power. The current chapter focuses on the phase of American grand strategy following the Spanish-American War: the struggle to consolidate the United States' newfound role and status in the international system between 1899 and 1903. The United States went to war to consolidate its control of the Philippines, participated in the pacification of the Boxer Rebellion in China, enacted the Platt Amendment (which increased American control of Cuba), and acquired what would become the Panama Canal Zone. Despite the expansion orientation of this time period, President McKinley found that expansionist policies were not worth the potential domestic cost and his successor President Theodore Roosevelt was forced to balance his preferences for an active, expansionist foreign policy with the realities of a powerful Senate and an American public infused with anti-imperialist norms.

If the previous chapter was the story of a rising expansionist wave being slowed by the institutional and normative friction of the American political structure, this chapter is a story of the further dissipation of the wave's energy as it bowed to the realities of domestic structural restraint. As McKinley and then Roosevelt attempted to mobilize national power to make it more useable in the international realm, they met strenuous resistance in the restraints of electoral, institutional, and normative politics. Their opponents in the Senate, the House of Representatives, and the citizenry used the restraining capacities of a divided political system to impose costs on the executive for any unpopular or potentially unpopular expansionist action. They could impose these costs because the American people lacked the normative commitment to expansionism necessary to support foreign policies that were burdensome, even in the short run. Thus the combination of separated powers, partisan electoral politics, and American normative commitment to anti-imperialism undermined the effort to build on the territorial gains of the War of 1898.

Extending Control over the Philippines (1899–1902)

The acquisition of the Philippines was undoubtedly the most important and controversial expansionist move made by the United States in the period of study for this project. As documented in the previous chapter, the decision to annex the archipelago was highly controversial and almost immediately became a potential political liability for the McKinley administration. Foremost in the mind of the president was the need to quickly establish American control and begin the process of "uplifting" the Filipino people. It was clear that the Philippines would be a proving ground for the viability of American political–military expansion. If the McKinley administration could successfully implement colonial policy in the Philippines, domestic opponents of expansion would be undermined and advocates of expansionism would be strengthened. Unfortunately for McKinley and other large-policy advocates, American political structure and Filipino nationalism could not be easily subdued. A careful analysis of American policy following annexation of the Philippines in 1899 suggests that American officials had difficulty developing a coherent policy, made decisions based on poor evidence and misperception, stumbled into an unwanted war, and faced enormous backlash for their ineptitude and incongruence with American values.[1] The brutality of the Philippine-American War and the fact that the United States was clearly using force to impose its will on a foreign people reinvigorated the opposition to McKinley and to expansionism in general.

The central issue is that the United States chose to implement a plan to extend its direct political–military control over the entire population of the Philippine Islands. The McKinley administration was willing to do so even though it required the large-scale deployment of US soldiers to violently pacify the native inhabitants. Alternatively, the United States could have worked out an arrangement to rule by, with, or through the existing nationalist government. Aguinaldo would have accepted protectorate status, but the United States was confident in its military prowess on the heels of its victory over Spain. To a certain extent the United States was also falling prey to the logic of sunk costs and vested interests. Once McKinley's proclamation of Benevolent Assimilation was issued, policymakers never seriously questioned the validity of its assumptions.

McKinley had to be exceedingly cautious about his policy toward the Philippines, and this caution played out negatively for the coherence and effectiveness of American policy. As documented in the previous chapter, McKinley had to carefully measure political support at home before pursuing his favored strategies abroad. The delays caused by the uncertainties of coalition building at home undermined American military strategy in the Philippines. In sum, the difficult process of employing state power undermined the objectives of the McKinley administration, which in turn undermined the further use of state power. In other words, the fragmented, balanced structure of the American state undermined the effectiveness of an expansionist foreign policy, which in turn decreased the attractiveness of expansionism.

The remainder of this section is divided into three parts. The first part describes the decision to exclude Filipinos from the governance of the Philippines and examines the implications of this decision to greatly expand American control of the archipelago. The second section analyzes the effect of the Philippine American War on the rise of the anti-imperialist movement and its effects on the election of 1900. And the third section evaluates the long-term impact of the Philippine-American War on American politics and foreign policy.

Benevolent Assimilation Proclamation

The main event leading up to the Philippine-American War was the December 21 executive order by McKinley to establish American sovereignty over the Philippines. Grania Bolton argues that McKinley's order to establish American sovereignty over the entire archipelago was the result of advice from military officers with direct experience in the Philippines: Otis, Merritt, and Dewey.[2] They all assured the President that Filipinos were unable to govern themselves and welcomed American control of the Islands. Furthermore, there was a faulty assumption in Washington that Dewey's victory at Manila Harbor put the United States in control of the entire Philippine Islands and American troops simply needed to establish a military government—Dewey himself shared this misperception. Linn bluntly sums up the situation: "even as the United States stood on the threshold of a great leap toward Pacific empire, no one knew what the agents of empire were supposed to be doing."[3]

McKinley's order to establish American control of the Philippines was called the Benevolent Assimilation Proclamation. The key passages read:

With the signature of the treaty of peace between the United States and Spain by their respective plenipotentiaries at Paris on the 10th instant, and as a result of the victories of American arms, the future control, disposition, and government of the Philippine Islands are ceded to the United States. In the fulfillment of the rights of sovereignty thus acquired and the responsible obligations of government thus assumed, the actual occupation and administration of the entire group of the Philippine Islands becomes immediately necessary, and the military government heretofore maintained by the United States in the city, harbor, and bay of Manila is to be extended with all possible despatch [sic] to the whole of the ceded territory.

. . . the authority of the United States is to be exerted for the securing of the persons and property of the people of the islands and for the confirmation of all their private rights and relations. It will be the duty of the commander of the forces of occupation to announce and proclaim in the most public manner that we come not as invaders or conquerors, but as friends, to protect the natives in their homes, in their employments, and in their personal and religious rights.[4]

With this statement of policy, McKinley "laid a claim to US sovereignty over the entire archipelago."[5] McKinley certainly knew that his claim of American sovereignty ran counter to the aspirations of Aguinaldo and his allies, but to him this seemed a minor issue that could be resolved through a policy of benevolent paternalism.[6] Brian Linn notes two crucial aspects of McKinley's proclamation: First, the 8th Corps mission was to establish control over the Philippines, which meant that any Filipino aspirations for independence were to be pushed aside. Second, McKinley established a benevolent policy of "protecting Filipino lives, property, and civil rights."[7] Putting these two elements together, McKinley committed the United States to enforce sovereignty over the islands and take responsibility for the well-being of the Philippine people.

The reception of McKinley's proclamation was perhaps not what he had hoped for. The commanding officer in the Philippines, General Elwell S. Otis, viewed the language of the proclamation as inflammatory and edited it before releasing it to Aguinaldo. Otis removed all mentions of the establishment of a military government over the Islands.[8] One of Otis's subordinates, General Miller, released the original, which not only demonstrated the American goal of total control over the Philippines, but also revealed General Otis's deception. Aguinaldo's government viewed both versions as "offensive," and Aguinaldo sent a reply that was "a virtual declaration of war."[9] As Bolton argues, "the so-called benevolent assimilation proclamation marks the last step toward violence."[10]

Additional negotiations between Otis and Aguinaldo in January 1899 went nowhere because the American representatives were unable to grant the Filipino negotiators their minimal demand—some form of sovereignty. During the negotiations the American representatives asked for guidance from Washington, but received no response. The conference ended badly with talk of violence. It had become clear to both sides that "a conflict of interest existed which was not amenable to concession. The Americans were circumscribed by Otis's narrow construction of the President's general policy statement and by the lack of further instructions to deal with the emergency. Rather than taking into account the long-range political implications that experienced diplomats might have considered, he viewed the situation in purely-immediate military terms."[11] General Otis was merely biding his time until reinforcements arrived. The start of hostilities on February 5, 1899 was not unexpected by the men on the front lines, but was a surprise in Washington.[12]

Bolton blames the escalation to war on the lack of "a firm coherent policy" from Washington and the absence of "flexible and creative local action" on the part of General Otis.[13] She sees the orders from Washington as being general guidance on policy, but argues that (1) they were based on bad advice from Otis, and (2) Otis could have worked within the constraints of McKinley's orders to establish better relations with Aguinaldo.[14] Otis did not seem to want to avoid war or at least did not try very hard to accommodate the Filipino nationalists. The key issue is that a policy of drift was politically expedient for McKinley.

At its root, the Philippine-American War began because McKinley was unwilling to govern the archipelago in cooperation with the Filipino nationalists. McKinley and his advisors did not respect the Philippine insurgents and did not view them as capable of establishing a legitimate government. At the same time, the nationalists would not accept American rule of the Philippines; "McKinley found it difficult to conceive that these little brown men could object to the authority and good intentions of their American friends."[15] In the final analysis, McKinley's "refusal to offer the Filipinos the promise of future self-government made war inevitable."[16]

The decision by McKinley to exercise control over the Philippines through military control of the territory caused the Philippine-American War. That is not to propose a monocausal theory, but simply to state a fact. This decision was an extension of the War of 1898—the successes at Manila Harbor and the occupation of Manila fostered the sense that control of the entire archipelago would be easy. McKinley was poorly advised by his agents in Manila, Dewey and Otis, and at least somewhat taken in by the imperialist rhetoric of energized expansionists. The United States also faced a loss of prestige if it could not successfully exert control over its new colony.

Anti-Imperialism and the Presidential Election of 1900

As the Philippine-American War commenced, the United States was heading toward the 1900 presidential election. As the election approached McKinley was beginning to feel the negative domestic political effects of the Philippine-American War. The inception of the war energized anti-imperialists, and many believed that McKinley was vulnerable to the charge of imperialism. Political scientist Melvin Small describes anti-imperialists as being a "sizeable minority" in 1900—certainly not a majority of Americans, but perhaps large enough to affect the outcome in key states.[17] The main goals of the anti-imperialists were to end the war and achieve self-determination for Filipinos.[18] Their ranks included conservative Republicans and mugwumps, but anti-imperialists tended to view the Democratic Party as most hospitable to their beliefs.[19] The full mobilization of the anti-imperialists was complicated by the divisive nature of the central issue of the early 1900s: monetary policy. Anti-imperialists were forced to choose between anti-imperialism and Free Silver on the one hand (William Jennings Bryan), or expansionism and the gold standard on the other (William McKinley). This division proved to be decisive in limiting the electoral influence of anti-imperialists. However, their attacks on McKinley forced him to conform to the rhetoric of anti-imperialism and strongly emphasized the humanitarian nature of American foreign policy. The rhetoric of anti-imperialism and humanitarianism contrasted with the policy of pacification in the Philippines, thereby creating an opportunity for rhetorical coercion—the process by which one side of a debate is forced to either deny the fundamental norms of a society or surrender their policy position.[20] The dissonance between the principles of anti-imperialism and the reality of US policy imposed political costs on expansionists and demonstrated the difficulty of maintaining a foreign policy of colonialism in a society with deep anti-imperialist traditions.

The platforms and campaign rhetoric of both parties demonstrate their rival positions on imperialism in general and the Philippines specifically. The Republican Party was the party of expansion, but Republicans disavowed the term "imperialism." They denied that imperialism was even a salient partisan issue since neither of the political parties favored it.[21] To reinforce the point that they were not the party of imperialism, Republicans tried to enhance their anti-imperialist credentials by emphasizing the Open Door notes of 1899 and 1900 as anti-imperialist in nature.[22] In their campaign rhetoric Republicans proclaimed their commitment to "independence and self-government" as well as establishing "the blessings of liberty and civilization."[23] They argued that the United States was protecting the people of the Philippines from the tyranny of Aguinaldo and his followers, and they accused anti-imperialists of cowardice and treason.[24] While the Republican Party took a clear position on imperialism and expansion, they preferred to make the presidential campaign about the return to economic prosperity under the McKinley administration and what they characterized as irresponsible economic policies supported by the Democratic presidential candidate, William Jennings Bryan.

In 1900 the Democratic Party took a strong position against "seizing or purchasing distant islands to be governed outside the Constitution and whose people can never become citizens."[25] They supported adding territories that would eventually become states, inhabited by people who would make willing and desirable American citizens. The Democratic platform also endorsed moving forward rapidly with full Cuban independence (the island was under US military occupation at the time). The Democratic position on the Philippines was that the Filipino people should be provided with a "stable form of government," then given independence and American protection from outside influence.[26] Despite their general anti-imperialist orientation, Democrats were worried about being labeled as "copperheads" and consistently voted to fund the ongoing Philippine-American War and to increase the size of the army as requested by the McKinley administration, and generally refused to totally condemn the war.[27] These anti-imperialist planks were the central focus of the 1900 Democratic platform and national convention, but for Bryan it took second place to the currency issue.[28]

The Democratic Party was divided sectionally on the issue of expansion, with the East and Midwest most strongly anti-imperialist while the South and West were more ambivalent. In fact, some of the most ardent expansionists were Southern Democrats.[29] The Democratic Party was also divided over the currency question. Free Silver was popular in the West, and Democrats from these states insisted that this was a winning issue for Bryan in 1900. Anti-imperialists and Eastern Democrats argued just as strongly that the desire for Free Silver had faded as gold had become more abundant and the economy had improved. They argued that anti-imperialism and trust-busting were winning issues for Bryan in 1900.[30] Regardless of the strength of the rival arguments, Bryan's identity as a politician was fundamentally tied to the currency issue, and he could not easily abandon it in 1900.

Bryan lost the election, performing worse in 1900 than in 1896 in almost every measure. His anti-imperialist stance does not seem to have helped him electorally, except perhaps in New England where he did perform better in 1900 than in 1896.[31] Anti-imperialism probably hurt Bryan in the West and South, though in the South he still produced large majorities.[32] But overall the role of foreign policy in the election should not be overestimated. The election of 1900 was not determined by the issue of imperialism or expansionism, but instead the ability of the McKinley campaign to maintain the focus on the current prosperity of the country and the risk implied in changing economic policy.[33] While anti-imperialism was the focus of the Democratic convention, during the campaign it took second place to Free Silver.[34] Democratic candidate William Jennings Bryan's signature issue continued to be Free Silver, and McKinley was happy to exploit the currency issue as much as possible throughout the campaign.[35] However, McKinley and the Republicans certainly were aware of a strong anti-imperialist movement and the importance of anti-imperialist Gold Democrats, independents, and Republicans who voted for McKinley (or abstained from voting) because they were afraid that the Democratic silver standard plank would cause economic chaos.[36] To assuage the qualms of these voters McKinley "skill-fully narrowed the foreign-policy differences between himself and Bryan."[37] This point is not trivial, because public discourse can have a causal effect on the future behavior of politicians. Disavowal of imperialism is both an acknowledg-ment that it is widely unpopular and tends to make future imperialist actions awkward to explain.[38]

Several lessons can be drawn from the 1900 campaign and election results. First, imperialism could hurt the Republican Party at the polls if the silver plank was withdrawn from the Democratic platform. Another way to look at it is that at least 45 percent of the country supported the party with a strong anti-imperialist stance. When you add the anti-imperialist independents and Repub-licans who supported McKinley because of the currency issue, you have a large portion of the American public.[39] Second, Republicans and Democrats learned that imperialism was not the most salient issue for most voters, and that in wartime patriotism had a normative appeal that rivaled anti-imperialism.[40] Third, the election of 1900 demonstrated that imperialist rhetoric was not a legitimate part of the American foreign policy debate. McKinley and his sup-porters had to justify their policy as "humanitarian and idealistic."[41] Further-more, because Democrats used "humanitarian-idealistic and moral arguments," Republicans were forced to justify expansionism in the same terms—duty—rather than emphasizing strategic and economic interests.[42] This made the expansionist position vulnerable to events that emphasized the nonhumanitar-ian, immoral, and blatantly self-interested aspects of expansionism such as the Philippine-American War and exploitative economic policies toward Puerto Rico and the Philippines. In general, expansionists could not generate the public support to propel the project forward—in part because of the normative disso-nance and in part because the promised gains of expansion never really material-ized. Neither radical anti-imperialism nor normal great power imperialism could gain dominance in the United States.[43]

In sum, the election of 1900 demonstrates both the power and the limits of electoral restraint on imperialism. Foreign policy is often not the decisive issue in a campaign. If this is the case, incumbents may have little incentive to moder-ate their foreign policy. At the same time, even issues that do not end up being decisive can still be important. In 1900 anti-imperialists were not a majority, but they put considerable pressure on McKinley to move away from imperialist rhetoric.[44] It is important that McKinley wanted to focus on currency and Bry-an's supporters wanted him to focus on imperialism, suggesting that political strategists on both sides saw the issue of imperialism as a strength for the Demo-cratic Party and a weakness for the Republican Party. Furthermore, as Republi-cans became aware of their vulnerability on the issue of imperialism, their enthusiasm for new colonial ventures began to decline.

Anti-Imperialism and the Prosecution of the Philippine-American War, 1900–1902

The Philippine-American War had long-term effects beyond the election of 1900. In 1900 the war was still relatively new and had largely consisted of conventional combat between the Philippine and American forces that ended in victory for the United States. Guerrilla operations by the Filipino forces started in the beginning of 1900, but American forces waited until after the election to intensify the pacification campaign.[45] Thus it was only after the election of 1900 that the most difficult and unpopular aspects of the war emerged. The length of the war and the atrocities committed during the pacification campaign gave new life to the anti-imperialist movement and highlighted the fundamental contradiction between the humanitarian justification for control of the Philippines and the atrocities committed against the Filipino insurgents and civilians. The major effect of the war was an increased reluctance among American leaders to become involved in colonial wars of pacification.

Anti-imperialists were very active in promoting opposition to the Philippine-American War. Through their muckraking investigations and publicity campaigns, anti-imperialists drew attention to the cruelty of the Philippine-American War.[46] Anti-imperialists "wrote letters, magazine articles, and pamphlets. They made innumerable speeches, including many on the floor of Congress. They organized themselves into anti-imperialist leagues, lobbied in Washington, and used virtually all the means at their disposal in an attempt to influence both popular opinion and government officials."[47] They were successful enough that Postmaster General Charles Emory Smith censored their mailings, which gave anti-imperialists another issue to use to attack the administration.[48] From these and other efforts Americans became aware of the atrocities committed by American troops. Historian Richard Welch counted "fifty-seven verifiable instances when American soldiers committed atrocities," including murder of prisoners and civilians, rape, and torture; in addition there were approximately sixty cases of assault that "closely approximate the category and definition of torture."[49] These incidents seem to have increased as the war proceeded and the Filipino forces turned to guerilla tactics.[50]

The efforts of anti-imperialists to publicized atrocities committed by American troops in the Philippines produced investigations by the War Department and the Senate.[51] Anti-imperialist Republican Senator George Frisbie Hoar was the man most responsible for the Senate investigation of the conduct of the war. Despite the fact that the committee responsible for the investigation was led by diehard expansionist Henry Cabot Lodge, evidence did surface of American brutality, including William Howard Taft's rather graphic description of the so-called water cure that was used by American soldiers to torture Filipino captives during interrogations.[52] These disclosures were followed by Associated Press reports that American Brigadier General J. Franklin Bell had set up reconcentration camps in Batangas province, and later, that Filipino prisoners had been summarily executed by Major Littleton Waller in Samar province. The establishment of reconcentration camps was especially damaging to the army and its supporters because it was this policy—*reconcentrada*—by the Spanish in Cuba that had spawned so much outrage prior to the War of 1898; comparisons between American officers and the hated Spanish General Weyler were common in the press. Press attention peaked in April and May 1902 with an army report that documented the brutal policy of retribution enacted by General Jacob H. Smith in the Philippine province of Samar. Newspapers across the political spectrum condemned the policies of General Smith, but most held back from condemning American policy or the war in general. Anti-imperialists stepped up their attacks on the Roosevelt administration, but were met with a successful counterattack repeating the well-tread argument that anti-imperialists were treasonous cowards who impugned the honor of the American soldier. Criticism of the war effort faded from the editorial pages rather quickly due to American success in the Philippines, lack of new revelations, the higher salience of domestic issues, issue fatigue, and the fickleness of public opinion.[53] Furthermore, anti-imperialists' effectiveness was diluted because they were divided by party, class, and domestic economic issues.[54]

The anti-imperialists had their strongest effect as the war was coming to an end, but even when the worst atrocities came to light, a strong public outcry against US military policy in the Philippines never developed.[55] Welch attributes the relatively low level of public opposition to American military policy to the lack of good information about the conduct of the war and to "the dominant mood of optimism and romantic nationalism" of the period.[56] He notes that there was "a presupposition in favor of the rightness of the diplomatic and military policies of the nation. Their opponents were required to fight that presupposition and prove that in rejection lay the path of patriotism."[57] During the Philippine-American War most Americans viewed the control of the Philippines as consistent with "national progress and national honor."[58]

Despite the lack of a large, sustained public backlash against the Philippine-American War, the long-term effects are clear and significant. The war "revived a moribund anti-imperialist movement," and most importantly, "brought disillusionment with the nation's imperial mission."[59] Historian Frank Freidel is worth quoting at length on the long-term impact of the anti-imperialist critique of the Philippine-American War:

> The dissenters were somewhat less than complete failures. They had called national attention to the horrors of the Insurrection, and were particularly successful in doing so after the election, in 1901–1902. In the end they brought about a

considerable degree of national revulsion, and in consequence an end to this sort of imperialistic venture. There were to be further interventions during the Progressive Era—in the Caribbean, Central America, and even Mexico—but never on the scale of the Philippines. The thirst for additional colonies had suddenly and permanently been slaked. There was not to be the grandiose building of empire that some jingoes had hoped would be America's future. Indeed, the consensus seemed to have shifted to the view that ultimately, when they were ready, the Filipinos must have their independence.[60]

Joseph Halle adds, "a decade later it would have been hard to find any responsible opinion, including that of Roosevelt and of Mahan, to dissent wholly from the view that our acquisition of responsibility for them [the Philippines] was unfortunate."[61]

In 1899 many argued that possession of the Philippines would enhance the great power status of the United States, but this was quickly shown to be a mirage. The acquisition of the Philippines fostered the entrenchment of a forward posture for the US navy and helped justify the maintenance of a large force, but there was little increase in trade or involvement in China. There was an increased sense of shared interests with Britain and an uptick in mutual suspicion with Germany and Japan.[62] Some viewed the Philippines as a stepping-stone to Asia, and it did help the United States take part in the suppression of the Boxer Rebellion in 1900. However, within a few years most viewed the Philippines as a "serious liability." It was acknowledged that the United States Navy could not defend the islands from a Japanese attack. Furthermore, American presence in Asia seemed to produce "tension and conflict among the powers in East Asia," and the security expenditures were higher than any economic benefit gained from possession of the islands. Soon even Theodore Roosevelt was saying that the Philippines had no strategic value.[63]

The Limits of Expansionism

The Philippine-American War was the peak of American political–military expansionism. It is the only case during the period of study where the United States uses military force to subjugate a foreign people and establish a US colonial government. This so-called small war is explicable mainly through the logic of conquest: the Philippines were gained through war, and therefore must be pacified. The United States was a country on the rise that had just demonstrated its capabilities through victory in war; it would be humiliating to simply give up its territorial gains.

When we speak of a peak in an historical process it suggests an immediate, if not steep, decline. This is exactly what happened to America expansionism. The Philippine-American War was a demonstration of power and the limits of power. Americans applauded the military victories in the Spanish-American War and Philippine-American War, but the outpouring of patriotism couldn't quite hide the sense of unease at the use of military force to subjugate a foreign people. There was an awareness of the costs in blood, treasure, and morale among politicians and the general public due to the advocacy of anti-imperialists, especially the American Anti-Imperialist League and politicians like Senator Hoar and William Jennings Bryan.

The Philippine-American War is a case of delayed expansion and backlash caused by the incongruence between the imperialist actions of the US government and anti-imperialist elements in the strategic culture of American society. As noted, Americans were not radical anti-imperialists who reflexively renounced all territorial expansion. In fact, most scholars see broad support for the US annexation and pacification of the Philippines. However, evidence from the election of 1900 and its aftermath suggests that American support for expansion was shallow, and the public quickly reverted to its traditional anti-imperialist beliefs when expansion began to look like imperialism. The lack of economic and strategic benefits did play a role in reducing the popularity of territorial expansion, but this was a second-order effect of the inability of the United States to effectively consolidate its overseas colonies. This point is developed in the next chapter.

The Boxer War and Occupation of Beijing (1900–1901)

In June of 1900 a multinational force of 2,078 troops from eight countries—Austria-Hungary, France, Germany, Great Britain, Italy, Japan, Russia, and the United States—led by British Vice Admiral Sir Edward Seymour landed at Dagu, near Tianjin, on the Northeast coast of China to relieve the foreign diplomatic legations in Beijing that were under threat from a nationalist (antiforeign, anti-Christian) uprising called the Boxer Rebellion.[64] The multinational force occupied Beijing and surrounding territory in Chi-Li province.[65] Each of the coalition members was allocated a section of territory to pacify. As a participant, the United States gained political–military control of part of Beijing and the surrounding countryside. Once the United States became involved there was pressure from some quarters for the United States to maintain its military presence in China, but fear of public backlash prevented McKinley from seriously considering a concession or naval base in China.

The Boxer War took place during the Philippine-American War, and in the diplomatic context of European and Japanese competition for concessions in China and the US opposition to the partition of China into exclusive economic zones. The emergence of the Boxer movement in the region around Beijing was the result of Chinese nationalism reacting to increasing foreign encroachment on Chinese sovereignty. The United States reluctantly cooperated with the other powers in the occupation of Beijing, implemented a highly benevolent policy in their area of control, pulled out their troops as quickly as possible, and refused to seek any territorial concessions in China. The restrained nature of American intervention in China was due mainly to the fear that public opinion would turn against the intervention if it became too difficult or if the United States became caught up in the imperial designs of the other intervening powers. The election of 1900 weighed heavily on McKinley's decision-making process, inducing a high level of caution and restraint.

Expansion by the United States was expected in this case due to several conditions hypothesized to foster territorial expansion. First, American strategic and economic interests in an independent China (as articulated in the Open Door notes) were in danger of being infringed upon by the great powers active in East Asia. American intervention and the establishment of permanent American bases in China would protect those interests. Second, many in the United States had an almost mythical attachment to the idea of the China market. Third, American diplomats and Christian missionaries strongly supported a hard line against the reigning Qing Dynasty, including a permanent presence in China. Fourth, American troops were already deployed in the Philippines and it would therefore be relatively easy to mobilize American power to expand into China. Fifth, there was a general sense in the United States that the country was now a great power and had to accept the responsibilities that came along with that status. Finally, the American presence in the Philippines created a strong incentive for the United States to involve itself in the power politics of the region in order to protect its new colony. For these reasons, the United States was expected to engage in territorial expansion in China if an opportunity presented itself.

Causes of the Intervention

The proximate cause of the multinational Beijing expedition was the threat to the foreign legations from Boxers and their allies.[66] The threat was exaggerated by the diplomats, but since the legations were their only source of information, the home governments were led to take actions in defense of their diplomatic missions, which in turn forced war onto China with a coalition of great powers.[67] The foreign powers were also caught in the logic of power politics in China. Each of the counties with an interest in China could not afford for their rivals to get the upper hand, so as long as at least one major country pushed for increased intervention, it was difficult for any of them to hold back.[68] Intervention was also fostered by the widespread belief that it would be easy to crush the Boxers with forces already in Far East. The underlying reason for intervention was the desire for European powers, the United States, and Japan for increased influence in China.[69]

The foreign crisis started with the December 21, 1899, murder of British Reverend S. M. Brooks, one of an increasing number of attacks on missionaries and Chinese Christians. Brooks was killed by bandits who were not part of any organized movement, but his death was seen by the British delegation and others as part of a larger antiforeign plot. To intimidate the Chinese government the British, American, German, French, and Italian legations first implemented a naval demonstration off the coast of Northeast China in April 1900 and then deployed legation guards in May of 1900.[70] Under foreign pressure, the Chinese government attempted to suppress the Boxers, but had neither the capacity nor will to do so. Largely in response to the arrival of the legation guards, the Empress Dowager Cixi (the dominant presence in the Manchu Court) went into collusion with the Zhili Boxers, and her envoy invited them to Beijing to help protect the city from a potential large-scale military invasion; on June 7, they arrived in large numbers.[71]

The timing of the Boxer Rebellion was politically and strategically inconvenient for the McKinley administration. As noted above, in 1900 McKinley was under pressure regarding the acquisition of colonies and the general issue of imperialism. He was up for reelection against an avowed anti-imperialist, and already under attack from anti-imperialists for annexing the Philippines. The United States could contemplate participation in the Beijing expedition because it already had thousands of US troops stationed in the Philippines. However, these troops were needed for pacification operations in the Philippines, so it complicated the situation to shift forces to China. Despite these problems, the compelling national interest in protecting American lives and preventing the partition of China by the European powers and Japan was enough to tip the scales in favor of the deployment of American forces. The central goal of the United States was to strengthen the existing government of China (the Qing or Manchu Dynasty) and restore stability in China. The presence of American troops would give the United States a voice in whatever settlement emerged from the intervention. McKinley was particularly worried that a difficult occupation would hurt his administration at home and wanted a strategy that emphasized the benign intentions of the United States. To do so, it was important to maintain American independence from the other detachments of foreign troops to prevent "participation in some dark intrigue irrelevant or even inimical to American interests."[72] Finally, American intervention in China would also have the positive externality of demonstrating the strategic importance of the Philippines at a time when its annexation was increasingly unpopular.[73]

The actions of President McKinley suggest that he felt the expedition was a potential political liability, and therefore he had a strong incentive to make it as unobtrusive and unremarkable as possible. The first hurdle was the deployment of troops. The constitutionality of McKinley's decision was questioned in the American press and the president considered calling a special session of Congress to approve the deployment of soldiers, but demurred because he did not want to give Democrats in Congress a forum for criticizing him as the election approached. He also believed that it was within his powers as commander in chief to deploy the US military. However, acting without the support of Congress meant that "McKinley had to insist upon the limited nature of the action."[74] Otherwise, he risked more widespread backlash. As the operation was underway, Secretary of State John Hay released the second Open Door note stating that American policy was to "preserve Chinese territorial and administrative entity, protect all rights guaranteed to friendly powers by treaty and international law, and safeguard for the world the principle of equal and impartial trade with all parts of the Chinese Empire."[75] This statement of American policy took pressure off the Republican Party electorally by dampening Democratic criticism of McKinley's China policy.[76] Hay's note was popular because it was an expression of American exceptionalism, and was "regarded by Americans as an example to the whole world of unselfish national purposes."[77]

The public was angered by reports of Chinese attacks on Christian missionaries and seems to have supported McKinley's China policy of independent and restrained action. However, missionaries and the business group Asiatic Association called for much more aggressive action by the United States. The missionary newspaper the *Independent* "called for an American occupation of Peking, the deposition of the empress dowager and restoration of [Emperor] Kuang-hsu [Guangxu] and the establishment of an international protectorate over China."[78] Later, the *Atlantic Constitution* suggested that American policy should be the "utter annihilation" of the ruling Chinese regime.[79] These calls for more forceful action against the Qing regime reflected the outrage caused by published accounts of Boxer attacks on missionaries operating in China.[80]

Historian Marilyn Young provides the best summary of the reasons for intervention and the form that it took, emphasizing McKinley's concerns about public opinion: McKinley "moved cautiously, but, perhaps fearing the even greater uproar that would ensue if he failed to rescue [American Minister] Conger, failed to demonstrate that America could protect its own interests, and failed to use what influence America had to prevent the very machinations the anti-imperialists condemned, he *did* move."[81] In sum, McKinley was aware of the problems involved in moving troops from the Philippines and his vulnerability to anti-imperialists, but was most concerned with public response if he did not protect the American legation and American interests.[82]

American Conduct and the Consequences of the Occupation

American officers and diplomats were given the somewhat contradictory orders to protect American interests, avoid collaboration with the other foreign powers whenever possible, support the Chinese government, and maintain good relations with the Chinese people. The military policy that was implemented suggests that commanders on the ground in China followed these orders quite closely, and the effect was what McKinley hoped for—the United States emerged on relatively good terms with China compared with the other great powers involved in the expedition.

The first use of force by the multinational expedition led British Vice-Admiral Edward Seymour (including a small detachment of American bluecoats) landed at Dagu, near Tianjin, on the Northeast coast of China to relieve the legations in Beijing.[83] The 2,078-man expedition turned back before reaching Beijing due to attacks by Boxers and Chinese soldiers. The second use of force was the Battle of the Dagu Forts, a naval bombardment of Chinese fortifications the United States did not participate in because it appeared to be an act of war against China rather than an operation against the Boxers. The third use of force was the second expedition to Beijing that left Tianjin on August 6 and entered Beijing on August 14; American forces were part of this second expedition and participated in the subsequent occupation of Beijing.[84]

The American occupation zone was in an area of Beijing called Chinese City, which was heavily damaged by fire and looting during the Boxer occupation of the city. US General Adna Chaffee's main goals were to establish security and better the living conditions of the inhabitants of the American sector. In order to achieve these goals he identified Chinese who would cooperate with the American occupation forces. Chaffee was able to win the support of certain prominent Chinese through his benign policies and their own desire for influence over the occupation government. By September 1900 Chaffee's goals had largely been achieved: order was restored, and normal life had returned to the American section of Chinese City. The success of American forces and their Chinese collaborators drew Chinese residents to the American sector from less well governed areas of the city, especially the German sector.[85]

Within weeks of the arrival of American troops in Beijing, the McKinley administration was struggling to develop a plan to get them out. As stability returned to Beijing in September 1900, talk of withdrawing American troops began to circulate. The exit strategy was to recognize Chinese authority and turn over responsibility to a reconstituted Chinese government. McKinley remained concerned that the imperialism issue would hurt him in the coming election, and wanted to free up the troops for service in the Philippines. He was also worried about increasing reports of European atrocities, the difficulties involved in supplying the American troops through the winter, and further entanglement with rival foreign powers in China. Secretary of War Root saw no good reason for American troops to remain in Beijing without a clear mission, and advocated withdrawal of US troops to the coast. But McKinley followed the advice of Chaffee, Conger, and Hay to keep some of the troops in place in Beijing and continue to cooperate with the European powers and Japan. The decision to reduce the American presence in Beijing to a legation guard had popular support. By fall of 1900 the crisis was diffused and on the way toward resolution; McKinley began a gradual withdrawal of troops, cutting Chaffee's force in half to about 1,900 men.[86]

As stability was being restored, the Department of the Navy and General Chaffee began to expand their ambitions for an American presence in China. By early winter Chaffee was arguing in favor of "acquiring military bases that would demarcate and safeguard an American sphere of influence in North China."[87] He believed the United States should establish control of a port city and use it to support a permanent American base in Beijing. Chaffee worried that instability would continue in China and that the United States needed to maintain a strong position vis-à-vis other foreign powers. Conger strongly opposed attempting to obtain any territorial cession in China, and he was backed by Secretary Hay. The navy continued to seek out locations for potential coaling stations in China throughout 1901 and 1902, but with no success. The McKinley administration had little interest in gaining a territorial concession in China. McKinley's goals were to strengthen the Chinese government, not undermine it further, and stay out of the competition for Chinese territory. Meanwhile, the American forces in Beijing continued to collaborate with local Chinese leaders to fund and implement programs to increase the quality of life in their zone, working to reestablish a working municipal government, continue to provide food and fuel for the population, and strengthen public health and justice systems.[88]

By November, the Chinese imperial government was beginning to reestablish its authority in Beijing with the acquiescence of the foreign occupiers. By March 1901 rumors began circulating in Beijing that the Americans were preparing to withdraw, and Chinese inhabitants of the American zone, worried they might come under the control of another occupation force, submitted a petition with 13,000 signatures asking the Americans to stay. The American occupation ended in May of 1901, well ahead of the withdrawal of other nations. German and British forces took over the American zone and in September the Chinese government reassumed control of the city. The American occupation was judged a success, marked by the "reasonableness and restraint of the American army in Peking."[89] The Chinese themselves viewed the American troops as the most benevolent among the foreign forces.[90]

The intervention was a short-term success: the siege of the Beijing legations was lifted and the Boxer movement destroyed. Troop reductions began to occur in 1901, and after the signing of the Boxer Protocol foreign troops were withdrawn to the legations and strategic positions around Beijing. The Boxer Protocol forced China to pay reparations equal to approximately $5 billion in today's currency and obliged them to execute several pro-Boxer Chinese officials. Also,

China was not allowed to import arms for two years, and the Dagu forts were destroyed.[91] Despite these concessions, intervention was a strategic failure: anti-Western sentiment increased following the Beijing expeditions, which helped bring to power Chinese nationalists in 1911. However, the United States maintained better relations with China than the other powers: "The United States, by withdrawing early, providing good government in the sector on Peking, and by refusing its share of the reparation money, was able to remain the best trusted Western state by the Chinese nationalist government. But even the American approach to China was not enough to ensure that the new social order in China would be friendly to the United States."[92]

Avoiding the Costs of Expansion

Participation in the multinational occupation of Beijing was clearly an expansionist action by the United States. American forces invaded foreign soil and took political–military control of foreign territory. The main reason for the expedition was McKinley's interpretation of American national interests—protecting the American embassy and preventing the European powers and Japan from eliminating American influence in China. Parochial interests and the propensity for expanding political objectives during war fostered proposals for a more expansionist policy.

This case illustrates an important ongoing theme in this study: the conflict between the continuing incentives for expansionism and US presidents' concern about the political costs of an expansionist grand strategy. In the case of the Boxer Rebellion, historians note McKinley's concern that the actions taken in Beijing could lead to political costs through congressional opposition and public disapproval manifested at the voting booth. These concerns led to a strategy that focused on getting out of Beijing quickly, ensuring humanitarian behavior by US forces, and avoiding any controversial actions. There were calls for a more political–military expansionist approach by business and religious groups, as well as the commanding officer of US forces, but these ideas were not seriously considered by McKinley due to the elections of 1900 and the ongoing battle with anti-imperialists over the annexation of the Philippines and the prosecution of the Philippine-American War. Security considerations also seem to have fostered restraint. The United States was already embroiled in the Philippine-American War, and US soldiers that were in Beijing could not also be on Luzon. McKinley therefore wanted the intervention in China to be as cheap, easy, and quick as possible. The United States was a reluctant partner in the expedition and wanted to avoid entangling itself in the imperialist games being played by European powers and Japan. Therefore this case is categorized as limited expansion caused by the fear of political costs made possible by electoral institutions, fear that territorial expansion in China would cause public opposition, and security concerns related to maintaining military capacity for pacification in the Philippines and desire to remain separate from European and Japanese schemes in China. As with other cases, the hypotheses of interest-group theory are not supported by the evidence. To the extent that economic interests played a role in decision making in Washington, they encouraged expansion and not restraint.

American Occupation of Cuba and the Platt Amendment (1899–1902)

During the War of 1898, an American army invaded and occupied significant portions of Cuba to defeat Spanish forces. Following the peace agreement between the United States and Spain, the United States moved to occupy the whole island and build a Cuban state. During this period annexationists sought to Americanize Cubans to foster annexationist sentiment among the people. It was thought that if Cubans demanded annexation, the restraint of the Teller Amendment could be overcome. Annexationists were opposed by anti-imperialists, but more importantly they were opposed by McKinley and others in his administration who feared the negative electoral effects of a prolonged occupation of Cuba. These fears were intensified by the election of 1900 and the fear that a long occupation of Cuba could lead to the same result as the Philippines: a costly war of pacification. Overall, the political costs of the occupation overrode any impulses for annexation. However, expansionists did win a victory by forcing Cuba to incorporate into the Cuban constitution the right for the United States to intervene in Cuban affairs.

This is considered a case of limited expansion because of the strong incentives for the annexation of Cuba matched with the outcome of protectorate status under the Platt Amendment. Annexation of Cuba was driven by many of the same factors that led to annexation of the Philippines. First, even though the United States had officially disavowed any intent to annex Cuba—and actually passed a law prohibiting it—there was a strong temptation to expand war aims once the shooting started, and the presence of American troops on the island removed any difficulties American leaders would have with mobilizing state power. Second, the ideological milieu in support of expansion was strong in the wake of the victory in the War of 1898 and had an advocate in the military governor general selected by the president, General Leonard Wood. Third, the United States had considerable economic, strategic, and paternalistic reasons to see Cubans recover from the war and establish political and economic stability. Some considered American control over Cuban domestic affairs to be the best way to ensure that these interests were protected. Political and military leaders were also beginning to see control of the Caribbean Basin as important for

American national security. This reasoning was based largely on the perennial goal of building a canal across the Central American isthmus.

The Aftermath of the Spanish American War

On July 17, 1898 Santiago de Cuba fell to American forces, resulting in the collapse of Spanish forces in Cuba. On August 12 the United States and Spain agreed to a suspension of hostilities and on December 10, 1898, signed a peace treaty. The United States officially took control of Cuba on January 1, 1899, but the Cuban Army of Liberation was governing much of the interior. For a time tensions were high between American and Cuban forces, but American leaders successfully co-opted leading Cuban generals and many of the Cuban veterans. Most importantly, leading Cuban generals Calixto Garcia and Máximo Gómez accepted a modus vivendi with the United States that allowed for temporary American control of Cuba. With the cooperation of Garcia, the United States implemented a food-and-jobs-for-guns policy and gave each veteran a lump-sum payment for their service in the Liberation Army. Many officers were also given administrative positions in the new government being formed by the United States. As a precaution against future violence, the US troop presence was increased to 45,000 by March of 1899—twice the size of the force that invaded Cuba to defeat Spain. Political activity by Cubans in the winter of 1899 was confined mainly to competition over American patronage. Overall most Cubans were unhappy with the American military presence, but they understood that the path to independence required that they bide their time.[93]

Deciding the Fate of Cuba

Between 1899 and 1901 the fate of Cuba was decided through a debate between US annexationists and opponents who hoped to establish Cuban independence as soon as possible. Despite the promise made in the Teller Amendment that the United States disclaim "any disposition of intention to exercise sovereignty, jurisdiction, or control over" Cuba, many in the United States favored annexation. In fact, annexationist sentiment was strong among some members of the McKinley administration and expansionist members of Congress during the first year of American occupation of Cuba.[94] Annexationists hoped to get around the explicit prohibition of American control of Cuba by relying on a potential escape clause in the Teller Amendment that allowed the United States to engage in "pacification."[95] Expansionists were opposed by antiannexationists made up of both anti-imperialists and McKinley administration officials who feared electoral backlash from a lengthy occupation of Cuba. The outbreak of war in the Philippines induced an extra bit of caution in the McKinley administration. The last thing the president needed was a costly political conflict over Cuba. Ostensibly, antiannexationists had the upper hand because the Teller Amendment prevented overt attempts at annexation and Cuban sentiment was clearly against annexation.

By late 1899 the McKinley administration was beginning the process of establishing Cuban self-government and independence. McKinley was feeling pressure from the guerilla war in the Philippines and needed to avoid any problems in Cuba as the 1900 election approached. McKinley felt that if he went back on the promise of Cuban independence and a Cuban insurgency developed, this would favor the Democratic candidate. As electoral pressure restrained McKinley's options in Cuba, American business interests tied to the Cuban sugar industry were warning against precipitous withdrawal. McKinley tried to implement a balanced policy of moving forward with a census, local elections, and then a constitutional convention in Cuba as quickly as possible while avoiding a precipitous withdrawal.[96] Along these lines, McKinley instructed Governor of Cuba Leonard Wood "to get the people ready for a republican form of government . . . Give them a good school system, try to straighten out their courts, and put them on their feet as best you can. We want to do all we can for them and to get out of the island as soon as we safely can."[97] Secretary of War Root and McKinley both wanted a rapid end to American occupation.[98] Root was in constant fear that an armed rebellion would break out in Cuba.[99]

Nonetheless, some in Congress and in the McKinley administration, such as Governor Wood, still hoped that a long-term transformation of Cuban public opinion could make annexation possible.[100] Wood's goal was to Americanize Cuba and not to prepare Cuba for independence. General Leonard Wood's strategy was to create "conditions leading to 'annexation by acclamation.'"[101] An important step in the process was gaining Cuban collaborators that could be made loyal to the United States and trusted to make the request for annexation. Achieving friendly relations with elites—especially military leaders—was done by providing jobs for them in the occupation government. However, Wood's choice of Cuban elites could not be indefinitely imposed on the population, so elections were a necessary next step. To increase the chances of American-friendly elites winning, US officials worked to foster a cohesive political party out of loyal Cubans and to shape the electorate through suffrage laws. Wood even went on the campaign trail for his favored candidates.[102]

Besides fostering collaboration with the "best" Cubans, Wood's main tool of influence was to institute reforms that would increase the legitimacy of the occupation forces and Americanize the Cuban people. Wood had significant success at working with the Cubans to reform the education system, eradicate yellow fever, and build up the infrastructure. Judicial and municipal reforms were less successful. But this was not enough. Wood's efforts were not instituting the deep cultural changes that he hoped for. As 1899 came to a close, Wood tried to convince McKinley to give him more time to develop his plan, but McKinley needed evidence of progress toward Cuban independence before the presidential election.[103] The failure of Wood's policy became clear when the Cuban people elected nationalists in the municipal elections in June 1900 and in the election for the constitutional convention in August.[104] The elections demonstrated that the Cuban people were not willing participants in Wood's plan for Americanization. Historian Louis Pérez views the strong Cuban public opinion against annexation as decisive in turning the United States away from that option in 1899.[105]

In the United States, much of the public felt their generosity was not being appreciated by the Cubans and were ready to pull out as quickly as possible.[106] American patience was tested by a series of scandals in 1900. The problems included an ongoing feud between Military Governor Wood and his subordinate General Wilson; a dispute between American and Cuban officials over a contract to pave roads and build a sewer system in Havana; an unflattering portrayal of the McKinley administration in an article published by Wood's aide James E. Runcie; and, most damaging, embezzlement of Cuban funds by American Postal Service employees. These scandals shook the public confidence in McKinley's Cuban policy and gave Democrats an opening to attack the competence and integrity of the administration. On May 16, 1900, Democratic Senator Augustus Bacon of Georgia gave a rousing speech on the floor of the Senate denouncing the McKinley administration for the Postal Service scandal and demanding to know why US soldiers remained in Cuba and under what authority the United States was governing the country. Republican Senator Orville Platt responded that the Postal Service scandal was a small blot on an otherwise pristine record of the military occupation, but agreed that an investigation was warranted. He also made a strong argument that American forces were merely engaging in "pacification" in accordance with the Teller Amendment. Furthermore, he asserted that it was the duty of the United States to establish a stable government in Cuba, and that this was the true meaning of pacification.[107] The main fear of the Republicans was a total collapse of support for McKinley's foreign policy: "The difficulties and scandals in Cuba, when added to the revolt which had raged for a year in the Philippines, threatened to discredit the administration's entire colonial policy, and there would be a presidential election in only a few months."[108] The scandal was finally contained due to the quick response to the problem by McKinley, Root, and Wood, including a thorough investigation and punishment of the perpetrators.[109]

Despite the growing controversy, Wood continued to advocate for extending the military occupation of Cuba, hoping to establish in a Cuban constitution the right for the American military governor to have a veto on all Cuban legislation. However, Wood's eagerness to join in the Boxer War in China led to a sudden epiphany that Cuba was ready for self-government and no longer needed Wood or a large number of American troops there to manage the process. He convinced Root and McKinley that a constitutional convention should be held in a month and he began organizing elections for it immediately (though he never did get to go to China).[110]

The Platt Amendment

On November 5, 1900, the Cuban Constitutional Convention began its work to draft a constitution and determine the future of Cuban-United States relations. On the issue of what form of government Cuba would have, American officials did not interfere with the Cuban deliberations. From the American perspective, the crucial issue was the relationship between Cuba and the United States, and in this American officials were not willing to let Cubans determine their own future. Both General Wood and Senator Platt (chair of the Senate Committee on Relations with Cuba) felt that the majority of Cubans were unfit for self-government and while formal US control was not possible, it was necessary for the United States to have sufficient influence to shape Cuban politics and policy. While the Cuban delegates worked to design a constitution, American officials worked to design a new relationship between the two countries.[111]

Despite the successful elections and progress on crafting a Cuban constitution, pressure continued to build in Washington to speed up the transfer of power to Cuban hands. Secretary of War Elihu Root wrote to Wood on January 9, 1901, that the Cuban occupation was a "burden and annoyance" both in terms of expense and political pressure from Democrats in Congress and in the press. The McKinley administration was still pursuing the goal of withdrawing as soon as possible, while at the same time doing what they could to build the foundations of political stability in Cuba. Root accepted that the Teller Amendment did not allow the United States to impose institutions and agreements upon the Cuban people, and therefore the Cuban people would have to be convinced to impose institutions upon themselves. Root and other prominent Republicans worried that Cubans could shield themselves behind the Teller Amendment, and, with the support of anti-imperialists in the United States, force the United States to withdraw its forces and negotiate with a sovereign Cuba. These concerns formed the basis for the Platt Amendment.[112]

In a February 9, 1901, letter to General Wood, Secretary Root laid out administration policy. Root identified the core American national interest "in the maintenance of that [Cuban] government free of foreign control and internal disorder."[113] In the letter he outlined the provisions that would form the core elements of the Platt Amendment: prohibition of any treaty between Cuba and a third party that would infringe upon Cuban sovereignty, a right for the United States to intervene to protect civil liberties and Cuban independence, leasing rights for American naval bases, and ratification of all acts implemented under the US military government.[114] Key to the Root plan was that the Cuban delegates would voluntarily include Root's provisions into the Cuban Constitution.

Wood communicated Root's plan to the Cuban committee on relations with the United States on February 15; some objections were voiced, but overall Wood thought the Cuban delegates would accept Root's proposal. In truth the Cuban delegation was shocked by the Root plan and hoped that Congress would attenuate the demands of the McKinley administration. The Cuban leaders were concerned about their political futures in Cuba if they acquiesced to the terms suggested by Wood. At most the Cuban committee was willing to recommend that the future Cuban government, once fully constituted, should pass laws in accordance with most of Root's proposals—excluding the right of US intervention, leasing of bases, or limits on debt. It thus became clear that the process would not be as voluntary as the American leaders hoped, and it appeared that the United States would have to insist on its proposals.[115]

The Platt Amendment was introduced to the full Senate on February 25, 1901, as part of an army funding bill. It was the result of an effort starting in 1899 with General James Harrison Wilson and modified by Leonard Wood, Root, and the Platt Committee, with oversight from McKinley.[116] The bill was denounced by the Democratic press and staunchly defended by Republican newspapers (though some Republican editorialists argued that it allowed Cuba too much freedom). Former advocates of war against Spain, Senators Morgan (Dem.) and Foraker (Rep.) attacked the provision calling for American intervention to protect life, liberty, and property to be eliminated. Foraker argued that the clause would encourage the losing party in elections to cause instability in order to force the United States to intervene and overturn the election (though in the end Foraker voted in favor of the bill). Democrats and anti-imperialists like Senators Money (Dem.) and Hoar (Rep.) supported the amendment, because it would end the military occupation of Cuba. In the end the vote was mainly by party line with 43 yeas (all Republican) and 20 nays (17 Democratic and Populist and 3 Republican). In the House, the bill passed 161 to 137, again along party lines. The bill was signed into law by McKinley on March 2, 1901. Some in the press accused Democrats of limiting their opposition to the bill because of the generous funding for pork barrel projects like the River and Harbors Bill, and funding for the St. Louis Fair and Charleston Exposition. After the bill passed Senator Platt stated that he wished he could have achieved greater US control over Cuba, but felt limited by what Congress would accept.[117]

The amendment began by authorizing the president to end the US occupation when a Cuban constitution and government had been established, but then went on to significantly curtail aspects of Cuban sovereignty. The United States claimed a right to intervene as necessary "for the protection of life, property, and individual liberty."[118] The amendment also limited the size of the debt the Cuban government could assume and gave the United States the right to naval stations in Cuban territory. The Platt Amendment was not strongly opposed by anti-imperialists because they wanted Cuban independence as soon as possible—even if it meant incomplete sovereignty.[119] Cuban approval was still needed for the treaty to go into effect. Root instructed Wood to make it clear to the Cuban delegates that they had no real choice but to incorporate the Platt Amendment into their constitution if they wanted to achieve self-government. He also noted that opposition to the amendment would cause negative feelings in the United States and might affect trade relations. The content of the Platt Amendment reached Cuba on March 2 and immediately caused a series of public protests across the island, with Article III on the American right of intervention the most controversial element. The Cuban press came out very strongly against the amendment. Some delegates thought that if they rejected the amendment, Congress would be forced back in session to reconsider.[120]

The delegates to the Cuban constitutional convention rejected the Platt Amendment 24 to 2 and sent a delegation to the United States to express their concerns in April 1901. Senator Platt tried to assure the Cuban delegation that ratification by the Cuban delegates did not amount to "the establishment of a protectorate or suzerainty."[121] Root also wrote a letter officially stating that the United States would not make Cuba a protectorate. He claimed that Article III was a formalization of the Monroe Doctrine; it was necessary because the Monroe Doctrine was not accepted in international law but the Platt Amendment would be, and therefore European countries could not complain if the United States was forced to intervene to maintain the sovereignty and internal stability in Cuba. Promises of tariff concessions and the American assurances noted above split the Cuban elite and dissipated the strength of the opposition.[122]

Advocates of the Platt Amendment in the United States attempted to rally support among Americans by publishing essays in popular journals taking care to show that it was consistent with the Teller Amendment. The anti-imperialist press strongly opposed the Platt Amendment. Anti-imperialist newspapers such as the *Evening Post* argued that the Platt Amendment violated the Teller Amendment and claimed it was a step toward annexation. On a 15 to 14 vote, the Cuban convention passed a constitution including the exact wording of the Platt Amendment along with the promises made by Root, and their own interpretation of the meaning of the controversial articles. This was not good enough for Root, because he felt some of the added material changed the meaning. Two weeks later the Cuban delegation gave in to Root's demands on a 16 to 11 vote with 4 abstaining.[123] Cuban delegates accepted the Platt Amendment because they saw it as the quickest route to independence.[124] Independence arrived on May 20, 1902, when Wood handed power over to the first elected president of Cuba, Estrada Palma.[125]

A Substitute for Annexation?

There is a vigorous debate among historians about the meaning and effects of the Platt Amendment and its relationship with the Teller Amendment. Historian Louis Pérez Jr. sees the Teller Amendment as a relatively unproblematic barrier to annexationists, and sees the Platt Amendment as something akin to annexation. He argues that the Teller Amendment was "something of a substitute for annexation [and] served to transform the substance of Cuban sovereignty into an extension of the U.S. national system."[126] However, Pérez's argument is inconsistent with the available evidence. The Platt Amendment did not lead to quasi-annexation. Cuba did become a protectorate of the United States, but as history shows, the United States was not eager to involve itself in Cuban politics.[127] The historical record shows that Cuba maintained its autonomy because it avoided annexation. A comparison with the Philippines and Puerto Rico illustrates the importance of nonannexation. The United States withdrew its military in 1902 and allowed Cubans to run their country. The United States did intervene in 1906 and 1917—not to impose specific policies, but instead at the request of Cuban leaders to help restore order. Cuba successfully resisted unwanted American intervention in 1912 and 1920 and in several cases took foreign policy actions that went against the interests of the United States.[128] The central point is that Cuba maintained its independence in domestic politics and largely in foreign policy as well, which suggests that the Platt Amendment did not effectively dissolve Cuban sovereignty and reinforces the importance of the Teller Amendment and electoral concerns that prevented annexation.

Political–military expansion did occur in the sense that the Platt Amendment formally gave the United States the right to intervene in Cuban domestic affairs whenever American leaders judged internal stability to be under threat. This in effect diminished Cuba's sovereignty, but not necessarily more so than any small state's sovereignty is diminished by living in the shadow of a great power. Furthermore, the United States did not pursue full annexation and withdrew its troops to allow Cubans to take control of their own affairs. Therefore the final result of this case is categorized as delayed and limited expansion, because American domestic institutions increased the time and resources it took to enact the Platt Amendment and restrained the ability of US expansionists to pursue their goal of annexation. If McKinley had not been concerned about the election of 1900 and not beset by constant partisan attacks, he might well have listened more closely to annexationists, especially those such as Generals Wood and Wilson. This episode shows continuing uncertainty on the part of McKinley about the capacity for the American people to support expansionist ventures. The president was clearly uncomfortable expending political capital to pursue external policies that had only weak public support. McKinley's vulnerability was exploited effectively by Democrats and anti-imperialists to make colonialism and expansionism costly endeavors for the Republicans. Expansionism retained its importance and was clearly entrenched in certain elements of the military, Congress, and the business community. However, it is possible to detect a shift in the reasoning behind expansion. Strategic and economic interests were beginning to play a primary role in the debate over expansion, while the idea that the United States should assert its status as a rising power began to play a secondary role.

Acquisition of the Panama Canal Zone (November 18, 1903)

The American acquisition of the Panama Canal Zone in 1904 is a clear-cut example of territorial expansion in service of American security and economic interests. The impetus behind the canal was a strategic weakness. Naval planners were worried that it would be difficult to defend both coasts of the United States if ships had to sail all the way around South America to move from one coast to another.[129] To quickly and efficiently project naval power, the United States needed a path across the isthmus. A shorter sea route between the two American coasts would also facilitate domestic and international trade. A canal would increase American ability to defend not only its own shores but also its newly acquired territories in the Pacific Ocean. Thus, American security and economic interests were very strong drivers behind expansion in Panama. Other background factors included the inauguration of one of the most unabashedly expansionist presidents in American history, Theodore Roosevelt. He certainly perceived the United States to be on the rise and strongly believed it should act according to its status as a great power. He also was confident of his ability to harness state power in the pursuit of national interests. For these reasons territorial expansion was highly likely whenever an opportunity arose.

However, security concerns and pursuit of national interests are only part of the story. Domestic institutional and normative restraints had two crucial effects on the acquisition of the Canal Zone. First, separation of powers and the open policymaking process in the United States caused a considerable delay in deciding on which canal route to choose and greatly complicated the process of making a deal with Colombia after the Panama route had been chosen.[130] Second, during the debate over the Panama Canal Treaty President Theodore Roosevelt was accused of forging a corrupt bargain with Panamanian rebels and French businessmen to deprive Colombia of one of the provinces. These partisan attacks were politically costly and forced Roosevelt to backtrack from an expansive notion of American interests. Third, the unseemly undercurrents to the whole Panama Canal affair left Roosevelt more vulnerable to future accusations of imperialism and induced caution on his future behavior, even though the Panama Canal itself was highly popular. In sum, while President Roosevelt successfully gained the Canal Zone for the United States through the use of his executive power, in the long run his actions and the actions of his opponents undermined the overall expansionist project.

The Path to the Panama Canal

During the 1800s several schemes developed to build an isthmus canal, but it was only at the end of the century that the United States was able to acquire the requisite territory to complete it.[131] The 1890s marked a renewed push to build an American-controlled canal across Central America. An isthmus canal was central to the dreams of the large-policy advocates such as Alfred Thayer Mahan, Theodore Roosevelt, Brooks Adams, Henry Cabot Lodge, and China market enthusiasts. Naval strategy required the rapid movement of ships from one coast to the other, and the exploitation of Asian markets would be facilitated by a canal. The lack of a canal hurt the United States during the War of 1898, and the possessions gained during and after that war both solidified the ability of the United States to protect an isthmus canal (naval bases in Puerto Rico and Guantanamo Bay, Cuba) and provided a new reason that the United States needed access to the Pacific Ocean (to protect the Philippines and Hawaii). In pursuit of these new interests, in 1900 Congress pressured the McKinley administration to move quickly on renegotiating the Clayton-Bulwer Treaty with Great Britain to allow the United States to unilaterally build and fortify an isthmus canal. A new treaty was reached in 1901 after Britain conceded to US demands. This is considered a signal that Britain viewed the United States as the predominant power in the Caribbean.[132] At the time, American emphasis was on a canal built through Nicaragua because a French company, the New Panama Canal Company, owned the rights to build in Panama and was asking for $109 million for its assets, which an American commission assessed at a value of $40 million. However, William Nelson Cromwell, American attorney and agent of the New Panama Canal Company, successfully lobbied (and perhaps bribed) Republican lawmakers between 1896 and 1902 to oppose the construction of a Nicaraguan canal. In 1901 the New Panama Canal Company dropped its price from $109 to $40 million; this move lowered the estimated cost of a Panama canal below that of one built in Nicaragua.[133]

The decision to lower the price of the New Panama Canal Company's rights and assets drew engineer and entrepreneur Phillipe Bunau-Varilla to the United States to represent the company. Debate over the two canal options raged in Congress, with the Nicaraguan faction led by Senator Morgan wining an early victory in the House with a 308–2 vote in favor of the Nicaraguan canal. A rival bill was passed in the Senate, the Spooner Act, instructing President Roosevelt to purchase the rights to a canal in Panama, but if that failed he was to begin negotiations with Nicaragua. Bunau-Varilla then used the eruption of a volcano on Martinique to illustrate the danger of a Nicaraguan eruption, and convinced the House to pass the Senate bill 260–8. Roosevelt signed the bill into law on June 28, 1902, and Secretary of State Hay began negotiations with the Colombian Ambassador. In January of 1903 a deal was struck and a treaty signed in which the United States would pay $10 million plus $250,000 per year for a 99-year lease on a six-mile wide canal zone. After Senator Morgan's obstruction-ist tactics were overcome, the US Senate ratified the Hay-Herran Treaty on March 17, 1903, by a vote of 73 to 5. The deal was rejected by the Colombian Senate in August of 1903, leading Roosevelt and Hay to contemplate other avenues.[134]

Acquiring the Canal Zone

The acquisition of the Canal Zone depended on the actions of Panamanians as much as it depended on the actions of Americans. For over half a century Pan-ama was a restless province of Colombia, rebelling dozens of times between 1840 and 1903, and gaining independence for two years in the 1840s. Thus from the perspective of Panamanian history, independence was only a matter of time and would require only minimal American support to occur.[135] Nevertheless, a proxi-mate cause was needed, and it was supplied when Phillipe Bunau-Varilla took the lead in connecting the strands of American expansionism and Panamanian nationalism in 1903. After consultation with American officials Bunau-Varilla concluded that the United States would tacitly support Panamanian secession from Colombia. The United States would justify its actions by referring to its right to maintain transit across the isthmus, a right given to the United States in their 1846 treaty with Colombia. Bunau-Varilla then made contact with Dr. Manuel Amador Guerrero, a leader of the independence movement in Panama and physician for the Panama Railroad, which was owned by the New Panama Canal Company. The alliance of the Canal Company and Panamanian nation-alists began planning for a new rebellion. In a personal meeting with President Roosevelt in October of 1903, Bunau-Varilla made it known that revolution in Panama was certain. Roosevelt did not encourage the revolution, but Bunau-Varilla inferred that the United States would take advantage of the revolution if it were to occur. US naval vessels were directed to take positions along the coast of the potential breakaway region to prevent the landing of any troops from either side and to establish control over the Panama Railroad. Bunau-Varilla was informed of these actions during conversations with American officials. On November 2 and 3, after Bunau-Varilla learned that the American cruiser *Nash-ville* would be passing through Panamanian waters, the plan went into action. The key component of the plan was paying off the Colombian troops and gain-ing the support of the governor of Panama, who was appointed by Bogotá. In a confused situation on November 2, the captain of the *Nashville* allowed Colom-bian troops to land at Colon on the Pacific Ocean side of Panama. Quick think-ing on the part of Railroad Superintendent Colonel James R. Shaler prevented disaster for the rebels. Shaler offered to transport the Colombian officers to Pan-ama City on a special rail car, promising that their troops would be following soon after. Once the officers reached their destination they were arrested by bribed Colombian troops. The next day American troops landed to establish control of the railroad and supervise the Colombian troops, but did not offer support to the rebels. Fighting in Colon was prevented by rebel bribes to the Colombian soldiers, who were soon sent back to Colombia after being reunited with their officers. The revolution was concluded on November 6, 1903, in an almost bloodless fashion—one civilian was killed accidentally in Colon. The United States, as well as European and Latin American countries, quickly recognized the new country of Panama and work began immediately on a canal treaty.[136]

After the successful rebellion, the center of the drama shifted to Washington, DC, where Bunau-Varilla desperately wanted to get a treaty passed before he was removed from his post as interim minister for Panama to the United States. Bunau-Varilla's main goal was to get the $40 million for the Canal Company before its concession ran out; his concern for Panamanian sovereignty was a distant second. To short-circuit potential opposition in the Senate, Bunau-Varilla and Secretary Hay agreed to a treaty that was much more favorable to the United States than the treaty submitted to Bogotá earlier that year. Most importantly, the new treaty gave the United States virtual sovereignty over a ten-mile-wide Canal Zone in perpetuity.[137] The previous version of the treaty had allowed Panama to maintain sovereignty over the Canal Zone and was limited to 99 years. Hay and Bunau-Varilla quickly signed the treaty before Panamanian representatives arrived to relieve the French engineer. The Panamanian government was unhappy with the treaty, but was presented a fait accompli and had few good options; if they held out for a better deal, the United States might simply take what they wanted without a treaty, or might build in Nicaragua instead and leave Panama to face an irredentist Colombia. The government of Panama approved the treaty on December 2, 1903, and it was submitted to the US Senate on January 4, 1904.[138]

Despite the rapid action of Roosevelt, Hay, and Bunau-Varilla—or perhaps because of the rapid action—a significant number of US newspapers and senators raised objections to the Panama Canal treaty. Not surprisingly, Democratic papers and politicians, along with anti-imperialists, responded with the most outrage. Democratic senators Arthur Gorman and John Morgan led the opposition, and with 33 out of 90 Senate seats the Democrats would have prevented the ratification of the treaty on a party-line vote. Roosevelt justified US aid to Panamanian nationalists by referencing the 1846 treaty, American national interests, and the imperative of promoting the cause of civilization. He went so far as to claim that American control of the Isthmus canal was "in the interest of its inhabitants and of our own national needs, and for the good of the entire civilized world."[139] In response, Democrats invoked anti-imperialist and republican norms to undercut Roosevelt's rhetoric. One Democratic paper retorted that

Roosevelt's justifications were nothing more than "a tyrant's plea of necessity."[140] Democratic senators attacked Roosevelt's aggrandizement of executive power, arguing that Roosevelt violated the Constitution by engaging in an act of war (deploying troops in Panama) without congressional authorization, and violated the Spooner Act when he did not pursue a canal treaty with Nicaragua after negotiations with Colombia fell apart. The attacks against Roosevelt forced him to emphasize the practical benefits to American interests rather than a mandate from civilization. One widespread justification for the Canal treaty was the possibility that France would intervene to protect the property of the French New Panama Canal Company if the company's assets were not purchased by the United State. There was worry that this would lead to a French-Colombian war in Central America. The debate was also colored by repeated Colombian threats to retake Panama by force. The most interesting part of the debate was the lengths to which Roosevelt and his defenders went to refute the claim by opponents that the Roosevelt administration instigated or encouraged the Panamanian rebellion.[141]

Republicans were able to hold the line and pass the treaty without amendments. Subsequent to the ratification of the treaty by both countries, American officials convinced Panamanians to include in their Constitution a right of US intervention to maintain order in Panama.[142]

Public opinion appeared to be strongly in favor of the treaty, because the American people wanted a canal. Many southern Democrats voted with the Republicans, because they had long viewed an isthmus canal as in the economic interests of the South.[143] Senator James Berry of Arkansas stated bluntly that "the people of the South want this canal."[144] The final vote in February of 1904 was 66 to 14 with about half of the Democrats voting for the treaty, most of them coming from the South, West, and Midwest.[145] Several Democrats who voted in favor of the treaty noted that they did not agree with Roosevelt's actions, but simply saw the value of the canal as too great and public support too strong to vote against it. Walter LaFeber argues that Roosevelt's victory in the Senate is best explained by "patriotism" and "pocketbooks."[146] In other words, Americans were unwilling to turn back an important national achievement and saw the canal as important for American economic interests. Strategic concerns may have also played a role. The outbreak of the Russo-Japanese War on February 8, 1904, brought into sharp relief the strategic value of the canal.[147] The canal was seen as vital for protecting the Caribbean from German encroachment and threats to American Pacific possessions from Japan.

Roosevelt's achievement was popular in the United States, but there was lingering unease about "how Roosevelt and his administration had used presidential authority and military muscle to accomplish the objectives of the United States."[148] President Roosevelt felt the necessity to justify his actions in his 1903 state of the union address to Congress and in a second message to Congress in

January of 1904. He laid out his actions in great detail and asserted that his administration had nothing to do with encouraging the Panamanian rebellion. Roosevelt justified his actions in terms of supporting the aspirations of the Panamanian people, the good of mankind, and the cause of progress.[149] However, doubts about the acquisition of the canal zone did not fade away immediately; in 1904 one editorial noted that the methods of acquisition "were subversive of the best principles of the republic."[150]

Years after the events detailed above Roosevelt gave a speech in California where he shows pride in his accomplishment and lingering frustration with Congress:

> The Panama Canal wouldn't have been started if I hadn't taken hold of it. Because gentlemen if I had followed the general conservative method I should have submitted an admirable state paper, occupying a couple of hundred pages detailing the fact to Congress[,] and asked Congress [sic] consideration of it; in which there would have been a number of excellent speeches made on the subject . . . and the debate would be proceeding at the moment with great spirit, and the beginning of the canal would be 50 years in the future.[151]
>
> Naturally the crisis came when I could begin the work unhampered. I took a trip to the Isthmus, started the canal and then left Congress not to debate the canal, but to debate me and in portions of the public press the debate still goes on as to whether or not I acted properly in getting the canal, but while the debate goes on the canal does too and they are welcome to debate me as long as they wish, provided that we can go on with the canal now.[152]

These passages from the speech also suggest that Roosevelt did not expect Congress to easily approve of his actions to gain the Canal Zone and that he was cognizant of the importance of public opinion.

Long-Term Effects of the Acquisition of the Canal Zone

Historian J. Michael Hogan argues that the approval of the Hay-Bunau-Varilla Treaty legitimized Theodore Roosevelt's "aggressive, interventionist approach to foreign affairs." Hogan argues that Roosevelt's philosophy would live or die on the merits of the canal building process. If the United States could master the isthmus, then the interventionist philosophy would "bear fruit" and receive the "ultimate endorsement."[153] This is essentially what Hogan argues did happen: the success of the Panama Canal construction ratified Roosevelt's doctrine of Big Stick diplomacy of battleships and interventionism, which only began to come under concerted criticism decades later.[154] Hogan is partially correct. His argument that policy success can reinforce the underpinning ideology has merit, but the history of American foreign policy after 1904 suggests that expansionism was not ratified by the American people and was even abandoned by Roosevelt himself.[155] Furthermore, the repeated, elaborate justifications given by Roosevelt highlight the extent to which he understood imperialism and even expansionism to be outside the realm of socially acceptable behavior in the United States.[156] Contrary to theories that see strategic interests or power maximization as suitable guides to grand strategy, American leaders could not simply state that territory had to be taken for reasons of national interest. American leaders have always been restrained by the checks and balances of American institutions and the enduring anti-imperialism of American strategic culture, and have to take these factors into account when implementing grand strategy.

The more important effect of the acquisition of the Canal Zone was stated by Elihu Root: "The inevitable effect of our building the Canal must be to require us to police the surrounding premises. In the nature of things, trade and control, and the obligation to keep order which go with them, must come our way."[157] The building of the canal obligated the United States to extend its security perimeter to encompass Panama and the possible avenues of attack. For decades to come American leaders would justify intervention in the Caribbean Basin by referencing the need to protect the Panama Canal. Despite the enhanced incentives for expansion, the taking of the Canal Zone would be the final territorial acquisition by the United States. Roosevelt's interventionism was actually on its last legs when it achieved its greatest success.

This case is coded as delayed expansion with backlash. The United States gained control of new foreign territory of high geopolitical importance. The result was highly popular, but the way in which it was achieved was highly unpopular and required decades of effort to achieve. The discomfort with process did not prevent the United States from completing the treaty with Panama for control of the Canal Zone, but it did add to the growing sense that territorial expansion was not consistent with American values and therefore could be politically costly. This episode of expansion is best explained by the overwhelming geopolitical value of an isthmus canal, combined with the ideological tenets of a large-policy approach to foreign policy and the crucial entrepreneurship of Bunau-Varilla and to a lesser extent Roosevelt and Hay.

Conclusion

Between 1899 and 1903 the United States fought in two wars of colonial pacification (in the Philippines and China) and gained two protectorates (Cuba and Panama). The United States was consolidating its territorial gains from the Spanish-American War and fulfilling a major strategic objective in starting construction on a canal across the Central American isthmus. In the Philippine-American War, American expansionism continued to be driven largely by the status, identities, and strategic ideas that tend to emerge from an increase in relative power. American expansionists argued that the United States must accept its role in international politics to civilize the Philippines, watch over the Cubans, and fulfill its destiny as the dominant power in the Western Hemisphere.

However, arguments that emphasize expansionism miss important features of American foreign policy between 1899 and 1903. As the cases above demon-strate, the American people and the legislative branch of government were not unambiguously supportive of these actions. War in the Philippines led to signifi-cant backlash that lasted a generation, while also jumpstarting the anti-imperialist movement. As the expansionist projects continued, negative feed-back began to strengthen and generate clearer effects. Intervention in China was carefully limited and McKinley rejected a permanent American naval base or concession due to concerns about public and congressional opposition. Elec-toral concerns and opposition in Congress caused McKinley to oppose annex-ation of Cuba, forcing annexationists to settle for a protectorate. Finally, the taking of the Panama Canal Zone fostered partisan attacks on Theodore Roose-velt and a good degree of public soul-searching by the American people. In sum, what should have been a series of stepping-stones to ever greater American political–military expansion was instead the outer limit of American territorial expansionism.

The synergy between separation of powers and strategic culture was beginning to be felt in this period, but exerted ever stronger effects during the presidencies of Roosevelt and Taft. The limiting effects of the costs imposed by congressional opposition and the fear of negative public opinion (and concomitant electoral concerns) were a strong force of negative feedback, fostering learning by advo-cates of expansion. As the analysis continues in the next chapter, institutional and normative restraint was increasingly robust and resilient against the efforts of expansionists.

Notes

1. On American ineptitude during the occupation of Manila and early stages of the Philippine-American War see May 1996, 287–288; Linn 2000, 5–7, 26–31; Halle 1985, xii–xiii, 1–2, 11–12; Bolton 1972.
2. Bolton 1972, 102.
3. Linn 2000, 7. See also Halle 1985, 11–12.
4. McKinley's executive order is reprinted in Blount 1912, 147–150.
5. Kramer 2006, 169–210.
6. Welch 1979, 15.
7. Linn 2000, 30–31.
8. Golay 1998, 47; Welch 1979, 20–21.
9. Bolton 1972, 103. See also Welch 1979, 20–21.
10. Bolton 1972, 103.

11. Bolton 1972, 104.
12. Bolton 1972, 103–104; Welch 1979, 21–24.
13. Bolton 1972, 104.
14. Otis consistently told McKinley that "Filipinos generally welcomed American rule" (Golay 1998, 37).
15. Welch 1979, 5.
16. Welch 1979, 20.
17. Small 1995, 32.
18. Welch 1979, chapter 3.
19. Mugwumps were northeastern Republicans-turned-independents infused with the spirit of moral reformers who opposed machine politics, imperialism, and anything else that seemed contrary to their view of the highest principles of American tradition. See Beisner 1968, 5–17; Blodgett 1962, 614–634.
20. Krebs and Jackson 2007, 42–48.
21. Welch 1979, 65–67.
22. Young 1968, 140; Small 1995, 32–33.
23. Quoted in Schoultz 1998, 147.
24. Welch 1979, 52–56, 59, 67.
25. Quoted in Schoultz 1998, 146.
26. Welch 1979, 64. For the struggle over the platform see Rystad 1975, 184–196, 206–218.
27. Welch 1979, 61, 65. Copperhead was a Republican term for Democrats who opposed the policies of the Lincoln administration during the Civil War and were viewed by many at traitors. See Curry 1972.
28. Rystad 1975, 215.
29. Welch 1979, 61–63; Rystad 1975, 303–304.
30. Rystad, 168–258.
31. Harrington 1935, 228; Rystad 1975, 291, 295, 297–298.
32. Rystad 1975, 302–305.
33. Rystad 1975, chapter 9; Gould 1980, chapter 9.
34. Although there was variation in Bryan's speeches as he traveled the country, in the East the main focus was trusts and foreign policy; Rystad 1975, 266–290.
35. Bailey 1937; Gates 1977, 61–62; Welch 1979, 67–70; Small 1995, 32.
36. Bailey 1937, 43–52; Harrington 1935, 217–218, 226–227; Rystad 1975, 168–258, 306, 309.
37. Gould 1980, 227.
38. See Krebs and Jackson 2007.
39. Rystad 1975, 309–311.
40. Welch 1979, 70–71.
41. Rystad 1975, 53.
42. Rystad 1975, 310; Gould 1980, 226–227.
43. Rystad 1975, 309–311.
44. Ferguson 2004, 51; Gould 1980, 226–227.
45. Welch 1979, 35–39.
46. On the Philippine-American War see May 1991; Linn 2000; Welch 1979.
47. Gates 1977, 52.
48. Freidel 1969, 178–182; Harrington 1935, 221.

49. Welch 1974, 234.
50. Welch 1974, 236.
51. Welch 1974, 239; Freidel 1969, 182; Herring 2008, 328.
52. Jones 2012, 272–273.
53. Welch 1979, 136–146; Jones 2012, 269–349.
54. Harrington 1935, 220, passim.
55. Freidel 1969, 183; Welch 1974, 247–253; Jones 2012, 348–349.
56. Welch 1979, 147. See also Harrington 1935, 230; Jones 2012, 349.
57. Welch 1979, 148.
58. Welch 1979, 149. See also Jones 2012, 349.
59. Herring 2008, 328–329; Jones 2012, 350.
60. Freidel 1969, 183.
61. Halle 1985, 3.
62. Welch 1979, 151–152.
63. Ninkovich 2001, 72–75.
64. In 1900 Europeans referred to Tianjin as Tientsin, and some historians who write on this topic continue to use the incorrect spelling. At the time of the Boxer Rebellion Beijing was called Peking. Some historians continue to refer to the "occupation of Peking," but I see no reason to perpetuate this anachronism.
65. At the time, Europeans used Peking instead of Beijing. I use Beijing except in the case of direct quotations because that is the correct spelling for the name of the city.
66. The Boxer Rebellion was started by sects of religiously motivated martial arts practitioners and would-be magicians reinforced by groups of criminals, peasants, and parts of the Chinese Imperial Army who hoped to capitalize on the instability of the Boxer uprising to express grievances and enrich themselves. The Boxers were reacting to European imperialism and Christian missionary activity, and therefore to a large extent was a nationalist movement. The Boxer Rebellion originated in Shandong Province just south of Beijing and within the German sphere of influence and the site of a railroad concession. The first major act of the Boxer Rebellion was the Shandong riots in reaction to German aggression and brutality in 1898–1899. For in-depth studies of the origins of the Boxer movement see Xiang 2003; Elliott 2002; Purcell 1963; Esherick 1987; Ouellet 2009, 509–510.
67. The threat to the foreign legations increased significantly after the multinational invasion began.
68. Xiang 2003, 153–155.
69. Ouellet 2009, 511–512.
70. Russia and Japan also sent legation guards in order to maintain parity with the other foreign legations, even though they were relatively unconcerned about the Boxer uprising.
71. Xiang 2003, 159–181, 185–232; Esherick 2009, 269–288; Ouellet 2009, 510; cf. Young 1968, 146–147.
72. Young 1968, 157.
73. Young 1968, 158.
74. Young 1968, 162–163. See also Gould 1980, 221–222.
75. Quoted in Gould 1980, 222.
76. Gould 1980, 222–223; Morgan 2003, 358–359; Young 1968, 158–171.
77. Leech 1959, 522.

78. Leech 1959, 155.
79. Quoted in Leech 1959, 169. Many missionaries continued their hard-line position well after the occupation of Beijing; see also Leech 1959, 187–196.
80. Axelrod 2007, 331–332.
81. Young 1968, 171.
82. Young 1968, 170–171.
83. In 1900 Europeans referred to Tianjin as Tientsin.
84. Ouellet 2009, 509–511, 513–519; Xiang 2003, 241–305; Elliott 2002, 497–537; Esherick 2009, 288–306; Young 1968, 147–148, 150–152.
85. Hunt 1979, 506–514; Sibley 2012, 216–218.
86. Leech 1959, 526–528; Gould 1980, 223–224; Young 1968, 183–187; Morgan 2003, 360; Hunt 1979, 514–515; Young 1968, 179–187.
87. Hunt 1979, 515.
88. Hunt 1979, 514–518; Young 1968, 204–206.
89. Hunt 1979, 525.
90. Hunt 1979, 518–525.
91. Ouellet 2009, 513–519; Esherick 2009, 306–311.
92. Ouellet 2009, 523.
93. Hernández 1993, 31–93.
94. Pérez 1983, 271–273.
95. Pérez 1986, 42–44.
96. Schoultz 1998, 143–144.
97. McKinley quoted in Morgan 2003, 339. See also Hitchman 1968, 394.
98. Morgan 2003, 339.
99. Leech 1959, 391.
100. Leech 1959, 393–394; Pérez 1983, 272; Cummins 1967, 377–378; Pérez 1983, 272.
101. Pérez 1983, 281.
102. Pérez 1983, 274–318; Schoultz 1998, 144–146.
103. Schoultz 1998, 145; Healy 1963, chapter 15; Hitchman 1968, 395–399.
104. Pérez 1983, 312–318; Pérez 1986, 40; Healy 1963, 148.
105. Pérez 1983, 273–274.
106. Leech 1959, 391–393.
107. Healy 1963, 135–142; Morgan 2003, 340–341.
108. Healy 1963, 142.
109. Morgan 2003, 340–341.
110. Pérez 1986, 32–41; Healy 1963, 144–146; Hitchman 1968, 399.
111. Schoultz 1998, 147–148.
112. Pérez 1986, 44–47.
113. Quoted in Healy 1963, 156.
114. Quoted in Healy 1963, 157.
115. Healy 1963, 156–162.
116. Root is considered to be the primary author, Hitchman 1967, 356–369; Cummins 1967, 370–389; Gould 1980, 238.
117. Healy 1963, 167.
118. Quoted in Schoultz 1998, 148.
119. Schoultz 1998, 148–150.

120. Healy 1963, 168–171; Pérez 1983, 324–325.

121. Quoted in Schoultz 1998, 150.

122. Healy 1963, 171–173; Cummins 1967, 370–389; Pérez 1983, 326; Gould 1980, 239; Morgan 2003, 341–342; Hitchman 1967, 345–350.

123. Healy 1963, 173–174, 176–178; De la Torriente 1930, 368–371; Hernández 1993, 97–98; Gould 1980, 239–240.

124. Hitchman 1968, 401; Pérez 1983, 32.

125. Hernández 1993, 92–102; Hitchman 1968, 401.

126. Pérez 1986, 49.

127. Healy 1963, 153.

128. De la Torriente 1930, 376.

129. Braisted 1957.

130. Panama was part of Colombia until it successfully seceded in 1903.

131. For historical background see LaFeber 1989, 8–12; Collin 1990, 132–146. It is interesting that the United States did nothing to stop the French from building an isthmus canal; if it had not gone bankrupt there would have been a French-Colombian canal instead of an American one.

132. Herring 2008, 326; Collin 1990, 170.

133. LaFeber 1989, 12–16; Collin 1990, 160, 169–176. For an extensive discussion of how intellectual undercurrents in the United States in the 1890s intensified the interest in an isthmus canal see Hogan 1986, 20–34.

134. LaFeber 1989, 16–19; Collin 1990, 177–179, 186–199, 215–236.

135. LaFeber 1989, 19–22; Collin 1990, 147–150. On the Colombian civil war see Collin 1990, 163–185, 199–209.

136. LaFeber 1989, 23–26; Collin 1990, 245–267; Gould 1991, 91–97.

137. It was claimed that Panama maintained "titular sovereignty" over the Canal Zone; LaFeber 1989, 33–36.

138. LaFeber 1989, 28–31; Collin 1990, 269–290; Gould 1991, 97–98; Major 1984, 115–124.

139. Quoted in Hogan 1986, 35. Roosevelt's reference to the 1846 Bidlack-Mallarino Treaty was based on a legal analysis claiming that the treaty established "joint American-Colombian sovereignty over the canal zone" (Collin 1990, 240–244).

140. LaFeber 1989, 32.

141. LaFeber 1989, 31–32; Hogan 1986, 34–35; Collin 1990, 290–302, 305, 309; see also Gould 1991, 98–99.

142. LaFeber 1989, 33.

143. Southerners wanted to break the transcontinental transportation monopoly held by the railroads. Senator Morgan also favored a canal, but thought that one located in Nicaragua would benefit the South even more, especially well-positioned cities on the Gulf of Mexico like New Orleans and Mobile. See Collin 1990, 153.

144. Quoted in Hogan 1986, 36.

145. LaFeber 1989, 32–33; Hogan 1986, 35–37; see also Gould 1991, 98–99.

146. LaFeber 1989, 32.

147. Hodge 2008, 721.

148. Gould 1991, 98.

149. Engel 2008, 682.

150. LaFeber 1989, 33.

151. Quoted in Vivian 1980, 99.
152. Quoted in Vivian 1980, 99.
153. Hogan 1986, 37.
154. Hogan 1986, 54–56.
155. See the following chapter.
156. Jones 2012.
157. Quoted in Schmidt 1995, 43.

4

---- ★ ----

ADAPTATION AND RECESSION

1904-1912

WHEN THEODORE ROOSEVELT took office for his second term as President of the United States it seemed that all the pieces were in place for significant increase in American territorial expansion: there was plenty of territory in the Western Hemisphere that had not been claimed by any great power; the political instability of the Caribbean and Central America provided the opportunity and justification to annex new territories; the United States had recently emerged as a colonial power; the proexpansionist Republican Party was dominant in American politics; and Roosevelt, a vigorous advocate of imperialism, had just won the presidential election by nearly 20 percent over his opponent.[1] Furthermore, the ongoing colonial project in the Philippines and new opportunities in Africa provided opportunities for the United States to continue to raise its status in the realm of great power competition.

Probably the most important expansionist impulse was caused by the acquisition of the Canal Zone in Panama, which extended the US security perimeter into the middle of Central America and the west end of the Caribbean Basin. From this point forward, protecting the Panama Canal (even before it was completed) was a core security objective of the United States. Perceived threats to the islands guarding the approach to the canal or from neighboring countries in Central America consistently triggered the consideration of political–military expansion. The key concern was that political instability in the Caribbean or Central America could encourage outside powers to intervene and potentially create protectorates or colonies in this geopolitically important area. Thus the logic of security through expansion was the major reason for the expansionist efforts of the executive branch. Finally, among a fairly small segment of the US elite, there was a paternalistic sense of mission to uplifting the nations viewed as less fortunate. These goals are all consistent with international relations theories that predict that an increase in power will lead to an expansion of interests.

Despite the favorable context for territorial expansion, in hindsight we know that the modest American empire had reached its height by 1904. Under Roosevelt's presidency the United States passed up several opportunities to gain control over new territory and even ended up losing territory.[2] Roosevelt's successor, William Howard Taft, shared both Roosevelt's imperialist predilections and his lack of success in implementing these preferences. Taft attempted to rebrand expansionism under the title of "dollar diplomacy," but failed in all of his attempts to gain formal control of the finances of foreign governments.[3] The reason for the dissipation of the American imperialist drive was the restraining influence of American anti-imperialist norms and decentralized institutions. No great public outcry against territorial expansion developed, but US presidents consistently saw imperialism as a potential electoral vulnerability and did what they could to avoid the perception that they supported imperialism. The reason for this electoral vulnerability is the consistent influence of anti-imperialism in American society. As shown in the cases below, Roosevelt and Taft were both highly cognizant of the potential electoral costs of expansionist foreign policies and consistently sought to minimize the scope and duration of intervention in foreign countries. Furthermore, because foreign interventions often required consent from the Senate (in the case of a treaty) or appropriations from Congress (for military deployments and development aid), the legislative branch had a veto over expansion and often used it. Congressional restraint was caused by a desire to limit the power of the president (institutional interests), prevent the increase in American foreign commitments (principled anti-imperialism), and for electoral advantage (personal and partisan interests).

This chapter covers eight cases of expansion or attempted expansion by the United States. Four cases concern the establishment of customs receiverships in the Dominican Republic, Honduras, Nicaragua, and Liberia; three cases discuss military intervention in Cuba and Nicaragua; and one concerns the retrenchment of imperial ambitions in the Philippines. In each case the struggle between expansion and restraint plays out in a slightly different manner, but overall we see the forces of expansion slowly degraded by the obstructionist forces of restraint.

Customs Receivership and Rejected Protectorate in the Dominican Republic (1904–1907)

In response to fears of European military intervention in the Dominican Republic, President Roosevelt attempted to establish US control of Dominican customs receipts and debt payments early in his first term. Developments in the Dominican Republic contributed to the creation of the Roosevelt Corollary to the Monroe Doctrine, and it was the site of the first attempt to implement the new strategy. Opposition in the Senate delayed the formal implementation of Roosevelt's policy and forced Roosevelt to significantly decrease the level of US responsibility over Dominican finances and sovereignty. The changes made by the Senate were also meant to rebuke Roosevelt for his novel interpretation of the Monroe Doctrine. At the same time, this is not a case of pure restraint. The Roosevelt administration succeeded in implementing a temporary customs receivership through an executive agreement before revising the policy to appease the Senate.

We have good reason to expect political–military expansion in the Dominican Republic because of security concerns about the intervention of European powers in the Western Hemisphere. With the acquisition of the Panama Canal Zone, the United States was even more concerned than it had been previously about the geopolitical implications of European intervention in the Caribbean Basin. A second factor is the continuing relevance of background conditions such as Republican control of the executive and legislative branches, status-seeking by the United States (something especially important to Roosevelt), jingoist political rhetoric, and activities by Americans and Dominicans to encourage American expansion.

Gunboat Diplomacy

By the mid-1800s countries in Latin America were taking out large loans from European and American investors, and soon the threat of debt default became pervasive. In response, European countries pursued a policy of "gunboat diplomacy," which was a form of coercion that entailed the use of naval power against weaker countries to collect outstanding debts.[4] As this practice became increasingly common in the Western Hemisphere, the United States grew concerned that European countries would escalate from intervention to occupation by turning weak, poorly governed Latin American countries into protectorates or colonies. This fear emerged during the 1902 Venezuelan crisis and culminated in the Roosevelt Corollary to the Monroe Doctrine and later Taft's concept of dollar diplomacy. The American experience with the Dominican Republic was vital to the emergence of this doctrinal shift to a more active US role in the domestic affairs of countries in the Caribbean Basin.

Dominican Debt and the Origins of American Interests

The financial troubles in the Dominican Republic began during the reign of military dictator Ulises Heureaux between 1886 and 1899. During Heureux's reign political stability was purchased using foreign debt to fund bribes and military force to stifle opposition. At the time of Heureaux's death the Dominican Republic was tens of millions of dollars in debt to the US-based San Domingo Improvement Company (SDIC) and to European creditors.[5] Over the next several years, political instability deepened as civil war became pervasive and foreign debt continued to mount. Both France and Germany sought to protect the investments of their citizens. France sent warships to collect a quarter million dollars in debt, while Germany turned down an offer for rights to Dominican territory at Samaná Bay and Manzallino Bay as payment for their debt. The United States increased its involvement in Dominican affairs in early 1904 as American naval forces began periodically using military force with the stated purpose of protecting American lives and property and to support the regime of Carlos F. Morales Languasco. Though distracted by the debate over the Hay-Bunau-Varilla Treaty and the Russo-Japanese War, President Roosevelt began to take a stronger interest in the Dominican Republic by 1904. Morales welcomed American interest; he knew his rule depended on American support. Between December 1903 and January 1904 several plans were floated by Morales and Dominican diplomats for an American protectorate over the Dominican Republic, American help to pacify the interior of country and manage government finances, and the leasing of Samaná Bay and Manzallino Bay to the United States for naval bases.[6]

US officials were lukewarm to the idea of increased political–military control over Dominican affairs; nevertheless, rumors of increased US and European military intervention pervaded the summer and fall of 1904, driven by continuing political instability and increased discord among the Dominican Republic's creditors. One trigger of the increased discord was the July 1904 arbitration judgment—from a panel made up of two Americans and one Dominican—that required the Dominican Republic to begin making payments to SDIC and gave the United States the right to appoint a receiver of customs duties if there was a default. The Morales government disputed the award, but under pressure from the State Department allowed SDIC's agent to begin collecting customs revenue at the main port city of Puerto Plata in October of 1904. European creditors wanted a share of the customs revenues and protested against the favorable treatment of the SDIC claims. Tension between the United States and European creditors continued to increase through the end of 1904, and rumors began to surface of European military intervention to gain repayment of loans. France, Belgium, Spain, Italy, and Germany discussed taking control of customs houses in the southern ports of the Dominican Republic.[7]

Why wasn't President Roosevelt more enthusiastic about a Dominican protectorate?[8] Roosevelt did not want European powers to gain more influence or territory in the Western Hemisphere, but did not think that annexing the Dominican Republic was a practical response by the United States. Roosevelt famously declared, "I have about the same desire to annex it as a gorged boa-constrictor might have to swallow a porcupine wrong-end-to."[9] Instead, as one scholar suggests, he sought to exercise "some control without formal responsibility."[10] The best evidence suggests that Roosevelt's reluctance was tied to fears of domestic opposition to additional territorial expansion. Schoultz argues that "Roosevelt had lost his appetite for annexation after seven years of nearly continuous involvement in Caribbean adventures."[11] Veeser concurs, noting that the "imperial burdens in Puerto Rico, the Philippines, and to a lesser degree in Cuba and Panama" made the American officials reluctant to take on an addition burden in the Dominican Republic.[12] Roosevelt's personal preference appeared to include taking "partial possession" of the Dominican Republic, but he did not follow through because he predicted strong domestic opposition and worried about the effect such action would have on the approaching presidential election.[13] Roosevelt had just faced a tough battle in gaining ratification of the Hay-Bunau-Varilla Treaty, "and he was not ready to face another contest with his Senate opponents, especially in an election year."[14] Roosevelt tried to answer charges of imperialism in the Philippines and Panama with references to nonintervention in Venezuela and withdrawal from Cuba; he did not relish the idea of having to explain a new colony in the Caribbean.[15] It was only after his election in 1904 that Roosevelt moved to take a more aggressive stance on the Dominican problem in conjunction with the announcement and explication of his corollary to the Monroe Doctrine.[16] However, even then, Roosevelt did not go so far as advocating annexation of the Dominican Republic.

The Roosevelt Corollary

As Roosevelt attempted to come to terms with the growing crisis in the Dominican Republic, he articulated a broad policy statement, later known as the Roosevelt Corollary. The public was first introduced to the doctrine in a letter written by Roosevelt and read by Elihu Root at a dinner celebrating Cuban independence on May 20, 1904. The negative public reaction to the letter led Roosevelt to wait until after the election to fully describe the new doctrine.[17] The venue for the more comprehensive articulation of the corollary was Roosevelt's annual message to Congress in December of 1904.[18] The key sentence of the address committed the United States to intervening in countries in the Western Hemisphere to repair sins of commission and omission: "Chronic wrongdoing, or an impotence which results in a general loosening of the ties of civilized society, may in America, as elsewhere, ultimately require intervention by some civilized nation, and in the western hemisphere the adherence of the United States to the Monroe Doctrine may force the United States, however reluctantly, in flagrant cases of such wrongdoing or impotence, to the exercise of an international police power."[19]

The Roosevelt Corollary was based on the realization that the Monroe Doctrine could only endure if the United States helped protect European interests
in the Western Hemisphere. By policing the behavior of Latin American countries—especially in the financial realm—the United States could eliminate the
main reason European powers would have for military intervention in the Western Hemisphere. Thus, in a sense the Roosevelt Corollary was a unilateral declaration of a multilateral commitment.[20] The new doctrine would also commit the
United States to putting the interests of "civilized" countries ahead of the interests of specific American businesses. For the doctrine to be successful, the United
States would have to fairly represent the interests of European powers and limit
its favoritism toward private American investors. The implications for US policy
in the Dominican Republic were quickly grasped by the relevant parties: SDIC
representatives were displeased with this shift in American policy, while European countries swiftly embraced it.[21]

Emergence of Congressional Opposition

With the election of 1904 behind him, Roosevelt was ready to move forward
and apply his Corollary to the Dominican Republic. The most effective way for
the United States to keep Europeans out of the Dominican Republic was to take
charge of Dominican finances to ensure the repayment of foreign debt, a policy
that would align neatly with the newly announced Roosevelt doctrine. The
recently appointed American minister to the Dominican Republic, Thomas C.
Dawson, was instructed to begin negotiations with the Morales government for
an American customs receivership. Roosevelt also sent Naval Commander
Albert C. Dillingham to help with the negotiations—a typical arrangement that
would lend so-called moral support to the actions of a US minister. The resulting
agreement concluded on January 21, 1905, sparked intense partisan opposition
in the United States.[22] Under the shadow of American naval vessels, US officials
negotiated a convention with the Dominican Republic giving the United States
a customs receivership and specifying that 55 percent of tariff receipts would
go to foreign creditors and 45 percent would be dispersed to the Dominican
government. Customs receipt and distribution would be managed by an American official appointed by the US Secretary of State. The agreement also committed the United States to helping the Dominican Republic renegotiate its private
debt and, more expansively, promised to "grant the latter [the DR] such assistance as the former [United States] may deem proper to restore the credit, preserve the order, increase the efficiency of the civil administration and advance
the material progress and welfare of the Dominican Republic." The expansive-
ness of the US commitment was a central reason for Senate opposition to the
convention. Opposition was also a result of the framing of the convention as an
application of the new doctrine of the Roosevelt Corollary.[23]

As the convention with the Dominican Republic was being negotiated and signed, a battle of institutional supremacy was being waged between President Roosevelt and the US Senate over a series of arbitration treaties signed between November of 1904 and January of 1905 and over domestic policy. The dispute over the arbitration treaties involved the inclusion of a "provision stating that before appealing to the Hague Court the two powers [that were party to the treaty] were to conclude a 'special agreement' defining the issue in dispute, the scope of the arbitrator's powers and the procedure to be followed."[24] The Senate argued that giving the president the right to make a special agreement with a foreign country infringed upon the treaty consent powers of the Senate, and demanded that the treaties be revised to eliminate the provision for special agreements. Following several attempts to pressure recalcitrant Republicans and Democrats, Roosevelt gave in and in 1908 signed a series of new arbitration treaties including the Senate amendment.[25]

It was in the context of this struggle that Roosevelt apparently hoped to conclude an agreement with the Dominican Republic without the advice and consent of the Senate. Roosevelt viewed the agreement with the Dominican Republic to be a simple extension of the arbitration judgment and a purely financial arrangement that did not rise to the level of a treaty requiring the consent of the Senate. Many members of the Senate disagreed and viewed the agreement as usurpation of senatorial power. Roosevelt was forced to submit the agreement to the Senate after news of the accord was greeted by a chorus of protests in the press and Democrats in Congress (news reached the American press on January 21). Republicans were also concerned, but confined their protests to private communications with administration officials. Soon after opposition arose in the press and in the Senate, the Roosevelt administration decided to modify the substance of the agreement. Roosevelt decided that approval by the Senate was necessary, and acting Secretary of State Francis Loomis rewrote the agreement to make it more palatable. A new protocol was signed with the Dominican Republic on February 7, 1905, that made the following changes: acceptance of the need for approval by the Senate, removal of any guarantee to protect Dominican sovereignty and instead a promise to respect its territorial integrity, removal of the commitment to help renegotiate Dominican debt, and invocation of the Monroe Doctrine to justify American intervention in the Dominican Republic. This change in policy was viewed at the time as a victory for the Senate.[26] Roosevelt submitted the revised treaty for approval by the Senate on February 15, 1905, with the message that the treaty was crucial to prevent foreign governments from gaining control of Dominican revenues. To obtain ratification of the treaty, Roosevelt needed all 54 Republicans and at least three Democrats. However, Senate Democrats were not fully mollified by the changes. According to Richard Collin, "Democratic Senators Augustus O. Bacon of Georgia, Hernando de Soto Money, and John Tyler Morgan . . . were determined to punish Roosevelt for what they perceived as a case of executive usurpation . . . and to use their minority party legislative veto as a political weapon."[27] Democrats and some conservative Republicans were determined to restrain the power of the executive branch and sought to use the Dominican treaty to do so. Opposition by Democrats, anti-imperialists, and conservative Republicans continued to prevent the treaty from coming to a vote before the Senate adjourned in March of 1905.[28]

With the Senate session over and the treaty still in purgatory, Roosevelt became convinced that something had to be done to stabilize the situation in the Dominican Republic until the treaty could be pushed through the Senate. Under the advice of Minister Dawson and with the endorsement of Dominican leaders, Roosevelt's cabinet, and prominent Republican senators, Roosevelt used an executive agreement to establish a temporary modus vivendi whereby he would nominate customs officials and the Dominican president would appoint them. The collector of customs would deposit the customs revenue in the National City Bank of New York until a permanent agreement was put into effect. Roosevelt appointed American Colonel George Colton as customs receiver and Jacob Hollander as a financial advisor in charge of reforming the Dominican financial system. Officially, Colton was employed by the Dominican government, but the arrangement amounted to an American customs receivership with American supervisors running the customs houses and the American navy providing security. Later Roosevelt would brag that he had essentially implemented the treaty against Senate objections; however, at the time "the President attempted to make his action appear as unlike defiance of the Senate as possible."[29] He argued that his actions were simply meant to maintain the status quo until the Senate made a decision on the treaty, though maintaining the status quo required de facto control of the customs houses and the use of the navy to prop up the Morales regime. The results of the new policy were positive and almost immediate. Creditors were reassured, and political and economic security increased substantially in the Dominican Republic. With the situation stabilized there was time for a lengthy debate in the Senate that was more about partisan politics and the balance of power between the branches than about the Dominican Republic. In the meantime, new Secretary of State Elihu Root worked to placate the Senate.[30]

The appeasement of critics coupled with the success of Roosevelt's policy helped quiet his critics and paved the way for a more positive reception to a new treaty. The new treaty responded to senatorial criticism by making several important changes: removal of any mention of the Monroe Doctrine, removal of any suggestion that the United States guaranteed Dominican territorial integrity, clarification that the United States was under no obligation to maintain order in the Dominican Republic, and removal of the promise to help the Dominican Republic renegotiate its debt with other creditors. The Dominican-American Treaty was signed on February 8, 1907, and ratified on a vote of 43 to

19 on February 25. The new agreement was approved by the Senate after three Democrats joined the Republican block and the Democrats decided not to implement further delaying tactics. One reason given for the lower opposition was public indifference to policy toward the Dominican Republic, thus removing the ability for Democrats to build political capital on opposing Roosevelt's policy.[31]

Stability reigned in the Dominican Republic until the assassination of President Ramótabiceres in 1911. In 1912 the Wilson administration would have to develop its own policy for the Dominican Republic—a policy that ended up looking very similar to the solution sought by President Roosevelt.

A Case of Strategic Restraint?

There are two ways to view the events in the Dominican Republic. First, like W. Stull Holt, one can view the passage of the 1907 treaty as "a remarkable triumph for the President" in that Roosevelt got what he wanted—a customs receivership in the Dominican Republic—and in doing so defied the Senate by implementing the modus vivendi.[32] This is a plausible interpretation. But a second interpretation that compares the initial policy aspirations of the Roosevelt administration to the end result shows that the final treaty dramatically scaled back the obligations of the United States toward the Dominican Republic, and this scaling back was the direct result of Senate opposition to Roosevelt's policy. Thus, while Roosevelt may have won by temporarily implementing a policy against the wishes of the Senate, the substance of this policy was dramatically changed by the presence of institutional restraints on political power. In other words, without the restraint caused by separation of powers, policy toward the Dominican Republic would have been significantly different.

Beyond the specifics of Dominican policy, this case touches on the content and direction of US grand strategy. One could argue that Roosevelt succeeded in implementing a new and important foreign policy, but in practice Roosevelt did everything he could to minimize the importance of the policy pursued in the Dominican Republic, going to the extent of removing any mention of the Monroe Doctrine from the treaty. Historian Richard Collin argues that the policy outcome in the Dominican Republic "was not a presidential defeat of the Senate's treaty-making power or an expansion of the Monroe Doctrine as much as a limitation on American expansion and an affirmation of responsibility to less prosperous Caribbean peoples."[33] Collin suggests that Roosevelt achieved something less than a total victory.[34]

In sum, the US Senate acted as a major obstacle for Roosevelt's foreign policy toward the Dominican Republic and his geopolitical vision of managing the Western Hemisphere for the good of civilization. Senate opposition delayed the formal implementation of the customs receivership treaty for two years and won many concessions from the Roosevelt administration that significantly decreased American influence over the Dominican Republic.

American action in the Dominican Republic did expand US control over foreign territory, but only in a limited sense. The Dominican government agreed to allow an American official to act as an independent collector and distributor of revenue, following the guidelines stated in their treaty with the United States. Thus to a certain extent, expansionist policy overcame the restraints of domestic institutions. Roosevelt implemented a customs receivership in the Dominican Republic against the opposition of the US Senate. Nevertheless, we do see domestic institutions working against expansionist policy by preventing Roosevelt from fully implementing his preferred policy and forcing him to significantly weaken American political investment in the Dominican Republic. Opposition (and potential opposition) in the Senate prevented the Roosevelt administration from establishing a protectorate or making any political commitments to the Dominican Republic and avoided legitimizing the new doctrine propounded in the Roosevelt Corollary. The primary cause of restraint was separation of powers articulated through the mechanism of Senate opposition to executive branch policy. Security concerns and economic interests did not play a role in causing restraint. The main security-based and economic arguments were voiced in favor of maximal control over the Dominican Republic. The basic reasons for intervention were to prevent European powers from colonizing the Dominican Republic and to support and facilitate the collection of foreign debt, including debt held by Americans.

Intervention in Cuba (1906–1909)

As the situation in the Dominican Republic was stabilizing, new problems were brewing in Cuba. The expulsion of Spanish forces in 1898 did not bring lasting stability to the new nation. Instability and civil war returned to Cuba in the early 1900s, leading Roosevelt to send in US troops in 1906 to restore order and put in place political and economic reforms to foster long-term stability. Long-term occupation and annexation were suggested and considered by political leaders. We would expect these expansionist measures to be implemented for several reasons. First, the United States had strong geopolitical and economic interests to protect in Cuba. American leaders like Roosevelt and Taft saw Cubans as unfit to rule themselves and unable to maintain stability; the implication is that American interests would be constantly at threat if the United States did not maintain long-term political–military control over Cuba. Second, once intervention occurred and the United States had troops occupying Cuba, there was a strong incentive to stay. In fact, we expect political goals to expand once troops are committed to resolve a conflict. Third, American agents in Cuba made a strong argument for staying until Cuban society was fundamentally altered.

Taking into account the various sources of restraint in this case, why did the United States intervene at all? For Taft the key reason for intervention was the US obligation to protect foreign property (especially American property), which required restoring order and establishing a stable government.[35] Foreign investment in Cuban sugar plantations and mills was between $75 and $100 million.[36] Strategically, Cuba remained important for its proximity to the US coast and relation to the site for the Panama Canal.[37] Historian Langley and historian-diplomat Dana Munro argue that the key reason for intervention was not strategic or economic; it was simply because the Cuban political system broke down and Roosevelt felt obligated to fix it under the Platt Amendment. Munro also notes that widespread destruction of European property would have put pressure on the United States to intervene under the logic of the Roosevelt Corollary.[38]

Roosevelt rejected both the long occupation and annexation options because both of these options would require military pacification of Cuba, which did not have had public support. Roosevelt was also attempting to foster better relations with Latin America at the time and did not want to further alienate fellow republics of the Western Hemisphere. In the end the Roosevelt administration policy toward Cuba was expansionist, but at the same time was highly circumscribed in both time and intensity because of the fear of potential political costs of imperialism.

Political Instability and American Commitments

Following the Spanish American War of 1898, US troops occupied Cuba to help ensure the removal of all Spanish forces and establish political stability. After the withdrawal of American troops in May 20, 1902, Cuban politics were contentious but peaceful. New president Tomás Estrada Palma faced a mildly intransigent Congress that was strongly influenced by leaders of the revolutionary army. However, as the 1905 presidential election approached, Estrada Palma aligned himself with the Moderate Party and purged Liberal officials from government posts in order to ensure his election. When it became clear that Moderates would sweep the elections through electoral fraud, the Liberals decided to boycott the elections. Estrada Palma won an overwhelming victory and was inaugurated on May 20, 1906. Within three months full-blown civil war had begun. The popular Liberal forces quickly gained control of most the countryside and threatened Estrada Palma's hold on power.[39]

Victories by Liberal forces continued to pile up and in early September of 1906 Estrada Palma requested American help to put down the rebellion. In a message to President Roosevelt he invoked the Platt Amendment, claiming that "government forces are unable to protect life and property" in Cuba, and in a subsequent message he implored Roosevelt to immediately send two or three thousand US troops.[40] Apparently US intervention was one of the few things that Moderates and Liberals could agree on. Liberal leaders requested American intervention to establish order and ensure a fair election. They were sure that if the United States intervened, it would not support the clearly unpopular and illegitimate Palma regime. To increase the probability of American intervention, the Liberals continuously threatened to destroy sugar fields and other foreign property.[41] In response to Estrada Palma's pleas, Roosevelt dispatched the USS *Denver* to Havana and the USS *Marietta* to Cienfuegos. By September 13, small contingents of American bluejackets were ordered to go ashore to protect American property and maintain stability in Havana.[42] The landing of American personnel was done without the approval of Washington, and in the case of Havana, the bluejackets were ordered to return to their ship.[43]

A New Occupation?

In two years' time, Cuba had gone from poster child to cautionary tale. In 1904 Cuba was held up by Roosevelt as an example of how American intervention could quickly reform a wayward Latin American republic into a paragon of effective government.[44] In 1906 President Roosevelt was looking for a way to avoid a new entanglement. He was reluctant to intervene, writing that "on the one hand we cannot permanently see Cuba a prey to misrule and anarchy; on the other hand I loathe the thought of assuming any control over the island such as we have over Porto Rico and the Philippines. We emphatically do not want it."[45] As noted above, by his second term Roosevelt had become more sensitive to the rising anti-American sentiment in Latin America and wanted to avoid any action that could be perceived as imperialistic. At the time of the Cuban crisis Secretary of State Root was on a goodwill tour of South America and had just committed the United States to intervene as little as possible in the affairs of other countries.[46] Fellow large-policy advocate Henry Cabot Lodge affirmed, "Nobody wants to annex them, but the general feeling is that they ought to be taken by the neck and shaken until they behave themselves."[47] Moreover, Roosevelt had come to believe that "the American people were reluctant to support prolonged military involvement in other countries."[48] Similarly, historian H. W. Brands concludes, "Certainly Americans at large did not want it [annexation of Cuba]; popular enthusiasm for colonial adventures had never recovered from the Philippine war. Roosevelt understood this, and it reinforced his own reluctance."[49] Finally, there was concern that a large-scale intervention in Cuba could hurt Republicans in the midterm elections in 1906. In sum, as several authors make clear, public opinion was a major restraint on American intervention in Cuba in 1906.[50]

Despite Roosevelt's reluctance to get involved in Cuban affairs, he felt that the United States had a responsibility (formalized in the Platt Amendment) to maintain order in the island republic. Thus, when President Estrada Palma and his entire cabinet threatened to resign and throw Cuba into chaos, President Roosevelt sent Secretary of War William H. Taft and Assistant Secretary of State Robert Bacon to Cuba to take stock of the situation and attempt to forge an agreement between the Cuban factions. Upon arrival on September 19, 1906, Taft immediately called for additional US naval vessels to take up positions around Havana. Taft saw fundamental problems with Cuban politics and culture that made Cubans unfit for self-government. He wrote to his wife that "the proper solution to the present difficulties would be annexation if we consulted the interest of the Cuban people alone but the circumstances are such that the United States can not take this course now, though in the future it may have to do so."[51] Taft's judgment about the fundamental dysfunction of Cuban politics catalyzed further preparations for military intervention, including a judgment from the Department of Justice stating that "intervention to maintain law and order and protect property was not an act of war requiring congressional approval"—a decision that outraged anti-imperialists.[52]

Both the Moderates and Liberals in Cuba intensified their efforts to force a decisive intervention by the United States, while the Roosevelt administration tried to resolve the crisis without arousing a hostile Congress or the skeptical public. A further complication was that it was unclear who the United States should support if it did decide to intervene. Taft saw the Liberals as unfit to rule, but could not ignore the unpopularity and illegitimacy of Estrada Palma's Moderate administration. It was clear that if the United States were to agree to Estrada Palma's request to help defeat the rebellion, the United States would be fighting the whole Cuban people."[53] As a future presidential candidate Taft had a strong incentive to quickly and effectively resolve the Cuban crisis: any mess that was made in 1906 might have to be cleaned up by him in 1908.[54] After negotiations between the Moderates and Liberals failed, Estrada Palma and his cabinet resigned, leaving Cuba without a working government and no constitutional means of installing one. With Roosevelt's reluctant support, Taft established a provisional government on September 25, 1906 with himself at its head and requested 6,000 American troops. Roosevelt's reluctance to take this step was due to congressional and public opposition, and he continuously implored Taft to avoid using the word "intervention." Roosevelt had a variety of concerns over the implications of intervention in Cuba. First, he was worried about the effect intervention in Cuba would have on the pending treaty with the Dominican Republic still being debated in the Senate. Second, at a broader level, by this time he believed that public opinion, conveyed through congressional action, made it problematic for the United States to manage tropical colonies. Military pacification was especially unpopular. Nobody wanted to repeat the

Philippine-American War of recent unpleasant memory, and no one wanted to reenact the scorched-earth tactics of Spanish General Weyler (see chapter 2). Third, concern about public opinion was especially salient due to the rapidly approaching midterm elections. Fourth, Roosevelt needed congressional acquiescence because the legislative branch controlled appropriations for Cuba under the Platt Amendment. To manage the countervailing incentives for and against intervention, the president tried to take the middle ground between expansionist Senator Albert Beveridge's advice to use military force to take control of Cuban and anti-imperialist Senator Joseph Foraker's advice to leave the matter to the Cubans. The United States would set up a provisional government, but it would be under Cuban law and with Cuban cooperation.[55]

Occupation Policy

Roosevelt hoped for a short occupation, and Taft immediately declared that the American presence would last only until order was restored and new elections could be held; in the meantime the provisional government would be primarily Cuban, not American. Because both major Cuban political factions supported American intervention, there was no resistance to US troops and officials went about their business of resetting Cuban politics. At the same time, US forces were careful not to avoid instigating resistance among the Cuban population. It was understood that there was very little support among Americans for a military campaign in Cuba. As one author notes, "the Roosevelt administration had no intention of arousing a storm of criticism in the United States by undertaking to pacify Cuba militarily."[56] This meant consistently acquiescing to those that could make the occupation difficult through military resistance; in other words, the Liberals.[57] More specifically, this approach meant that the 6,000 marines and soldiers stationed in Cuba performed no military operations; instead as Roosevelt ordered, "their mission was to provide the 'moral force' behind the provisional government."[58] US forces made their moral presence felt through long marches through the countryside and the establishment of intelligence networks. The Army of Cuban Pacification (as the US force was called) also made major contributions to road building and other public works. However, the real work of pacification had to be done by Cubans, which required that the Rural Guard be reformed, retrained, and depoliticized to prepare it for this task.[59]

Charles E. Magoon was chosen to replace Taft, who returned to Washington to recommence his duties as Secretary of War after about two weeks as provisional governor of Cuba. Magoon was a lawyer and diplomat with recent experience in Panama and a strong expertise in Hispanic law (as it was called at the time). When Magoon took up his new post in October of 1906, his first order of business was to begin spending the Cuban budget surplus on public works to foster higher employment and decrease the chance of renewed armed rebellion.[60] Second, he reversed some the most blatantly fraudulent election results and replaced Moderates with Liberals. These policies of public largesse increased the number of requests for patronage, requiring Magoon to create positions that required no actual work (called sinecures or *botellas*). Pardons and well-funded trips abroad were also used to foster peace. Third, Magoon established a Cuban army dominated by Liberal former insurgents that would coexist with the Rural Guard, which was still associated with the Moderates. The army would be a regular military force, and the guard would remain the national police. Fourth, Magoon instituted electoral reform and expanded suffrage. In sum all these policies amounted to a strategy of avoiding conflict by buying off the opposition. For both Roosevelt and Taft the key goal was to keep Cuba quiet to prevent it from impinging upon American domestic politics, and to achieve this they were willing to countenance a policy subservient to the short-term demands of certain Cuban factions.[61]

Magoon's approach was generally in line with the goals of his superiors, but as his supervision of Cuban politics continued, differences emerged. Magoon determined that the Platt Amendment had fostered a sense of dependence on the United States as guarantor of political stability, but more importantly, the Hispanic race was culturally or biologically unfit for responsible self-government. Magoon wanted to go beyond the reforms listed above; he recommended a permanent American presence in Cuba as military and legal advisors. Army officers also supported a long-term occupation of Cuba, perhaps lasting a generation. Roosevelt vetoed any extended American presence in Cuba.[62] Despite Roosevelt's wishes, completing a census and voter registration list took time, so it wasn't until summer of 1908 that local elections could be completed, followed by congressional and presidential elections a few months later. José Miguel Gómez was installed as the new Cuban president on January 28, 1909, the same day that Magoon left the country.[63]

A Reluctant Occupation

The most surprising aspect of the second occupation of Cuba is that it ended so quickly. If in 1902 the United States had to withdraw because the stated war aim of Cuban independence had been achieved, in 1906 the United States could easily argue that the Cubans had been given their chance at self-government and had failed. Withdrawal was also out of step with international norms. Europeans were shocked that the United States kept its word to leave Cuban both in 1898 and again in 1906.[64] The reluctance to become involved followed by the quick withdrawal also suggests that the United States was not tempted to follow a strategy of aggressive expansionism. As Richard Collin notes, "Never has an intervention been undertaken with as much reluctance and distaste as America's second Cuban intervention."[65] Hill concurs: Roosevelt intervened in Cuba with the utmost reluctance, not to assist Cubans who had been unjustly deprived of their political rights by a corrupt government, but to satisfy treaty obligations and to reestablish law and order."[66]

Louis A. Péres Jr., a prominent historian of Cuba, argues that the 1906 intervention was motivated by economic interest in the island and interconnected with American establishment of hegemony in the Caribbean and the establishment of markets there for American products. However, he does not explain why the United States was so reluctant to intervene nor why they left with the Liberals fully entrenched in power.[67] Furthermore, it is hard to discern any clear economic benefit the United States accrued from intervention, except to protect plantations that were probably not in serious jeopardy anyway. In a material sense it was Cuba that benefited from American intervention: roads and other public works were built, education was improved, and political stability was restored. Roosevelt biographer Lewis Gould provides a succinct summation of Roosevelt's approach to the 1906 Cuban crisis:

> Theodore Roosevelt and his administration intervened reluctantly and sought to leave as soon as was politically feasible. The president did not endeavor to reshape Cuban society or to guide the island's political developments into new paths. By 1908/9, Theodore Roosevelt wanted no more expansive imperialism for the United States; he wanted only the orderly management and eventual liquidation of the tutelary duties the nation had assumed a decade earlier.[68]

The available evidence suggests that a more expansionist policy was possible in terms of scope and duration, and such a policy was recommended by some of Roosevelt's top advisors. The cause of restraint is less clear in this case than in the Dominican case, and therefore the argument has to be more nuanced and is dependent on the statements of participants and the views of historians cited above. The general explanation offered here is that Roosevelt lost his appetite for an expansionist foreign policy not because he changed his own preferences, but instead because he determined that Americans would not support a strongly expansionist foreign policy and that the American political system made it virtually impossible to sustain such a policy. Previous foreign policy experience taught Roosevelt that if he wanted to avoid costly political battles, he should reduce his ambitions abroad. The historiography on the 1906 Cuban intervention supports this line of argumentation. Roosevelt was worried that opponents in Congress could impose political costs if his Cuba policy was deemed too expansionist. Specifically, he was concerned that the U.S.-Dominican treaty could be held hostage to Cuban policy and that imperialism could become an issue in the midterm election.

H. W. Brands notes that separation of powers (and political competition in general) restrained Roosevelt's actions, but he also argues that Roosevelt was less interested in intervention in Cuba in 1906 that he had been in 1898 because

"now Spain was long gone, and the hegemony of the United States in the Caribbean was essentially unquestioned."[69] However, this explanation is questionable
in light of evidence from the Dominican Republic case that suggests the United
States continued to fear European intervention in the Caribbean up through
1906.

Throughout his adult life Roosevelt viewed imperialism as the best policy for
the United States in its relations with "uncivilized" areas of the globe. However,
by the time he had the opportunity to annex the Dominican Republic and enact
a long-term occupation of Cuba, Roosevelt had come to realize that the American public opinion and political system could not support the demands of imperialism. The American public was too attached to the anti-imperialist traditions
of the past and too selfish to spend the resources required to successfully civilize
the barbaric peoples of the world. Furthermore, the political system of separated
powers fostered a high level of partisan competition that made unpopular, farsighted policies extremely difficult to develop and maintain.

Consonant with Roosevelt's understanding of the structure of American politics, the US occupation of Cuba in 1906 was done reluctantly and ended as
quickly as possible due to fears that the Republican Party would be punished by
the American electorate. The Roosevelt administration believed that the American people did not have the stomach for any more long-term occupations of
foreign lands and had no interest in annexing more territory, no matter how
close to American shores or how economically valuable. Because of the Roosevelt administration's skillful management of the second Cuban occupation, Congress did not have to take restraining action. Roosevelt was sure to make the
intervention as shallow and short as possible, giving anti-imperialist critics little
to criticize. In conclusion, the Cuban occupation of 1906 is coded as a case of
limited expansion caused by fears of public and congressional opposition. Secondary causes of restraint include the desire to foster better relations with Latin
American countries and the changing geopolitical context, mainly the weak
European presence in the Western Hemisphere. Therefore, security-based causes
of restraint cannot be totally refuted, especially the argument that the United
States did not have to annex Cuba because of Spain's exit from the hemisphere.
Nevertheless, this argument is not convincing because it is clear that the United
States continued to be concerned about European—especially German—
intervention in the Caribbean. Groups with economic investments in Cuba were
in favor of greater American control over Cuba.

Attempts to Strengthen the US Position
in the Philippines (1907)

In the Dominican Republic and Cuba President Theodore Roosevelt suggested
through his words and deeds that he had lost interest in acquiring new colonial

territories for the United States. In both cases Roosevelt recognized that public opinion was against further territorial aggrandizement and that Democratic opposition in the Senate, and even some Republicans, would make him pay politically for any policies smelling too strongly of imperialism. Nevertheless, Roosevelt maintained his personal belief that a central goal of US foreign policy should be "to extend 'civilization' to backwards lands."[70] Even if it was not possible to bring new areas under American control, he still hoped that the Philippines could serve as an example of the American ability to successfully uplift a backward people. However, Roosevelt's attempts to civilize the Philippines were defeated by the American political structure of anti-imperialist norms and institutional checks and balances.

Similar to the Dominican Republic case, President Roosevelt's attempts to implement an expansionist foreign policy in the Philippines were vetoed by Congress, demonstrating to Roosevelt that the American system was incompatible with imperialism.[71] Roosevelt came to this conclusion after his attempts to implement policies meant to foster economic development in the Philippines were blocked by Congress. More specifically, there was constant pressure from Congress to move toward Philippine independence and a strong reluctance to make a long-term investment in Philippine political and economic development. Most importantly, Congress refused to lower tariffs on Philippine goods entering the United States, thereby undermining Philippine economic growth. Because Roosevelt could not trust the American political system to support the burden of civilizing the Philippines, he came to see America's largest colony as a vulnerability rather than a strength. Roosevelt never lost faith in the need to spread civilization by transforming barbaric peoples through imperialism. Instead he lost faith in the capacity of the American system to live up to the responsibility of a civilized nation. This argument is supported by evidence of Roosevelt's continued advocacy for imperialism after he left office in 1909.[72] In sum, Roosevelt's commitment to imperialism—conceptualized as spreading civilization to all corners of the globe—was constant, but his ability to enact an imperial foreign policy was blocked by American norms and institutions.

From the perspective of our theory of rising power expansion, the Philippines is an especially important case. As a rising power with expanding interests the United States would be expected to take the opportunity to use its new foothold in Asia to expand American influence in that area. We would expect the United States to continue to expand its sphere of influence in the Asia-Pacific region and compete with other great powers for influence. Therefore, if the United States could turn the Philippines into a solid power base, it could be used to expand to other areas of the Asia-Pacific. This scenario is what expansionists planned on when they advocated for annexation. Also, because the United States expended so many resources to pacify the Philippines, and the McKinley-Roosevelt administration spent so much energy defending the American presence in the archipelago, it is a good candidate for ideological entrapment. There is some evidence that this did occur, at least with President Roosevelt. He repeatedly emphasized how important the Philippines was as a demonstration of American superiority, and that failure in the Philippines would be a demonstration of lamentable weakness.

Roosevelt's Views on Imperialism and the Importance of the Philippine Project

Two main arguments support the contention that Roosevelt attempted to build a stronger American commitment to the Philippines than what actually occurred. First, Roosevelt's consistently positive view of imperialism and his desire for the United States to take up the cause of civilization (especially in the Philippines) suggest a preference for keeping the Philippines under American control until Filipinos became a civilized people. In fact, Roosevelt saw the American policy in the Philippines as a model of how a civilized country could uplift a barbarous nation. Beyond his general beliefs about the desirability of imperialism, Roosevelt had a strong personal commitment to the Philippines and a commitment to successfully civilizing the largest US colony.[73] Second, large-policy advocates viewed the American presence in the Philippines as a means for the United States to project American influence into Southeast Asia and East Asia for geopolitical and economic reasons. However, for the Philippines to be a strategic asset it had to be politically stable, economically productive, and home to a significant US military presence and protected by a naval squadron. But early in Roosevelt's term the archipelago became a strategic liability because the United States was unwilling to make the necessary investment, politically, economically, and militarily.

Theodore Roosevelt's writings suggest that he maintained a positive view of imperialism throughout his life. The form of imperialism supported by Roosevelt was the expansion of civilization through the conquest, occupation, and uplift of barbarous areas of the world. He therefore viewed imperialism as a positive, progressive force for all of humanity. It was the duty of civilized countries to uplift the uncivilized peoples of the world.[74] His consistent views on imperialism are demonstrated by the fact that Roosevelt's views on imperialism changed very little between the publication of his four-volume history of American continental expansion published prior to the Spanish American War (1889–1896), his public statements regarding the Spanish American War in 1898, and his series of lectures given in 1910 on British imperialism in Africa.[75] Only during the years of his presidency was Roosevelt more circumspect about his views on imperialism.

Roosevelt's first extensive discussion of the benefits of imperialism occurred in his four-volume work The Winning of the West published between 1889 and 1896, and was expanded upon in subsequent writings and addresses. For Roosevelt, the

central purpose of imperialism was the spread of civilization, which he believed
to be inherently good, whether it was the United States expanding across the
North American continent or the British exerting control over Sudan. The
important point was that civilized countries brought with them peace and order,
which was good for all humankind. These points are made repeatedly in Roosevelt's writings. In his discussion of US continental expansion Roosevelt argued,
"It was all-important that it [the West] should be won, for the benefit of civilization, and in the interests of mankind."[76] In an essay published in 1899 called
"Expansion and Peace," written in the aftermath of the Spanish-American War
and annexation of the Philippines, Roosevelt remarked, "every expansion of a
great civilized power means a victory for law, order, and righteousness."[77] In a
September 2, 1901, speech in support of American colonial policy toward the
Philippines, Roosevelt argued, "It is our duty toward the people living in barbarism to see that they are freed from their chains, and we can free them only by
destroying barbarism itself."[78] During his tour of British Africa in 1909 and 1910,
Roosevelt reaffirmed his belief in the power of imperialism to civilize the world
and benefit mankind. In his 1910 speech in Khartoum, Sudan, Roosevelt celebrated the "genuine progress . . . made by the substitution of civilization for
savagery" in Sudan under British rule.[79] Later that same year in a London speech
he congratulated the British: "Your men in Africa are doing a great work for
your Empire, and they are also doing great work for civilization. This fact and
my sympathy for and belief in them are my reasons for speaking." Furthermore,
he declared, "the great fact in world history during the last century has been the
spread of civilization over the world's waste spaces."[80] Roosevelt also implored
all civilized nations to work together in the common endeavor of "subduing the
savagery of wild man and wild nature, and of bringing abreast of civilization
those lands where there is an older civilization which has somehow gone
crooked."[81]

Roosevelt's views on the Philippines are consistent with his views on civilizational imperialism.[82] He saw the United States as a civilized nation that had the
responsibility to conquer and civilize the Philippines. In 1900, Roosevelt's vision
for US policy was to "help our brethren of the Philippine Islands forward on the
path of self-government and orderly liberty that that beautiful archipelago shall
become a center of civilization for all eastern Asia and the Islands around
about."[83] The key to becoming a civilized people was to develop character
through the process of self-government. It was the duty of civilized nations to
help uncivilized nations develop the capacity for self-government. It was unclear
how long the civilizational process would take, but Roosevelt noted that Anglo-
Americans took over a thousand years to perfect their civilization and he was
unwilling as president to specify how long the Philippines would have to be
under American tutelage. Failure to follow through on the duty to civilize could
lead to a reversion to barbarism. It was the responsibility of the United States to

act selflessly to guide the Philippine people through the process of obtaining sufficient character to be worthy to join the civilized world.[84]

Success or failure in the Philippines would determine the future of the American imperial project and the role of the United States in East and South Asia. As Hans Schmidt notes, "the taking of the Philippines made the United States an Asiatic Power;" however, it remained to be seen if the United States could translate its new geopolitical position into regional influence.[85] Successful modernization of the Philippines could provide a model for future American colonial projects and facilitate access to the East Asian market. Advocates of long-term control of the Philippines saw the archipelago "as a springboard for the penetration of the China market and an Open Door for home manufactured goods and investment surplus capital." They also believed that American colonial policy "would introduce 'moral regeneration in an otherwise hostile oriental environment, and be a beacon of progress, law and order, demonstrating America's superiority in colonial management to Europe and the world."[86] In sum, possession of the Philippines made it possible for the United States to achieve the strategic and economic ambitions that drew the United States into a more expansive foreign policy in the late 1890s.

Roosevelt's Change of Heart

By 1906–1907, reforming Philippine policy was high on President Roosevelt's agenda. Economic and political development on the islands was lagging and the civilizational mission was at risk of failure. To make matters worse, Japanese power was growing in East Asia and was perceived to be a threat to the American position in the Philippines. Roosevelt was aware of and highly concerned about the vulnerability of the Philippines to Japanese attack.[87] One author even states that following a 1906 confrontation with Japan, "defense of the Philippines . . . became the uppermost preoccupation" for Roosevelt.[88] While Philippine policy was becoming more urgent, Roosevelt's ability to achieve his legislative goals was decreasing. Hostility between Roosevelt and Congress had reached the point of mutual hostility and contempt, limiting his ability to implement policies to strengthen the colonial presence of the United States in Asia. By 1906 "congressional enmity crippled the president's already circumspect conduct of foreign relations."[89] In short, between 1902 and 1907 Roosevelt faced worsening relations with Congress, growing strategic vulnerability in Asia, and the approaching collapse of the American civilizational project in the Philippines.

The change in Roosevelt's perception of the Philippines can be seen in his change of heart about the rapidity of granting independence to the Philippine people. In 1902 a Philippine legislature was established by Congress through the Philippine Government Act, but Roosevelt delayed the implementation for six years, writing to a friend in 1904 that the Philippine people would not be ready for independence for 40 years at the earliest.[90] However, Roosevelt seemed to change his mind in the summer of 1907, when he began advocating for rapid independence for the Philippines. Taft had to convince Roosevelt not to act too precipitously in the move toward ending American rule. In public Roosevelt claimed that his change in policy was due to an increase in Philippine capacity for self-government. In private, Roosevelt stated he felt that independence was coming too early. Why would he push so hard for increased Philippine autonomy if he believed the colony was not ready for it? One possible explanation for the premature move toward independence was a desire to disengage from Southeast Asia to prevent conflict with Japan—in other words, geopolitical concerns outweighed his commitment to civilizational imperialism.[91] However, this is not how Roosevelt explained his change of heart. In a private letter he stated that he was concerned that the necessary long-term occupation and civilizing mission in the Philippines was impossible under the American system because the American people "do not desire to hold foreign dependencies, and do believe in self-government for them."[92] This sentiment is contrary to his personal preference that "the best thing for the Philippines would be to have a succession of Taft's administer them for the next century."[93] In sum, Roosevelt accepted that American beliefs made it impossible to civilize the Philippines.

This explanation for the change in policy is rendered more credible by its timing and its relationship to Roosevelt's perception of Japan. Roosevelt's discovery of the power of American anti-imperialism occurred after he failed in his third attempt to lower tariffs for Philippine goods entering the United States and his relationship with Congress was at its nadir. In an August 21 letter to Taft, Roosevelt elaborated on the impact of domestic politics on the situation in the Philippines: Americans were not "prepared permanently, in a duty-loving spirit . . . to assume the control of the Philippine Islands for the good of the Filipinos." And, "it is impossible to awaken any public interest in favor of giving [the Philippines] tariff advantages; it is very difficult to awaken any public interest in providing any adequate defense of the islands."[94] Roosevelt was also concerned that Congress would overthrow his policy and complained that no policy was likely to last for longer than the end of his four-year term.[95] Furthermore, "to keep the islands without treating them generously and at the same time without adequately fortifying them and without building up a navy second only to that of Great Britain, would be disastrous in the extreme."[96] In sum, Roosevelt came to the conclusion in August of 1907 that Congress and the American people did not have the normative commitment to imperialism that was necessary to successfully civilize the Philippines and make the United States a true imperial power.[97] The Philippines was a strategic liability, but only because domestic factors prevented the United States from civilizing and fortifying the archipelago.

Throughout his time as president, Theodore Roosevelt was highly conscious of the restraint of public opinion and congressional opposition. Roosevelt recognized that a major foreign policy initiative that lacked domestic political support was likely to result in strategic failure. Significant evidence emerged during Roosevelt's presidency that there was only weak public support for American colonialism. First, the opposition Democratic Party was strongly anti-imperialist and consistently attacked Republicans on the issue. From 1900 on, anti-imperialism in general, and independence for the Philippines specifically, was a part of the Democratic platform. Second, important parts of the Republican constituency tended toward anti-imperialism, especially in the West and Midwest. Roosevelt's vulnerability on the issue of imperialism was reinforced by the deepening of conflict between the executive and legislative branches during Roosevelt's second term. The Republican Party was fracturing into conservative and progressive wings, making it difficult to maintain party cohesion. To make matters worse, Roosevelt displayed open contempt for Congress, especially the Senate. As noted earlier in this chapter, Roosevelt's conflict with the Senate created problems in foreign policy toward the Dominican Republic between 1904 and 1907. He also faced opposition to the minor treaty that resulted from the 1906 Algeciras Conference and The Hague arbitration treaties. Roosevelt entered the Cuban crisis in 1906 cautiously and highly concerned with public opposition. He had an opportunity to provide long-term, civilizing policy for Cuba, but never seriously considered the possibility.[98] In sum, available evidence suggests that Roosevelt had a consistent goal of civilizing the Philippines, but that between 1902 and 1907 he came to realize that this goal was impossible due to American norms and political institutions. More specifically, the public, the Democratic Party, and parts of the Republican Party opposed imperialism, colonialism, and most forms of expansionism.

Failure of Measures to Strengthen the Philippines

Despite his awareness that new colonial projects would not be acceptable to the American people, Roosevelt hoped to complete the most important ongoing project. The key policy proposal to strengthen the US position in the Philippines was the reduction of the tariff on Philippine goods coming into the United States. Roosevelt called tariff reduction "of the utmost consequence to the islands."[99] Roosevelt made three attempts to reduce the tariff—1902–1903, 1904–1905, and 1906–1907—each of which was defeated in Congress by protectionist sentiment and partisanship. The first attempt would have reduced the tariff to 25 percent of Dingley rates, but failed to pass the Senate. The second attempt would have reduced the tariff to 50 percent of Dingley rates, but failed to make it out of the Senate Committee on the Philippines. The third attempt also failed in the Senate. During the final push for passage of the bill Roosevelt wrote to his son Kermit that he was "having every variety of hard time in the Senate," and he noted that the Senate was attempting to "revenge themselves by trying to beat . . . the Philippine tariff bill."[100] Roosevelt experienced these failures even though the tariff reduction on the Philippines was consistently a high priority for his administration, and he put his prestige on the line in making personal attempts to persuade senators to support the bills. He found that the public, press, and Congress were not interested in supporting his Philippine project. The defeat of the tariff legislation demonstrated to Roosevelt that domestic restraints would prevent him from implementing a successful policy to civilize the Philippines.[101]

It seems clear that reducing the tariff on Philippine goods was a policy priority for Roosevelt and that the president viewed it as crucial to American success in the Philippines. However, it is important not to overemphasize the role of tariff policy; in fact there were several other measures taken by Congress to undermine the Philippine colonial project. Not only did Congress refuse to lower tariffs during Roosevelt's term, it also restrained the size of the navy, and often let narrow interests define economic policy in the Philippines.[102] In February of 1907 Roosevelt complained that "Congress has resolutely refused to provide any system of adequate fortification for the Philippines and Hawaii, and has greatly hampered me in building up the navy."[103] US colonial policy in the Philippines was a general failure, including the areas of economic development, education, and political development. Annick Cizel argues that "America's transpacific 'center of civilization' never stood up to Roosevelt's expectations, either in his lifetime or after." Roosevelt blamed poor harvests due to unfavorable weather and inadequate investment and revenue for the failure of the Philippines project. Cizel suggests the problem was more fundamental: imposition of nation-building from outside is self-contradictory. Filipinos resisted American attempts to mold their government and society, just as other colonized peoples have done. To the extent that nation-building occurred in the Philippines, it was in the form of anti-Western nationalism.[104]

In general, the unwillingness to devote sufficient funding to Philippine political and economic development and defense undermined Roosevelt's goals. This unwillingness was a result of the fragmentation and conflict intrinsic to a decentralized political system. For example, in the area of education reform in the Philippines, funding problems and administrative disagreements led to only minor achievements. In the area of economic reform, supporters of American sugar and tobacco producers in Congress blocked the efforts of the US Philippine Commission from implementing policies that would foster increased American investment in cash crop production in the Philippines. Furthermore, the historiography of Philippine communities suggests that American policies had little effect on the lives of the Filipino people except to perhaps worsen economic inequality already present.[105] All of these policy outcomes were possible because of separation of powers and the decentralized nature of the American political system, which gives voice to a wide range of interest groups.

In this case, domestic politics and strategic assessment were highly interconnected. During his second term President Roosevelt did not believe that war with Japan would occur in the short or medium term, but he did see two reasons to worry about the long-term vulnerability of the US position in East Asia: (1) decreasing support among Americans for fulfilling their imperial duty, and (2) the rising influence of Japan in East Asia. For a time, Roosevelt was optimistic about his ability to influence the first trend. However, the lack of public interest in improving the economic situation in the Philippines combined with the decreased enthusiasm for naval spending caused Roosevelt's shift to pessimism about colonial policy in the Philippines.[106]

Because of his failure to fully implement civilizational imperialism in the Philippines, Roosevelt came to believe that American public opinion, separation of powers, and frequent elections would undermine any attempt at a coherent and comprehensive imperial policy. Americans were fundamentally anti-imperialist: Congress was thoroughly hostile to Roosevelt's foreign policy agenda and American electoral institutions caused frequent changes in political leadership. Therefore he gave in to the inevitable and set to work preparing the Philippines for early independence. He presided over the creation of a Philippine legislature in 1907 that was granted a role in governing the country and advocated independence within one generation.[107] The promise of independence moved toward fruition during Wilson's presidency, and his policy of "Filipinization" gave Filipinos a larger say in their own government. The Jones Act of 1916 promised independence when a stable government was established.[108] As one prominent historian notes, "No imperial nation to this point had promised independence or even autonomy."[109]

Roosevelt's change of heart—from fortifying the Philippines to cutting them loose—was a direct result of his inability to persuade Congress to pursue a rational imperial policy in the Philippines. Roosevelt came to the conclusion that American public opinion, institutions, and ideals could not support a long-term, costly occupation of the Philippines. Lack of support for doing what was necessary to civilize and defend the Philippines led Roosevelt to label the territory "our heel of Achilles."[110] It was US lack of commitment to the colonial project that made the Philippines a geopolitical liability for the United States: "American occupation of the Philippines was not inherently dangerous. What made Roosevelt regard the islands as the heel rather than the arm of Achilles was the public's lack of imperial commitment, transmitted through Congress."[111]

In conclusion, the attempted strengthening of the Philippines between 1902 and 1907 is a case of restraint caused by congressional and public opposition to executive branch policy proposals to invigorate the economy and military defenses of the Philippines. Security concerns played a role in the decision making in this case, but were more of an effect of restraint rather than a cause. Some economic interest groups fought against lowering tariffs on Philippine goods, thereby playing a small role in causing restraint.

Failed Customs Receivership in Liberia (1910–1912)

As Roosevelt was becoming increasingly pessimistic about the US position in the Philippines, events in Liberia and Central America began to draw his attention and the attention of his protégé, William Howard Taft. Between 1910 and 1912 three major attempts to install American customs receiverships were made; the first of these attempts was in Liberia.[112] The attempt to establish a customs receivership in Liberia began under the Roosevelt administration, but was formally proposed under the Taft administration. The Liberian case provides the first illustration of the failure of dollar diplomacy.

Liberia was potentially America's entrance into the scramble for Africa. There is good reason to expect that the United States would take up this opportunity. In theory, the United States should have pursued opportunities to expand its influence and prestige to match that of other great powers. Establishing a colony in Africa is clearly consistent with the incentives faced by the United States. The proximate cause of intervention was security-related; the Roosevelt administration wanted to prevent Great Britain from gaining control of Liberia.

The Origins of American Interests in Liberia

Liberia has its origins in an African American colony on the west coast of Africa established in the 1820s by ex-slaves with support from the US government. From that time until the early 1900s there was little American interest in the African country, despite numerous requests for aid from Liberian political leaders. Britain had a larger influence on Liberia due to large loans in 1870 and 1906, British training of the Liberian constabulary, and periodic British control of Liberian customs receipts. Throughout the late 1800s both France and Britain seized territory long considered to be part of Liberia, and both appeared to covet the rest of Liberian territory. The United States began to consider a larger role in Liberia in 1907 and 1908 as the British Foreign Office began to push for increased control over Liberia. In March of 1908 the American minister to Liberia, Dr. Ernest Lyon, sent word to Washington that Liberia's sovereignty was in jeopardy and the government in Monrovia sent a delegation to the United States to ask for diplomatic assistance in dealing with Britain, Germany, and France, and for development aid.[113]

The United States failed to take action until January 1909 when the imminent absorption of Liberia by Britain caused a variety of US officials, influential individuals, and interest groups to call for American action in support of Liberian independence. Secretary Root appeared to favor making Liberia an American protectorate, but both Liberians and African Americans wanted to maintain Liberian independence and saw limited American involvement as preferable to

British domination. African Americans lobbied for American intervention in Liberia, especially Booker T. Washington, who would become President Taft's unofficial advisor on "Negro affairs."[114] The United States also wanted to keep Liberia open as a destination for African American emigrants, which required that it remain an independent country or become a US protectorate.[115] The Roosevelt administration saw increased US control of Liberia as consistent with "its desire to make the United States a world power." In their eyes, "Liberia could become an American base in Africa."[116] Assistant secretary of state Alvey A. Adee thought Liberia needed total rehabilitation that would require the United States "to assume an administrative protectorate, in short a colonial control in all but the name."[117] In sum, there was broad consensus that the United States should intervene in Liberia, but there was no consensus on what long-term US goals should be.

In February 1909 the situation came to a head with Liberia strongly resisting strong British military intimidation in the form of a gunboat in Monrovia harbor and the occupation of Liberian territory by British-sponsored forces from Sierra Leone. American minister Dr. Lyon convinced the diplomatic community in Liberia to oppose British aggression, forcing the British to back down. The British kept up the pressure, but were restrained by the imminent involvement of the United States.[118]

Pursuit of a Customs Receivership

In April of 1909 the Roosevelt administration sent a Senate-approved committee to investigate the continuing problems between Liberia and European colonial powers. The fact that the commission was escorted by three cruisers from the US Navy demonstrated the seriousness of the mission.[119] The purpose of the American delegation was primarily a fact-finding mission to determine the best way for the United States to aid Liberia.[120] The commission's report was highly critical of both British and French infringements on Liberian sovereignty. It was also expansive in its notion of US interests in Liberia. The commissioners recommended that the United States provide a loan to fund Liberia's entire foreign debt, help define the borders of Liberia, establish a customs receivership, and train the Liberian Frontier Force.[121] The report also hinted at the potential payoff for the United States by noting the "stores of wealth" available in Liberian territory that were ripe for exploitation.[122] William Taft (now president of the United States) took up the issue in March of 1910, proposing to Congress that the United States take control of Liberian finances, take responsibility for training a Liberian constabulary, and possibly establish a coaling station in Liberian territory. However, the majority of US senators were not interested in expanding the role of the United States in Africa. The Senate refused to move forward with Taft's proposal in May 1910. Opponents of Taft's plan were not convinced that the United States had a clear national interest in Liberia, viewed the racial issues surrounding Liberia as too controversial, and saw Taft's proposals as being too favorable to American financial interests. In general, the US Senate saw Liberia as well outside of the legitimate sphere of formal influence of the United States.[123]

After the failure to obtain the consent of the Senate, the State Department (under Taft's instructions) encouraged a consortium of American banks to contribute to an international loan to Liberia—the United States, Britain, France, and Germany would provide equal shares. A message from Secretary of State Philander Knox to Minister Lyons dated June 11, 1910, states, "the President has decided to lend Liberia assistance in the financial, military, and agricultural departments; that the financial assistance is to take the form of a loan to be negotiated by American bankers who are to have as partners British, French, and German associates."[124] The loan agreement included compromises with Britain over territorial boundaries between British colonies and Liberia, and with France and Germany over market access to Liberia. Under the agreement Liberia would appoint four financial advisors (one from each country, led by the American official) that would oversee customs revenues. The loan agreement went into effect in early 1912, but relations within the international consortium were dysfunctional from the start. German, British, and French officials continuously jockeyed for position and only deferred to the American official when it suited their interests.[125]

Support in the military and agricultural arenas also took on an informal cast. In a June 11, 1910 memo, Knox wrote to Minister Lyons, "in the military department the President proposes to secure American officers for service in the frontier force, and in the matter of agriculture, it is proposed to select for Liberia an expert for the position of director of agriculture, the salaries of these officials to be a charge upon the customs."[126] Liberia accepted Taft's offer of military assistance and in 1912 the United States sent three retired African American army officers—Major Wilson Ballard, Captain Arthur Brown, and Captain Richard Newton—to Liberia to command and train their Frontier Force. Due to the lack of a formal agreement between the United States and Liberia, active American soldiers could not be assigned as trainers. The US military attaché to Liberia, Major Charles P. Young (also African American), would oversee the training, but did not have any authority over the former US military officers or the Frontier Force. Young was ordered to "advise and assist" but prohibited from "exercising command."[127]

A Limited Intervention

Despite the efforts of the Roosevelt and Taft administrations, the limited intervention by the United States did not establish an American base in Africa, as some had hoped. Because American involvement occurred through the private sector, the United States did not establish an official American footprint in Liberia. The US government did not take responsibility for loans made by American bankers and did not retain control over the military advisors. The Liberian experience had several broad implications. First, it suggests that separation of powers, manifested through congressional opposition to executive branch policy, restrained American expansionism in Africa. Given a pliant Congress or a more unified political system, the United States could have easily established a protectorate or colony in Liberia, which would have injected the United States into the so-called scramble for Africa. One can easily imagine the potential for conflict if the United States established itself formally in Liberia: it would have greatly increased the potential for war with European powers over colonial borders and spheres of influence. Also, the multilateral agreement ensured that American influence would be balanced by British, French, and German influence. Second, Liberia demonstrates how opposition in Congress forced the Taft administration to shift to an informal approach to dollar diplomacy. Therefore separation of powers caused US expansionism to shift to a shallower form of influence based on private sector involvement. In sum, this case is coded as delayed and limited expansion due to congressional opposition. Economic and security-based theories of restraint are not supported by the data. Security concerns caused expansion, not restraint, and no major economic groups opposed expansion.

Failed Customs Receivership in Honduras (1910–1912)

Like Liberia, Honduras was a country of interest for the State Department because of the presence of Americans in the country, the high level of foreign debt, the unstable political situation, and the continuing concern about the security of the Panama Canal. Honduras was a buffer state between rivals Manuel Estrada Cabrera of Guatemala and José Santos Zelaya of Nicaragua, and therefore frequently used as a site for their competition for influence in Central America.[128] At the time Nicaragua was considered something of a rogue state because Zelaya was pursuing policies contrary to American interests. Zelaya negotiated with European powers to build a canal in Nicaragua to rival the Panama Canal and hoped to unite Central America into a single country with himself as its president. Toward that end, he aided rebel groups in unfriendly neighbors. For example, in 1907 Miguel R. Dávila came to power in Honduras through an armed rebellion aided by Zelaya.[129] The rebellion deposed Manuel Bonilla, a leader known to be friendly to banana company interests and an ally of Cabrera. By 1909 a crisis was brewing in Honduras caused by increasingly strong pressure from the British on Dávila to repay Honduras's debt of $120 million from loans made in 1866 and 1870.[130] To American officials the problem looked familiar, and it did not take long for the State Department to suggest an American solution. However, Hondurans did not welcome American interference in their politics or finances. The US Senate also found American intervention in Honduras distasteful. Thus, in this case the United States was restrained by its own legislature and the legislature of Honduras.

We expect expansion in this case mainly because of Honduras's proximity to Panama and the potential for foreign intervention to resolve debt problems. The central US geopolitical goal was to remove British influence in Honduras. The Roosevelt and Taft administration was also hostile to Zelaya and his allies, and saw the growth of their influence as contrary to American interests. Expansion of US control over Honduras would alleviate both security concerns. The United States also had economic interests in Honduras due to the presence of the large banana-growing operation of the United Fruit Company.

Pursuit of a Customs Receivership

From the perspective of the Taft administration the solution to the financial problems and strategic vulnerability of Honduras was clear: an American customs receivership.[131] Secretary of State Root suggested to the American minister in Honduras that the United States would look favorably upon a request from President Dávila for assistance from the United States in securing a new loan backed by an American customs receivership. US officials warned the Honduran government that they had to either accept a US customs receivership or Honduras would be left at the mercy of Great Britain. Dávila accepted an arrangement proposed by J. P. Morgan and endorsed by British bondholders in December of 1909, despite public opposition in Honduras. The deal depended on the willingness of the United States to pledge to protect Honduran independence and establish an American customs receivership. A treaty was signed by American and Honduran officials on January 10, 1911, and submitted to the US Senate on January 26. This treaty was to be a model for Nicaragua and potentially other troubled Latin American republics.[132]

In the meantime, a new revolution commenced in Honduras under the leadership of former president Manuel Bonilla and American mercenary Lee Christmas with funding from Sam "the Banana Man" Zemurray, an American entrepreneur and sometime employee of the United Fruit Company. Bonilla and Christmas obtained and outfitted a yacht in New Orleans with Zemurray's help and landed in Trujillo, Honduras, on January 10, 1911. The United States took (unsuccessful) measures to prevent Zemurray's troops from reaching Honduras and declared several towns on the north coast a neutral zone enforced by American and British naval forces. However, the unintended consequence of the United States forbidding any fighting was to allow the Bonilla-Christmas-Zemurray forces to set up base in Honduras unmolested. As Dávila attempted to gain American support he submitted the customs receivership treaty to the Honduran Congress; it was defeated 33–5 on January 31, 1911. American mediation of the conflict led to the resignation of Dávila and the selection of Bonilla supporter Francisco Bertrand to become president; it was also agreed that the two sides would split political appointments in the provisional government and elections would be held to replace the provisional president.[133] In sum, up to early 1911, the cautious attempts at intervention by the United States were initially rejected by the Honduran Senate. However, continued instability in Central America drew the United States deeper into Honduran politics.

A Second Attempt at a Customs Receivership

Bonillistas dominated the provisional government and ensured that Bonilla was elected in October 1911. Negotiations over a customs receivership treaty and American loan continued through 1912. The treaty passed the Senate Foreign Relations Committee over the opposition of all Democrats on the committee. The united Democratic opposition suggested that the treaty had almost no chance of getting sufficient support in the full Senate, leaving it to languish in legislative purgatory. This legislative failure shifted the initiative to the private sector. Zemurray stepped in with a new loan offer—still contingent upon passage of the treaty—and J. P. Morgan withdrew. However, in April of 1912 Bonilla publicly announced his opposition to an American customs receivership and in May the Honduras customs receivership bill failed to make it out of the Senate Foreign Relations Committee after a renewed push by the Taft administration to have the Senate reconsider the convention. The Zemurray loan fell through, which led to loan offers from El Salvador and the United Fruit Company. Both parties were attempting to increase their influence in Honduras. The Salvadorian deal was not taken seriously by Honduras and the United States discouraged an increase in the influence of United Fruit.[134]

As the discussion above demonstrates, the failed attempt at creating a US customs receivership in Honduras is a clear-cut case of restraint caused by opposition in the US Senate. The Senate failed to ratify the Taft administration plan for a US loan and customs receivership due to partisanship, fears of the negative consequences of increased involvement in Central America, and mistrust of executive power. Emily Rosenberg provides a succinct explanation for the bill's failure: "Drawing on antibanking arguments, they [congressional critics] claimed that such a controlled loan might lead to wider political and even military commitments. They expressed distrust of executive branch power, especially when allied with large banks."[135] Interestingly, separation of powers in Honduras was also a factor in limiting American influence. Even if the US Senate had ratified the treaty, the opposition in Honduras would have been difficult to overcome. The United States clearly inserted itself into Honduran politics, but restrained itself from gaining any control over the institutions or policymaking apparatus of Honduras. This case is coded as a case of restraint caused by separation of powers. Security concerns and economic interests both played a role in this case by encouraging expansion. British influence was seen as a threat that could be resolved by replacing British credit with American credit. The United Fruit Company welcomed increased American involvement, but there is no evidence the company had influence on US policymaking.

Nicaragua Intervention (1910)

The Nicaraguan case is in some ways similar to the Liberian and Honduran cases, but is distinct in terms of the level of intervention by the United States. Instead of just attempting to implement a customs receivership, the United States became a participant in the civil war in Nicaragua by landing marines to protect the town of Bluefields (and not incidentally the main rebel group in the country). More extensive intervention to occupy large portions of Nicaragua and install a government were considered but rejected due to concern about congressional and public opposition. Part of the reason for a more intervention-ist policy was the hostile relations that developed between the United States and Nicaragua during the Roosevelt and Taft administrations referenced in the previous case. Relations between the United States and Nicaragua deteriorated between 1903 and 1909 as it became clear that Nicaraguan Liberal leader José Santos Zelaya and American leaders had different visions of the future of Central America. Zelaya believed Nicaragua should be the dominant state in the region, and the United States was not convinced this was best for regional stability and American interests. One cause of the divergence was the 1903 decision by the United States to build an isthmus canal in Panama instead of Nicaragua. In response, Zelaya threatened to allow Europeans to build a canal in Nicaragua, and displayed a hostile attitude toward the United States and Americans doing business in Nicaragua.[136]

Zelaya saw Guatemalan leader Manuel Estrada Cabrera as his main rival for regional predominance. This rivalry did not bode well for the buffer states of El Salvador and Honduras, which were under threat from invasion and subver-sion.[137] By 1906 the region was "inflamed" by the rivalry as fighting broke out between Guatemala, Nicaragua, Honduras, and El Salvador.[138] An American- and Mexican-sponsored conference was convened in Washington, DC, in 1907 to mediate the conflict in Central America and set up institutions to resolve future disputes peacefully. The main result was the creation of the Central American Court of Justice and general peace treaty. However, these achieve-ments did not bring peace and stability to the region because internal conflict continued to be a problem.[139] The United States was in a contradictory position of supporting stability, but also trying to influence Central American republics to select pro-American leaders and pursue pro-American policies.

Civil War and Intervention

Taft administration officials continued Roosevelt's policy of diplomatically isolating President Zelaya and supporting the sovereignty of El Salvador and Honduras. The Taft administration saw Zelaya as hostile to US interests and was looking for opportunities to eliminate his influence in the region by expanding US influence in Nicaragua. In October 1909 a rebellion against Zelaya was launched by Nicaraguan Conservatives led by a provincial governor, general, and disenchanted Liberal, Juan Estrada. The rebellion may have been inspired by American disenchantment with Zelaya and definitely had support from Americans living in Nicaragua (including American consul Thomas Moffat and consular agent José de Olivares), but it lacked official US support and was met with hostility by American naval officers deployed in the area.[140] During the fighting two Americans serving Estrada's forces as demolition experts were captured and executed by Zelaya's forces. In response, the United States broke off relations with Nicaragua and threatened to use force to capture Zelaya. A plan suggested by Assistant Secretary of State Huntington Wilson to occupy the cities of Corinto and Managua to restore order was rejected due to concern that Congress would have to be involved. Under American pressure, Zelaya resigned in December of 1909 and sought asylum in Mexico.[141]

The United States was not much happier with the new president José Madriz and dispatched an expeditionary force to the waters off the coast of Corinto on the west coast of Nicaragua. Rear Admiral William Kimball, leader of the expeditionary force, requested authority to set up a provisory government in Nicaragua, but his request was rejected and instead the force was slowly withdrawn. The civil war continued through early 1910, and by May forces loyal to President Madriz surrounded the rebel force in Bluefields, Nicaragua, on the Atlantic coast and threatened to bombard the town. Commanding officer Captain William Gilmer of the USS Paducah deployed 100 marines to prevent fighting from occurring in the town. This action was primarily to protect American lives and property, but also had the effect of preventing government forces from finishing off the rebels—a result consistent with the preferences of the Taft administration. US naval forces also prevented Madriz's troops from searching ships for contraband, thereby preserving Estrada's supply route. Stymied in their attempts to end the rebellion, the government troops withdrew. The "neutral" US policy sapped the morale of the Madriz forces and undermined its legitimacy. By August the rebel forces were victorious. American intervention fostered a rebel victory and an Estrada government.[142]

Send in the Marines! (But Not Too Many)

During the Nicaraguan civil war of 1909–10 the United States did not formally take sides and only briefly landed a small number of marines to establish a neutral zone in the town of Bluefields. However, even this small intervention had a significant impact on the outcome of the rebellion and is a clear example of the United States intervening in the domestic affairs of a foreign country. The actions taken by American forces did not seem to be controversial at the time and relied primarily on the judgment of naval commanders in the field rather than any grand strategy emanating from Washington. In fact, the State Department had to scramble to find precedent for Captain Gilmer's actions.[143] The conflict never reached a level of importance that required Congress to address the issue. However, the knowledge that Congress might be hostile to more extensive involvement in Nicaragua acted as a restraint on American foreign policy, preventing the State Department from ordering the navy to occupy portions of Nicaragua on the recommendation of Assistant Secretary of State Wilson and Rear Admiral Kimball. In sum, even without any action from Congress, separation of powers restrained the Taft administration from implementing a more expansionist foreign policy.

Rejected Customs Receivership and Rejected Protectorate in Nicaragua (1910–1911)

The United States was happy with the newly installed pro-American Juan Estrada as president of Nicaragua. After a long feud with Estrada's predecessors José Santos Zelaya and José Madriz, the United States was eager to capitalize on the chance to increase their influence on Nicaragua. In pursuit of this goal, the Taft administration signed a treaty establishing a customs receivership, but the treaty was rejected by the US Senate. Instead, an agreement between the Nicaraguan government and for a small loan led to a private American customs receivership. The Taft administration rejected a Nicaraguan protectorate offer because it was clear that the Senate would not approve a protectorate treaty.

Pursuit of a Customs Receivership

Under presidents Zelaya and Madriz Nicaragua did not suffer from high levels of debt, but the Taft administration was sure Nicaragua needed the same remedy as the Dominican Republic—private American loans guaranteed by a State Department customs receivership.[144] Soon after the successful rebellion in the summer of 1910, State Department officials began pushing for a customs receivership agreement and an initial agreement was negotiated and signed by American emissary Thomas Dawson and Estrada as the provisional president.

Nicaragua did not need the funds, but the Estrada government needed American diplomatic recognition to help establish its legitimacy. The price for American support was a customs receivership, a pledge to hold elections within six months (later changed to twelve months), punishment of those complicit in the killing of the two Americans, and the settlement of war claims by a mixed commission. The "Dawson agreements" were incorporated in a new Nicaraguan Constitution in 1911. The agreements were highly unpopular in Nicaragua, and by March 1911 an increasingly beleaguered Estrada requested an American protectorate. After a clumsy attempt to preempt a coup, Estrada resigned and Vice President Adolfo Díaz ascended to the presidency.[145]

Despite the strong anti-American sentiment among Nicaraguans, the customs receivership was formalized in the 1911 Knox-Castrillo Treaty and was ratified by the Nicaraguan Congress on June 6, 1911. The treaty stipulated that Nicaragua would negotiate a private loan to pay off government debt, and that loan payments would be made through customs duties collected by a collector general appointed by the government of Nicaragua. The collector general would be chosen from a list provided by the creditor and approved by the president of the United States. Any changes in customs duties would have to be approved by the US government. Both Knox and Taft lobbied hard for passage of the Knox-Castrillo Treaty—Taft reportedly sent personal letters to 57 senators. However, the pact never made it out of committee in the US Senate, receiving a tie vote in the Senate Committee on Foreign Relations in May of 1912. Opponents of the treaty were motivated by partisanship, electoral politics, continued unhappiness with the use of presidential power, belief that the terms of the agreement were unfair, and a belief that the United States should not become more involved in the Caribbean.[146]

The failure of the Knox-Castrillo Treaty to make it through the US Senate forced President Díaz to work out his own agreement with a consortium of US banks for a private loan. Two American banks offered loans to Nicaragua without requiring an American customs receiver, but the State Department "was interested in the customs collectorship as an instrument of policy."[147] It was argued that a Dominican-like arrangement was necessary to maintain political stability in Nicaragua. A deal was reached with American bankers Brown Brothers and Seligman for a $15 million loan contingent upon passage of the Knox-Castrillo Treaty. The deal would also give American banks controlling shares of the new National Bank of Nicaragua and the national railroad. However, there was no decrease in the level of opposition in the Senate, and so Diaz was forced to negotiate a short-term $1.5 million loan that required the installation of a collector general nominated by the creditors and approved by the US Secretary of State. Secretary Knox supported the agreement and gave his approval for Colonel Clifford D. Ham to become collector general, but Knox made it clear to the creditors that they were not going to be given any special protection by the US government. As the political situation deteriorated, Díaz became unsure of his support among Nicaraguans and requested an American protectorate. Without a trace of irony, Diaz stated that "the grave evils affecting us can be destroyed only by means of more direct and efficient assistance from the United States like that which resulted so well in Cuba."[148] However, congressional opposition to the Knox-Castrillo Treaty prevented serious consideration of protectoral status for Nicaragua.[149]

Some Moral Obligation

By failing to act on the Knox-Castrillo Treaty, Congress prevented the establishment of a formal American customs receivership in Nicaragua, significantly decreased the size of the loan from American bankers to Nicaragua, and signaled that an attempt to turn Nicaragua into a protectorate of the United States was not feasible. However, through a private contract an American official, approved by the American secretary of state, was in position to exercise considerable influence over Nicaraguan government finances. Historian and former diplomat Dana Munro argues that this imposed "some moral obligation" on the United States to continue to help Nicaragua restore its financial health.[150] Munro's statement foreshadows the increased political and military involvement by the United States in Nicaragua in 1912 and after. In sum, the United States did increase its influence over foreign territory, but not as much as the Taft administration wished because of opposition by the Senate. However, even that small increase in US control had important implications for the future of US-Nicaraguan relations, as will be analyzed in the next section.

Intervention in Nicaragua (1912)

In 1912, Nicaragua was once again beset by civil war. President Díaz requested American help and US marines and sailors were ordered to Nicaragua to help pacify the country. The mission was successful and the United States quickly withdrew most of its forces, but maintained a legation guard of 100 marines as a symbol of American commitment to peace and stability in Nicaragua (or some would say a symbol of American imperialism). There was little opposition to this intervention, but a significant backlash led by Senator Bacon helped turn the phrase "dollar diplomacy" into an epithet.

Send in the Marines

In June of 1912 a new rebellion engulfed Nicaragua, led by Minister of War Luis Mena. In the initial phases of the war, Mena's forces took two steamships owned by the national railroad and bombarded the capital of Managua, endangering the lives of many Nicaraguans, Americans, and other foreigners. President Díaz asked for and received American military assistance; by September of 1912, approximately 2,700 US marines were stationed in Nicaragua. After their arrival the first priorities for the marines and bluecoats were to protect American lives and property, stop attacks on the capital, and end rebel attacks along the rail line from Managua to Grenada. US forces were not involved in the fighting between government and rebel forces. The commanding officer of American forces, Rear Admiral W. H. H. Southerland, took a neutral stance toward the combatants and saw no reason that US Marines should fight the battles of the Nicaraguan government. Marines only fought to maintain the security of the railroad. In September, after several battles along the rail line between US forces and insurgents, Marine Major Smedley Butler convinced Mena to cease attacks on the railroad and respect American lives and property. This concession was followed quickly by the surrender of Mena, due largely to illness. However, General Benjamín Zeledón continued the fight and maintained control of the town of Leon and the hills above the rail line near the towns of Coyotepe and Measaya. Admiral Southerland was reluctant to attack the rebels but was ordered to do so by his superiors in Washington. On October 3 and 4, an estimated 850 US marines and bluejackets attacked Zeledón's forces dug in near Coyotepe. In the most difficult fight of the intervention, American forces defeated the rebels, suffering four dead and seven wounded. Nicaraguan government forces then defeated Zeledón at Masaya, killing Zeledón in the process. US Marines then cleaned up the remaining rebel forces at Leon.[151]

Establishment of the Legation Guard

US forces remained in Nicaragua to supervise the November election, after which the force level was reduced to around 100 marines, which remained as a legation guard. The continued American presence meant no revolution would be tolerated and therefore the minority Conservative party would remain in power.[152] The legation guard remained until 1925; after they departed, civil war again erupted in Nicaragua.[153] American interest in Nicaragua was primarily geopolitical in that the United States wanted to maintain political stability in its sphere of influence.[154] The 1912 intervention marked the first time that "American forces had actually gone into battle to help suppress a revolution."[155] The public seemed generally supportive of the American military action, but there was also opposition. The use of military force to prop up a "receivership government" triggered anti-imperialist backlash in the United States.[156] A resolution introduced by Senator Augustus Octavius Bacon (D. Georgia) calling for an investigation of State Department actions in Nicaragua passed unanimously. The main concern was whether the State Department had implemented a policy that was previously rejected in the Senate.[157] Concern over American expansionism dovetailed with the antibanking sentiment in the years following the panic of 1907. Congressional and journalistic investigations brought to light the concentration of financial power in the United States in the hands of a small number of investment banks. In the context of suspicion over financial interests in the United States and the use of military force in Nicaragua, "the term 'dollar diplomacy' became increasingly pejorative and took on the connotation of a foreign policy directed by a money trust."[158]

Informal Involvement

Informal involvement in Nicaraguan finances and the limited military involvement that followed the 1910 revolution led to a more direct and invasive involvement in 1912. Military intervention led to a public backlash against intervention in Nicaragua and also against the concept of dollar diplomacy, and may have impacted the decision to leave only a legation guard in Nicaragua. However, even that small force was a promise of continued US commitment to Nicaragua and cast a shadow over the political process there. Therefore this case is coded as expansion combined with backlash. American intervention was clearly an example of political–military expansionism. Even though it was restrained in certain ways, the United States intervened militarily in the affairs of another country and maintained a military force in that country for over a decade. Nevertheless, military intervention is not the whole story. The investigations that occurred after the intervention in Nicaragua triggered increased scrutiny of dollar diplomacy, which in turn led to increased opposition and potentially increased the political costs of future interventions. Security-related concerns and economic interests did not play a major role in restraining American foreign policy in Nicaragua. Security concerns in the form of protecting the Panama Canal and preventing an increase in European presence in the hemisphere continued to be referenced to justify expansion.

Conclusion

The evidence presented here suggests that the United States exhibited restraint relative to the overall potential for expansion and our general expectation for rising powers to be strongly expansionist. The one case of generally unrestrained expansionism triggered a significant backlash in American domestic politics that undermined the expansionist project. The causes of restraint in six of the cases were the reinforcing effects of separation of powers and anti-imperialist norms. Separation of powers operated through the mechanism of congressional opposition to executive branch policies made possible by the requirement for senatorial consent on US treaties and the appropriations power of the US Congress. Anti-imperialist norms operated through the mechanism of public opinion and the potential electoral costs of unpopular executive action. These two causes are interconnected: members of Congress were also affected by public opinion and electoral concerns and, at times, their own commitment to anti-imperialist norms. The delays and political embarrassment created by the failures of Presidents Roosevelt and Taft created negative feedback on their expansionist efforts. Both presidents, especially Roosevelt, learned that implementing a truly imperialist grand strategy was impossible and increasingly settled for a much less robust form of expansion.

In each case in this chapter the restraints of domestic political structure played out in different ways depending upon the form of restraint and the specific context of each case. The Dominican Republic case contains examples of both the restraining power of congressional opposition to executive branch power and the ability of the president to partially overcome that opposition. In the end President Roosevelt partially got what he wanted, but the Senate demonstrated its ability to obstruct the president's agenda and extract political and policy costs for what they saw as overreach by the executive. In the case of the Philippines, congressional opposition and unfavorable public opinion prevented Roosevelt from devoting sufficient resources to successfully modernize and fortify the Philippine colony. As a result, the Philippines became a strategic liability instead of the foundation for greater influence in East Asia. In Liberia, Honduras, and Nicaragua, formal American control of domestic policy was rejected by the Senate. Opposition to dollar diplomacy treaties in Congress was based on the fear that involvement in collecting and distributing customs receipts would inevitably lead to further involvement in domestic politics of foreign nations—a fear that came true in Nicaragua. Opponents also "distrusted . . . . executive branch maneuvering, power, and alliance with large banking establishments."[159] In Cuba and Nicaragua military occupations were limited and shallow due to the fear of the electoral consequences of public disapproval. President Roosevelt and Secretary Taft deftly managed the occupation in Cuba to avoid opposition and backlash. These cases provide considerable supporting evidence in favor of the argument that the domestic political structure of the United States restrained US foreign policy from 1906 to 1912.

The evidence and analysis offered in this chapter may be unconvincing, because it downplays the importance of American expansion between 1904 and 1912. At least two groups of scholars may take issue with the interpretation made in this chapter: Open Door historians and neoclassical realists. First, the Open Door school of US diplomatic history regards the actions of Roosevelt and Taft to be a form of imperialism that is not quite like European imperialism, but imperialism nonetheless.[160] Historians of this school view dollar diplomacy as "colonialism-by-contract" or "informal imperialism."[161] More specifically, "contracts replaced treaties as the mechanisms to introduce and to legitimate economic supervision over potential dependencies. In these cases, contracts reinforced, though they altered, a neocolonialist, hierarchical order in which people with money and presumed expertise held critical financial power over debtor nations."[162] However, even scholars who view American action as imperialistic note that the central reason for privatizing imperialism was the opposition of Congress to formal US commitments.[163] It was assumed that this policy approach would lead to financial and economic reforms in Latin American countries, which would foster political and economic stability in the region and increased American investment.[164] Rosenberg and Rosenberg assert that "State Department officials regarded loan controls as a means to advance United States strategic, economic, and humanitarian interests by introducing North American-guided financial stability to the region."[165] In the economic arena US interventions were seen to favor banana interests in Honduras and sugar planters in Cuba by protecting American property and supporting leaders friendly to the United States.[166] Perhaps most importantly, work on the Panama Canal began on May 4, 1904, which created the most important strategic interest for the United States in the Western Hemisphere (beyond the borders of the United States).[167]

Historians are correct in noting that the United States did increase its involvement in the affairs of Central American and Caribbean nation-states in the early twentieth century. In other words, the United States did expand its political–military control over foreign territory. In addition, the scholars cited above and throughout the case studies convincingly demonstrate that there were strong incentives for expansion. However, their analysis obscures a taken-for-granted fact of enormous importance: the US projection of power in the age of dollar diplomacy was extremely limited compared to other great powers in other regions of the world and compared to the opportunities available for expansion. Using the terms "colonialism" and "empire" vastly overstates the amount of control that the United States exercised through the private financial arrangements made between American banks and Latin American countries. From our broader perspective on the foreign policies of rising powers, what is striking about American foreign policy toward the Caribbean and Latin America is that separation of powers and anti-imperialist norms effectively restrained the United States from significantly expanding and deepening its control over foreign territory.

Second, neoclassical realists might point out that the outcome in most of the cases in this chapter was some form of expansionism, from military intervention to informal customs receiverships. They might highlight the point that the increased relative power of the United States led it to intervene abroad, just as predicted by neoclassical realist theory. The specific form of expansion was determined by domestic institutions, but the overall outcome was determined by the international-structural incentives for expansion—again, just as neoclassical realism would predict. If we look at the cases in isolation, then this interpretation makes sense. However, if we look at the evolution of US foreign policy toward the periphery during this period, it is clear that form of expansion is a more important outcome than whether or not any expansion occurred. Put another way, because of the continuous delaying, limiting, and prohibitory actions of Congress, the United States was prevented from pursuing an unrestrained political–military form of expansionism, the form of expansionism that has proven to be most disruptive in world politics. Neoclassical realists are correct that international incentives matter a lot, but in the cases analyzed in this chapter, domestic factors mattered more.

The logic of territorial expansion typically involves slowly increasing commitment to ever larger areas of foreign territory. Initial commitments can foster a path-dependent process involving the logic of sunk costs and vested interests.[168] Eschewing any formal commitments to Honduras, Nicaragua, and Liberia and implementing a highly limited formal commitment to the Dominican Republic, the United States mostly escaped the logic of security through expansion emphasized by defensive realists and avoided the temptation to capitalize on territorial control emphasized by neoclassical and offensive realists. The clear lack of enthusiasm for customs receiverships in Honduras, Nicaragua, and Liberia undermined attempts to make financial control the basis of American policy in Central America and elsewhere. Proposals to implement this policy in Guatemala, Costa Rica, and China quickly dissipated after the earlier failures of dollar diplomacy.[169] In addition, by implementing a foreign policy of strategic restraint, the United States appeared less threatening to other great powers including, most importantly, the predominant power of the period, Great Britain. As a benign rising power the United States encouraged Great Britain to look elsewhere for potential rising challengers during this period.

This chapter demonstrates that the imperialist drive that emerged in 1898 had all but faded from the American foreign policy discourse by 1912. Opportunities for annexation of new territory in the Dominican Republic, Nicaragua, and Liberia were turned down, and the opportunity to strengthen the American foothold in Asia was rejected. This evidence of strategic restraint runs contrary to the predictions of our theory of rising power expansion. Some expansion did occur, which suggests the continued value of the theory. However, the most important aspect of American foreign policy during this period was its restraint, not its expansionism.

Notes

1. Or more accurately, his first elected term. Roosevelt became president on September 14, 1901, after President McKinley was assassinated less than one year into his second term.

2. The only territory officially added to the United States during Theodore Roosevelt's presidency was the Canal Zone in Panama; territory was lost by the United States in the final agreement with Canada over the boundary with Alaska. See Tilchin 2008, 667.

3. On Taft's failures see the cases below. For a brief overview see Collin 1995, 491–492.

4. James Cable (1994, 14) provides a widely used definition of gunboat diplomacy: "the use or threat of limited naval force, otherwise than as an act of war, in order to secure advantage or to avert loss, either in the furtherance of an international dispute or else against foreign nationals within the territory or jurisdiction of their own state."

5. Veeser 2003, 304–305.

6. Collin 1990, 372–392; Veeser 2002, 128–132; Healy 1988, 112–119.

7. Veeser 2003, 307; Schoultz 1998, 184; Rosenberg and Rosenberg 1987, 63; Veeser 2003, 309–315; Collin 1990, 403–408, 414–418.

8. On Roosevelt's lack of interest in establishing a protectorate or annexing the Dominican Republic see Collin 1990, 394–395; Brands 1997, 525; Healy 1988, 113.

9. Quoted in Gould 1991, 176; Ferguson 2004, 56.

10. Herring 2008, 371.

11. Schoultz 1998, 183.

12. Veeser 2002, 127.

13. For the Roosevelt quote and an analysis of its context and meaning see Collin 1990, 396; Gould 1991, 176; Brands 1997, 525–526.

14. Collin 1990, 396. Healy (1988, 113) makes a similar point.

15. Schoultz 1998, 184; Collin 1990, 399.

16. Schoultz 1998, 184–185.

17. Brands 1997, 526.

18. Gould 1991, 175. For the full text see Theodore Roosevelt: "Fourth Annual Message," December 6, 1904 (Peters and Woolley 2009–2014).

19. Brands 1997, 527.

20. See Veeser 2002, 137.

21. Veeser 2003, 316–321; Veeser 2002, 137–142, 148–154. On European support for American intervention in the Dominican Republic see Collin 1990, 430, 446.

22. Schoultz 1998, 184; Rosenberg and Rosenberg 1987, 63; Veeser 2003, 309–315.

23. Schoultz 1998, 186–188; Langley 2002, 111–112; Hollander 1907, 287–290. The quote from the text of the 1905 convention is from Hollander, 289.

24. Holt 1933, 204.

25. Holt 1933, 204–207. The first of the arbitration treaties was amended by the Senate on a vote of 50 to 9 to replace the term "special agreement" with "treaty," thereby giving the Senate a vote on all arbitration agreements. The wide margin of the vote demonstrates the bipartisan opposition to delegating foreign relations powers to the president. On domestic policy disputes between Roosevelt and the Senate see Collin 1990, 427.

26. Collin 1990, 212–218.

27. Collin 1990, 427.

28. Schoultz 1998, 188; Langley 2002, 111–112; Gould 1991, 178; Munro 1964, 106.

29. Holt 1933, 223.

30. Collin 1990, 418–435, 441–453; Gould 1991, 178; Munro 1964, 106, 116–117; Hill 1965; Hollander 1907, 288–296. Financial stability was maintained even during

regime change. American forces did not prevent the overthrow of Morales in early 1906 and his replacement by Vice President Ramón Cáceres. During the revolution Root prohibited the landing of US troops.

31. Holt 1933, 219–229; Schoultz 1998, 188; Langley 2002, 111–112; Gould 1991, 178; Munro 1964, 106, 116–117; Collin 1990, 441–453; Hill 1965, 167; Gould 1991, 179.

32. Holt 1933, 229.

33. Collin 1990, 598.

34. Collin 1990, 441–453.

35. Minger 1961, 80–81, Minger 1975, 126–127.

36. Minger 1975, 123.

37. Minger 1975, 118.

38. Langley 2002, 28; Munro 1964, 135; Brands 1997, 570.

39. Hernández 1993, 102–129; Collin 1990, 529–530; Pérez 1986, 91–95; Puente 1906.

40. Hernández 1993, 130.

41. Hernández 1993, 130–131; Collin 1990, 531–533; Langley 2002, 32, 37; Munro 1964, 128. See also Pérez 1986, 95, 97.

42. Bluejacket was the term used for enlisted naval personnel.

43. Langley 2002, 30–31.

44. Hernández 1993, 117.

45. Quoted in Schoultz 1998, 198. See also Pérez 1986, 98; Gould 1991, 252.

46. Hernández 1993, 129; Gould 1991, 251–252.

47. Quoted in Schoultz 1998, 199.

48. Langley 2002, 61.

49. Brands 1997, 570.

50. Hill 1965, 99–100; Minger 1961, 77; Minger 1975, 122–123; Collin 1990, 532–533; Munro 1964, 132; Gould 1991, 251–253; Brands 1997, 570.

51. Quoted in Schoultz 1998, 200; Minger 1975, 133.

52. Collin 1990, 533–534. Minger states that Taft wanted a judgment from the attorney general but Roosevelt refused because he saw the Platt Amendment as the indisputable "law of the land" and did not want to undermine executive power. Minger 1961, 78–79; Minger 1975, 124–125. See also Brands 1997, 572–573.

53. The quote is from a report by William Taft and Robert Bacon. See Hernández 1993, 134.

54. Hernández 1993, 133–134.

55. Schoultz 1998, 200–201; Collin 1990, 534–539; Hill 1965, 99–100; Minger 1961, 77, 82–85; Minger 1975, 122–123, 130–131; Langley 2002, 32–35; Munro 1964, 133–135; Gould 1991, 252–253; Brands 1997, 570, 572.

56. Hernández 1993, 142.

57. Hernández 1993, 139–142.

58. Hernández 1993, 143.

59. Minger 1961, 86.

60. Unfortunately he awarded many of the public works contracts to American firms that failed to complete the work after the US occupation ended (Langley 2002, 39).

61. Hernández 1993, 145–156; Munro 1964, 136–139. See also Collin 1990, 540–541; Langley 2002, 42–43.

62. Langley 2002, 41; Schoultz 1998, 202–203.
63. Hernández 1993, 156–158; Schoultz 1998, 202–203.
64. Hill 1965, 104; Munro 1964, 140.
65. Collin 1990, 540.
66. Dalton 2002, 320.
67. Pérez 1986, chapters 4 and 5.
68. Gould 1991, 253.
69. Brands 1997, 569.
70. Wertheim 2009, 495.
71. In this case the policy was not to expand control of foreign territory, but instead to strengthen control of foreign territory.
72. Wertheim 2009, 496–498.
73. Cizel 2008, 690–711.
74. Burton 1961, 356–377; Burton 1965, 103–118; Burton 1968, 203; Ninkovich 1986, 221–245; Wertheim 2009, 494–518; Scott-Smith 2008, 637.
75. See Burton 1961, 356–377; Burton 1965, 103–118; Burton 1968, 203; Wertheim 2009, 497–505.
76. Roosevelt 1894, 44; quoted in Wertheim 2009, 498 and Burton 1965, 109–110.
77. Roosevelt 1902, 32; quoted in Wertheim 2009, 498.
78. Ninkovich 1986, 232. This speech was given 12 days before the assassination of President McKinley.
79. Roosevelt 1910, 3.
80. Roosevelt 1910, 159.
81. Roosevelt 1910, 161.
82. Ninkovich 1986, 221–245.
83. Roosevelt quote in Burton 1965, 111.
84. Burton 1965, 112–113; Wertheim 2009, 497–505.
85. Schmidt 1995, 4.
86. Cizel 2008, 701.
87. Ricard 2008, 649.
88. Ricard 2008, 649.
89. Wertheim 2009, 511.
90. Wertheim 2009, 506.
91. Esthus 1967, 194–195; Wertheim 2009, 507.
92. Roosevelt quoted in Wertheim 2009, 508.
93. Roosevelt quoted in Wertheim 2009, 508.
94. Roosevelt quoted in Wertheim 2009, 509.
95. Roosevelt quoted in Wertheim 2009, 510.
96. Roosevelt quoted in Wertheim 2009, 509.
97. Cizel (2008, 706) agrees that public support was the cause but argues that Roosevelt didn't lose hope until 1915.
98. Wertheim 2009, 510–513; Schoultz 1998, 198; Pérez 1986, 98; Gould 1991, 252.
99. Roosevelt quoted in Wertheim 2009, 513.
100. Roosevelt 1946, 130.
101. Wertheim 2009, 513–514. Tariff reduction did occur in 1909 under the Taft administration. The Payne-Aldrich Tariff Act established free trade between the Philippines and the United States. This measure shifted Philippine trade from Europe to the

United States but did not have a large effect on the size of Philippine exports. The act also significantly decreased the amount of revenue taken in by the colonial government through import and export duties. See Hooley 2005, 467, 468, 472, 478.

102. On Congress's role in restraining naval spending see Stillson 1961, 18–31; Oyos 1996, 649–650.

103. Roosevelt 1946, 179.

104. Cizel 2008, 704–706. See also Hunt 1998, 32.

105. May 1996, 289, 294–295.

106. Wertheim 2009, 514–515. This pessimism grew over time until he advocated the end of US colonial control of the Philippines. Roosevelt (1915a, 1915b) makes his argument in two letters to Cameron Forbes.

107. Wertheim 2009, 496, 505–507.

108. Herring 2008, 365–367.

109. Herring 2008, 367.

110. Quoted by Wertheim 2009, 508.

111. Wertheim 2009, 509.

112. Liberia was viewed as having the same problems as Caribbean and Central American republics and therefore in need of the same remedy—customs receivers and financial advisors.

113. Lyon 1981, 232; Duignan and Gann 1984, 195; Wilson 1947, 16–25; Erhagbe 1996, 56–57.

114. Lyon 1981, 233–235; Erhagbe 1996, 55–65; Harlan 1966, 441–467.

115. Lyon 1981, 235–236.

116. Lyon 1981, 236. Assistant Secretary of State Huntington Wilson (1916) referred to Liberia as "a pied-d-terre [foot on the ground] in Africa" for the United States.

117. Harlan 1966, 455.

118. Lyon 1981, 236–237.

119. DeRoche 2003, 103–104; Lyon 1981, 221–234; Rosenberg 1985, 192–193; Duignan and Gann 1984, 196. For the commission's assignment see *Foreign Relations of the United States 1909*, 705–707. (The *Foreign Relations of the United States* series is the official record of American diplomacy and is produced by the State Department's Office of the Historian. Subsequent citations are abbreviated *FRUS*.)

120. Lyon 1981, 235.

121. Harlan 1966, 456. See also Lyon 1981, 235–240; Rosenberg 1985, 193–194; Duignan and Gann 1984, 196–197; Wilson 1947, 26–27.

122. Quoted in Kilroy 2003, 82.

123. Lyon 1981, 236–240; DeRoche 2003, 104; Harlan 1966, 457; Rosenberg 1985, 195. Another author uses similar language, Taylor 1956, 10. Rosenberg 1982, 61; Rosenberg 1999, 75. *FRUS 1909*, 705. For the text of Taft's statement on the issue see Peters and Woolley 2009–2014.

124. *FRUS 1910*, 709.

125. Lyon 1981, 240–242; Rosenberg 1985, 195–196; Duignan and Gann 1984, 198–199. Lyon and Rosenberg also disagree on this point. Lyon states that each of the four participating countries contributed equally to the loan, while Rosenberg states that Britain, France, and Germany contributed "minority amounts": Lyon 1981, 240; Rosenberg 1985, 195.

126. *FRUS 1910*, 710.

127. Duignan and Gann 1984, 197–198. See also Kilroy 2003, 82–85; Clegg 1996, 51–60.

128. Langley 2002, 52. On the dangers facing buffer states see Fazal 2007.

129. Langley 2002, 53.

130. LaFeber 1993b, 44; Munro 1964, 217–218.

131. American officials were attempting intervention in Honduras practically simultaneously with its efforts in Nicaragua and Liberia, and so the outcomes were perceived to be interdependent. See Schoultz 1998, 214; Rosenberg 1999, 66.

132. Munro 1964, 218–225.

133. Munro 1964, 225–231; Rosenberg 1999, 68.

134. Munro 1964, 193–194, 231–235; Rosenberg 1999, 68–69.

135. Rosenberg 1999, 68.

136. Herring 2008, 374; Walker 2003, 18; Munro 1964, 167–169.

137. Schoultz 1998, 210–211; LaFeber 1993b, 40–41; Langley 2002, 52; Munro 1964, 170–171.

138. LaFeber 1993b, 41.

139. LaFeber 1993b, 41–42; Langley 2002, 54–55; Musicant 1990, 138.

140. Munro 1964, 173–175; Challener 1973, 294–299. At the time, some suggested that American merchants hoped to trigger an American intervention that would increase the value of their investments in Nicaragua; see Schoultz 1998, 212. It appears that the independent banana producers on the Atlantic coast of Nicaragua had ongoing grievances with the Zelaya government regarding the monopoly granted to the Bluefields Steamship Company (Munro 1964, 172–173).

141. For an these events see Schoultz 1998, 212–213; Langley 2002, 56–59; Musicant 1990, 138–139; Munro 1964, 175–179; Healy 1988, 153–155. Secretary of State Knox summarizes the US position in his letter to the Nicaraguan chargé d'affaires in FRUS 1909, 455–457. For a discussion of the reluctance to involve Congress in diplomacy with Nicaragua see Munro 1964, 176; Perkins 1981, 26.

142. Musicant 1990, 139–142; Schoultz 1998, 213; Langley 2002, 59–60; Walker 2003, 18; Munro 1964, 181–186; Challener 1973, 299–301.

143. Challener 1973, 300–301.

144. Schoultz 1998, 214. However, corruption and poor fiscal policies under Estrada left the country in poor financial shape; Walker 2003, 18–19.

145. Munro 1964, 186–191; Langley 2002, 60–62; Musicant 1990, 142–143.

146. Schoultz 1998, 214–216; Munro 1964, 193, 203; Pringle 1939, 698–699.

147. Munro 1964, 185.

148. December 21 letter from Diaz to Knox in FRUS 1911, 670–671.

149. Munro 1964, 194–204; Rosenberg and Rosenberg 1987, 67; Langley 2002, 62. On the growing anti-American sentiment and instability in Nicaragua in late 1911 and early 1912 see FRUS 1911, 670–671 and FRUS 1912, 993–996. Schoultz (1998, 218) makes the inference that potential congressional opposition prevented consideration of making Nicaragua protectorate.

150. Munro 1964, 203–204.

151. Langley 2002, 64–69; Schoultz 1998, 218; Munro 1964, 204–210; Musicant 1990, 144–156.

152. The assumption being that the ruling party would not allow a free and fair election. Schoultz 1998, 218–219; Langley 2002, 69–70; Munro 1964, 216.

153. Walker 2003, 20.
154. Walker 2003, 20.
155. Munro 1964, 215.
156. Rosenberg 1999, 77.
157. Munro 1964, 215.
158. Rosenberg 1999, 79.
159. Rosenberg and Rosenberg 1987, 64.
160. For an overview of the historiography of the Roosevelt-Taft period see Collin 1995.
161. Rosenberg and Rosenberg 1987, 65; Lyon 1981, 221.
162. Rosenberg and Rosenberg 1987, 66.
163. Rosenberg and Rosenberg 1987, 65, 67.
164. Rosenberg and Rosenberg 1987, 67–68.
165. Rosenberg and Rosenberg 1987, 68.
166. LaFeber 1993b, 42–46, 62–64; Pérez 1997, 117–169.
167. Ricard 2008, 19–20.
168. See Snyder 1991, 1–20, 31–65.
169. Rosenberg 1999, 69, 75–76; Munro 1964, 235–245.

5

---- ★ ----

EXPANSIONISM
TRANSFORMED

1913–1921

THE FIRST WAVE OF American expansionism stretched from 1898 to 1912 and was characterized by the struggle for the United States to reconcile its rapidly expanding national power with its highly circumscribed role in world politics.[1] Growth in the material power of the United States resulted in strong incentives for an expansionist grand strategy. The United States certainly expanded, as documented by the previous chapters. However, the United States expanded much less than we would expect, judging from the enormous increase in material power that occurred during the late 1800s and early 1900s. The United States rose higher and faster than any country in history, and yet its expansionism was mainly confined to one major outburst in 1898 that was limited in scope and, over the long run, undermined the expansionist project by triggering an anti-imperialist backlash in the United States. As I demonstrate in chapters 2 through 4, the best explanation for American strategic restraint is the friction created by the domestic political structure of the United States. The institutional balance of powers among multiple branches of government and the decentralized electoral system both acted as checks on American expansionism by increasing the difficulty and costs of aggregating and employing state power for imperialist ventures. The norms and traditions of American strategic culture reinforced the institutional restraints and had an independent effect through public opinion and the personal principles of American political leaders.

In many ways, the presidency of Woodrow Wilson marks a second wave of expansionism in American foreign policy. Wilsonian expansionism was distinguishable from the first wave due to four shifts in the importance of preexisting conditions favorable for expansion. First, security concerns came to play a larger role in fostering expansionism during the Wilson presidency. Security concerns had been present since the days of McKinley, but the beginning of World War I and then American entry into the war intensified these concerns. The grand rhetoric calling for the United States to help civilize the barbaric peoples of the world was submerged by fear of European (mainly German) penetration of the Western Hemisphere. Second, Wilson was more committed to anti-imperialist values than his predecessors, though clearly his belief in spreading constitutional government was not always consistent with his belief in upholding the right of nations to self-government. Wilson and his secretary of state William Jennings Bryan were well known for their anti-imperialist principles, which they believed to be consistent with American values and interests. However, Wilson also famously proclaimed: "I am going to teach the South American republics to elect good men!"[2] Thus, like Roosevelt, Wilson had an ideological predisposition for an expansionist policy, and like Taft and McKinley, Wilson believed disorder in the American near-abroad was a national security threat. However, unlike Roosevelt's civilizational imperialism and Taft's dollar diplomacy, Wilson's belief system included strong anti-imperialist elements.

Fourth, Wilson administration policy was shaped by policy legacies left over from McKinley (Cuba), Roosevelt (the Dominican Republic), and Taft (Nicaragua). Wilson entered the White House believing that a considerable part of the problem in Latin America and the Caribbean was the economic imperialism of the United States and Europe. But the Wilson administration continued to use many of the same tools as previous administrations to foster stability in the Western Hemisphere, and in some cases went further than previous administrations.[3] Thus the legacies of past policies played an important role, putting pressure on Wilson and Bryan to maintain influence established through dollar diplomacy and perhaps more importantly to uphold previous commitments to maintain stability. Taft's general approach toward the Caribbean emphasized order and stability, and by the time Wilson took office these guiding principles had become goals in themselves rather than means to achieve more fundamental political objectives.[4] In the emergence of policy legacies, we see the potential for the development of a path-dependent process favoring an expansionist grand strategy.

During Wilson's term in office the United States embarked on its most expansionist policies since 1898: the occupation of Haiti and the Dominican Republic, major military interventions in Mexico and Cuba, and a continued military presence in Nicaragua.[5] Nevertheless, expansionist acts by the United States were limited (and in one case prevented) by separation of powers, electoral incentives, public opinion, and the personal principles of Woodrow Wilson. In Mexico, public opinion and Wilson's personal principles limited the scope and duration of the occupation of Veracruz (1914) and the Punitive Expedition in northern Mexico (1916). These same factors, along with separation and balance of powers, prevented the United States from intervening in Mexico in 1919. In the

Dominican Republic and Haiti, restraint was noticeably absent from US policy. Congress and public opinion were both supportive of American military occupation of both these countries. Restraint was absent because the policy was being implemented by the party of anti-imperialism. The Democrats did not want to undermine their own president and the Republicans had a hard time criticizing a policy they had been promoting for over a decade. Wilson's policy toward Nicaragua was characterized by limited expansion of American political influence. The United States finally gained formal control over customs receipts, but Wilson failed in his attempt to turn Nicaragua into a formal protectorate of the United States because of Senate opposition. Wilson intervened with a rather light touch in Cuba, providing moral support and matériel to the sitting government and deploying marines to protect sugar production, but not overturning election results or imposing policy.

In the end, Wilson significantly expanded the amount of foreign territory under the control of the United States by embarking on the long-term military occupation of the island of Hispaniola. However, normative and institutional restraints at the domestic level prevented what would have been a massive increase in American-controlled territory: the occupation or colonization of Mexico. Less importantly, institutional and normative restraints prevented the establishment of a Nicaraguan protectorate. Thus, on balance, institutional and normative restraints at the domestic level continued to play an important role in shaping the broad contours of American grand strategy. The second wave of American expansionism surged forward under President Wilson, but was consistently restrained by the domestic normative and institutional structure of the United States.

Occupation of Veracruz
(April 21, 1914–November 23, 1914)

President Wilson's first foray into political–military expansion was the invasion of the Mexican city of Veracruz in the spring of 1914. The proximate cause was Mexico's unwillingness to respect the honor of the United States, but the more fundamental cause was Wilson's continuing frustration with Mexican leader Victoriano Huerta's dictatorial rule and his belief that it was the duty of the United States to bring democracy to Mexico. German connections to Huerta were also a motivating factor. The objectives of the initial war plan were to occupy Veracruz and neighboring Tampico and blockade of the east coast of Mexico. After American forces landed in Veracruz, senior military leaders and Wilson's top diplomatic advisor in Mexico advocated an escalation of the political objectives to include occupation of Mexico City. Members of the Senate and Wilson's close advisor Colonel House advocated the occupation of all of Mexico.

Wilson did not follow any of this advice. Instead he reduced his war aims and halted his forces at Veracruz. Wilson was shocked by the difficulty of the fight in Veracruz and the unified hostility in Mexico to US actions, and so were the American people. He expected an easy victory that would energize the anti-Huerta opposition. Due to the American public opposition, unified Mexican hostility, and the military loses incurred in the fighting, Wilson exercised restraint.

Wilson's Response to the Mexican Revolution

The dynamics of the Mexican Revolution dominated US-Mexican relations from 1910 until the 1920s. The revolution was largely a reaction to Mexican President Porfirio Díaz's authoritarian policies and encouragement of foreign investment in Mexico. The most important issue was the economic grievances of the people, which were based on the widespread perception that Díaz was enriching himself and foreigners by impoverishing the rest of Mexico. The proximate cause of the revolution was a recession in 1910, which coincided with the presidential election. As in the past, Díaz was ensured victory due to election fraud. However, unlike past elections, this election led to a violent uprising, and in 1911 Díaz was convinced to resign and flee Mexico. Francisco Madero assumed the presidency, but in February of 1913 his government was overthrown and he was murdered by General Victoriano Huerta and his supporters. Soon a group calling themselves the Constitutionalists (led by Venustiano Carranza and Francisco "Pancho" Villa) emerged in armed resistance against Huerta. Several European countries recognized the Huerta government, but the Taft administration delayed recognition and Woodrow Wilson continued this policy when he took office in March 1913.[6]

For a time Wilson remained aloof from the struggle in Mexico, but over time he slowly shifted American policy to support the Constitutionalists. Wilson's first major attempt to resolve the conflict in Mexico was his proposal for a cease-fire in July of 1913, followed by an election that would not include Huerta as a candidate. However, neither side was willing to submit to an election. As the fighting continued, Wilson's agent in Mexico, John Lind, advised the president that there seemed to be no other option for restoring democracy except "recognition of the belligerency of the rebels or outright American intervention."[7] By October of 1913 Wilson moved toward the second option: "He made preliminary plans for military action, telling his friend Colonel House that he was considering declaring war in order to blockade Mexican ports and force Huerta out of office. At the end of October he actually drafted a message to Congress and a joint resolution authorizing the use of the armed forces of the United States to force Huerta out and to return power to the Mexican Congress."[8] Talk of war was silenced for the moment when Senator Augustus Bacon, chairman of the

Foreign Relations Committee, helped to end talk of military action by advising President Wilson that Congress would not support the use of force. Wilson then publicly repudiated the idea of military intervention, but returned to a more belligerent tone in a November 24, 1913 speech: "If General Huerta does not retire by force of circumstances, it will become the duty of the United States to use less peaceful means to put him out."[9]

As late 1913 turned into early 1914, Wilson moved to aid the Constitutionalist cause and again began to consider US military action to remove Huerta. Discussions with representatives of the Constitutionalists through 1913 slowly overcame Wilson's suspicions and led to the lifting of the arms embargo against them in early 1914. At the same time, Wilson was facing demands from many in the United States and in Europe for intervention against the Constitutionalists, who were viewed by some as thieves and murderers. Anti-Constitutionalist sentiment was especially strong among the American business community and in Great Britain. As it became clear that Huerta would remain in power indefinitely, American policy moved toward intervention. Lind's reports from Mexico were now consistently pushing Wilson to intervene to remove Huerta. By the end of 1913 Wilson advisor Colonel House favored installing an American consul general in Mexico, like the British had done in Egypt. Interventionist sentiment was reinforced by concerns that European powers (especially Germany) were poised to become more involved in Mexican affairs. In August of 1914 the War and Navy Departments developed plans for an invasion of Mexico.[10]

Incident at Tampico

Strong forces were aligned in favor of intervention, and on April 9, 1914, Wilson was granted an excuse for military action when several US sailors were briefly detained in Tampico, Mexico, by Mexican authorities. The commander of the sailors' naval squadron, Rear Admiral Henry Mayo, demanded an official apology, punishment for the offending officials, and a 21-gun salute to the American flag. Mayo was acting on his own judgment, but once word reached Wilson about the incident the president gave Mayo his full support. Huerta rejected the demands as an affront to Mexican sovereignty. After Wilson and Huerta could not agree on an appropriate apology, Wilson asked for congressional authority for the use of force in the name of national honor.[11] The goal of military action was "to obtain from Gen. Huerta and his adherents the fullest recognition of the rights and dignity of the United States."[12] The objectives of the proposed intervention were the occupation of both Tampico and Veracruz and a blockade of the east coast of Mexico. The House of Representatives approved the use of force resolution 337 to 37. The Senate debated the measure for two days while Elihu Root and Henry Cabot Lodge tried to drum up support for a stronger resolution that would allow Wilson to occupy all of Mexico. Events forced Wilson's hand, and the decision was made to quickly take the customs house at Veracruz before the Senate finished its debate.[13]

Why Veracruz and not Tampico, where the incident occurred? First, Tampico was not a suitable target, due to sandbars that guarded the port and the lack of fortifications; international law made it problematic to attack an unfortified city. Furthermore, it was not a particularly important city, and occupying it would not significantly undermine the Huerta regime. Second, Veracruz was Mexico's primary port, and its loss would be a major economic blow to Huerta. Luckily for Wilson, an incident occurred in Veracruz on April 10—again a Mexican official mistakenly arrested an American seaman. Third, as Wilson and his advisors were preparing invasion plans, the State Department discovered that the German ship *Ypiranga* was on its way to Veracruz to unload a shipment of machine guns and ammunition for Huerta's forces. This third factor ended up being decisive.[14]

Invasion of Veracruz

Military action in the port city of Veracruz occurred on April 21 (the day before the Senate approved the use of force resolution) in order to prevent a shipment of German arms from reaching Huerta's forces. Secretary of the Navy Josephus Daniels gave the orders: "Seize custom house. Do not permit war supplies to be delivered to Huerta government or any other party."[15] The mission was expanded by commanding officer Rear Admiral Frank F. Fletcher to include seizure of the customs house, telegraph office, and railroad yard. Upon landing in the city, American marines and bluecoats faced fierce resistance from Mexican soldiers and armed irregular forces, causing the mission to be expanded again to encompass the occupation of the entire city. The city was pacified in two days. The number of marines and bluecoats reached 3,000 on the second day and then 6,000 by day three, and a week later 7,150 when the US Army's Fifth Brigade took over the occupation. The invasion of Veracruz took three days and cost the lives of approximately 200 Mexicans—mostly noncombatants—and 19 Americans, a far higher cost than Wilson expected.[16] Wilson thought that American marines and bluecoats would be welcomed by Mexicans, his action would be supported by the Constitutionalists, and the small-scale military intervention would help bring about the fall of Huerta. Instead, the invasion triggered an outpouring of Mexican resistance and nationalism from all political factions.[17]

Wilson was faced with a difficult choice: should he follow the previously agreed-upon plan and occupy additional Mexican territory and implement the blockade? Should he go even further and send American forces on to Mexico City to depose Huerta? Should he take action to ameliorate the backlash against the invasion of Veracruz? Wilson's advisors were split on how to proceed. Secretary of War Garrison argued in favor of a full-scale invasion, and Secretary of State Bryan and Secretary of the Navy Daniels were opposed to further offensive action. Outside of the administration there were more votes for continued escalation: "aome hotheads, including his future archenemy, Republican senator Henry Cabot Lodge of Massachusetts, preferred all-out war, military occupation of Mexico, and even a protectorate."[18] The troops on the ground were also eager to take the fight to the Mexican army and the war correspondents were eager to cover it, which led military officers and many journalists to favor war. Lind and Rear Admiral Fletcher also advocated for the occupation of Mexico City.[19] But Wilson followed Bryan's advice and took steps to de-escalate the conflict. Wilson pulled back from the planned full blockade of Mexico and attack on Mexico City and rejected proposals to broaden the invasion. He even refused to further reinforce the American forces at Veracruz. Instead, he looked for a way to pull back from the confrontation with Mexico. In response to the unanticipated resistance, increasing Mexican public support for Huerta, and negative American and Latin American public opinion, Wilson agreed to foreign mediation on April 25th. US troops did not pull out until November 1914, several months after the Constitutionalists had forced Huerta from power.[20]

Huerta's flight from Mexico did not end the fighting in Mexico. The Constitutionalists fractured and Pancho Villa and Emiliano Zapata turned their guns on Carranza's forces, presenting Wilson with several more opportunities for intervention in Mexican affairs. Secretary of War Garrison, American businessmen (especially twine manufacturers), the Catholic Church, Colonel House, and eventually American farmers, foreign governments, and Americans with relatives in Mexico all pushed Wilson for increased military intervention.[21] Garrison even suggested that American forces should be used to prevent Carranza from taking power.[22] However, withdrawal from Veracruz ended the US attempt to determine who would lead Mexico: "Despite provocations and temptations of various sorts, the president henceforward objected to and resisted all plans for forcible interference in Mexican affairs that came to his attention."[23] In the end, Wilson had plenty of opportunities to gain control over Mexico, but consistently rejected these opportunities.[24]

Explaining Wilson's Restraint

It is important to determine why Wilson shifted to a more restrained strategy after the invasion and occupation of Veracruz. More specifically, Wilson changed his mind about a blockade of the east coast of Mexico and the invasion of Tampico after the invasion of Veracruz.[25] Furthermore, it seems that Wilson did contemplate a more widespread intervention as plans for the occupation of Veracruz were being developed, but rejected advice to take up this option after American troops were in Veracruz.[26] Wilson biographer John Milton Cooper Jr. argues that the number of casualties shocked and saddened Wilson, but public opinion was not the cause of Wilson's shift because American public opinion was not known to Wilson by the time he decided to de-escalate the crisis. Instead, the change resulted from "self-criticism. He knew he blundered."[27] In other words, Wilson shifted from a strategy of escalating military pressure to multilateral mediation because he saw almost immediately that military intervention would fail to achieve regime change in Mexico.[28] Cooper certainly identifies an important factor that shaped Wilson's decision; however, he dismisses the causal force of American public opinion too quickly. It is clear that Wilson knew what the public reaction was in the four days between the invasion and the move toward mediation. Editorials, petitions, and letters to the president during that four-day period show that condemnation of American aggressiveness began immediately after the invasion.[29] Schoultz concurs with the argument that public opinion mattered, suggesting that it was "core Democratic constituents" that played the strongest role in restraining Wilson.[30] World opinion also appears to have had an effect on Wilson's thinking. Following the American attack on Veracruz, anti-Americanism swept through Latin America. As Arthur Link suggests, "Altogether, it was an unhappy time for a President and a people who claimed the moral leadership of the world."[31]

It is most likely that public dismay at home and abroad, combined with the perceived ineffectiveness of the military intervention, shifted Wilson's perspective on intervention in Mexican affairs. In this case the public opinion of copartisans seemed to affect Wilson through the logic of persuasion, which contrasts with the logic of coercion that was prevalent in previous cases. Because Wilson led the party of anti-imperialism he was more concerned with maintaining the support of coalition members than fighting off the criticism of the opposition. Anti-imperialism was also part of Wilson's personal value system, and therefore he was more susceptible to being persuaded by anti-imperialist logic and reasoning.

Wilson's approach to the Mexican Revolution was at once anti-imperialist and interventionist. He supported self-determination and believed that developing countries needed to free themselves from the power of foreign capitalists. Wilson also had faith in democratic elections to resolve domestic conflicts. At the same time, he believed that the United States could intervene and foster progressive reforms.[32] Wilson surely would have agreed with his advisor's characterization of the problem in Mexico as being rooted in the fact that Mexico was "a European annex, industrially, financially, politically."[33] Since external influence was the root of Mexican problems, it might be necessary for the United States to intervene to weaken the negative impact of European imperialism. Wilson thought that the Mexican people should rule themselves, but he also thought they needed American help to do it correctly. Removing Huerta was not an infringement on the Mexican right of self-determination; it was a prerequisite of self-determination.

In April of 1914 the United States invaded the territory of a foreign country. This is a clear act of aggression and a clear example of increased control of foreign territory. However, the most remarkable aspect of the intervention is that it remained confined to Veracruz. It would have been a perfect opportunity to occupy all of Mexico, as Lodge and many others advocated, or at least force regime change. Instead, the occupation lasted for only seven months and was never extended beyond Veracruz.

This case confirms that rising powers expand their interests and seek increased control over territory and international prestige. Nevertheless, what is most important about this episode is that the expansionist impulse was halted by the restraining power of anti-imperialist norms that operated through public opinion and the personal values of President Wilson. Wilson's de-escalation was a rational response to the unexpectedly high cost of the invasion of Veracruz. However, the cost was only significant in light of the reinforcing dynamics of American, Mexican, and international outcry against the military operation with Wilson's own values that opposed imposing American will by force on a weaker country. Therefore, this is a case of limited expansion caused by anti-imperialist norms through the mechanisms of public opinion and personal values. Security considerations were also important because of concerns that further extending American military power in Mexico would lead to a very difficult—and possibly counterproductive—operation. Though it should also be noted that security concerns about German aid to Huerta was a significant reason for intervention.

Economic interest groups did not play a significant role in determining US foreign policy. The most significant reference in the historical literature is the anti-Constitutionalist perspective of American business, which would have worked against intervention. However, there is no evidence that business groups influenced Wilson's thinking on Mexican intervention.

Haitian Intervention and Occupation (July 1915)

Less than a year after exiting from Mexico, American marines and bluecoats found themselves intervening in another country to its south. This time the target was Haiti, a country unimportant to American commerce but strategically important due to its proximity to the Panama Canal. Unlike the operation in Veracruz, the intervention in Haiti transitioned into a long-term military occupation that almost completely subverted Haitian sovereignty. The main cause of expansion is the defensive realist logic of security through expansion. World War I increased American fears of German infiltration of the Caribbean Basin, and continuing political and financial instability in Haiti gave the United States an incentive to act before a European power could marshal its forces to intervene. A revolution in the summer of 1915 provided the opportunity for the United States to land its forces in the Haitian capital. Congress and the public were supportive of American involvement in Haiti because of security concerns and a sense of racialized paternalism toward the Haitian people. President Wilson was reluctant to intervene and delayed American military action in deference to Haitian sovereignty because of his personal values. But any principled objections he felt were eventually overcome by strategic imperatives and his desire to promote constitutional government in the Western Hemisphere.

American Interests in Haiti

American Haitian policy was shaped by the interconnected factors of foreign influence, political instability, and geography. Both France and Germany had considerable investments in Haiti in the 1910s, much more than the United States. Investment led to influence, especially for Germans who intervened in Haitian politics by funding the frequent rebellions.[34] Between 1908 and 1915 Haitian politics were increasingly unstable as revolution followed revolution in quick succession. High public debt in Haiti was an outgrowth of political instability, and the State Department worried that the high debt would provide an opening for European influence.[35] The concern about European influence and Haitian instability was heightened by the geostrategic location of Haiti. The United States was mainly concerned about the security of the Panama Canal, and saw the potential for a European naval base at Môle Saint-Nicolas in northern Haiti as a significant threat to American interests. The fear was that Haiti would offer a base at Môle Saint-Nicolas as repayment for debt to a European country. After the beginning of World War I security concerns increased significantly, especially regarding German intentions in the Caribbean. Robert Lansing, Secretary of State after Bryan's resignation in 1915, viewed German aggression in Latin America as a major threat to American security. The concern over the power vacuum in the Caribbean Basin was widely discussed. One editorial argued, "If we are wise we shall get a better control over events in Central America and the Caribbean than we have now, and get it while we are comparatively free of interference."[36] American interest in Haiti stemmed from three interconnected goals: protection of the Panama Canal, elimination of foreign influence in Haiti, and establishment of American influence over Haitian politics and finances.[37]

Military Intervention

In 1914 the State Department began to pressure Haitian leaders to accept a US customs receivership to prevent financial control by a European power and to

lease rights to a naval base at Môle Saint-Nicolas to the United States. A customs receivership would also end a leading cause of the frequent revolutions—
the struggle for control of customs revenue. These efforts came to naught;
Haitian leaders resisted US infringements of Haitian sovereignty because they
feared domestic backlash. The United States received assurances that Haiti
would not allow any other country to establish a naval base at Môle Saint-
Nicolas, but no formal agreement was signed. Haitian assurances were insufficient, and the Wilson administration came to the conclusion that intervention
would be required to establish order and stability and ensure American interests
were protected. However, Bryan and Wilson were reluctant to actually act on
these conclusions and instead attempted to shape Haitian policy through diplomatic efforts throughout 1914 and 1915.[38] American intervention was thus
delayed for years because of Wilson's and Bryan's reluctance to violate Haitian
sovereignty. They stood by the principle that the United States would only intervene if Haiti asked for US assistance.[39]

Intervention occurred unexpectedly when Haitian President Vilbrun Guillaume Sam was deposed on July 27, 1915, in a particularly bloody rebellion.
Admiral William B. Caperton of the US Navy was on the scene when Sam was
killed.[40] He witnessed the anarchy of mob violence unfold from his ship and
decided on July 28 to land his marines and sailors to restore order in Port-au-
Prince. Five hours later Secretary of State Lansing ordered American forces to
intervene, thereby confirming the actions taken by Caperton.[41] The State
Department claimed that humanitarian intervention was necessary to provide
peace and security for the Haitian people. Hostility greeted American marines
and sailors, but little organized resistance occurred. American forces quickly
brought order to the city and naval medical personnel began providing humanitarian assistance to the residents of Port-au-Prince. There were no orders detail-
ing what Caperton should do after he reestablished order in the capital. Admiral
Caperton was simply instructed to maintain control of Port-au-Prince until policy could be formulated in Washington. In the meantime, Caperton's emissary
to Port-au-Prince, Captain Beach, worked with the newly created Haitian Committee of Safety to administer the city.[42] The delay in American policy suggests
that the Wilson administration was not looking for any opportunity to occupy
Haiti and implement an existing plan of conquest and occupation. Much as in
other US expansionist adventures, policymakers had to muddle through the
process of establishing political control.

The landing of marines and sailors in Port-au-Prince itself did not necessitate
a prolonged occupation of Haiti. For years Americans and Europeans had been
landing troops as needed to protect the foreign nationals during Latin American
and Caribbean revolutions.[43] This happened in Haiti multiple times: the United
States sent forces to Haiti almost every year between 1903 and 1915, and sent
gunboats 28 times between 1912 and 1915.[44] Admiral Caperton seemed to

believe that the US occupation would be short-lived. He reported to the American press that "occupation of Port au Prince by the forces of the United States will be of short duration if the people will calm themselves and abide by the orders which have been issued looking to disarmament and the restoring of peace."[45] Thus, while armed intervention in Haiti was certainly an important assertion of American influence on Haitian politics, it became a much more expansionist policy only after occupation commenced. At the time of Caperton's occupation of Port-au-Prince, there is little evidence of domestic restraint on American foreign policy. Congress was not involved, and public opinion seemed supportive of intervention—or at least the press coverage and editorializing was positive.[46]

American-Haitian Treaty of 1915 and American Occupation (September 1915)

Despite its decision to assert military control over Port-au-Prince, the Wilson administration had not settled on a clear policy for Haiti in the summer of 1915. Boaz Long, the chief of the Latin American division at the State Department, argued in favor of the installation of a military government and a long-term occupation of Haiti lasting "for a period of 33 years at the end of which period, and each succeeding 33 years, it shall be decided by the President and Congress as to whether the United States shall withdraw."[47] Secretary of State Lansing was more cautious, but his fear of "a European resurgence in parts of Latin America" was enough to put him on the side of a long-term US presence in Haiti. Wilson echoed Lansing's concerns and thought it imperative to establish a stable, constitutional government in Haiti.[48] Lansing—the former State Department Counsel—struggled to find a legal basis to justify American control of Haitian finances and finally settled on a humanitarian argument. Wilson agreed that it was the duty of the United States to restore order and constitutional government in Haiti, and he deployed reinforcements to allow Caperton to cement his hold on Port-au-Prince and the surrounding area.[49] Wilson wrote to Lansing on August 4: "I suppose there is nothing for it but to take the bull by the horns and restore order."[50] However, a comprehensive policy would have to be implemented through a treaty agreement, which would involve Congress and take time to implement. Thus for several more weeks Caperton was left to muddle through the best he could.

The next logical step in the process of restoring order was to find Haiti a new president. The former president Guillaume Sam had been literally torn to pieces in the violence that precipitated American intervention. The Haitian tradition was that the Haitian Congress would elect as president whoever deposed the previous president or controlled the strongest *caco* force. In this case Dr. Rosalvo Bobo had the strongest *caco* support, but since his revolutionary forces had not reached Port-au-Prince at the time President Sam was killed, there was some confusion over how to proceed. The inability of the Haitian Congress to immediately elect a new president after Sam's death provided the opportunity for the United States to maintain and extend its influence. As US forces strengthened their hold on the capital, Caperton worked to delay the presidential election until he could find a suitable candidate. He wanted to find a leader who would be cooperative, and settled on the president of the Senate, Sudre Dartiguenave. This choice was generally agreeable to the Haitian Congress, and they elected him with a strong majority on August 12, 1915. Caperton did not directly coerce the Haitian Congress to get the outcome he desired, but it was no secret that Dartiguenave was the candidate favored by the Americans and the ubiquitous presence of American marines must have had a certain persuasive influence.[51]

By the time Dartiguenave was elected, the Wilson administration had developed a more specific plan for Haiti. Wilson and his advisors desired some kind of legal sanction for the occupation and so within a day of his election Dartiguenave was presented with a treaty that amounted to an American wish list for controlling key aspects of Haitian government. Historian Hans Schmidt summarizes the main elements of the treaty:

> The treaty provided that the United States would aid Haiti in economic development and establish Haitian finances on a firm basis. An American-appointed financial adviser and general receiver of customs would have extensive control over Haitian government finances, and Haiti was forbidden to modify its customs duties or increase its public debt without United States approval. The United States would organize and officer a Haitian gendarmerie, and the Haitian government agreed to execute an arbitration protocol with the United States for settlement of foreign claims. The treaty was to remain in force for ten years from the date of exchange of ratifications, which was May 3, 1916.[52]

The main author of the treaty, Secretary Lansing, worried that US Senate might take a negative view of the lack of respect the executive branch was showing Haiti and balk at approving a treaty that legitimized these actions. But he saw no other realistic option. Wilson agreed, but worried that it might turn Latin American opinion against the United States.[53]

The first obstacle to overcome was to obtain the signature of President Dartiguenave. This was no easy chore considering the widespread anti-American sentiment that had emerged in Haiti and the increasingly restive *cacos*. As negotiations stalled in the middle of August, Caperton was ordered to take control of the customs houses in Haiti's major port cities and use the tax receipts to fund local government operations. The increased anti-Americanism and unrest led Caperton to declare martial law and institute press censorship on September 3, 1915. After considerable American pressure Dartiguenave signed the treaty on September 16, 1915, despite the fact that the president, his cabinet, and the

Haitian Senate viewed the treaty as an infringement on Haitian sovereignty and national honor. After the signing of the treaty the Dartiguenave government was officially recognized by the United States. While the treaty was under consideration by the Haitian Congress, US Marines moved to subdue the *cacos* in northern Haiti.[54] With peace established in the north, the State Department increased its pressure on the Haitian government to approve the treaty, giving Dartiguenave only a small allowance from the customs receipts until the treaty was fully implemented by the Haitian government. The approval of the Haitian legislature was achieved on November 11, 1915. A modus vivendi was signed on November 29 to implement the treaty while waiting for the ratification of the US Senate.[55]

The US Senate approved the treaty "unanimously and without debate" on February 28, 1916.[56] Calhoun calls the resulting regime "an American puppet regime" and Haiti a "de facto protectorate of the United States."[57] The press and public supported US involvement in Haiti and generally seemed to believe that the United States had a duty to reform Haitian government and uplift the Haitian people: "The Americans perceived themselves as the saviors of Haiti, not its tyrants."[58] In other words, the mission to civilize was back, but with a Wilsonian twist. This approach was not without its critics. For example, Booker T. Washington predicted that the occupation would inevitably end badly. *The Nation* was highly critical of US policy in Haiti, the Dominican Republic, and Nicaragua. Republicans offered mild criticism, noting the contradiction between Wilson's rhetoric and actions, but hamstrung by their own expansionist platform. Anti-imperialists spoke out against US actions in Haiti, the Dominican Republic, and Nicaragua, but had little impact on policy.[59] Lansing, Daniels, and Wilson all expressed regret at the "high handed" actions of the United States in Haiti, but justified it as being the only realistic option.[60]

Full implementation of the treaty began in June of 1916. The central mechanisms of the treaty included services such as "the Customs Receivership, the Office of the Financial Advisor, the Constabulary, the Public Works Service, and the Public Health Service."[61] These agencies were nominally under the control of the Haitian government, but the lead officer of each agency was nominated by the President of the United States and appointed by the President of Haiti. Not surprisingly, American officials were chosen for all treaty positions. Through the general receiver and financial advisor the United States could control Haitian finances, through its officer corps the United States controlled the gendarmerie, and through the Public Works Service and Public Health Service the United States controlled economic development in Haiti.[62] Despite Haitian hopes for increased autonomy, implementation of the treaty did not lead to increased civilian control of the government or economic development.

By September 1916, Secretary of the Navy Daniels was inquiring as to when the marines might be brought home, since it appeared that Haiti was quite stable. State Department officials, including Secretary of State Lansing, did not agree, and Lansing ordered the occupation to continue. Marine Colonel Little- ton W. T. Waller, now in command of US forces on the ground in Haiti, agreed with Lansing.[63] There was still much to be done.

Occupation Extended (March 1917)

Haitian economic development required refinancing of its debt. Financial advi- sor to Haiti Addison T. Ruan recommended a $30 million loan for Haiti to pay off its existing debt. Such a large loan would require extending the treaty, because the lender would only trust the Haitian government to continue pay- ments as long as the United States controlled Haitian finances. Wilson con- ferred with Senate leaders and the State Department looked for American bankers willing to offer such a loan. On March 29, 1917, the treaty was extended from 10 to 20 years. But the entry into World War I made the United States unwilling to support a large loan to Haiti, so nothing came of Ruan's plan.[64] Another attempt to strengthen the Haitian financial system was made after Haiti declared war on Germany in 1918 under the War Loan Act, but this too failed.[65]

Also in 1916 and 1917, officials in the State Department and navy revised the Haitian constitution. When the Haitian assembly rejected the new constitution Marine Major Smedley Butler convinced President Dartiguenave to order the assembly dissolved, giving the president and his Council of State control of the Haitian government. In 1918 the revised constitution was approved by a Haitian constitutional convention and a popular vote—though opponents of the consti- tution decided not to vote rather than vote against it, and those who voted for it didn't seem to know what they were voting for. The constitution was fairly liberal, except for a clause that gave the president almost dictatorial powers for a temporary but indefinite period and substituted a presidentially appointed Council of State for an elected legislature. It also made it legal to sell land to foreigners and ratified the actions of the occupation government.[66] By 1917 "the façade of an independent Haitian government had collapsed . . . Haiti was ruled by an American military regime which acted, when it pleased, through the president."[67]

The Emergence of Haitian Resistance and American Domestic Opposition

Beginning in 1918 Haitians developed an increasingly organized resistance to the American Occupation while journalists and activists in the United States began to portray the occupation in a more negative light. In northern Haiti the use of forced labor for road building fostered a rural *cacos* insurgency lasting from 1918 to 1920 before being suppressed by the gendarmerie and Marines, causing the death of approximately 1,500 Haitians.[68] In the aftermath of the suppression of the Haitian insurgency, the Haitian group Union Patriotique and the NAACP in the United States protested the brutal tactics by American marines and Haitian gendarmes. *The Nation* magazine ran critical investigative articles. Both Secretary of the Navy Josephus Daniels and the Senate ordered investigations between 1920 and 1922. The navy investigation documented "almost twenty instances of specific acts of unjustifiable violence against Haitians by American military personnel," but found that systematic brutality did not occur.[69] The accusations of brutality and the subsequent investigations gave Warren G. Harding a campaign issue for the 1920 election—he began denouncing the "rape of Haiti" in his campaign speeches. Evidence of brutality by American forces led to widespread criticism in the American press. In Haiti, Union Patriotique was advocating for the end of American occupation and gaining thousands of members.[70] By 1919 mainstream journalists were beginning to make note of the contradiction between the Wilsonian rhetoric of self-determination and the American practice of subjugation in Haiti and the Dominican Republic. Many newspapers began turning from cheerleaders to critics, and by "1920 a majority of American periodicals criticized the United States for its intervention in Haiti and the Dominican Republic."[71]

Lack of Restraint

American intervention in Haiti was driven mainly by strategic, paternalist, and humanitarian motivations. Wilson's interventionism in the Caribbean and Central America was driven by the specific circumstances in the individual countries and the general strategic situation—protection of the Panama Canal and the exigencies of World War I.[72] Wilson's motivation was also humanitarian; he sincerely believed that some countries needed American assistance. His goal in "Mexico, Haiti, and Santo Domingo [Dominican Republic] was to help the poor and the powerless gain some level of democracy and freedom."[73] Intervention was also motivated by a sense of racial paternalism and imperial destiny.[74] Some supporters were nakedly imperialistic, advocating annexation of the island of Hispaniola (containing both Haiti and the Dominican Republic). A 1916 editorial in the Chicago *Tribune* declared, "the American destiny goes south, and it is imperial."[75] Most newspaper editorials favored intervention, but rejected annexation.[76] Long-term intervention would be cheaper than annexation, and would avoid adding more nonwhites to the US population. Some also argued that the United States should gain access to Haitian natural resources, but the most common argument was made "on the basis of a paternalistic regard for a degraded people" and the need to establish political stability in Haiti and the Dominican Republic for the good of the unfortunate peoples of Hispaniola.[77] In his survey of American newspapers, Blassingame found that a majority of the publications endorsed intervention in Haiti and the Dominican Republic between 1904 and 1919.[78] Contemporary newspapers also claimed that the majority of Americans endorsed intervention, even though the American public was generally ignorant about events in the Caribbean.[79] The Haitian case is almost a textbook case of attempting to achieve security through expansion. The rising power of the United States led to expanded interests and control of new territory, which in turn led to an expansion in the US security perimeter. More specifically, the acquisition of the Canal Zone and the building of the Panama Canal made control of approaches to the canal a strategic necessity. The United States expanded its defensive perimeter and its definition of security to include the guarantee of stability in strategically placed foreign countries in the Caribbean Basin. When handed control of the Haitian capital by Admiral Caperton and the State Department, strategic, ethnocentric, paternal, and humanitarian reasoning convinced the President Wilson to commit to the occupation of Haiti. We can thus categorize this case as expansion. There were no particular security-based or economic reasons to delay intervention in Haiti. In fact, security concerns compelled the United States to act as soon as possible in 1914, and therefore provided incentives for expansion, but none for restraint.

As one of the few cases of outright expansion, the occupation of Haiti requires some further explanation. Why were domestic restraints so easily cast aside? First, separation of powers was a less effective restraint, because the president and the opposition party in Congress basically agreed on expansion in this case. Second, in a country overtly hostile to territorial aggrandizement, the logic of security through expansion combined with ethnocentric humanitarianism should be among the most convincing reasons for expansion. Even anti-imperialists would have to agree that expansion was acceptable if it could mitigate a clear threat to the security of the United States. Anti-imperialists would be further disarmed by humanitarian objectives. Finally, from the outset, the intervention did not generate large human or financial costs because of Haitian quiescence. This combination of factors strongly reduced incentives to oppose political–military expansion in Haiti. Opposition would increase only when Republicans converted to anti-imperialism, the security threat diminished, the humanitarian argument was undermined by the killing of Haitian protesters, and the costs were more heavily scrutinized.

Occupation of the Dominican Republic
(November 29, 1916)

American intervention in the Dominican Republic was similar in many ways to the intervention in Haiti. In both cases strategic imperatives and paternalistic-humanitarian motivations dominated a decision-making process that took place entirely within the executive branch. In both cases Wilson was reluctant to intervene but saw no other choice, given his perception of American national interests. It was assumed that protection of the recently completed Panama Canal required the United States to maintain the Caribbean as part of its sphere of influence and prevent other great powers from challenging American dominance of the region. With respect to the Dominican Republic specifically, the main interest was in preventing a European power from gaining a naval base at Samanáa Bay on the north coast. Part of American interests was a result of important economic relations in the Caribbean, but the Dominican Republic itself was not important economically.[80] One major difference between the two countries was that intervention in the Dominican Republic was encouraged by the policy legacy of the Theodore Roosevelt administration. By 1916 the United States had been collecting Dominican customs for over a decade. The hope in 1904–1907, when the customs receivership was being negotiated, was that a customs receivership would stabilize the Dominican Republic; however, control of Dominican customs receipts did not end the cycle of revolution in that country. The main result of customs receivership was to create the perception that the United States was responsible for Dominican stability. The general sense among policymakers and American public was that the Dominican Republic "had become the peculiar responsibility of the United States when Theodore Roosevelt intervened in 1904 to put the country's finances in order in the face of threatening European creditors."[81] A second difference is that Haiti maintained at least the appearance of independent government while the Dominican Republic was governed directly by the US military. Regardless of the differences, the reaction in the United States was the same, at least at first. As military intervention shifted to full military government of the Dominican Republic there was little if any opposition from Congress or the public. Toward the end of World War I the press turned against the interventionist policy in the Caribbean, but this criticism was not strong enough to end the military occupation for several more years.

From Dollar Diplomacy to the Promotion of Constitutional Government

Between 1911 and 1916 Dominican politics became increasingly unstable, with power changing hands eight times during this period.[82] Dominican politics were dominated by two competing factions: the Horacistas led by Horacio Vásquez and the Jimenistas led by Juan Isidro Jiménes. During this period the United States was highly involved in the domestic politics of the Dominican Republic, using gunboats, control of customs receipts, and threats of military occupation in attempts to coerce successive Dominican leaders to establish a stable, constitutional government. The main goal of the Wilson administration was to assist the Dominicans in electing responsible leaders who were supportive of US interests and could bring stability to Dominican politics. Things didn't quite go according to plan. General José Bordas Valdez was elected in 1913 in a reasonably free and fair election supervised by American officials, but neither the Horacistas nor the Jimenistas were satisfied, and by summer of 1914 Jimenista Desidario Arias and Horacio Vásquez were both leading revolts against the Bordas regime. Bryan promised Bordas US support but insisted that Bordas accept the appointment of an American financial advisor who would have veto power over government spending and the authority to prepare the Dominican government's budget.[83] State Department officials were beginning to see the situation as hopeless and declined to observe the June 1914 election, which Bordas won easily. The Wilson administration did not recognize Bordas as president. The Dominican policy of the Wilson administration was in disarray.[84]

From 1914 forward, the United States attempted to increase its influence on the Dominican Republic. A new major effort to reform Dominican politics took place in 1914 with the arrival of an American commission (with gunboats and marines at the ready), sent to implement the Wilson Plan. The plan required an end to revolutionary activity, the resignation of Bordas, and the selection of a provisional president followed by an American supervised election to select a full-term president and Congress. The plan pledged American support for a Dominican government chosen according to the plan.[85] Wilson made it clear that the United States would not allow any further revolutions in the Dominican Republic; political change would occur through elections only. The commission was successful in convincing the reigning president Bordas to step down, and convinced all of the important Dominican political elites except Arias to accept the plan. Ramón Baez was appointed provisional president until a new president could be elected to a six-year term. Elections were held in October of 1914, but the results were challenged and a new election was held in November. Former president Juan Isidro Jiménez won and was inaugurated in December of 1914 with full American support. The elections were observed by American officials and considered to be generally free and fair, with limited fraud and intimidation.[86]

Despite the successful implementation of the Wilson Plan, American officials were not completely satisfied with the level of American influence on Dominican politics and began pressuring Jiménez to recognize the powers granted to the financial advisor and director of public works under his predecessor but never formalized under Dominican law. These American designated officials would practically control all government expenditures, and, combined with the American customs receivership, would give the United States total control over Dominican finances. President Jiménez appeared open to these demands, but the Dominican Congress was strongly opposed and some members threatened to depose the president if such a deal was made. The public outcry in the Dominican Republic against these new demands was so great that it soon became clear that Jiménez could not implement them and survive as president. Bryan responded by retracting his demand for an American financial advisor. However, after Lansing took over as Secretary of State in June of 1915, the new US minister, William Russell, demanded the reinstatement of the American financial advisor (or the transfer of the financial advisor's powers to the customs receiver) and American control of the Dominican armed forces, which would be turned into a constabulary force. In return the United States would advance $120,000 to Jiménez to pay the salaries of government employees, which were far in arrears and causing much discontent. News of the demands caused a wave of anti-Americanism to sweep through the country. After vacillating, Jiménez officially rejected the American proposals on December 8, 1915. US policy then was simply to wait for an occasion to deploy an occupying force.[87]

Military Intervention in the Dominican Republic (May 1916)

A split between Jiménez and his Secretary of War Desidario Arias was the proximate cause of American intervention. After turning down the American offer of cash for control the Jiménez administration was under increasing financial pressure, causing Jiménez to fear for his hold on power. Jiménez attempted to arrest Arias to preempt a coup attempt, but Arias outmaneuvered Jiménez and took control of Santo Domingo. The United States refused to provide Jiménez with customs funds so that he could raise and supply troops to put down the rebellion. The United States was willing to intervene militarily to support the regime, but was unwilling to allow it the resources it needed to defend itself. Jiménez would not support American military intervention and instead resigned. The commanding officer of US forces, Rear Admiral William Caperton, was given orders to take what action he felt was necessary. He convinced Arias to flee the capital on May 14, and on the next day took control of the city. Caperton then moved to take other major cities in June and July, and a force of marines commanded by Colonel Joseph H. Pendleton ended the resistance by Arias and his fighters. In June, Minister Russell declared that all revenue would be collected and disbursed by American officials. The Dominican Congress quickly elected Dr. Francisco Henríquez y Carbajal as provisional president, but the United States withheld recognition and customs receipts from the new government, hoping to force Henríquez to agree to American demands of total control of Dominican finances and the Dominican military. Negotiations continued between Russell and Henríquez until Russell finally concluded that the situation required "complete control by the United States in Santo Domingo [sic] until such time as the country can get together and prove its ability to work out its own destiny."[88] The US intervention faced little resistance because "no one, not even US officials, realized in May and June of 1916 that the intervention would expand into a military government which would rule the Dominican people for the next eight years."[89]

Military Occupation of the Dominican Republic (November 29, 1916–1924)

By the end of October of 1916, American officials were looking for a pretext to allow them to implement full military control over the Dominican Republic. They found one when Henríquez took steps to select a new legislature. The State Department feared that electors would give allies of Arias control of the legislature, which was considered unacceptable. Herbert Stabler, chief of the Latin American Division, recommended military occupation and Secretary Lansing forwarded this recommendation to President Wilson. Wilson approved the plan for military occupation on November 26, 1916, "with the deepest reluctance," and on November 29 Captain (soon Rear Admiral) H. S. Knapp put this order into effect and declared himself military governor.[90] Knapp proceeded to replace the Dominican cabinet with military officers and put the Dominican Congress on an indefinite recess. Governors and city councils maintained their offices at the pleasure of the new military government. Military Governor Knapp, ruling by executive order, issued censorship and disarmament proclamations and set up military courts to try cases that involved the military government.[91]

The intervention and occupation was based on the premise that the Dominican government had violated the 1907 treaty with the United States by increasing its debt above the allowed limit and by failing to maintain peace and order in the country.[92] Dominican nationalists rejected American claims that the Dominican Republican had violated the treaty and asserted that the American occupation was illegal. Furthermore, they argued that even if the Dominican government had violated the treaty, the United States had no right under the treaty or international law to invade and occupy a sovereign country.[93]

The occupation of the Dominican Republic did not cause much public reaction in the United States. Newspaper editorials consistently supported the interventionist policy of the Roosevelt, Taft, and Wilson administrations toward the Dominican Republic and took a paternalist–racist perspective that the Dominicans were unable to govern themselves. There was a widespread belief that American national security required the United States to bring about political stability in the Dominican Republic. Some editorials even called for annexation of the country.[94] Criticism was found in the pages of *The Nation*, which consistently opposed military intervention. Criticism also emerged from other quarters after World War I concluded. Journalists began emphasizing the normative dissonance in American foreign policy by juxtaposing the idealist rhetoric of self-determination that emanated from Versailles with the military governments

imposed on Haiti and the Dominican Republic.[95] By 1920 "a majority of American periodicals criticized the United States for its intervention in Haiti and the
Dominican Republic."[96] Wilson appeared to view intervention and occupation
as the least bad option in the context of instability in the Dominican Republic
and the strategic importance of the Caribbean during wartime.[97] Wilson consistently admitted that he was quite ignorant of the situation in the Dominican
Republic, didn't know what to do about the situation, and essentially followed
the advice of his secretaries of state, first Bryan and then Lansing.[98]

Completing the Occupation of Hispaniola

The list of reasons why the United States invaded and occupied the Dominican
Republic is long: "the desire to protect US interests in the Caribbean and Panama Canal region, especially against the possible encroachments of Germany;
the Wilson administration's 'missionary impulse,' the desire to set things right
in Latin American republics by imposing good leaders, democracy, and stability;
and the wish to protect North American economic interests in the Dominican
Republic."[99] These motivations were reinforced by the legacy of past policy decisions. More so than the interventions in Veracruz and Haiti, American policy
in the Dominican Republic was driven by the "accrued weight" of American
diplomacy.[100] Well before the crisis that led to the military occupation of the
Dominican Republic, the United States was using its authority over customs
receipts to manipulate Dominican politics.

The forces of restraint were weak in this case, and the outcome is coded as
expansion. Many of the same factors that reduced the incentive for opposition
to Wilson's policy in Haiti also facilitated the occupation of the Dominican
Republic. Congress was not involved, and most of the decision making was done
within the State Department and the Department of the Navy. The repeated
interventions into Dominican politics by the State Department from 1912 to
1915 occurred without any complaints from Congress or anti-imperialist groups.
In this situation there was no avenue for Congress to intervene directly—no new
treaty was proposed, no new expenditures were required—and there were few
political incentives for other forms of cost-imposing strategies. Regardless, Democrats in Congress were not inclined to oppose the policy of their party leader
and Republicans supported Wilson's Caribbean policy. The lack of opposition
to the increasingly invasive American management of Dominican politics
removed any external restraint on Wilson's policy and paved the way for full US
political–military control of the Dominican Republic to the United States. Wilson did seem personally conflicted over the invasiveness of US policy, but could
reconcile himself with the assurance that he was helping to uplift a less advanced
people.

To the extent that the public was aware of what was happening in the Dominican Republic between 1916 and 1920, it was supportive of American policy and therefore electoral pressures for restraint were absent. Dissent became widespread only after World War I ended and the press devoted more attention to US Caribbean policy. Even after the war ended, other issues were more prominent including peace talks in Europe, the domestic fight over the League of Nations, and growing demand for intervention in Mexico. Any change in policy toward the Dominican Republic would have to wait for Wilson's successor, Republican Warren Harding. Security-based concerns fostered expansion and not restraint and economic interests did not play a role shaping the decision making in this case.

Nicaragua Customs Receivership and Rejected Protectorate (1916–1917)

Under the Wilson administration the United States sought increased control over Nicaragua in order to prevent any European powers from gaining influence in the unstable Central American republic. The Wilson administration and the president of Nicaragua sought to make Nicaragua the protectorate of the United States and sought to gain exclusive rights to a naval base and canal. This effort failed when the proposed treaty was rejected by the US Senate Committee on Foreign Relations, twice. A treaty finally passed without the protectorate clause. Passage of the treaty occurred during an increase in German submarine warfare in the Atlantic Ocean, ensuring that international security concerns provided the backdrop for debate. The United States followed up the treaty with an effort to help the Conservatives stay in power, and in return for this support the Nicaraguan government agreed to put a mixed commission (two Americans, one Nicaraguan) in charge of customs receipts. An expansion of US infringement of the sovereign rights of Nicaragua certainly occurred, but it was significantly delayed and reduced in scope because of opposition in the US Senate.

Failed Protectorate

When Wilson took office as president of the United States, Nicaragua was viewed as highly unstable by State Department officials. Under President Taft a formal customs receivership had been rejected by the Senate, but through a private agreement with American banks, Nicaragua had an American collector of customs and had Americans in other financial advisory posts.[101] Just before Wilson's inauguration, George Weitzel, chief of the Division of Latin American Affairs and US minister to Nicaragua, negotiated a treaty with Nicaragua that would give the United States exclusive rights to a canal and a naval base on the

Gulf of Fonseca in exchange for $3 million, but his treaty was blocked by the Senate.[102]

Wilson and his Secretary of State Bryan had to quickly decide how to deal with the fact that Nicaraguan President Adolfo Díaz had an empty treasury, and American bankers were unwilling to loan more money without further reassurances by the United States government. At the same time concerns arose that Díaz would look to Europe for new loans if American banks proved unwilling. It was widely believed that more stable finances were necessary to prevent a revolution. In June of 1913 Díaz's lobbyist in Washington, Charles Douglas, passed on a request from the Nicaraguan president for a treaty with the United States similar to the Weitzel treaty rejected by the Senate (rights to build a canal and naval base), but with an amendment that would give the United States the right to intervene militarily in Nicaragua to maintain order (similar to the Platt Amendment). Secretary of State William Jennings Bryan and President Wilson both agreed to Díaz's proposal. Opposition arose immediately in the United States and abroad. The proposed treaty was criticized in the American press as "Dollar Diplomacy Outdone."[103] Anti-imperialist Senator William E. Borah declared, "It is the beginning of that policy whose irrefutable logic is complete dominance and control."[104] Other Central American countries were strongly against the treaty because it undermined the sovereignty of Nicaragua (which set a bad precedent) and because the clause granting naval bases to the United States in the Gulf of Fonseca infringed on the territorial claims of neighboring countries. On August 2, 1913, the Senate Committee on Foreign Relations rejected the treaty on an 8–4 vote because of the protectorate clause. After failing to convince Wilson that the US government should provide a loan to Nicaragua, cutting out the bankers completely, Bryan was forced to help Díaz find private financing. Díaz was able to reach an agreement with the American banks Brown Brothers and J. and W. Seligman, but this was only a short-term solution to Nicaragua's financial troubles.[105]

In early 1914 Nicaraguan foreign minister Emiliano Chamorro again requested a treaty with the United States, including the protectorate clause. Wilson worried that the discussion of making Nicaragua a protectorate was undermining American "moral prestige" in Central America, but Bryan assured him that the United States would not lose prestige because Nicaragua would publically request the protectorate clause.[106] With Díaz and American diplomats predicting an imminent descent into anarchy, Wilson agreed to resubmit the treaty to the Senate Committee on Foreign Relations with the protectorate clause still included. The Committee took up the treaty in June of 1914. Several senators attacked the close cooperation between US bankers and the State Department, and others protested the presence of American troops in Nicaragua. Chamorro seemed to win over some votes when he mentioned that Germany was willing to make Nicaragua a better offer, playing on the ever-present

American fears of German influence in Central America and the Caribbean. Chamorro also made clear that Nicaragua requested American help with the loans and needed the marines to maintain political stability. The anti-imperialist press again harshly criticized the treaty. Despite Wilson's lobbying, the treaty was again rejected by the US Senate.[107]

The Bryan-Chamoro Treaty

Following their second defeat, Wilson and Bryan finally got the message that the Senate would not approve of a Nicaraguan protectorate. Bryan renegotiated, and the Bryan-Chamorro Treaty was signed on August 5, 1914. It was basically a copy of the Weitzel treaty excluding the clause giving the United States the right to intervene and excluding any mention of a protectorate. However, trouble was not over for the treaty. Costa Rica and El Salvador began lobbying the US Senate to reject it, and Republican Senator Elihu Root argued that the treaty merely prolonged the rule of an unpopular president in Nicaragua (Díaz). Anti-imperialist Senator Borah threatened to filibuster. Opponents succeeded in delaying the vote, but after considerable delay the Senate ratified the Bryan-Chamorro Treaty on June 19, 1916. Democrats in the Senate voted overwhelmingly in favor of the treaty (40 to 5) even thought they had rejected an identical treaty at the end of the Taft administration. Republicans also switched sides and denounced the Bryan-Chamorro Treaty as undermining Nicaraguan democracy, even thought they had previously supported an identical treaty. One reason that the vote finally occurred was that renewed conflict with Germany over submarine warfare in the Atlantic Ocean led to increased fear of German intervention in the Caribbean. The final vote tally in the Senate was 55 to 18.[108]

In the treaty, the United States received "exclusive rights, in perpetuity, to build a canal in Nicaragua, a renewable 99-year lease to the Great and Little Corn Islands in the Caribbean, and a renewable 99-year option to establish a naval base in the Gulf of Fonseca. In return, Nicaragua was to receive payment of three million dollars."[109] Parts of the agreement were ruled illegal by the Central American Court of Justice, but the ruling was ignored by the United States, which contributed to the dissolution of the court the United States helped create.[110]

Establishment of a Joint High Financial Commission and Public Debt Commission

The Bryan-Chamorro Treaty did not stabilize Nicaragua, at least not enough to remove American influence from Nicaraguan politics. During the 1916 election US Minister Benjamin Jefferson and the ubiquitous Admiral Caperton helped

unify the Conservatives behind Emiliano Chamorro and made certain the Liberal candidate was not an associate of former President Zelaya, which eliminated
the top Liberal candidate Julián Irias and led to a Liberal boycott of the election.
The persuasive power of American officials was facilitated by the presence of US
naval ships and the strengthening of the legation guard in Managua. President
Chamorro took office on January 1, 1917, gaining control of what was again an
empty treasury. The United States was now withholding customs receipts and
pressuring Chamorro to accept a US financial advisor. Chamorro negotiated a
new loan as part of "the Lansing Plan, which provided for another bank loan in
return for the creation of a three-member High Commission to supervise Nicaragua's finances."[111] Two members of the commission were appointed by the US
State Department and one appointed by the President of Nicaragua. The agreement led to the disbursement of customs receipts. Nicaraguan commerce fared
well over the next few years with increases in timber and coffee sales leading to
budget surpluses. In the 1920s Nicaragua was able to buy back its National Bank
(1920) and its Pacific Railroad (1924) from foreign creditors.[112] By 1925 the
Conservatives felt confident enough for US forces to withdraw their oversized
legation guard, thereby ending the US military presence in Nicaragua.[113]

Wilsonian Dollar Diplomacy

The Wilson-Bryan Nicaraguan policy was virtually indistinguishable from its
predecessors. Like the Taft administration, the Wilson administration increased
US control over the functions of the Nicaraguan state. However, also like Taft,
Wilson achieved less control that he wanted. The United States gained de facto
control over Nicaraguan finances through the Joint High Commission, but the
repeated attempts to turn Nicaragua into an American protectorate were
rejected by the US Senate. The Wilson administration's expansionist policy
toward Nicaragua was driven largely by William Jennings Bryan's understanding
of American interests in Central America. Bryan came to support a policy indistinguishable from dollar diplomacy for several reasons. First, he argued that a
change in US policy away from supporting Díaz would have led to instability and
insurrection in Nicaragua, which would benefit no one. Thus, Bryan felt it was
the morally right thing to do to continue its paternalist oversight of Nicaragua.
Second, as long as there was the possibility of a canal being built by a foreign
power in Nicaragua, American security would be threatened. Furthermore, a
naval base in Fonseca Bay would help protect the Panama Canal.[114] In sum,
American Nicaraguan policy was expansionist because of the perceived threat of
European influence in Central America and the opportunity presented by
friendly and dependent Nicaraguan leaders. However, policy was much less
expansionist than it otherwise would have been without the institutional separation and balance of powers in the American state.

Invasion of Northern Mexico (March 15, 1916–January 1917)

In the spring of 1916 the United States invaded Mexico for the second time during President Wilson's tenure in office. The "punitive expedition" was launched in response to Pancho Villa's raid on an American town and military fort in New Mexico. Despite the repeated calls for a full invasion of Mexico, Wilson was committed to avoiding war and gave orders to General Pershing to avoid conflict with Carranza's forces. If not for Wilson's personal commitment to restraint, war would have been almost certain. Wilson believed that a predatory war against Mexico was immoral, and was committed to preventing territorial aggrandizement at Mexico's expense. Public opinion confirmed and reinforced Wilson's personal beliefs. Wilson also had important security-based concerns about war with Mexico. He was worried about committing American military capacity in a war with Mexico when war with Germany was becoming increasingly likely—though the German threat could also be seen as a reason to attack Mexico immediately, before the German-Mexican alliance could solidify. At the time of the Punitive Expedition there were reports of German aid going to both Villa and Carranza, though at best only circumstantial evidence has been uncovered.[115]

Pancho Villa's Raid on Columbus, New Mexico (March 9, 1916)

While the State Department took the lead in handling the instability in Nicaragua, Wilson's attention was focused on events across the Atlantic in Europe and across the border in Mexico. After the resignation of Huerta in 1914, civil war continued to rage in Mexico with Emiliano Zapata and Francisco Villa fighting against the Constitutionalist Carranza government. Wilson was indecisive about which leader to support, but finally settled on Carranza. On October 19, 1915, Wilson formally recognized the Carranza regime as the "*de facto* government of Mexico" and lifted the arms embargo against the Mexican government.[116] Wilson also decided that the United States should stay out of Mexican politics. In his annual message to Congress on December 7, 1916, Wilson communicated his commitment to nonintervention. He declared, "We will aid and befriend Mexico, but we will not coerce her; and our course with regard to her ought to be sufficient proof to all America that we seek no political suzerainty or selfish control."[117] In private, a day later, he told members of the Democratic National Committee, "If the Mexicans want to raise hell, let them raise hell. We have got nothing to do with it. It is their government, it is their hell."[118] However, events would conspire to pull the United States into the fires raging across its southern border.

Villa felt betrayed by American support for his rival and began attacks on Americans in Mexico and on American soil. His violent anti-Americanism culminated in a raid that killed 17 Americans (10 civilians) and 100 Mexicans in

Columbus, New Mexico on March 9, 1916.[119] This was the second deadly attack on Americans by Villa's men. Two months earlier, 16 or 17 American mine workers had been killed in Chihuahua, Mexico. Villa's attacks, though extreme, were part of the criminal and revolutionary activity that was common on the Mexican-American border in beginning in 1915. Before Villa's attack the US War Department had already deployed a large number of soldiers along the border. Tensions were high due to the Plan of San Diego—a declaration of the intent of Mexican revolutionaries to carve new countries out of the part of the American Southwest lost by Mexico in 1848. The area would include a Spanish-speaking country and a country inhabited by African Americans and American Indians. President Wilson responded to the plan and the increased border violence by asking Carranza to increase patrols along the border. However, the Mexican side of the border was home to criminals and various revolutionary factions, none of which could be fully controlled.[120]

US Response: The Mexican Punitive Expedition (March 15, 1916)

The pressure on Wilson to retaliate against Villa was high. First, Villa's raids came during an election year, and Wilson would surely be punished at the polls if he did not respond to the attacks. Republicans generally advocated harsh retaliation and would certainly make Mexico into a campaign issue.[121] For example, following Villa's raid, Republican Senator Fall introduced a resolution to send 500,000 American troops into Mexico.[122] The American public (especially long-time opponents of the Mexican Revolution) seemed largely supportive of strong retaliation. American hardliners—including business and Catholic leaders—demanded action, and outrage was widespread among the public. As one author observes, "Americans had . . . been killed in their homes and the demand for intervention in Mexico mounted."[123] Second, the Wilson administration was concerned about its reputation in Latin America if Villa got away with killing Americans on American soil.[124] Third, there was virtual unanimous agreement within the Wilson administration that strong action had to be taken. Wilson's cabinet all agreed on intervention, and experts at the War College pushed strongly for a full-scale attack on Mexico and argued that a limited campaign against Villa would "invite local disasters and delay."[125] Fourth, Wilson also wanted to prevent revolution from spreading in Central America and wanted to look tough in the context of the war in Europe.[126]

Wilson quickly realized some sort of military intervention in Mexican territory was necessary, but his determination to avoid war with Mexico strongly shaped the form of intervention he chose. Wilson responded to Villa's raid by first asking Carranza to find and punish the men responsible for the attack. Within hours of this request Wilson decided that he had to send American troops into Mexico to pursue Villa. Under Wilson's orders, on March 15 General John Pershing crossed into Mexico on a mission to disperse Villa's army. Publicly, Wilson stated the goal was to capture Villa. In truth, the purpose of the punitive expedition was to punish Villa and pressure Carranza to secure the border region while avoiding any conflict with Mexican government forces. Two days after Pershing crossed the border, Congress passed a concurrent resolution in support of the president's actions.[127]

The actual crossing of the border was a tense moment and demonstrates the level of restraint Wilson was willing to employ even as he ordered American troops into action in foreign territory. Wilson almost did not authorize Pershing's forces to cross the border because of last-minute rumors that Carranza's troops would engage the American force. Wilson ordered Pershing to cross the border only if he could do so without opposition from Carranza's forces. Luckily, Carrancista forces acquiesced in the crossing of Pershing's expedition; however, "it is instructive that Wilson shrank from any circumstance that would have involved the United States in a full-scale war."[128] Wilson may have been thinking of the deadly Veracruz operation when he told his secretary,

> I shall be held responsible for every drop of blood that may be spent in the enterprise of intervention. I am seriously considering every phase of this difficult matter, and I can say frankly to you, and you may inform the Cabinet officers who discuss it with you, that "*there won't be any war with Mexico if I can prevent it*," no matter how loud the gentlemen on the hill yell for it and demand it.[129]

In this conversation Wilson also noted the probability of war with Germany and the need to keep all resources at the ready for war in Europe.[130]

Pershing's force of 4,000 men was quite successful at punishing Villa's forces, even though they could never trap his army in a decisive conventional engagement. By June of 1916, US and Constitutionalist troops had killed over 400 of Villa's troops and his army was in total disarray. The expedition had achieved its primary goal of breaking up Villa's bandits, but Wilson did not recall Pershing because the secondary goal of forcing Carranza to secure the Mexican border region was not achieved. Raids continued along the Mexican-American border, and Wilson wanted to compel Mexico to implement a long-term solution to border violence. As tensions increased Wilson called up the National Guard from the border states for increased security and increased the pressure on the Carranza government.[131]

Confrontation with Constitutionalist Troops

Wilson made a calculated risk in maintaining American troops in Mexican territory, a risk that almost resulted in catastrophic consequences. In the course of traveling 350 miles into Mexican territory over the course of several months, violence between American and Constitutionalist forces was probably inevitable. On April 12 US soldiers exchanged fire with Carrancistas in the Mexican town of Parral. Carranza blamed the American soldiers and demanded the removal of all American forces from Mexico. Pershing's response was to request permission to occupy Mexican territory instead of just patrolling it: "In order to prosecute our mission with any promise of success it is therefore absolutely necessary for us to assume complete possession for time being of country through which we must operate; and establish control of railroads as means of supplying forces required."[132] As Edward Haley notes, acceding to this request would have changed the basic purpose of the expedition and been a major step toward all-out war with Mexico. Wilson rejected both Carranza's demand and Pershing's request and instead ordered a policy review, took measures to dampen conflict between Pershing's forces and Carrancistas (such as concentrating expedition forces near the US border), and redoubled American diplomatic efforts. As diplomacy was beginning to bear fruit, Pershing again emphasized that success would require military occupation of large areas of Mexican territory. But Wilson's commitment to restraint and the increasingly tense relations with Germany fostered a conciliatory policy toward Mexico.[133]

Soon after the incident in Parral, additional raids occurred on American territory—some possibly carried out by Carrancistas—and tensions increased with the Mexican government. On May 5 and 6 two small towns in Texas were attacked from across the border and American forces crossed the border in pursuit. Again, Americans felt outrage at the attack and the governor of Texas called for the occupation of all of Mexico. Mexican troops began to concentrate in northern Mexico with orders to oppose with force any further incursions into Mexican territory and any movement by Pershing's forces to the east, west, or south. A confrontation of massed US and Mexican forces seemed likely. Further negotiations between the two countries demonstrated that Wilson would not back down until he had some assurance that raids on American towns from Mexican territory would cease and Carranza was willing to risk war to force the complete withdrawal of American troops from Mexican territory immediately. On June 16, 1917, Wilson's close advisor Colonel House wrote in a letter to Wilson that war "looks . . . inevitable."[134] The War College was ordered to draw up plans for an invasion Mexico. Two historians have uncovered evidence that Mexico even began planning an invasion of south Texas, hoping to trigger an uprising by Mexican Americans and Native Americans.[135]

On June 21, 1916, Colonel House's prediction almost came true. While out on reconnaissance, American Captain Charles T. Boyd disobeyed orders and attempted to lead his troops through the Mexican town of Carrizal. Constitutionalist forces warned Boyd that they had orders to prevent him from moving through Carrizal, but Boyd ignored the warning and led his troops into town looking for a fight. Mexican forces resisted and Boyd led his men in a frontal assault against well-entrenched Mexican troops armed with at least one machine gun. In the firefight that ensued the American forces were scattered; between nine and 14 Americans were killed and 24 taken prisoner, and approximately 45 Mexicans were killed. The first reports that reached the United States claimed the American soldiers had been attacked without warning, and General Pershing, thinking this was the beginning of a Mexican attack on his forces, advocated attacking Carranza's forces and taking the Mexican state of Chihuahua. Wilson ordered that no action be taken until it was clear what had happened in Carrizal. Wilson demanded the release of the prisoners and a statement of Mexican policy from Carranza while also preparing for war by deploying the entire National Guard along the border ("the largest deployment of US military forces since the Civil War") and drafting a resolution asking for congressional authorization to invade Mexico.[136]

The confrontation with Carranza's forces occurred during the presidential campaign and in the same month as the Democratic National Convention. One historian observes, "If domestic US politics had mandated the Pershing expedition in the first place, they clearly prohibited anything but a forceful response to the Carrizal encounter."[137] Wilson wrote a draft of his message to Congress on June 26; in it he asked Congress for the authorization to deploy additional troops in Mexico to use "in any way it may be necessary to guard our frontier effectively, if necessary to enter on Mexican soil."[138] But this request was never made. Wilson did not want to take action that would lead to full-blown war with Mexico. Instead of giving the address, he waited.[139]

Avoidance of War with Mexico

Forces of restraint took hold in both countries. Carranza released the American prisoners on June 29, 1916. Wilson responded with a speech arguing that war with Mexico was against American principles and would be a black mark on the reputation of the United States.[140] In the United States, peace groups lobbied against another war with Mexico and it appeared that the public had lost some of its belligerency: a large majority of the letters the president received was against war. Arthur Link argues that the widespread sentiment favoring peace with Mexico had a significant effect on Wilson's thinking: "We can be certain that the catalyst prompting him to consider a new course was an extraordinary eruption in public opinion that had just occurred."[141] Wilson discovered that US soldiers were to blame for the Carrizal incident, and he wanted to avoid a replay of 1846. He also knew it would take hundreds of thousands of troops to occupy Mexico and continued to worry about conflict with Germany. Wilson declared publicly on June 30 that the United States had no intention of invading Mexico. He appealed to "ideals of America" to avoid "dictation into the affairs of another people."[142] His moderation was criticized by the Republican Party, but Wilson clearly saw further confrontation with Carranza's forces as dangerous politically and responded "by limiting the mission of the Expedition and by pulling it back into northern Chihuahua."[143] Wilson agreed to negotiations with Carranza, and a joint high commission was created for this purpose. After several months of negotiations and after the 1916 election, Wilson made the decision to withdraw US troops in January 1917 as Germany recommenced its attacks on US shipping. The last American soldier crossed back into the United States on February 5.[144]

Crisis De-escalation

From the earliest days of the crisis Wilson was committed to avoiding war with Mexico. In both public and private Wilson gave the same two reasons for his restraint. First, he believed that war with Mexico was immoral, and American public opinion reinforced this belief. He felt that a predatory war against a weaker nation was wrong.[145] He also believed that Mexico had a right to settle its own affairs without outside interference, and he was ashamed of past US interference. Wilson's personal commitment to restraint was reinforced by American public opinion. Historians agree that public opinion favored a military response to the attack on Columbus, but public opinion was solidly against all-out war with Mexico. Link argues that public opposition to war following the Carrizal incident was decisive in shifting Wilson away from the path to war.[146]

Second, Wilson was concerned about committing American military capacity in a war with Mexico when war with Germany was becoming increasingly likely. Wilson "did not want one hand tied behind him at the very moment the nation might need all its forces to meet the German situation."[147] However, the German threat was potentially a casus belli for conflict with Mexico. At the time of the Punitive Expedition there were reports of German aid going to both Villa and Carranza, though at best only circumstantial evidence has been uncovered.[148] In sum, Wilson and the majority of Americans were morally against war with Mexico, and Wilson's perception of the strategic situation favored preparing for potential war with Germany rather than committing resources to war with Mexico.[149]

The analysis above shows that American intervention in Mexico in 1916–1917 was carefully limited by Wilson, despite the strong advocacy for more aggressive strategies like outright occupation of Mexican territory, regime change, and turning Mexico into a protectorate. While the difference between patrolling a piece of territory and formally occupying it may seem slight, it was the difference between tense relations and all-out war. In this case American expansionism was limited by Wilson's personal moral beliefs, his understanding of American ideals (or norms), the strong public opposition to war with Mexico, and the need to conserve military resources during a time when war with Germany was increasingly likely. There is no single reason that allows us to determine the true fundamental reason for Wilson's restraint. The strategic situation was ambiguous, while the normative incentives all pointed toward restraint. Economic interest groups did not push for restraint. The most vocal economic interests advocated for strong action against Mexico. The outcome of this case is limited expansion caused by American strategic culture acting through Wilson's personal beliefs and public opinion.

Political Intervention in Cuba (1917–1922)

As Wilson was managing the Punitive Expedition in Mexico, political instability reemerged in Cuba in 1916. The central problem was that Conservatives were in power and had to rely on electoral fraud and intimidation to remain in power. Liberals knew they would win a fair election, but could not count on the Conservatives to run a fair election and therefore had to either accept minority status or take up arms to overthrow the Conservative regime. With the initiation of the 1917 February Revolution, they chose the latter option. The Wilson administration was caught in the dilemma of opposing both electoral fraud and armed insurrection, and therefore could not fully support either the Conservatives or the Liberals. There was significant pressure to resort to another military intervention, but instead the United States used a variety of other, less intrusive tools. Wilson attempted to influence and shape Cuban politics without resorting to military intervention.

US officials decided that the least bad option was to support the sitting Conservative president Mario García Menocal, while trying to clean up the elections and to bring the Liberals back into the political process. First, several hundred US marines were sent to protect American sugar plantations, which allowed Menocal to concentrate his forces on putting down the revolution. Second, US General Enoch H. Crowder was invited by Menocal to analyze the Cuban electoral system and recommend reforms to decrease the prevalence of electoral fraud. Third, American observers monitored the 1920 election. When none of these measures worked, General Crowder was sent back to Havana as Wilson's personal representative on special mission to Cuba with the moral authority to dictate whatever changes he thought were necessary to reestablish stability.

The decision to intervene, even in this more limited manner, was driven by the policy legacy institutionalized by the Platt Amendment, Wilson's commitment to spreading constitutional government, and security concerns. Because of the history of American involvement in Cuba and the still-operative Platt Amendment, American leaders felt a responsibility to intervene to help resolve episodes of instability and violent internal conflict. This sense of responsibility dovetailed with Wilson's personal beliefs that the best way to bring stability was through constitutional government. American security fears were heightened during this period, which was just after the resumption of unlimited German submarine warfare in the Atlantic (February 1917), the revelation of the Zimmerman telegram (March 1917), and finally the entrance of the United States into World War I (April 1917). US forces remained in Cuba until 1922.[150]

Revolution of February 1917

In 1917 the stage seemed set for a replay of the 1906 US occupation of Cuba. In fact, Liberals hoped for US intervention and supervision of a new election, which they were sure they would win. However, Wilson sought to avoid a major intervention in Cuba and saw stability of the Conservative Menocal regime as the key to keeping the United States out of Cuba. To strengthen Menocal the United States implemented a strategy of providing moral support to Menocal and sending a clear message to the Liberals that there would be no intervention to force a new election. The US State Department released statements directly to the Cuban press conveying American support for the constitutional government of Cuba and opposition to any and all revolutionary activity. The main effects of US efforts were to prevent further defections to the Liberal cause and to foster the surrender of some of the Liberal leaders of the rebellion. The United States also attempted to mediate between the two factions, encouraging Menocal to hold new elections in the disputed districts and grant amnesty to the rebels. In fact, the US Navy (and US sugar interests) took a more favorable view of the Liberals, in some ways shielding them from government forces.[151] At the same time, the United States sold large amounts of matériel to the Menocal government and eventually sent marines to protect foreign property—plantations, mines, and railroads—in Camagüey and Oriente in eastern Cuba, where they remained until 1922.[152] Many Liberals did fight, including Gómez, and they were defeated by Menocal's forces. On May 20, 1917, Menocal was inaugurated for his second term as president of Cuba.[153]

American Observation of the Cuban Election of 1920

Menocal's inauguration did not end the US role in Cuban politics. As the 1920 presidential election approached, American officials sought to prevent another round of political violence. The centerpiece of US strategy in Cuba was electoral reform and supervision. The Menocal government reacted positively on this issue and invited General Enoch H. Crowder to devise a plan for the reform of electoral institutions in Cuba.[154] However, Menocal opposed US supervision of elections, which he saw as inconsistent with Cuban sovereignty. Crowder completed a comprehensive analysis of the Cuban electoral system and devised a set of reforms to eradicate the most egregious forms of electoral fraud. Liberals wanted even more US involvement and argued that the United States was responsible for ensuring free and fair elections in Cuba because the United States opposed political change by revolution. The State Department renewed pressure on Menocal to request American supervision of elections but Menocal stood firm, again arguing that he could not agree to such an affront to Cuban sovereignty. Crowder and the US minister in Havana agreed with Menocal. The issue was diffused when Menocal personally pledged to ensure the integrity of the 1920 elections.[155]

Optimism about a free and fair election quickly dissipated. As the 1920 election approached, the Conservatives began frantically passing legislation to undermine the Crowder reforms. It quickly became clear that the Conservative Party would not allow a Liberal victory and were reverting to the most egregious forms of fraud and intimidation. In response, the Liberal Party announced a boycott of the election. The US State Department warned both parties to abide by electoral laws and maintain the integrity of the electoral process in Cuba. Secretary of State Bainbridge Colby demanded that US officials supervise the election; Menocal acquiesced, and Liberals rescinded their boycott. US observers reported on numerous examples of fraud, intimidation, and violence, but Menocal ignored Colby's demands to clean up electoral practices. The election took place on November 1, 1920, and failed to designate a clear winner. As the electoral bureaucracy attempted to sift through all the complaints of fraud, a growing sense of crisis emerged. Concurrently, a financial crisis hit Cuba in October after a sharp drop in the price of sugar led to a run on the banks. The Wilson administration, tired of arguments about respect for Cuban sovereignty and believing that Cubans had proved that they could not run a clean election, appointed General Crowder as the personal representative on special mission to Cuba to clean up both the electoral and financial mess.[156]

Crowder arrived in Havana on January 6, 1921, on the US battleship USS *Minnesota* to aid President Menocal in resolving the political and financial crisis. Crowder arrived without a formal agreement with the Cuban government and without any formally specified powers or duties beyond being instructed ito confer with President Menocal as to the best means of remedying the situation" of the contested election and financial crisis.[157] Crowder was sent in place of a formal military intervention, which the Wilson administration sought to avoid "after attacks on its Caribbean policy during the recent presidential campaign in the United States."[158] Cuban Conservatives were not happy about Crowder's appearance, but Liberals viewed American intervention as necessary to ensure a fair election. Under Crowder's guidance the Cuban Supreme Court ordered new elections in about 20 percent of the voting districts. However, the Liberals wanted a completely new election, and their subsequent boycott handed the election to Alfredo Zayas—a former Liberal who had become allied with the

Conservatives. Crowder remained in Havana to advise the new government on financial and administrative reforms. He did not officially have authority over the Cuban government, but it was inferred that a rejection of Crowder's advice could lead to more invasive intervention by the United States.[159]

Moral Support

The Wilson administration policy toward Cuba between 1917 and 1921 was one of limited intervention. American troops were stationed in the economically most important areas of the country, but did not take an active role in the fighting. The most important tool by the United States was its moral support of the Menocal regime. National security imperatives were probably the primary reason for intervention, at least until the end of World War I. The Liberal revolution was seen as distinctly unhelpful at a time when the United States was preparing for war with Germany, especially because sugar was seen as a strategic resource and Cuba was a major sugar producer.[160] While Wilson also sent a personal representative to advise the Cuban government and even though General Crowder's advice was backed by the threat of a full military occupation, the Wilson administration did not force regime change or impose any specific policies on the Cuban government. Wilson clearly was not interested in a full-scale occupation like the one that had taken place in 1906. Thus, while the United States continued to intervene in Cuban affairs under Wilson, "Washington was increasingly loath to exercise the military option in Cuba."[161] US forces were already deployed along the border with Mexico and in Hispaniola, and war with Germany was declared as the rebellion was underway. There was little enthusiasm to tie down more the military power of the United States in stabilization missions.[162] Also, it is clear that there was little desire among policymakers or the public for another military occupation of Cuba. Within the Wilson administration, there appears to have been a simple loss of appetite for micromanaging the politics of foreign countries.

This is a case of limited expansion. The situation in Cuba in 1917 was very similar to the situation in 1906. The Roosevelt intervention was reluctant and more limited than many argued for at the time. The intervention of 1917 was even more restrained than 1906. Because of Wilson's personal feeling of distaste for military intervention and his belief that the American public was also skeptical of another military occupation of Cuba, the United States resorted to the less intrusive measures of advice and instruction. National security concerns can be seen to have motivated both restraint and expansion. The United States did not want to waste soldiers in Cuba that could be used in Europe to fight World War I. At the same time, sugar was seen as a strategic commodity, and therefore sugar production in Cuba needed to be protected by US troops. Economic interests played a role in encouraging the United States to deploy troops to guard sugar plantations and, overall, encouraged increased US involvement in Cuban politics.

Push to Intervene in Mexico (1919)

By 1919 a strong prointerventionist movement developed in the United States built on frustration with the limited nature of the Punitive Expedition and new fears over the Mexican Constitution of 1917. Article 27 of the constitution gave the Mexican people ownership of all subsoil resources in Mexican territory, potentially endangering foreign ownership of mines and oilfields in Mexico. The possibility of expropriation catalyzed a well-funded interventionist movement made up of American businesses with interests in Mexico (especially oil companies), members of Congress (led by Senator Albert B. Fall of New Mexico), and officials in the State Department. This coalition moved the country toward intervention while Wilson was distracted by peace negotiations in Europe and then sidelined from policymaking by his stroke. Some in the prointerventionist movement hoped to establish a "Cuban arrangement with Mexico"—that is, establishing a protectorate in Mexico.[163] Others simply contemplated the seizure of Mexican oilfields or the overthrow of Carranza.[164] Americans doing business in Mexico feared the loss of their property and Americans living in Mexico feared their lives were in danger. American government officials, including members of Congress, noted the strategic importance of Mexican oil in light of the drawdown of American oil supplies during World War I. Furthermore, animosity continued between Mexico and the United States because they were on opposite sides of World War I—Mexico was neutral, but tacitly supported Germany.[165] Boaz Long, chief of the Division of Latin American Affairs at the State Department, even claimed that the hated Article 27 "was inserted at the last moment upon the suggestion of a German lobbyist, and was paid for by German money."[166]

The path to intervention was blocked only after Wilson recovered sufficiently to regain command of the policy agenda and end collaboration between interventionists in the State Department and US Senate. Wilson's anti-imperialist values were the most important cause of restraint. All other factors, including economic and security interests, favored intervention. This case is a clear example of restraint.

The Push for Intervention

By 1919 a significant coalition of groups had joined forces to advocate for another round of American intervention in Mexico. In the private sector, "border businessmen and refugees from Mexico, who had established the American

International Protective Association, and . . . large corporate interests represented in the International Committee of Mexico City" had been promoting counterrevolutionary propaganda in the United States since 1916.[167] By 1919 these groups were joined by the Association of Oil Producers in Mexico, which represented large oil companies with drilling operations. Oil producers came into conflict with the Mexican regime because they were concerned that they were heading toward nationalization of the oil industry. Oil producers helped fund counterrevolutionaries in Mexico and prointerventionist activities in the United States. In 1918 and 1917 oil companies submitted a plan to the Wilson administration that included going to war with Mexico. Wilson rebuffed their advice. In December of 1918 oil producers and other corporations with business in Mexico formed the National Association for the Protection of American Rights in Mexico (NAPARIM) to develop a concerted public opinion campaign against the revolutionary government in Mexico. A Senate subcommittee to investigate Mexican affairs was created in August of 1919.[168] One author observes, "Oil producers, miners, smelting and allied industries, British entrepreneurs, cattle and landed interests, 'the orthodox Catholic Church strongly backed by the Catholic societies of America, and former *porfiristas* agreed almost unanimously that Carranza must go."[169]

The push for intervention was led by Senator Fall and his subcommittee on Mexico. Fall had a long history of opposing the Mexican Revolution. He had significant investment in Mexico and believed that American investment could not be safe under a revolutionary government. Fall consistently advocated for aggressive measures against Mexico. During the occupation of Veracruz, Fall pushed for an expanded intervention to protect Americans throughout Mexico. After the raid by Pancho Villa, Fall introduced a resolution to send 500,000 American troops into Mexico. President Wilson consistently pursued policies more restrained than those advocated by Senator Fall and his allies.[170]

The interventionist movement was restrained as long as Wilson was overseeing Mexican policy, but because of the prointerventionist sentiment in the State Department, the direction of policy shifted quickly once Wilson became immersed in the peace talks at Versailles and the campaign for the League of Nations at home and more fundamentally preoccupied with his recovery from a stroke. As Wilson became fully involved with peace negotiations in Europe in early 1919, Undersecretary of State Frank Polk and Ambassador to Mexico Henry P. Fletcher "unilaterally initiated a harsher policy." The State Department continued to issue warnings to the Mexican government throughout the summer of 1919, and border violence caused brief American raids into Mexico. Without success Fletcher implored Wilson to give Carranza an ultimatum to ensure the security of American property and lives or the United States would sever diplomatic relations with Mexico.[171] By June 1919, the War Department had completed a plan for invading Mexico. By July approximately 60,000 US troops were stationed on the border and the navy made plans for taking the port cities of Tampico and Veracruz and the surrounding oil fields.[172]

Border violence led to increased demands for harsher action against Mexico, but Wilson made it clear to State Department officials that he was only interested in using diplomacy to shape Mexican behavior. While touring the United States in support of the League of Nations, Wilson suffered a stroke. Soon after, relations with Mexico reached a low point. New pressure from the Carranza government led to intensified conflict with American oil companies in Mexico. Mexican troops began seizing oil drilling operations that refused to comply with Mexican oil laws on November 12, 1919. More importantly, US Consular Agent William O. Jenkins was kidnapped in Puebla Mexico. In the United States it was assumed that Carranza had something to do with it, but in reality Jenkins was kidnapped by counterrevolutionaries seeking to undermine the legitimacy of the Carranza administration. Jenkins allegedly collaborated with his abductors and told supporters back in the United States, including Senator Fall, that he had been kidnapped by revolutionaries. Jenkins's kidnapping caused outrage in the United States, but before any action could be taken, he was released. The slight easing in tension was quickly reversed when Puebla officials arrested Jenkins for giving false statements. With Wilson ill, Secretary of State Lansing took control of Mexican policy. By the end of November Mexico was preparing for an invasion by the United States.[173]

Lansing pushed American policy in a more belligerent direction, with the support of Congress and the public. Lansing demanded Jenkins's release and threatened tougher American action if Mexico did not give in. According to historian Clifford Trow, Lansing's approach "moved the two countries to the brink of war."[174] Anti-Mexican sentiment, expressed in newspaper editorials, was strong among the American public. Lansing proceeded, knowing that Wilson would probably not approve. State Department officials collaborated with Senator Fall to produce a Senate resolution asking Wilson to cut diplomatic relations with Mexico and vacate recognition of the Carranza government. A day later "another resolution was introduced into the Senate which authorized the President to 'employ the naval and military forces of the United States and to take such measures as may be necessary to accomplish the payment and satisfaction of claims held by United States citizens against Mexico."[175] Newspaper editorials supported the Senate and State Department policy. Due to the efforts of by his wife, Edith Bolling Wilson, and his secretary, Joseph Patrick Tumulty, Wilson became aware of the action in the Senate and made his opposition to the resolutions known.[176] Following Wilson's lead, Senate Democrats quickly moved to revise Fall's resolution in line with the preferences of the president, while Fall argued that Wilson lacked the capacity to deal with the crisis. The Senate appointed a committee led by Fall to visit President Wilson to determine if he was well enough to conduct policymaking.[177]

Wilson's Restraint

By December 5, 1919, Wilson had improved enough to become fully abreast of the situation and consented to a conference with Senator Fall. Fall presented his case against the Carranza government. Wilson's clear interest and knowledge of the Mexican situation and overall lucidity convinced Fall that the president was capable of handling relations with Mexico. Wilson was not convinced by Fall's auguments, and sent Fall a letter stating his opposition to the resolution calling for breaking off diplomatic relations with Mexico and instructing the Senate that diplomacy was the responsibility of the presidency and Congress should follow Wilson's leadership. Chairman of the Foreign Relations Committee Henry Cabot Lodge tabled the resolution, acknowledging that the Senate was infringing upon the duties and powers of the executive. Lansing and the rest of the State Department were brought to heel, and US policy reverted to "watchful waiting." Lansing later resigned, in part due to the Mexico imbroglio.[178]

Only Wilson's recovery and quick intervention halted the drift toward military intervention in Mexico. He was able to rein in State Department officials and stymie attempts by the Republican Senators to take control of foreign policy.[179] Prior to Wilson's intervention, "the preconditions for military activity in Mexico were established."[180]

Wilson had two main reasons for avoiding more belligerent policy. First, he made an institutional argument: "I am convinced that I am supported by every competent constitutional authority in the statement that the initiative in directing the relations of our Government with Foreign Governments is assigned by the Constitution to the Executive and the Executive only."[181] In other words, he saw Congress (with the support of some of his cabinet) attempting to determine the foreign policy of the United States, which Wilson viewed as unconstitutional. His assertion of authority over foreign policy with Mexico was therefore a clear attempt to check the power of Congress in national policymaking. Second, Wilson was determined to maintain a policy consistent with the norms of self-determination and anti-imperialism.[182] Wilson consistently asserted a preference for nonintervention or, if necessary, limited intervention.[183] Pragmatic concerns also certainly played a role, such as the cost of mobilizing sufficient military forces for intervention and the fact that Carranza would likely be leaving office after the 1920 Mexican election.[184] However, too much should not be made of these issues. The United States was willing to intervene in 1916 despite having a small, unprepared army, and the United States had no assurance that Carranza would actually leave office or that his replacement would be more sympathetic to American concerns. The failed interventionist movement had an effect on American foreign policy beyond the events of 1919. The push to intervene in Mexico led to a backlash against US economic interests that pushed for an interventionist US foreign policy. In Congress and the press, oil companies and bankers were vilified for advocating increased American control over weaker foreign countries.[185]

The events of 1919 demonstrate the significance of the reinforcing tendencies of institutional and normative restraints in American foreign policy. First, Wilson's reigning in of Congress is an example of separation of powers preventing the implementation of expansionist foreign policy. In this case the executive is restraining the legislature. Wilson explicitly stated that his actions were partially motivated by the need to defend executive power in opposition to congressional infringement. Second, Wilson was motivated by his personal commitment to liberal norms of self-determination and anti-imperialism. This case eliminates the security issue (since World War I was over) and allows us to isolate the effect of norms and institutions.

Conclusion

By the end of Woodrow Wilson's second term as president the United States had two major colonies (the Philippines and Puerto Rico), two protectorates (Cuba and Panama), political–military control of two countries (Haiti and the Dominican Republic), and partial financial control in two countries (Nicaragua and Liberia).[186] The colonies, protectorates, and financial arrangements were left over from previous eras. The most important cases of territorial expansion during the Wilson era were in Haiti and the Dominican Republic. Policy toward Hispaniola shows little evidence of restraint beyond Wilson's initial reluctance to order military intervention. Haiti and the Dominican Republic were militarily occupied, and their internal politics and policies were directly or indirectly controlled by the United States. While some protest did occur, there was no significant outcry from the American public or Congress until after Wilson left office. Haiti and the Dominican Republic are clear examples of a strategy of security through expansion emphasized by defensive realists. In the shadow of World War I, the Wilson administration calculated that the United States could not afford to allow chronic instability so close to its shores. The central goal of the occupation of Hispaniola was to prevent a European power from gaining a naval base in a position to threaten the Panama Canal. The lighter political–military intervention in Cuba was propelled by similar logic.

Despite these clear instances of relatively unfettered territorial expansion, the rest of the cases covered in this chapter show that the overall narrative of the Wilson era was one of limited expansion. In Mexico, Cuba, and Nicaragua the United States had the opportunity to gain control over large sections of foreign territory, but failed to do so because of separation of powers, public opinion, and anti-imperialist norms. In 1914, 1916, and 1919 the United States and Mexico were on the brink of wars that would inevitably result in American occupation of Mexico. In all of these cases the United States pulled back from war. The thread that connects all of these cases of limited expansion is Woodrow Wilson's personal commitment to norms of self-determination and anti-imperialism. Wilson fundamentally believed that Mexico should have the opportunity to govern itself and that it would be wrong for a strong country to commence a predatory war against a weaker neighbor. In 1914 and 1916 public opinion and electoral considerations also played significant roles in reinforcing Wilson's normative commitment to peace. In 1916 national security considerations played a strong role in restraining the United States. Wilson repeatedly voiced the concern that war with Mexico in 1916 would leave the United States unprepared for war with Germany. In 1919 separation of powers played a major role in preventing war, as Wilson viewed belligerent congressional actions as a usurpation of presidential powers. The cases of personal restraint provide an excellent illustration of how structural redundancy creates more robust and reliable restraint. Even under conditions where institutional restraints and public opinion were not operative, restraint occurred due to the personal values of Wilson. Without the multiple layers of redundancy, increased expansion would have occurred.

Interventions in Cuba and Nicaragua were of lesser importance to the broad sweep of American foreign policy under Woodrow Wilson. Cuban policy did not seem to be a major concern of Wilson, and is completely omitted from several recent biographies.[187] The driving assumption of Cuban policy was that the United States should minimize its intervention while doing its best to ensure political stability. As in Hispaniola, American interests in Cuba were defined in terms of national security. However, in this case the threat came from the security of a strategic commodity—sugar. Since instability in Cuba practically coincided with American entry into World War I, strategic concerns appear to have been dominant until the end of the war, and again suggest that defensive realism provides the best explanation for expansion. After 1920, Wilson attempted to manage Cuban policy through a personal envoy rather than a military occupation.

Nicaraguan policy is the only clear example of Congress acting as a restraint on an attempt at territorial expansion by the executive during Wilson presidency. Wilson repeatedly asked the Senate to consent to a treaty that would make Nicaragua a protectorate. The Senate repeatedly refused to do so. In the end, a treaty was signed that gave the United States rights to build a canal and establish naval bases, and later the United States gained significant control over Nicaraguan finances. However, separation and balance of powers clearly restrained American foreign policy in the Nicaragua case.

The Wilsonian attempt to spread constitutional government in the Caribbean Basin reveals the enduring relevance of expansionist incentives up through the 1910s. Nevertheless, this second wave of expansion was delayed, limited, prevented, and undermined by the reinforcing restraint of domestic institutional structure and a strategic culture that fundamentally rejected the use of state power to subjugate foreign nations. The enduring relevance of domestic restraint is especially important during the Wilson presidency because of the reduction in incentives for the legislature to balance the executive. Since the opposition party (Republicans) favored expansionism, and members of the majority party largely supported their leader (Wilson), there was only weak institutional balancing. This institutional configuration brought personal values and executive restraint to the forefront of analysis in several of the cases and demonstrates the many pathways of restraint possible in a decentralized state.

Notes

1. This chapter includes seven cases of expansion or potential expansion. Missing from the list of cases is the US entry into World War I. There are two main reasons why this excluded. First, it seems unlikely that the United States would want to or be able to hold territory in Europe. To my knowledge there was no consideration of implementing any territorial expansion, and so it would be hard to justify this as a case study for the purposes of this book. Second, war itself is not necessarily an expansionist act. For example, the War of 1898 is not a case for the purposes of this book; the nonannexation of Cuba and the annexation of the Philippines are cases. Similarly, the Philippine-American War is a case because it was a war of conquest by the United States.

2. Munro 1964, 271.

3. Munro 1964, 269–274.

4. See Schmidt 1995, 46.

5. Wilson was fundamentally anti-imperialist in his thinking, but sometimes viewed American political–military expansion as the best way to alleviate or prevent European imperialism. Thus he had something of a double standard when it came to comparing European and American territorial expansion.

6. Herring 2008, 390–391; Clements 1980, 114; Schoultz 1998, 238–242; Langley 2002, 72–77; Link 1956, 347–348; Gardner 1982, 4–11. Taft-appointed American Ambassador to Mexico Henry Lane Wilson was indirectly involved in the plot to depose and murder Madero (Schoultz 1998, 240; Langley 2002, 75–76).

7. Clements 1980, 116.

8. Clements 1980, 118.

9. Clements 1980, 114–118; Schoultz 1998, 241–245; Cooper 2009, 240–242. See also Herring 2008, 391–392; Langley 2002, 77–82; Link 1956, 387.

10. Clements 1980, 119–123; Herring 2008, 391–392; Link 1956, 382–391; Haley 1970, 123–131; Gardner 1982, 11–23.

11. Herring 2008, 393.

12. Quoted in Schoultz 1998, 246.

13. Clements 1980, 123–124; Schoultz 1998, 245–246; Herring 2008, 391–394; Langley 2002, 82–84, 86–89; Cooper 2009, 242–243; Link 1956, 395–399; Quirk 1962, 1–77. Estimates on the dead and wounded vary; see Schoultz 1998, 246; Langley 2002, 95.

14. Langley 2002, 85–86; Quirk 1962, 69–70.

15. Quirk 1962, 85.

16. In fact, the United States was lucky to take so few casualties; Quirk 1962, 95. Estimates on the dead and wounded vary. See Quirk 1962, 103; Schoultz 1998, 246; Langley 2002, 95. Wilson was assured by Lind and Fletcher that the occupation would be achieved "without the loss of a single life"; Haley 1970, 131.

17. Clements 1980, 123–124; Schoultz 1998, 245–246; Herring 2008, 391–394; Langley 2002, 82–84, 86–95; Cooper 2009, 242–243.; Link 1956, 399–400; Quirk 1962, 78–120, 123.

18. Herring 2008, 393; Trow 1971, 49.

19. Haley 1970, 130.

20. Clements 1980, 124–126; Herring 2008, 393–394; Langley 2002, 97–108; Cooper 2009, 243–245; Link 1956, 400–416; Quirk 1962, 104–105, 126–128; Haley 1970, 133–134; Clements 1992, 99. For a detailed description of the American occupation of Veracruz see Quirk 1962, 121–155.

21. Clements 1980, 127–130.

22. Gardner 1982, 26.

23. Clements 1980, 127.

24. Clements 1980, 129, 133, passim.

25. Link 1956, 397, 401.

26. Link 1956, 399.

27. Cooper 2009, 244.

28. Cooper 2009, 244–245.

29. See the sources cited in Link 1956, 403–405. Quirk argues the American public reaction was positive except for Republicans that wanted Wilson to take Mexico City, though the source of this argument is unclear. Quirk 1962, 113–114.

30. Schoultz 1998, 246.

31. Link 1956, 405.

32. Clements 1980, 115, 117, 119–120, 125; Gardner 1982, 3–48.

33. John Lind quoted in Clements 1980, 120. See also Schoultz 1998, 244.

34. Schmidt 1995, 35–41; Baker 1961, 99; Langley 2002, 117, 119.

35. Baker 1961, 277–278; Calhoun 1986, 89; Schmidt 1995, 42–43; Langley 2002, 119; Musicant 1990, 158–160.

36. Healy 1976, 123.

37. Schmidt 1995, 54–63; Baker 1961, 97–125; Langley 2002, 111, 117, 120; Munro 1964, 326–327, 349; Calhoun 1986, 87–89; Blassingame 1969, 27–43; Healy 1976, 123–124.

38. Baker 1961, 100–125; Schmidt 1995, 61–63; Calhoun 1986, 87–99.

39. Calhoun 1986, 86–94.

40. It was common for the United States and European powers to send gunboats or briefly land marines to protect foreign property in the event of violence in foreign countries.

41. Calhoun 1986, 100; Langley 2002, 123;

42. Schmidt 1995, 64–70; Baker 1961, 272–277; Calhoun 1986, 100–102; Langley 2002, 121–124; Healy 1976, 43–65.

43. For example, American, British, and German forces landed during a 1914 revolution. Baker 1961, 102–103; Calhoun 1986, 89.

44. Baker 1961, 97; Musicant 1990, 158.
45. Caperton quoted in Healy 1976, 69.
46. Baker 1961, 282; Blassingame 1969, 27–43; Healy 1976, 122–123.
47. Long quoted in Healy 1976, 126.
48. Healy 1976, 127–131.
49. Munro 1964, 351–354; Calhoun 1986, 101–102; Calhoun 1993, 57–58.
50. Quoted in Baker 1961, 276; Healy 1976, 129.
51. Munro 1964, 354–356; Schmidt 1995, 74; Langley 2002, 123–125; Baker 1961, 279–280; Healy 1976, 66–67, 71, 75–84, 91–117.
52. Schmidt 1995, 77; see also Baker 1961, 288–289.
53. Healy 1976, 131–132.
54. See Bickel 2001, 69–105.
55. Schmidt 1995, 76–77; Munro 1964, 360–361; Baker 1961, 280–287, 292; Langley 2002, 127–129; Healy 1976, 131–137, 144–185.
56. Schmidt 1995, 77; see also Munro 1964, 361.
57. Calhoun 1986, 102.
58. Calhoun 1986, 103.
59. Baker 1961, 287–288; Blassingame 1969, 37–40, passim.
60. Baker 1961, 281–283.
61. Munro 1964, 364.
62. Munro 1964, 361–365; Musicant 1990, 206–207. On the functioning of the constabulary see Baker 1961, 296–297.
63. Baker 1961, 299–300.
64. Munro 1964, 367–368; Baker 1961, 302–304.
65. Munro 1964, 374; Baker 1961, 301–304.
66. Langley 2002, 150–151; Munro 1964, 369–371; Healy 1976, 202–205, 211.
67. Healy 1976, 205.
68. Munro 1964, 371–374; Langley 2002, 152–157.
69. Langley 2002, 158; Shannon 1996, 54–56.
70. Shannon 1996, 54–55; Blassingame 1969, 41–42.
71. Blassingame 1969, 42, 40.
72. Cooper 2009, 248.
73. Calhoun 1986, 70–72.
74. Calhoun 1986, 88–89.
75. Quoted in Blassingame 1969, 33.
76. Blassingame 1969, 34.
77. Blassingame 1969, 35, 36.
78. Blassingame 1969, 37.
79. Blassingame 1969, 37.
80. Calder 1984, xii; Atkins and Wilson 1998, 38, 40–41; Baker 1961, 62–63. A survey of newspaper editorials shows that these concerns were common knowledge in early twentieth-century America (Blassingame 1969, 27–43).
81. Baker 1961, 62; Blassingame 1969, 35–37; MacMichael 1964, 278–282.
82. Calder 1984, 5; MacMichael 1964, 304–336.
83. MacMichael 1964, 271–441.
84. MacMichael 1964, 330–347; Baker 1961, 75–87.
85. For the text of the Wilson Plan see *FRUS 1914*, 247–248.

86. Calder 1984, 5–6; Munro 1964, 274–295; Herring 2008, 388; MacMichael 1964, 353–361; Atkins and Wilson 1998, 45–47; Baker 1961, 87–90.

87. Calder 1984, 6–7; Munro 1964, 295–307; MacMichael 1964, 362, 388–406; Atkins and Wilson 1998, 47–48; Baker 1961, 90–95, 249–256. See also the correspondence in FRUS 1915, 279–339.

88. Munro 1964, 306–314; MacMichael 1964, 407–427; Langley 2002, 133–141; Atkins and Wilson 1998, 49–50; Baker 1961, 256–264. Russell quoted in Baker 1961, 264. The debt figures are from FRUS 1915, 321–325, 326–327.

89. Calder 1984, 10.

90. Wilson quoted in Langley 2002, 144. MacMichael argues that Wilson was almost totally ignorant of what was going on in the Dominican Republic and that Secretary of State Lansing (who had replaced Bryan) misrepresented the situation, making it sound as if revolution were imminent unless the United States acted. See MacMichael 1964, 432–434.

91. Munro 1964, 313–316; MacMichael 1964, 427–439; Calder 1984, 16–19; Langley 2002, 144–145; Baker 1961, 264–268.

92. Munro 1964, 314; Calder 1984, 21–22; MacMichael 1964, 437–438.

93. Calder 1984, 22.

94. Blassingame 1969, 27–43.

95. Blassingame 1969, 39–43.

96. Blassingame 1969, 42.

97. Baker 1961, 270; Cooper 2009, 248–249.

98. Baker 1961, 85, 96, 266; Cooper 2009, 248. See also MacMichael 1964, 256–441.

99. Calder 1984, 22.

100. Calder 1984, 22.

101. Schoultz 1998, 221.

102. Schoultz 1998, 224; Baker 1961, 31.

103. New York Times headline quoted in Baker 1961, 35.

104. Borah quoted in Link 1956, 36–37.

105. Schoultz 1998, 221, 224–226; Baker 1961, 31–46; Link 1956, 336–338.

106. Wilson quoted in Baker 1961, 46.

107. Schoultz 1998, 226–227; Baker 1961, 46–52; Link 1956, 338–339.

108. Schoultz 1998, 221, 224–227; Baker 1961, 52–61; Link 1956, 339–340.

109. Walker 2003, 21; FRUS 1916, 849–852.

110. Walker 2003, 21.

111. Schoultz 1998, 229.

112. Schoultz 1998, 228–229; Rosenberg and Rosenberg 1987, 67; Link 1956, 340–341.

113. Walker 2003, 21.

114. Link 1956, 34–35.

115. Clendenen 1961, 296–304; Harris and Sadler 1978, 402–405.

116. Clendenen 1961, 193.

117. Wilson quoted in Link 1964, 200.

118. Wilson quoted in Link 1964, 200.

119. Columbus was garrisoned by the Headquarters and Machine Gun Troops and 7 Rifle Troops of the 13th Cavalry, with about 553 soldiers, some of which were deployed along the border when Villa attacked; Hurst 2008, 23. The number of killed and wounded on each side ranges from 15 to 19 Americans killed and 67 to 167 Mexicans killed.

120. Sandos 1981, 295–301; Hall and Coerver 1997, 176–177, 180–182; Haley 1970, 187–188; Clendenen 1961, 225–242, 249–250; Link 1964, 205. For a detailed description of the Plan of San Diego see Harris and Sadler 1978, 381–408.

121. Haley 1970, 190.

122. Trow 1971, 49–50.

123. Sandos 1981, 301. See also Hurst 2008, 37–38, 42; Clendenen 1961, 247; Link 1964, 206–207; Herring 2008, 396. For a discussion of Catholic opinion see Link 1964, 197–199.

124. Schoultz 1998, 248–249.

125. War plan quoted in Hall and Coerver 1997, 186. See also Link 1964, 207, 211, 213.

126. Herring 2008, 396.

127. Sandos 1981, 301–302; Herring 2008, 396; Haley 1970, 188–195; Hurst 2008, 40–42; Clendenen 1961, 249–257.

128. Link 1964, 215; Haley 1970, 194; Hall and Coerver 1997, 190. See also Link 1964, 212–213.

129. Wilson quoted in Link 1964, 213. Emphasis in the original.

130. Link 1964, 214.

131. Sandos 1981, 302–304; Herring 2008, 394–395; Hurst 2008, 44–100. The older interpretation of the Punitive Expedition was that it was a failure; see Katz 1978, 101–130. Some argue that the cross-border raids against American towns were sponsored by the Carranza government; see Harris and Sadler 1978, 381–408.

132. FRUS 1916, 522.

133. Haley 1970, 195–212; Clendenen 1961, 266–269; Link 1964, 282–285. For a detailed account of the skirmish at Parral see Hurst 2008, 76–81. For a detailed analysis of how the threat of war with Germany affected US policy toward Mexico see Clendenen 1961, 296–304.

134. House quoted in Haley 1970, 214.

135. Haley 1970, 212–215; Herring 2008, 396; Sandos 1981, 303–306; Schoultz 1998, 249; Hurst 2008, 89–97; Clendenen 1961, 270–278; Harris and Sadler 1978, 398–402; Link 1964, 291–303. On the planned Mexican invasion of Texas see Harris and Sadler 1978, 395–398. The invasion was scrapped and instead Carranzistas contented themselves with cross-border raids.

136. Haley 1970, 215–219; Hall and Coerver 1997, 186–187; Herring 2008, 396; Sandos 1981, 306–307; Schoultz 1998, 249; Hurst 2008, 89–97; Clendenen 1961, 278–288; Link 1964, 203–314.

137. Schoultz 1998, 249.

138. Wilson quoted in Schoultz 1998, 249.

139. Schoultz 1998, 249–250.

140. Schoultz 1998, 250; Cooper 2009, 321–323.

141. Link 1964, 315.

142. Link 1964, 317.

143. Hall and Coerver 1997, 191.

144. Sandos 1981, 308–310; Haley 1970, 219–223; Cooper 2009, 322–323; Link 1964, 314–318.

145. Link 1982, 36. See also Cooper 2009, 322.

146. Link 1964, 315–318. See also Link 1982, 36.

147. Link 1982, 36. See also Cooper 2009, 322.

148. Clendenen 1961, 296–304; Harris and Sadler 1978, 402–405.

149. Cooper 2009, 321–323; Link 1964, 292.

150. Schoultz 1998, 297; Pérez 1986, 167–168; Baker 1961, 359–368; Meyer 1930, 138–145, 158–159.

151. For example, Commander Reginald Belknap prevented Cuban government forces from using the Santiago harbor in return for a pledge by the Liberals not to close the harbor by sinking ships at its entrance. Domínguez 1978, 16–17; Munro 1964, 495–496.

152. In March 1917 Cuba requested the withdrawal of the US Marines, but the State Department believed the situation was still too unstable. See Baker 1961, 366–367. Later Menocal formally approved of the presence of American troops on Cuban soil to train for deployment to Europe (Baker 1961, 368).

153. Chapman 1927, 362–385, 388; Pérez 1986, 168–170; Hernández 1993, 175; Baker 1961, 363–367; Meyer 1930, 145–163; Musicant 1990, 73–74, 76–78; Munro 1964, 490–497.

154. Crowder worked on electoral reform during the 1906–1909 occupation of Cuba.

155. Pérez 1986, 70–74; Chapman 1927, 400–402; Baker 1961, 424; Munro 1964, 503–507.

156. Pérez 1986, 175–181; Chapman 1927, 402–407; Baker 1961, 424–425; Pérez 1973, 5–8; Schoultz 2002, 407; Munro 1964, 509–521.

157. *FRUS 1921*, 672. See also *FRUS 1920*, V. II, 43.

158. Munro 1964, 521.

159. Pérez 1986, 190–195; Domínguez 1978, 18–19; Schoultz 2002, 407; Munro 1964, 521–524; *FRUS 1921*, 672.

160. Baker 1961, 366–368; Meyer 1930, 151, 160–162, 165; Musicant 1990, 76–78.

161. Pérez 1986, 194.

162. Pérez 1986, 72–73.

163. Henry Cabot Lodge quoted in Trow 1971, 46–47. See also Weaver 1985, 58.

164. Schoultz 1998, 251; Rosenberg 1975, 125.

165. Machado and Judge 1970, 3–7.

166. Schoultz 1998, 251.

167. Trow 1971, 50.

168. Trow 1971, 50–55; Schoultz 1998, 251; Machado and Judge 1970, 7–8; Rosenberg 1975, 123–152.

169. Machado and Judge 1970, 7.

170. Trow 1971, 49–50.

171. Trow 1971, 55–59; Machado and Judge 1970, 5–13.

172. Machado and Judge 1970, 8–9, 13–14.

173. Trow 1971, 59–62; Weaver 1985, 58; Machado and Judge 1970, 14–17.

174. Trow 1971, 64. See also Machado and Judge 1970, 17.

175. Machado and Judge 1970, 18.

176. Trow 1971, 46–72; Schoultz 1998, 251; Weaver 1985, 58–59; Machado and Judge 1970; Rosenberg 1975, 123–152.

177. Trow 1971, 63–66; Machado and Judge 1970, 18–20.

178. Trow 1971, 66–71; Machado and Judge 1970, 19–20; Clements 1992, 103.

179. Trow 1971, 71–72.

180. Machado and Judge 1970, 22.

181. Wilson quoted in Machado and Judge 1970, 20; Trow 1971, 70.
182. Machado and Judge 1970, 22; Clements 1987, 131–132.
183. For example see the record of Wilson's 1916 interview with Ray Stannard Baker (Link 1982, 36).
184. Machado and Judge 1970, 23.
185. Rosenberg 1999, 91.
186. Rosenberg 1999, 92.
187. Nordholt 1991; Clements 1987; Clements 1992; Cooper 2009.

6

★

REPUBLICAN
INTERREGNUM

1921–1933

T HE YEARS FOLLOWING Woodrow Wilson's second term as president mark the recession of the second wave of American expansionism. As demonstrated in the previous chapter, the second wave, like the first, was limited in its reach by the political structure of the United States. During the Wilson years American norms and institutions did not prevent expansion from occurring, but did significantly limit the scope and intensity of American expansionism. The Republican interregnum (1921–1933) was a transition period between the Wilson era when mainstream American leaders still advocated for political–military expansionism, and the ultimate disavowal of interference in the internal politics of foreign countries by the Franklin D. Roosevelt administration. During the interregnum, the general goal of presidents Harding, Coolidge, and Hoover was to reduce the level and amount of American political–military control over foreign territory. Success came in fits and starts, and was interspersed with moments of reversion such as the military intervention in Nicaragua in 1926 and the attempts at gaining further control over Liberian fiscal and military affairs in 1922. But in general, the United States tried to make up for what was now perceived to be past mistakes. For example, a payment of $25 million was made to Colombia as compensation for Theodore Roosevelt's encouragement of Panamanian secession and the Roosevelt Corollary was quietly revoked. The Republican administrations also began liquidating US protectorates by ending the US occupation of the Dominican Republic in 1924 and Nicaragua in 1933.[1]

Republican foreign policy of the 1920s was largely a reaction to the foreign policy of Woodrow Wilson—or, more precisely, public reaction to Wilson's foreign policy. The election of 1920 can only be seen as a rebuke to Wilson and the Democrats; the Republican Party regained the presidency and majorities in both Houses of Congress. Not only did Republicans reject the League of Nations, they also stepped back from Wilson's strategy of teaching our neighbors to the south to "elect good men" and were distinctly more differential toward Congress.[2] The slogan of the day was "Back to Normalcy."[3] The shift in mainstream Republican thinking was consistent with the attitudes of an American public that had become more anti-interventionist since the end of World War I.[4] Warren G. Harding was the first president of the post-Wilson era and set the stage for his Republican successors. Harding's central goals included "reduction of United States commitments in the area [Western Hemisphere], replacing military intervention with diplomatic persuasion, and relying on the resulting good will to promote ties and trade."[5] Intervention was not renounced, but was relabeled "interposition" by Harding's Secretary of State Charles Evans Hughes and de-emphasized as much as possible.[6] The outlook of the new president and his Secretary of State Charles Evans Hughes was fundamentally different from the approach of the Wilson administration. They sought to improve relations with Latin American countries and rejected military intervention as a tool of foreign policy in the Western Hemisphere: "They believed that abandoning armed intervention in favor of advice and counsel would foster good will in Latin America and ultimately benefit the United States by enabling it to garner the trade and support of the region. The president and secretary of state also contended that such a policy could stabilize the area and thereby render the military interventions of the past unnecessary."[7]

Presidents Coolidge and Hoover followed in the path created by President Harding and Secretary of State Hughes. Latin American policy was largely viewed through an economic lens (with some important exceptions), with political–military intervention perceived as being deeply unpopular and inappropriate. Coolidge presided over the final withdrawal from the Dominican Republic, but also the military occupation of Nicaragua and a war scare with Mexico. Hoover consistently practiced restraint, most importantly in refusing to consider intervention in the Dominican Republic in 1930–1931 and withdrawing from Nicaragua. It was also under Coolidge and Hoover that the Roosevelt Corollary was quietly revoked with the Clark Memorandum.[8]

Despite the increased restraint, several conditions that favor expansion are still relevant to American foreign policy between 1921 and 1933. First, the United States maintained its relative material power advantage over other countries in the world. Second, the relative US power advantage continued to grow until the late 1920s. Third, policy legacies weighed heavily on the presidents of this era. Even though US presidents generally sought to reduce American political–military control of foreign territory, they did not perceive immediate pullout of US forces to be practical in the short run. Fourth, power vacuums and political instability in the near abroad remained a problem in the Caribbean

Basin, providing justification for intervention. Fifth, American leaders began to perceive communism as a growing threat in the Western Hemisphere. The desire to prevent the spread of communism provided a new ideological rationale for expansion.

The following nine cases illustrate how the few attempts at expansionism were restrained by norms and institutions and how some of the vestiges of previous episodes of political–military expansion were liquidated during the Republican interregnum.

Attempted Increase in Financial Oversight in Liberia (1917–1922)

Beginning in 1912 the United States exercised considerable, if informal, influence over Liberian politics and policy through its leadership in the multinational customs receivership that included Great Britain, France, and Germany. As the multinational receivership fell apart with the beginning of World War I, the United States looked to gain more control over the fiscal and military policy of Liberia in order to increase political stability in the West African country. Between 1917 and 1920 the two countries agreed to increase American oversight of Liberian finances and formalize American control through a treaty. American officials felt an obligation to Liberia because of prior commitments. The treaty was first delayed by Liberian opposition and then killed in 1922 when the US Senate failed to give its consent.

Lansing's Ultimatum and the 1920 Financial Plan

The multinational banking consortium installed in 1912 as receivers of customs in Liberia was dysfunctional from the start, and by 1917 the agreement was falling apart. In April of 1917 Secretary of State Lansing sent a message to the Liberian government warning that a new financial arrangement must be agreed upon or else the United States would "withdraw the friendly support" it was providing Liberia.[9] Lansing's memo contained a list of reforms that Liberia should implement, and in return they would receive a loan from the US government through a World War I loan program for allies.[10]

The most important aspect of the new agreement proposed by Lansing was to empower the American financial advisor to supervise all government receipts and expenditures. This supervision was specified through a list of duties the financial advisor would perform, provided in Lansing's memo. Throughout his memo Lansing made various demands, ranging from requiring the Liberian government to consult with the financial advisor to giving the advisor veto power over Liberian policy.[11] The Liberian government agreed to Lansing's demands and the suggested reforms were adopted by the end of the year, at least on paper.[12] In return, the United States established a $5 million credit for Liberia.[13]

The reforms agreed upon in 1917 were to be formalized in a 1920 agreement providing for the disbursement of a $5 million dollar loan from the United States to Liberia. The draft of the 1920 financial plan sent to the Liberian government gave American officials almost complete control over Liberian government finances and a good deal of authority over the Liberian Frontier Force. Under the agreement, the US Receivership Administration—including the general receiver, the financial advisor, and other officials as needed—had authority over "the administration and collection of all the Assigned Revenues and Receipts and the application of the Assigned Revenues and Receipts" for the life of the loan. The Receivership Administration officials were to be designated by the President of the United States and appointed by the President of Liberia.[14] Under the 1920 plan, the general receiver would control all customs and internal revenues and the commissioner general of the interior would manage relations with the native tribes in Liberia and the Frontier Force.[15] The financial plan was not submitted to the US Senate as a treaty, but was instead to be implemented under the wartime authority granted to the Secretary of the Treasury; American officials knew that such a treaty would not receive senatorial consent in the United States.[16]

Liberian President C.D.B. King opposed the draft financial plan and did not recognize the authority granted the financial advisor in the 1917 agreement. The Liberian Congress approved a revised financial plan that reduced the authority of American officials. Control of revenue was crucial for the ability of Liberian leaders to stay in power and to enrich themselves and their supporters. Furthermore, the financial advisor serving in 1920 (H. F. Worley) was highly incompetent, which not only discouraged Liberia from giving him more power but also significantly reduced American influence over Liberian finances. Later it would become clear that Worley was not actively supervising Liberian finances.[17]

President King came to Washington in 1921 to renegotiate the treaty, arriving two days after the inauguration of Warren G. Harding. After consultation with American officials, a new treaty with some symbolic changes was signed and quickly approved by the Liberian legislature. However, by this time the US Senate had begun an investigation of the American wartime loans program. To avoid a confrontation with the Senate, the Treasury Department decided the financial plan was not a wartime loan and therefore would have to be approved by the US Congress. The State Department disagreed, but President Harding supported the Treasury Department and the agreement was submitted to Congress. In testimony to the House Ways and Means Committee, Secretary of State Hughes argued that the United States had "a moral obligation" to Liberia to go ahead with the loan.[18] The House passed the loan bill on a vote of 148 to 139 on May 10, 1922. Hughes and Harding encouraged the Senate to approve the financial plan, but on November 27, 1922, the Senate voted to recommit the bill to the Finance Committee on a vote of 42 to 33, thereby assuring that the joint resolution to authorize the loan would not reach the Senate floor again.[19] Congressional opponents of the plan were upset over profligacy of the wartime loan program and concerned that speculators would end up benefiting the most from the loan.[20]

The 1912 informal custom receivership continued, but the Liberian government reduced the influence of the general receiver of customs by increasing the hut tax and thereby decreasing Liberian reliance on customs revenues.[21] Various other reforms were undertaken to increase government revenues, leading to revenues in 1925 that were 275 percent more than in 1918.[22]

In conclusion, between 1917 and 1922 the United States attempted to gain almost total control of Liberian finances and military power. For a time control did increase, at least on paper, but resistance of the Liberian government and the refusal of the Senate to approve the 1920 financial plan prevented the American aims from being achieved. Thus the institution of separation of powers prevented the expansion of American control over the sovereign responsibilities of the Liberian government. The US Congress was empowered by a growing sense of executive deference to the role of the legislative branch. Senators were unhappy with executive branch policy and therefore vetoed it. Security and economic interests did not play major roles in decision making.

The Moral Readjustment of Cuba (1921–1923)

When Harding took office General Enoch Crowder was serving as Woodrow Wilson's personal representative on special mission to Cuba. Harding retained Crowder and entrusted him with the task of establishing sufficient stability in Cuban politics to alleviate the need for American military intervention.[23] Secretary of State Hughes ordered Crowder to make financial stability his highest priority. Crowder was instructed to "advise the Cuban Government, in particular, as to the solutions which may be found for the present disturbing financial conditions."[24] The financial crisis and years of deficit spending had left the Cuban government almost bankrupt. A loan was vital to shore up public finances and bail out sugar producers devastated by the drop in sugar prices. This situation gave Crowder considerable leverage in dealing with the Zayas government, because no bank would loan money to Cuba without the support of the State Department. Crowder forced Zayas to implement a variety of reforms in Cuban finances and governance to solve the problems of profligate spending and widespread corruption. Opposition to austerity measures was high, but it was Crowder's pressure to reduce corruption that struck at the foundation of political power in Cuba. Many of his recommendations were reluctantly accepted or successfully opposed through delaying tactics.[25]

By the fall of 1921, General Crowder decided that President Zayas required a firmer approach. His chance to increase his pressure on Zayas came when Cuba applied for a $5 million short-term loan from J. P. Morgan. Crowder succeeded in getting Zayas's commitment to budget reductions in return for State Department approval of the loan. Zayas agreed to a reduced budget and committed to reforming the tax system as conditions for the $5 million loan and the promise of a $50 million loan to be granted later. When Zayas's commitment to reform was found to be insufficient, Secretary Hughes expanded Crowder's authority through a reinterpretation of the Platt Amendment. According to Hughes's interpretation, fiscal insolvency threatened life, liberty, and property, and therefore the United States had full authority to intervene in Cuban fiscal policy.[26] Pérez argues that Hughes "effectively if not formally conferred parallel executive authority on Crowder."[27] At the same time, the United States sought to lessen the impact of Crowder's imposition by withdrawing the marines from Camagüey province at the request of the Cuban government in January of 1922.[28]

By the spring of 1922 Crowder was issuing a series of ultimatums to the Cuban government with the goal of "moral readjustment in the National Administrative life of the Cuban government."[29] In practice this meant a reorganization of public administration at all levels of government in Cuba. Crowder's crowning achievement was compelling Zayas to accept the installment of the "honest cabinet" chosen by Crowder. Many of Crowder's reforms became lost in a bureaucratic maze of overlapping authority and obstructionism, but he was also able to extract some level of compliance by holding out the promise of the $50 million loan and consistent diplomatic pressure from the State Department.[30]

Crowder originally sought to threaten Zayas with American military intervention, but this approach was vetoed by Secretary Hughes, who proclaimed that military intervention was not an option "because public opinion would not stand for it."[31] Hughes consistently instructed Crowder to avoid the implication that he was giving the Cuban government ultimatums.[32]

The End of American Intervention

In 1923 Cuba received the loan and began running budget surpluses. Crowder left his post as proconsul and became ambassador to Cuba. With Crowder out of the way and the financial crises ameliorated, Zayas could get to work reversing Crowder's reforms. The accomplishments of Crowder's two years as de facto coexecutive were quickly done away with, starting with the dismissal of the honest cabinet. Patronage politics replaced Crowder's moral readjustment program, and the only response from the United States was a series of warnings that were promptly ignored by President Zayas. Military intervention was no longer considered an option. Intervention on the scale of 1906 (or even 1921) had proven to be ineffective and even counterproductive. The total reform of the Cuban political system was not possible, and attempts to do so threatened to cause further political instability. The 1921–1923 intervention demonstrated that the United States could only shape Cuban politics while it exercised direct control. With the passage of the Cuban financial crisis the United States had little leverage with the Cuban government except through the threat of intervention, which Hughes was not willing to use. By the early 1920s US policy shifted decisively to nonintervention in Latin America and the Caribbean.[33]

The existing evidence suggests that American leaders believed that military intervention (or at least the threat of military intervention) was necessary to maintain good government in Cuba, but that they were restrained from even making the threat of intervention because American public opinion and Latin American public opinion would be against it. As noted above, Secretary Hughes cited public opinion when explaining why military intervention was not even considered to be an option. He did not question the efficacy of the use of force; he specifically stated that public opinion would not allow it. Hughes even refused to discuss the possibility of military intervention with Liberal leader General Gómez when he traveled to Washington in 1921 to ask for US military intervention to force a new election.[34] In addition, top Republicans were aware that even the hint of imperialism could be costly in the 1924 election, which fostered restraint during the period when Zayas rolled back Crowder's reforms. Finally, the Harding (and later Coolidge) administration was concerned about public opinion in Latin America during the lead-up to the Pan-American Conference of 1923, and did not want its policy in Cuba to stand in the way of its broader policy of rapprochement with Latin America.[35]

In this case the United States clearly exercised significant political control over Cuban politics through the efforts of Omar Crowder. For the two years that Crowder served as virtual copresident in Cuba he made significant achievements, especially in the area of fiscal policy, turning deep deficits into a budget surplus. However, the overall effect of Crowder's reforms was shallow and temporary. As soon as the United States approved the $50 million loan to Cuba it lost its leverage. Maintenance of Crowder's reforms would have required additional political–military pressure and possibly another round of military occupation. The leadership in Washington was restrained by its unwillingness to risk the negative public opinion in the United States and Latin America that would have resulted from increased political–military pressure on the Zayas regime. Therefore, unlike in 1906, the United States rejected the military occupation option and accepted its declining influence on Cuban politics.

This case is coded as limited expansion caused by elements of anti-imperialism in American strategic culture, which operated through the mechanisms of American public opinion and electoral incentives. Another important factor was the desire to court Latin American public opinion. The general belief among American leaders was that better, more equal relations with Latin American countries would be beneficial in both the economic and strategic arenas, and thus this was a secondary restraining factor. There were no specific economic interest groups pushing for restraint, nor were there any security concerns that fostered restraint.

Withdrawal from Dominican Republic (1924)

The United States began its occupation of the Dominican Republic under the Wilson administration with the intention of putting Dominican finances on more solid ground and establishing stability through constitutional government. The occupation quickly succumbed to mission creep, and the military government, ruling by decree, set to work reengineering the infrastructure of Dominican society. As the occupation reached its fourth year without any end in sight, Dominicans increased their opposition to American occupation and established a sophisticated lobbying apparatus in the United States and across Latin America. They were aided by an increasingly critical American press, public, State Department, and Congress. As President Harding took office, efforts to end the occupation increased in urgency. Through a long and torturous process, Harding administration officials managed the end of the occupation. However, Harding's policy was not without critics. The American occupation forces believed that the goals of maintaining security and long-term stability in the Dominican Republic were being undermined by ending the occupation so soon. American agents such as the military governor Rear Admiral Samuel S. Robinson did their best to slow down the process of American withdrawal for reasons of national security.

Negotiating the End of US Military Occupation

Extricating the United States from the Dominican Republic was high on President Warren Harding's list of foreign policy priorities when he took office on March 4, 1921. Harding's plan for withdrawal was announced on June 2, 1921, by Rear Admiral Samuel S. Robinson, the military governor of the Dominican Republic. The plan called for a committee of Dominicans chosen by Robinson to achieve the following: ratify all the acts of the occupation government, extend the powers of the American customs receiver to include supervision of all government revenue if needed to fund loan repayment, extend the life of the customs receivership until loans taken out under the occupation government were repaid, and increase American control of the Guardia Nacional until it was ready to take over the task of providing peace and stability. Dominican leaders strongly opposed Harding's plan. The most objectionable provision was the last: Dominicans feared that American control of the Guardia Nacional could be extended indefinitely, and would amount to an indefinite de facto military occupation. Dominican leaders were constrained by public opinion due to the assumption that whoever agreed to the conditions proposed by the Americans could not win an election in the Dominican Republic after the Americans left. The Dominican nationalists were also encouraged by a US Senate investigation of the occupations of Haiti and the Dominican Republic and the continuing diplomatic problems caused by the occupations. Robinson attempted to mollify the opposition but this effort went nowhere, resulting in a standoff—Harding and Hughes were committed to withdrawal but felt it was necessary to preserve the achievements of the occupation government. By the summer of 1921, one clear change had taken place: the prowithdrawal State Department had gained control of US policy from the Navy Department and occupation government, which had consistently favored a prolonged occupation.[36]

At the same time, the Harding administration was suffering from a prowithdrawal "propaganda barrage."[37] The campaign for Dominican independence came from several quarters. Dominican leaders hired former US minister to the Dominican Republic Horace G. Knowles to lobby the US Congress and American newspapers. He accused US occupation forces of brutality and decried American imperialism. Former Dominican president Francisco Henríquez y Carvajal also represented Dominican interests in the United States, and was a constant reminder that the United States had overthrown the last elected president of the Dominican Republic. The Haiti-Santo Domingo Independence Society also contributed to the prowithdrawal lobby. *The Nation* magazine continued its attacks on American military intervention in general and the continued occupation of the Dominican Republic in particular. Republican Senator William E. Borah was the major political spokesperson for the cause of American withdrawal. The result of the lobbying and media campaign was the establishment of a Senate Foreign Relations Subcommittee to investigate the occupation of Hispaniola, chaired by Republican Senator Medill McCormick. The investigation and hearings lasted from 1921 through 1922, including a trip to the Dominican Republic. The subcommittee released a report in 1922, but withheld the section on the Dominican Republic at the request of Harding due to ongoing negotiations with the Dominicans.[38]

Negotiations within the Harding administration between Hughes and Secretary of the Navy Edwin Denby resulted in a new proposal for withdrawal that made only minor concessions to Dominican leaders'rprevious objections. The navy position had carried the day. When Russell and Robinson informed Dominican leaders of the revised American proposal in February of 1922, it was quickly rejected. Dominican leaders suggested that they could accept most of the American demands, except for a continued military mission. The Harding administration was unwilling to give in on this point, and so the occupation continued.

The focus was shifted to finishing public works programs and the training of the Guardia Nacional, and negotiation of a loan for the purposes of completing these projects. In the meantime, efforts were made to decrease the tension between the occupation forces and the Dominican people.[39]

By early 1922 the Dominican nationalist movement was stagnant, fragmented, and losing support among the people. The nationalists suffered from financial and organizational problems throughout 1922. Nationalists continued to take a hard line, while support for accommodation and compromise grew among the people. It had become clear that the Harding administration was not going to give in to nationalist demands, and that the Senate investigation was not likely to force a change in this position. After issuing an ultimatum, Military Governor Robinson revoked the Harding Plan and declared July 1, 1924, as the planned withdrawal date of occupation forces (later than under the Harding Plan), and soon after announced a $10 million loan to pay debts incurred under the occupation. The Dominican people were growing impatient and public sentiment was shifting toward making the necessary compromises to end the occupation. Leading politicians from Dominican political parties, Federico Velásquez and Horacio Vásquez, approached the military government with offers of compromise.[40]

Compromise and Withdrawal

Negotiations with Dominican leaders recommenced after a loan of $6.7 million for completion of the existing public works projects was arranged. The navy had pushed for a $10 million loan to cover a larger set of projects, but Hughes advocated loaning the minimum needed to complete existing projects, and Harding supported Hughes. This time the talks were held in Washington with Hughes and Sumner Welles, Chief of the Latin American Division, representing the United States and Francisco J. Peynado, General Horacio Vásquez, Federico Velasquez, and Elias Brache representing the Dominicans. The United States finally agreed to hand over complete control of the Guardia Nacional at the time of American withdrawal, and in return the Dominican leaders agreed to ratify the acts of the occupation government and acquiesced to an extension of the customs receivership. The deal also reduced American control of internal Dominican finances and eliminated American supervision of Dominican elections. After the announcement of the agreement June 30, 1922, all major Dominican political factions gave their support and it received positive coverage in the American press.[41]

The 1922 negotiations were successful largely because Dominican lawyer, businessman, and former cabinet official Francisco Peynado was able to establish a rapport with US officials, was willing to compromise, and able to come up with the proposal for an interim Dominican government during the withdrawal. In addition, Peynado's mission was aided by continuing nationalist attacks in the press coordinated by lobbyist Horace Knowles and an important antioccupation speech by Senator Borah. The work of Knowles increased the effectiveness of Peynado's negotiations by keeping up the public pressure on Harding administrative officials. Knowles continued to lobby the Senate committee, investigating the occupation of Hispaniola to continue gathering information on abuses and investigating the $10 million loan proposed by Military Governor Robison.[42] It was also important that Harding and Hughes were committed to withdrawing as quickly as possible.[43] The Harding administration was anxious to end the occupation and willing to make new concessions in order to move forward. Secretary Hughes captured the heart of the issue when he stated that the occupation was "proving gravely prejudicial to our prestige."[44]

Some Dominican nationalists and American military occupation officials opposed the Hughes-Peynado agreement, and considerable work was necessary to push through the final implementation of the withdrawal. Sumner Welles was dispatched to the Dominican Republic as Harding's personal representative to work out the details of the American withdrawal and measure Dominican public opinion. His major Dominican opponent was the Junta de Abstención Electoral, which advocated an immediate full withdrawal or "withdrawal *pura y simple*."[45] Nationalists were especially upset that the laws imposed on the country during the occupation would stand after the occupation ended. Welles and Dominican allies toured the country to promote the Hughes-Peynado agreement among the Dominican people, achieving considerable success. Welles also worked with Dominican political leaders to determine the details of the withdrawal agreement and convened a conference of political leaders to choose a provisional president. The final agreement was released to the public on September 23, 1922, with general support from the Dominican public and press. Nationalists followed the lead of the major political parties and prepared for the elections of the provisional government. Dominican supporters in the United States and abroad also accepted the agreement.[46]

However, Welles's most vital role was to ensure that US military officials in the Dominican Republic could not sabotage the agreement. Admiral Robinson continued to work to modify and delay the implementation of the Hughes-Peynado plan, because he did not view it as being consistent with military goals of maintaining security and long-term stability in the Dominican Republic. Military Governor Robison consistently raised objections to aspects of the agreement he found objectionable on military grounds. He saw the Washington agreement as "tentative" and subject to modification as needed. Welles, fearing that even slight changes would revive Dominican opposition, made it clear that the agreement was final. Both officials appealed to Washington. Harding's desire for a rapid withdrawal led him to side with Welles and the State Department; Robinson was instructed that Welles was the highest-ranking American official in the

Dominican Republic. Nevertheless, the military governor continued to stall, forcing Harding to intervene personally on occasion to keep the process moving forward. The president consistently supported Welles's conciliatory approach toward Dominican leaders. The conflict was between "military logic" and "political expediency," and the latter consistently won out.[47]

The Convention of Evacuation was signed on September 12, 1922. A provisional government was elected by the US-appointed Comision de Representates and the new president, Vicini Burgos, was inaugurated on October 21, 1922. The Burgos government was in charge of preparations for the election of a new president and Congress in 1924 and for day-to-day administration of the country. Marine commander Brigadier General Harry Lee took over for Robinson as military governor and concentrated on completing the training of the Guardia Nacional Dominicana and the public works projects. Marines transferred policing authority to the Guardia Nacional and were pulled back to several main bases. Welles also departed, but returned to help facilitate the election of a regular government. On March 15, 1924, General Horacio Vásquez was elected president and was inaugurated on July 12. The last American marine left on September 18. American withdrawal immediately helped US standing in the Dominican Republic and Latin America.[48]

After the withdrawal of American military forces one final issue remained to be settled: control of Dominican finances. Since the Dominican Republic had several outstanding loans, a customs receivership had to continue in some form. At the beginning of the negotiations the United States suggested several modifications to the existing Customs Convention of 1907. First, the limit on Dominican debt was increased, and a provision for arbitration of disputes between the United States and Dominican Republic was added. Second, the amount of customs revenue contributed to the retirement of bonds was decreased. Third, the Dominican Republic was given the right to set its own tariff rates as long as sufficient customs revenue to service their debt was maintained. In conjunction with this concession by the United States, a most favored nation agreement was concluded between the two countries. On December 27, 1924, the Customs Convention of 1924 was signed, and it was ratified a month later by the US Senate. Opposition was significant in the Dominican Republic, but the treaty was ratified by the Dominican Senate in October of 1925 after four "explanations" were accepted by the United States as clarifying the treaty rather than changing its meaning.[49]

Explaining the End of an Occupation

In 1916 the United States intervened in the Dominican Republic with the goal of establishing political stability. In the years that followed, the means of establishing stability grew to include a total transformation of Dominican society through institutional change and large-scale investment in infrastructure and public works. In the process the United States established a military dictatorship—a benevolent dictatorship, but a dictatorship nonetheless. This was one of the most illiberal acts of the United States during the period of study. However, by the end of World War I, several factors combined to transform American policy from comprehensive reform of the Dominican Republic to rapid scaleback of responsibilities and total evacuation or American military forces. Most important was the reversion to an understanding of American national interests that privileged nonintervention. This reversion is clear in the public and private statements of American leaders as well as newspaper articles and editorials. What was the cause of this change?

In part, the retrenchment of American policy in the Dominican Republic is explained in the same way as previous examples of retrenchment described in earlier chapters: the US political structure is not well suited for long-term, resource-intensive projects such as military occupations. From this perspective, Dominican nationalists successfully implemented a cost-imposing strategy against the American occupation. Bruce Calder, the most important historian of the American occupation of the Dominican Republic, puts it this way: the propaganda and lobbying efforts of Dominican nationalists in the United States, Europe, and Latin America "were responsible . . . for withdrawal of the US forces from Santo Domingo. Their campaign made the military government's rule of the republic increasingly difficult, caused President Wilson's interventionist foreign policy to become a liability in US domestic politics, and brought extreme embarrassment and difficulty to the United States in its international relations."[50]

The fundamental reason that the cost-imposing strategy was successful is explained by focusing on American political structure. Because American political institutions are fragmented and characterized by checks and balances, the growing opposition to the occupation had many avenues for affecting American policy. When Dominican lobbying did not gain access to the executive branch it switched its efforts to influence Congress, the press, the public, and international opinion, and was successful. Because of the preexisting norms of antiimperialism, American foreign policy was always vulnerable to the imperialist critique. US policy was especially vulnerable to this critique in the 1920s because the hypocrisy of the American position was highlighted by the Wilsonian rhetoric of self-determination. Wilson himself recognized this issue, which led him to commit to nonintervention in Mexico and Cuba and move toward withdrawal in the Dominican Republic (at least rhetorically). Harding's election increased the pressure for withdrawal because he ran against Wilson's interventionist foreign policy, and therefore interpreted public opinion as being antiinterventionist. The aftermath of World War I was a time when Americans were growing tired of spending blood and treasure abroad. Harding's approach resonated during the election and was implemented as policy after the election.

This case is one of retrenchment caused by anti-imperialist norms and separation of powers. The public and many political leaders turned fundamentally against territorial expansion and occupation. Arguments for expansion that previously helped sway public opinion no longer seemed valid. Arguments on the grounds of security, prestige, mission, and economic prosperity were now primarily made in favor of restraint and withdrawal. Lobbying by advocates of Dominican independence gained support first from the press, public, and members of Congress, and then gained the support of the executive branch with the election of President Harding. Only agents of occupation in the Dominican Republic supported extending American political–military control and their arguments were rejected.

Withdrawal from Nicaragua (1925)

Between 1912 and 1925 the United States maintained a force of 100 marines in Nicaragua to maintain peace and stability. The so-called legation guard was not sufficient to prevent revolution through force of arms, but was seen as a symbol of American support for the ruling regime in Managua. As long as the United States maintained its small military presence, no one in Nicaragua would dare upset the existing political order. However, the situation was unsustainable for two reasons. First, the existing political order was Conservative, but the Liberal party enjoyed the support of a clear majority of the population. Therefore, Conservatives could only sustain their rule through intimidation and fraud, practices opposed by the United States. Second, the US political context was not conducive to a continued American military presence in Nicaragua. The post–World War I Republican foreign policy was strongly anti-Wilsonian, especially in the area of foreign interventions. The decision to end the US military deployment in Nicaragua was a result of the widespread understanding among political leaders that political–military intervention in foreign territory was deeply unpopular in the United States and was a detriment to US interests in the Western Hemisphere. Withdrawal proceeded even though all involved knew that civil war would be the result. American and Nicaraguan officials advocated for extending the American presence, but arguments based on the need to maintain stability in Central America no longer had the power that they once had.

Election of 1924

Under the political settlement formalized by the Bryan-Chamorro Treaty of 1916 and financial plan of 1917 and with the support of the 100-marine legation guard, the United States and Nicaraguan Conservatives established stability in Nicaragua. The economic boom during World War I led to budget surpluses, and "by 1924 the [Nicaraguan] government had repurchased its national bank and railroad, reduced its indebtedness by two-thirds, and begun to pay the awards of a claims commission."[51] However, Liberals chafed under Conservative rule and their dissatisfaction exposed the weak foundations of Nicaraguan political stability. With US support, Conservatives had maintained power at the cost of undermining democracy through three fraudulent elections between 1912 and 1920.

Protests by Liberals convinced the State Department to extract a pledge from the winner of the 1920 election—Diego Chamorro—that election laws would be reformed and a free and fair election would be held in 1924. The United States believed that long-term political stability could be established if a truly popular candidate was democratically elected president. Toward this end, the United States convinced the Nicaraguan government to institute electoral reforms between 1922 and 1923 authored by Harold Dodds of the US National Municipal League. The State Department also arranged for US officials to help implement the new electoral laws and for US marines to train a *Guaria Nacional*. However, by the time of the elections reforms were only partially implemented, and President Bartolomé Martínez refused an American offer to supervise the election. A Conservative-Liberal coalition ticket—Conservative Carlos Solórzano as president and Liberal Juan Sacasa as vice president—won a 1924 election marred by fraud. President Martínez supported the fusion ticket, but most Conservatives supported the candidacy of Emiliano Chamorro.[52] It was through Martínez's efforts that the Solórzano and Sacasa ticket won. Solórzano requested the continued presence of marines to support his regime, but American decision makers saw no reason for them to stay and they were pulled out several months after Solórzano's inauguration on January 1, 1925.[53]

Decision to Withdraw

Because of the protests by Solórzano and high-ranking American officials serving in Nicaragua, the United States maintained the legation guard for several months after the election. In the meantime it was the duty of the Nicaraguan government to train a Guaria Nacional (with US help) to maintain order. Despite last-minute complications, the United States kept its promise and US forces left Nicaragua on August 3, 1925.[54]

The end of the American military presence was part of the general strategy of Republican foreign policy—developed by Charles Hughes as a member of both the Harding and Coolidge administrations—to increase the popularity of the United States in Latin America by substituting diplomacy for military intervention. It was also based on a domestic political strategy built on the assumption that military interventions were unpopular and potentially costly at the ballot box. However, many American and Nicaraguan officials believed that the withdrawal of the final 100 marines would lead to a renewed civil war. Despite these warnings, the United States proceeded with the withdrawal. Part of the reason may have been that State Department officials were not entirely pleased with the results of the 1924 election, and therefore were not that concerned about the fate of the Solórzano-Sacasa therefor regime.[55] However, the most obvious reason for the withdrawal was that "from Washington's perspective nothing more remained to be done: Nicaragua's claims had been paid, its finances put in order, its foreign relations stabilized, and Dodds had done his best to set the government upon a democratic foundation."[56] The United States had come to view its military presence in Nicaragua as "a heavy political burden, especially with respect to public sentiment in Latin America.[57] Thus from the US perspective, there was no compelling reason to remain in Nicaragua. Furthermore, the legation guard itself was becoming more problematic. Its presence fostered anti-Americanism by frequently getting into trouble, at times even engaging in gunfights with local police.[58]

The withdrawal of the small American military force in Nicaragua occurred for several reasons. First, the presence of the American troops was always intended to be temporary; therefore it was simply an issue of specifying a date of withdrawal. Although it is certainly true that occupations can begin as temporary measures and then find reasons for perpetuating themselves. Second, and more importantly, public opinion in the United States and Latin America fostered withdrawal. Wilson's successors were committed to establishing a more positive image in Latin America and therefore took the opportunity to end the American military presence in Nicaragua to further that goal. Harding and Coolidge also viewed foreign policy retrenchment in the political and military spheres to be popular positions that would benefit them electorally.

The outcome of retrenchment is explained by the norm of American anti-imperialism acting through the mechanisms of public opinion and electoral calculations and the broader interest in improving relations with Latin America. A more long-term cause of the withdrawal from Nicaragua was the reduced power of expansionist incentives. The United States was still on the rise and maintained a large material power advantage over other countries in the world, but was becoming more reluctant to invest its power for territorial expansion. Opportunities remained viable, agents of empire maintained their faith in expansionism, and policy legacies continued to impose obligations on US leaders, but experience had shown that political–military expansion was not a viable option for the United States because its political structure would not allow it.

Nonintervention in Mexico (1925–1927)

Under President Harding a modus vivendi was established between Mexico and the United States that resolved the tension between the two countries left over from the Wilson-Carranza era.[59] The good feelings between the United States and Mexico lasted until 1925, when paranoia about President Calles's purported Bolshevism took hold among American political and business elites. Calles intensified the land redistribution program that was long a central pillar of revolutionary Mexico and ended international cooperation over debts, land, and oil issues. In response, President Coolidge and his secretary of state Frank Kellogg took a confrontational posture that triggered multiple diplomatic crises with Mexico that threatened to escalate to the use of military force. However, clear public and congressional opposition to taking a hard-line approach with Mexico signaled to the Coolidge administration that the use of military force was not an option.

Red Scare

Frank Kellogg, who took office as the new secretary of state in 1925, exemplified the trend toward communist-inspired paranoia. On the advice of his Latin American team at the State Department, Kellogg decided that the United States need to take a harder line with Mexico and force President Calles to provide more protection for American investors in Mexican natural resources. One of the voices in favor of a harder line was the new ambassador to Mexico, James Rockwell Sheffield. He was particularly prejudiced against Mexicans who, in his words, "recognize no argument but force."[60]

The increasingly hostile position of the State Department provoked a marked worsening of US-Mexican relations between 1925 and 1927. President Coolidge decided to take a more aggressive approach with Mexico in early June of 1925. The new policy went public when Kellogg sparked a diplomatic crisis with his statement on June 12, 1925, that "the Government of Mexico is now on trial before the world."[61] The United States was particularly concerned about the Petroleum and Alien Land Laws passed by Mexico in late 1925 that put conditions on foreign ownership of oil and land in Mexico. American hardliners advocated an embargo of Mexican oil to demonstrate the seriousness of American opposition to Mexican land and oil regulations, and acknowledged that "war was the logical terminal point of this policy."[62] President Coolidge himself was highly suspicious of Bolshevik influence in Mexico and nefarious Mexican influence on the ongoing instability in Nicaragua. It appears that Coolidge even considered military intervention in Mexico.[63] The diplomatic crisis reached its peak after Coolidge's January 1927 message to Congress accusing Mexico of threatening the legitimate government of Nicaragua and threatening the security of the Panama Canal.[64] Kellogg followed this statement by warning the Senate Foreign Relations Committee that Mexico was coming under the influence of Bolshevik Russia and posed the threat of "Mexican-fostered Bolshevik hegemony intervening between the United States and the Panama Canal."[65] The

Secretary of State noted that the situation was perhaps "preparing the way for possible military intervention."[66] President Calles declared Kellogg's statement "a threat to the sovereignty of Mexico that she cannot overlook," and "threatened to 'light up the sky all the way to New Orleans' by setting fire to Mexico's oil wells" in the event of US military intervention.[67]

Avoidance of War

Despite the tough rhetoric, there was little enthusiasm in the Coolidge administration for a policy that would end in war. Despite Calles's warning to set fire to the oil wells, Mexico signaled a conciliatory line when Foreign Minister Aarón Sáenz declared that Mexico had no interest in Nicaraguan internal politics. Senator Borah responded by advocating arbitration with Mexico and leading the Senate to a unanimous vote (79 to 0) on a resolution recommending arbitration.[68] The Coolidge administration's hostile stance toward Mexico was criticized in Congress on the grounds that it undermined US relations in Latin America. The House of Representatives conducted multiple investigations into American policy toward Mexico and Nicaragua and the majority of newspapers opposed the hard-line policy. Progressives in Congress repeatedly introduced legislation to prevent the deployment of American troops abroad.[69] Finally, many peace, labor, and religious groups and academics supported a conciliatory approach to Mexico. The peace movement was important in mobilizing public opinion against conflict with Mexico, especially the National Council for the Prevention of War and the Federal Council of Churches of Christ in America. Schoultz argues that "Congress and the solidarity groups deserve most of the credit for helping President Coolidge see the need for a more moderate U.S. approach."[70] Kellogg and other administration officials were reluctant to push the more aggressive policy too hard mainly "because they were afraid of repudiation by the American people" and the reaction in Latin America.[71] Drawing on contemporary newspaper reports, statements by Kellogg and other State Department officials, and reports by Mexican agents in the United States, historian James Horn provides extensive evidence that congressional and public opinion was the major factor fostering restraint.[72] Progressives like Borah, Senator Burton Wheeler from Montana, and Senator George Norris led the attack on Coolidge's hostile Mexican policy. Coolidge publicly signaled his more conciliatory approach and sent J. P. Morgan partner and former college roommate Dwight Morrow as his special representative to Mexico.[73] Coolidge instructed Morrow "to keep us out of war with Mexico."[74]

Morrow was an inspired or lucky choice and succeeded in extricating the United States from the diplomatic crisis with Mexico. Morrow had opposed previous US interventions in the affairs of Latin American countries and acted in the interests of the United States and not the large oil companies—some of which were represented by J. P. Morgan. Morrow was appointed and confirmed as ambassador to Mexico. He soon found the State Department staff opposed to compromise with Mexico. Morrow hired his own staff, proceeded to Mexico, and "accomplished in exactly three weeks what his predecessors had been unable to do in two years—convince President Calles that it would not violate any basic principle of the Mexican Revolution to void the most offensive sections of the 1925 petroleum law."[75] Morrow took the simple but effective steps of showing respect for Calles, Mexican sovereignty, and the people and culture of Mexico. He also arranged for Charles Lindberg and Will Rogers to visit Mexico as part of "the best public relations effort in U.S. diplomatic history."[76] In 1928 the Coolidge administration announced it was satisfied that American interests in Mexico were sufficiently protected; most of the US oil industry was not satisfied and worried about the precedent set by Mexico for the rest of Latin America.[77]

From 1910 until World War II important sectors of American society consistently pushed for the US government to use its power to interfere in the internal affairs of Mexico. Their favored policies ranged from economic coercion to military occupation and establishment of an American protectorate. The voices advocating a hard-line or interventionist policy toward Mexico influenced the thinking of policymakers such as Secretary of State Kellogg, and at certain junctures in American history, such as 1925–1927, these interests were able to foster crises in US-Mexican relations.[78] However, Congress, led by anti-imperialist Progressives and peace groups, pushed for restraint and were able to convince Coolidge to take a more conciliatory approach and pursue a diplomatic solution with Mexico.

Despite the fact that the two most important foreign policy decision makers in the US government were convinced that Mexico represented a clear threat to American national interests, the United States implemented a policy of reconciliation and restraint. Coolidge and Kellogg both seemed convinced that Mexico was a communist country and was looking to spread its influence throughout Central America, especially in Nicaragua. However, both men understood that sentiment in Congress and the American public was strongly against the use of coercive force against Mexico. Conciliatory diplomacy eventually diffused the crisis with Mexico, but as a subsequent section of this chapter demonstrates, the fear of Mexican influence in Central America was a central cause of future US military intervention in Nicaragua. Overwhelming evidence shows that the key factors causing restraint were congressional, public, and press opposition to coercive action against Mexico. Proponents of peace could draw the strong anti-imperialist public sentiment in the United States.[79] Both economic interest groups and security interests pushed the United States toward confrontation with Mexico, and therefore alternative explanations for restraint based on these factors cannot explain American restraint.

Occupation of Nicaragua and Failed Protectorate (1926–1927)

Less than a year after the legation guard was removed from Managua, American Marines and bluecoats were back in Nicaragua to protect foreign lives and property endangered by a civil war between Liberals and Conservatives. The motivation behind the renewed military intervention was the same as in the past: Nicaraguans failed to settle their political differences peacefully and American leaders continued to be unwilling to allow for disorder in the strategically important area between the Rio Grande and the Panama Canal.[80] However, to a large extent the usual reasons for intervention were not sufficient to quiet criticism in the United States, and the Coolidge administration quickly began looking for a way to get out of Nicaragua. The offer by President Díaz to make Nicaragua an American protectorate was not seriously considered because Coolidge administration officials knew it could not pass Congress and would have triggered public backlash. Within a year of sending in the Marines, Coolidge commissioned Henry L. Stimson to go to Nicaragua to find an exit strategy.

Conservative Revolution

When the American legation guard left Nicaragua in 1925 an uneasy truce existed between the Conservatives and Liberals. The Solórzano and Sacasa, Conservative–Liberal hybrid regime ruled uneasily under the constant threat of a Conservative rebellion. Conservative pressure and rumors of rebellion throughout the fall of 1925 led Solórzano to request the presence of American warships at the coastal cities of Corinto and Bluefields; the United States reluctantly complied. The tension decreased but did not dissipate. Sensing the vulnerability of the Solórzano regime, former president Chamorro instigated a coup d'état on October 25 that led to the removal of the Liberals from the coalition government to be replaced by Conservatives and Chamorro being installed as general-in-chief of the army. Chamorro then had Sacasa's office ruled vacated by Congress, engineered the resignation of Solórzano, and had himself elected president by Congress in January 1926.[81] Secretary Kellogg announced that the United States would not recognize the Chamorro administration as the legitimate government of Nicaragua, but lack of US recognition was not fatal to the Chamorro administration and he succeeded in consolidating his hold on power.[82]

Liberal Counterrevolution

By summer of 1926 the counterrevolution had begun, led by Luis Beltrán Sandoval's successful attack on Atlantic coast city of Bluefields. Soon Liberal forces controlled significant portions of the east coast. On May 6, 1926, US Marines took control of the town of Bluefields and made it a neutral zone. The State Department made it clear that US forces were not there to support one side or the other, and that their only purpose was protection of American and foreign lives and property. A policy of strict neutrality was in place. Chamorro's forces were able to regain most of the lost territory by the end of May and the Marines left.[83] Chamorro's victory was short-lived. He was running out of money and without American support, foreign loans were unavailable. Fighting recommenced in August of 1926 and soon marines and bluejackets were back in Bluefields. The new campaign by the Liberals appeared to be funded by Mexico and Guatemala, and was having considerable success. The United States was faced with the problem of accepting continued civil war in Nicaragua or putting their moral authority behind a particular faction. At this point both factions had engaged in unconstitutional actions, so it was not obvious what faction the United States should support.[84]

Secretary of State Kellogg took the advice of J. H. Stabler, head of the Latin American division, and instructed US chargé d'affaires ad interim Lawrence Dennis to support a negotiated settlement that would result in the resignation of Chamorro. Liberal and Conservative leaders were brought together at the Corinto conference that resulted in Chamorro's resignation and the instatement of Conservative Senator Sebastián Uriza as provisional president. Chamorro also pledged to reinstate the Solórzano Congress and gain their approval for the selection of Conservative former president Adolfo Díaz as the next president. The proposal was implemented more or less according to plan; Díaz was inaugurated on November 14, 1926, and quickly recognized by the United States. The situation was stabilized temporarily, but the causes of instability were still present: liberals were again living uneasily under a Conservative government supported by the United States.[85]

Landing the Marines

The American brokered agreement did not last long, and civil war soon brought American forces back to Nicaraguan soil. On December 1, 1926, former vice president Sacasa returned to Puerto Cabézas, Nicaragua, to declare himself president, set up a provisional government, and reinvigorate the Liberal revolution. Mexico immediately recognized Sacasa as president of Nicaragua. Kellogg and Coolidge began to fear Mexican Bolshevik influence in Nicaragua and worried that a Mexican-supported Sacasa regime might declare the Bryan-Chamorro Treaty void and reopen the possibility of a non-US Nicaraguan canal. There was also fear among some Coolidge administration officials that communism could spread to Panama and threaten the canal. After the Díaz government declared that it could not guarantee the protection of foreigners living in Nicaragua,

Coolidge decided to send in American forces. In August of 1926 marines landed at Bluefields, and then in December at Rio Grandé Bar and Puerto Cabézas to protect American lives and property—mines, timber operations, and fruit operations—and American rights to build a canal in Nicaragua. Another important issue was US status in the Americas. The Coolidge administration would not countenance another state (i.e., Mexico) exercising influence beyond their borders. As Wood notes, a victory for the Liberals in Nicaragua "would have resounded throughout Latin America as a Mexican triumph over the United States."[86] Over 5,000 US troops were in Nicaragua by February of 1927.[87]

The second occupation of Nicaragua occurred incrementally and without a clear strategic objective. Beginning with the establishment of a neutral zone in Puerto Cabézas, US forces slowly spread out to control all of the major cities in Nicaragua. The country became an archipelago of American neutral zones. The core mission was protection of American lives and property, but it was inevitable that the US presence would have an effect on the conflict between the Liberals and Conservatives. Because the marines were supporting the status quo, their presence favored Díaz. The Coolidge administration hoped that strict neutrality would limit criticism of the intervention, but the location of the neutral zones seemed intended to stymie the progress of Liberal insurgents. When Conservatives were in danger of losing ground to Liberal forces they simply informed the United States that the Nicaraguan government could no longer guarantee the safety of Americans in that area, and Marines would arrive to establish a neutral zone. This relieved Díaz of the burden of protecting the main urban areas of Nicaragua. Despite these impediments Liberal forces continued to make progress and gained control of the eastern half of Nicaragua (except for US neutral zones). By January of 1927 Liberal forces threatened Managua in the west. The United States quickly reestablished a garrison in the capital and pressured Díaz to find a way to end the conflict.[88]

Protectorate Proposal

After negotiations failed and Managua was in danger of being cut off from the coast, American forces took responsibility for the main rail route between Managua and the Pacific Ocean at the city of Chinandega. The neutral zone established by US forces covered the length of the railroad and the towns of Corinto, Chinandega, León, and Managua. This deployment made violence between the Liberals and Americans highly likely. By March these two forces had exchanged gunfire. Then in February 1927 Díaz suggested a treaty to the State Department that would make Nicaragua a protectorate of the United States. Minister Eberhardt supported the proposal because he saw it as a comprehensive solution to the chronic instability in Nicaragua, and it would allow for an early exit for US troops.[89]

Eberhardt's superiors were not as enthusiastic. As one historian observes, "Even if the treaty were favored by the State Department, it was unlikely that the Senate would ratify such an agreement."[90] Another states, "With its policy already under heavy fire at home and abroad, the Coolidge administration lost no time denying that it had any intention of taking Adolfo [Díaz] up on his offer even though it came with the endorsement of Minister Eberhardt."[91] The State Department also vetoed the Díaz plan to sell the national railroad and National Bank to private investors, because it was too reminiscent of dollar diplomacy.[92] By early 1927 the State Department was reevaluating policy toward Nicaragua. The Coolidge administration sought less involvement and responsibility, not more. By mid-March there were 2,000 American troops in Nicaragua, but Liberal forces under the leadership of Moncada continued to defeat Conservative forces. The United States was again in the uncomfortable position of using its military power to prop up an unpopular regime. Former secretary of war Henry L. Stimson was sent to extract the United States from Nicaragua before they found themselves in another small war.[93] Coolidge "was tired of the Nicaraguan mess and wanted to get it off his hands."[94]

Congressional opposition and negative public opinion were major factors in producing Coolidge's frustration with the Nicaraguan situation. The military intervention in Nicaragua was strongly criticized in the United States by members of Congress and the press. Senators William E. Borah and Burton K. Wheeler immediately criticized the deployment of Marines, and several major newspapers, including the *New York Times*, ran negative editorials. Coolidge responded with a special message to Congress on January 10, 1927, emphasizing Mexican interference, the threat to American lives and property, and the danger to American canal rights. Secretary Kellogg followed up with a statement emphasizing the communist threat to Central America emanating from Mexico. Congressional critics were far from convinced by these justifications. Borah, Wheeler, and Senator George Norris introduced resolutions calling for investigations to probe the veracity of the Coolidge administration arguments in favor of intervention. Representative Fiorello La Guardia rebuked Coolidge for deploying American troops to protect private interests, and Borah and Wheeler repeatedly introduced legislation that would prevent the use of the American military in Nicaragua. By early 1927 Coolidge faced an "increasingly skeptical and hostile public."[95] Opposition to American involvement in Nicaragua was in part tied to the fear that the Coolidge administration was attempting to create a justification for war with Mexico. Abroad, public opinion in Latin America was strongly against US policy, while the European press, with some satisfaction, made note of American hypocrisy.[96]

The second American military occupation of Nicaragua was unequivocally an act of political–military expansion. However, it occurred only after other attempts to bring peace to Nicaragua failed, and, as military interventions go, it was quite tentative and thoroughly lacking in resolve. The United States went to significant trouble to avoid having to actually fight anyone and Coolidge had little appetite to persevere against the wave of opposition from Congress, the press, and world opinion. The United States limited its expansionism by responding negatively when Díaz offered up Nicaragua as an American protectorate. Within less than a year Coolidge was looking for a way out. Unfortunately, it took much longer to get out than to get in, as is often the case with military occupations.

Economic interest groups and security concerns are not a viable explanation for restraint. In fact, security concerns were the major cause of expansion. At least four arguments were made in favor of American military intervention: "the alleged need to protect life and property, including investments, the 'Bolshevik menace to the Panama Canal area, the need to safeguard the Nicaraguan canal option, and the Monroe Doctrine—intervening to forestall intervention by Europeans."[97] The geostrategic importance of Nicaragua and the fear that Mexico hoped to gain hegemony over Central America appear to be the most important motivations for intervention.

Nonintervention in the Dominican Republic (1930–1931)

The United States withdrew its troops from the Dominican Republic in 1924 with the hope that constitutional government would provide long-term political stability. Long-term stability did emerge, but it happened through the 30-year dictatorship of Raphael Leonidas Trujillo and not through constitutional government. While some may blame the United States for supporting a ruthless tyrant like Trujillo, the relevant question for this study is why the United States did not intervene in the Dominican Republic in 1930 when Trujillo gained power through fraud and intimidation. In previous cases the United States saw unconstitutional practices as a justification for military intervention, and American State Department officials advocated a more interventionist approach by the United States. The reason the United States did not intervene in this case is that by 1930 US foreign policy had shifted decisively toward Good Neighborism. In short, the United States didn't do interventions anymore; the domestic costs were too high.

Revolution of 1930

In 1928 Horacio Vásquez announced that he would run for reelection in 1930 despite the fact that a second term was unconstitutional in the Dominican Republic. This move by Vásquez was sure to trigger armed opposition, but he proceeded, secure in the knowledge that the *Guardia Nacional* could put down any uprising. Vásquez successfully achieved the necessary amendment of the Dominican Constitution and began implementing a plan that would insure his reelection. A free and fair election was clearly not going to happen, and, even if it did, the opposition was too fragmented to challenge Vásquez. The American chargé d'affaires John Moors Cabot and then new Minister Charles Curtis attempted to forestall revolution throughout late 1929 and early 1930 by encouraging Vásquez to provide for a fair election. Opposition candidate Velásquez implored the United States to supervise the coming election, but according to Cabot this was not possible because it was "contrary to our Latin-American policy and would raise a storm of resentment in other Latin American countries."[98] These efforts ended up being irrelevant because the main threat of revolution was General Trujillo, not opposition political parties. On February 22, 1930, the revolution began, led by Rafael Estrella Urena and Trujillo (though the general's role was concealed for a time). Curtis and Cabot did their best to negotiate a peaceful end to the conflict.[99]

As a precaution, Curtis asked Washington to dispatch a naval vessel to protect Americans in the Dominican Republic in the event intense fighting did break out. The State Department refused the request; a warship would be dispatched only in the event of imminent danger to American lives or the operations of American officials. The State Department response demonstrates the "great reluctance to take any action reminiscent of intervention." Curtis was instructed to provide what help he could in mediating the conflict provided Dominican leaders welcomed his help. Furthermore, he was prohibited from taking any position regarding the support of the United States and was prohibited from threatening the use of force by the United States. He could merely provide his own personal advice.[100]

Rebel forces quickly gained control of Santo Domingo with the support of the Guardia Nacional under the command of Trujillo. President Vásquez quickly gave in to all rebel demands. He resigned, and Estrella was appointed Secretary of the Interior and provisional president. In addition, Vásquez promised not to run for president in the election later that year and Estrella promised that Trujillo also would not be a candidate. Finally, the election law of 1924 was to be reinstated (to repeal recent changes made by Vásquez), and all revolutionary groups would voluntarily disarm.[101]

The revolution of 1930 demonstrated a significant change in American foreign policy. The State Department was completely disinterested in the resolution of the political crisis in the Dominican Republic. It even refused to take a position on the outcome other than encouraging Minister Curtis to foster a peaceful solution. There were two main reasons for the passivity of the United States. First, the Great Depression made all other issues insignificant. All political energy in the Hoover administration was spent on economic policy. Second, nonintervention was the standing US policy with respect to the Dominican

Republic since 1924. Therefore, the lack of interference was in line with existing policy. On the ground in Santo Domingo, American diplomats wanted to take a more active approach, but were consistently overruled by Washington.[102]

Election of 1930

It quickly became clear that Trujillo had no intention of abiding by Estrella's promise. He came to dominate the Estrella administration and in March 1930 accepted the nomination as presidential candidate for the Confederación party led by Estrella and Elias Brache. Estrella was unhappy with this outcome and asked Minister Curtis to announce that the United States would not recognize a Trujillo regime. Curtis forwarded the request to Washington, but to his dismay was told the United States would recognize whoever won the election. Curtis was authorized to appeal to Trujillo's patriotism and provide friendly personal advice to the effect that a Trujillo presidency would be bad for the Dominican Republic. Curtis was very aware of the dilemma facing the United States. It was the same dilemma it continued to face in succeeding decades in Latin America: it could oppose the rise of a potential dictator and be charged with interfering in the domestic affairs of a foreign country, or it could maintain neutrality and be charged with support of a military dictator.[103] Neither option was very attractive.

As expected, Trujillo's main campaign strategy was violent intimidation by the Guardia Nacional. Assaults, assassinations, and kidnappings were common. The main party opposing Confederación, Alianza, dropped out of the election and encouraged supporters to boycott the election. Even so, Trujillo ended up with considerably more votes than the total registered voters in the Dominican Republic. Curtis's reports of Trujillo's tactics did not persuade the State Department to change its policy of nonintervention. The United States would recognize the winner of the election no matter what. Acting Secretary of State Joseph P. Cotton understood that the choice was to either accept the results of the election or send in the Marines, and the latter could only be considered in extreme circumstances. The United States was strictly abiding by the new policy of nonintervention and noninterference. The reason for this policy was that "the United States did not wish to risk the damage to its goodwill in Latin America that interference in the Dominican election would bring."[104] American officials felt that "the political price would have been too high to violate Dominican sovereignty again."[105] The political price would come in the form of negative public opinion in the United States and Latin America. Contrary to the claims of critics that the United States supported Trujillo because he would favor American economic interests, the United States never supported Trujillo and in fact opposed his candidacy (unofficially). Furthermore, all the candidates and parties were friendly to the United States, and thus there was no reason for the United States to favor one over another.[106]

US policy toward the Dominican Republic at the end of the Hoover administration demonstrates the shift that had taken place in American foreign policy. Not only was intervention almost completely off the table, any interference in the political process of the Dominican Republic was also prohibited. Many times in the past the subversion of constitutional principles was a trigger for military intervention. However, in this case intervention was not even considered, because of the negative impact it would have on domestic and regional public opinion. Again we have a clear case of restraint that was fundamentally caused by the shift in policy that increasingly viewed intervention as a nonviable option. This shift in policy was caused by the inability of expansionists to fundamentally alter the strategic orientation of the United States. The domestic structure of the United States imposed enough friction to delay and limit expansion to the extent that expansionism was discredited as a foreign policy tool. Because the United States was unsuccessful at spreading its influence through political–military expansion, it had to turn to softer tools like fostering a positive reputation among its neighbors in the Western Hemisphere.

In this specific case, American restraint was caused by norms against expansion and the view that positive Latin American opinion was important for US interests. Neither of the competing hypotheses—economic interest groups or security concerns—can explain restraint in this case.

Withdrawal from Nicaragua (1933)

By early 1927, US troops practically occupied Nicaragua by way of the archipelago of cities and towns they controlled. Coolidge was faced with a decision to either defeat the Liberal insurgency, allow the Liberals to gain power through force, or impose some kind of lasting settlement on the two sides. Coolidge chose to attempt the third option, and in this decision he was strongly influenced by the strong criticism of his use of American troops in Nicaragua. However, creating long-term political stability required a significant investment in the short run. Officials in the Coolidge administration believed that respect for Nicaraguan sovereignty had to take a backseat to the effort to develop a political system capable of managing the peaceful succession of power from one party to another. Thus, the United States supervised three successive elections and trained what they hoped was a nonpartisan national guard. Like other Republicans of the era, Coolidge was not interested in long-term occupation or the establishment of protectorates. Even if he had been tempted, it is clear that American public opinion and Congress would have made it extremely difficult to implement policies that appeared in any way to resemble imperialism.

Criticism of Coolidge and a Policy Shift

The Coolidge administration faced considerable criticism for its use of military force in Nicaragua. The criticism was especially strong in the Senate, which had become more Democratic after the 1926 election. As with relations with Mexico, Coolidge was pushed to shift to a policy that emphasized diplomacy instead of the use of force.[107] In messages to the public and Congress in late 1926 and early 1927 (December 31 and January 10), President Coolidge defended his Nicaraguan policy. He stated that the United States was in Nicaragua only to protect American lives and property and was a neutral party in the civil war between Liberals and Conservatives. The response from critics was not positive. In January of 1927, Democratic Senator Burton Wheeler and Representative Huddleston introduced resolutions calling for the withdrawal of American troops from Nicaragua. Wheeler argued that "the State Department has literally gutted the sovereignty of Nicaragua."[108] He claimed that US national interests of peace and commerce were being undermined by State Department bureaucrats and their masters on Wall Street.[109]

The continued criticism led the Coolidge and Díaz administrations to emphasize the connection between Mexico and Nicaraguan Liberals. The argument was made that Mexican communists were attempting to gain hegemony in Central America, starting with installing a friendly regime in Nicaragua. Coolidge claimed that US business and strategic interests were threatened by a Liberal takeover in Nicaragua, shifting rhetorically from neutrality to support for the Díaz regime. This change in justification backfired. It raised fears in the United States that Coolidge was moving toward war with Mexico, and outside the country Coolidge's comments were regarded as totally without merit.[110]

Thus by early 1927, the State Department was reevaluating policy toward Nicaragua and the Coolidge administration sought to extricate itself from what was becoming a costly foreign military adventure. Former secretary of war Henry L. Stimson was sent to extract the United States from Nicaragua before things got any worse.[111] Cohen states that "the absence of public support for the use of force" led Coolidge to send Stimson to find a diplomatic solution.[112] The choice to send Stimson quickly paid dividends: "The move was a public relations success even before Stimson's departure, as previously critical newspapers greeted the Stimson mission as a sign that Coolidge was backing away from military intervention in favor of a negotiated settlement."[113]

The Stimson Plan

Stimson arrived in Managua on April 17, 1927, with the full authority of the President of the United States to solve the Nicaraguan problem. His exit strategy depended on a truce and disarmament followed by a free and fair election in 1928. The United States would supervise the election and train a constabulary force. Conservatives and Liberals agreed to the basic principles of Stimson's approach, but the main sticking point remained in place: the Díaz presidency. Liberals could not make peace with Díaz because he symbolized the treachery of the Chamorro coup, but Stimson felt that there was no adequate replacement and that Díaz was the recognized president of the Nicaragua. Stimson's unwillingness to give in on this point and the willingness of Coolidge to order American troops to disarm insurgents by force left the Liberals little choice but to accept the Stimson plan. Liberal military leader General José María Moncado communicated his initial acceptance of the Stimson plan after a meeting with the American envoy in early May. A series of Conservative concessions and the offer of payment for Liberal insurgents that left the field facilitated disarmament. The Liberal military leaders (except for Augusto Sandino) agreed to stop fighting, and by June of 1927 the war was over—at least for a time. Most Nicaraguans applauded the settlement and the end of the fighting and generally viewed American intervention as laudatory. However, former Liberal Vice President Sacasa only accepted the agreement after it became a reality.[114] The drawdown of marines occurred quickly and soon only 2,000 remained.[115]

From Civil War to Guerilla War

One important military leader did not accept the Stimson plan—Augusto Sandino. At first his intransigence did not worry US leaders, and the drawdown of US forces began in June of 1927. It was assumed that the Guardia Nacional de Nicaragua could handle any holdouts among the insurgents. The Sandinistas demonstrated their seriousness by attacking a marine detachment at Ocotal, and were only driven off by airstrikes that killed between 40 and 300 Nicaraguans.[116] Officials in Washington were surprised and dismayed by the level of violence. This initial incident set the stage for what was to come: a hard-fought guerilla war in the forests and mountains of northern Nicaragua with Sandino ambushing and retreating and marines pursuing. The US Marines fought a five-year guerilla war in Nicaragua against Liberal Augusto Sandino involving up to 5,673 Marines and leading to 135 killed in action. Hundreds of Nicaraguans also lost their lives. The Coolidge administration justified their actions by labeling Sandino an anti-American, communist bandit and making outlandish, exaggerated claims about his motivations and exploits. They attempted to define Sandino as a mere brigand and then contradicted themselves by calling him a grave threat to Nicaraguan peace and stability, thereby justifying the continued presence of the Marines. Nicaragua came to represent American foreign policy in the Western Hemisphere and was at the center of debates over the US role in world affairs in the 1920s.[117] The central question was to what extent the United States would be involved in the affairs of other countries. In the Western Hemisphere the question was: whither military intervention?

American Opposition to US Occupation

The return of US troops to Nicaragua in 1926 became a focal point for the emergence of a new set of actors in American foreign policy. A solidarity network of citizen groups formed to lobby against American occupation of Nicaragua and, more generally, interventionism in the Caribbean Basin. These groups were opposed to US intervention in the affairs of Latin American and Caribbean countries for moral reasons. The most important group was the Committee on Cultural Relations with Latin America (CCRLA) led by Hubert Herring. William Green, president of the American Federation of Labor, also spoke out against American troops in Nicaragua. The All American Anti-Imperialist League began sending mail stamped with the slogan "Protest Against Marine Rule in Nicaragua," which was quickly banned by the US Postal Service.[118] Anti-imperialist journalists also emerged to criticize American interventionism. Through articles published in *The Nation* and other outlets, journalists like Carleton Beals routinely challenged the assertions of the Coolidge administration and claimed that marines were using brutal tactics against Nicaraguans. These critics had a significant effect on Coolidge administration officials, causing them to put pressure on General Frank McCoy to end the war quickly. Many critics blamed moneyed interests in the United States for imperialist foreign policy.[119]

Opponents of Coolidge in Congress were also very active. They questioned the president's authority to order the US military into combat in Nicaragua. They accused American forces of killing innocent civilians and wantonly destroying property in Nicaragua, and repeatedly attempted to defund the military operation. Most of these votes failed, but in 1929 the resolution to prohibit the use of navy funds in Nicaragua passed the Senate by eight votes. The resolution vote was quickly overturned on reconsideration, but demonstrates the power of opponents of the war. In fact, by that point they had all but won—neither presidential candidate in the 1928 presidential campaign supported a prolonged stay in Nicaragua. The Democratic platform that election year was strongly anti-imperialist and noninterventionist, and advocated the invalidation of any agreements that made the United States responsible for the political stability of foreign countries. The victor, Republican candidate Herbert Hoover, publicly agreed that rapid withdrawal was necessary. There was no outpouring of American public outrage against the military action in Nicaragua, but there was a consensus by the late 1920s that "the United States was becoming increasingly tired of directly running Nicaragua's internal affairs," and more generally that "the American public had little tolerance for presidential warmaking."[120]

Election of 1928

The campaign rhetoric of 1928 only sped up the existing effort to disengage from Nicaragua. The lame duck Coolidge administration was already pursuing an exit strategy: establishment of a legitimate regime through a supervised election and training a nonpartisan Guardia Nacional (i.e., the Stimson plan). Brigadier General Frank R. McCoy was appointed by Coolidge to serve as his personal representative and chair of the Nicaraguan electoral commission. The commission would have complete control over all things to do with the election: "in election matters Nicaraguan sovereignty would practically have to cease."[121] After electoral reforms were forced through by Díaz's presidential proclamation, an American supervised election took place on November 4, 1928. Except for convincing Chamorro to stay out of the election, US supervision was neutral, and for the first time in Nicaraguan history the incumbent party did not win. With 90 percent turnout of eligible voters, Liberal José María Moncada was elected and took office on January 1, 1929. The United States spent the next three years training the Guardia Nacional as it continued to fight Sandino's forces.[122]

After the election General McCoy returned to Washington, advocating a long-term American presence to fundamentally reform the politics and economics of Nicaragua. Secretary Kellogg rejected McCoy's plan because it would require the United States to arrange for a large loan to fund the reforms suggested by McCoy. Regardless of Kellogg's predilections, such a plan was impossible: "American public opinion was against imperial adventure, believing that because the United States had created an empire 30 years earlier, anything accomplished in foreign relations partook of imperialism. To be sure, the Great Depression that began in 1929 would have made American participation doubly impossible."[123]

Marines Withdraw

Hoover took office in 1929 and hoped to begin the removal of American forces quickly, but the continued Sandinista insurgency convinced him that a precipitous withdrawal was unwise. To many in Washington the lesson from past interventions in Nicaragua (and elsewhere) was that peace and stability could not be assumed and violence and disorder could reemerge quickly. However, insurgent activity declined following the 1928 election and remained low. Therefore the United States was able to begin the second drawdown of marines in early 1929 and by the end of the year 1,800 remained in Nicaragua. This drawdown was also made possible because the Guardia Nacional and a volunteer force of Nicaraguans began to take over policing duties and suppression of the Sandinistas. Since 1926 the United States had put considerable energy into developing the

Guardia, though interagency rivalry between State Department and navy officials and Nicaraguan partisan politics complicated matters. Congress even
allowed current US military personnel to train and command the Guardia. Hoover agreed to supervise Nicaraguan elections in 1930 (congressional) and 1932
(presidential) after a request from President Moncada. As in 1928, an American
naval officer was appointed to head the election commission in 1930 and US
forces supervised the election. The election occurred without incident and Liberals won majorities in both houses of Congress.[124]

Sandinista activity increased in late 1930 and 1931 and counterinsurgency
became more difficult after the start of the Great Depression.[125] According to
Coolidge biographer Robert Ferrell, "What should have been done was to double
or triple the marine force under forceful commanders and, with Honduran cooperation [to take away the safe zone], end the rebellion. Unfortunately, that would
have been impossible during such an anti-imperialist era. American opinion
would never have stood for it."[126] The resurgence of Sandino was demonstrated
by an ambush on December 31, 1930, that led to the deaths of eight marines
who were repairing telephone wires. This event and Sandino's renewed propaganda attacks led to a rethinking of counterinsurgency strategy in Nicaragua and
renewed criticism of foreign policy in the United States. Complete military victory seemed impossible, and opposition to a continued American presence was
spreading. Henry Stimson, now Secretary of State, ordered that preparations for
withdrawal be implemented, especially procedures and timetables for transferring
command of the Guardia Nacional to Nicaraguan officers. He informed Moncada that "public opinion in the United States would not support indefinite
retention of Marines."[127] January 1, 1933, was designated as the date when command of the Guardia would be turned over to the Nicaraguan officers, which
alleviated some of the pressure from American critics. The State Department
also announced June 1 as the date when all combat Marines would leave Nicaragua, leaving only those involved in training the Guardia. This move further
deflated criticism.[128] Stimson's announcement was certainly encouraged by congressional action to force the withdrawal of US troops. A House vote was held
hours after Stimson's announcement on a bill that would have required Hoover
to withdraw US forces from Nicaragua. The bill was defeated 191 to 133, but
the vote may have come out differently if not for Stimson's announcement of an
exit date.[129]

As the withdrawal date got closer, increasingly hysterical reports of rebel
activity reached Washington from the east coast of Nicaragua. Foreign citizens
repeatedly called for protection and American warships were sent to provide
security at port cities along the Atlantic. Controversy emerged over how much
protection foreigners required and deserved. Secretary of the Navy Adams
wanted to send in additional forces, but Stimson opposed introducing more
American troops. He announced that any foreigners who felt unsafe should

move to coastal cities where US warships could protect them without putting boots on the ground. There were strong pressures to deploy more Marines, but Stimson and Hoover resisted and kept on the path to total evacuation. By May the Sandinista uprising in the east had been suppressed, though insurgent activity continued in other parts of the country.[130]

The final task for the US occupation was supervision of the 1932 presidential election. The State Department rejected the navy's request for 1,800 marines to provide security for the election plus 1,115 election workers at a cost of $750,000 because they wanted to avoid any impression that the withdrawal was stalled or reversed. This decision was certainly shaped by legislation passed by Congress to deny funding for sending Marines to supervise the 1932 election. Instead Hoover and Stimson decided to use existing funds to send 643 election workers, but no extra protection. Liberal Juan Sacasa won the presidency in 1932 and Anastasio Somoza was installed as commander of the Guardia Nacional. The last marines left on January 2, 1933, the day after Sacasa was inaugurated.[131]

Choosing Restraint

During the second American intervention in Nicaragua the United States played a predominant role in Nicaraguan politics while providing for the most democratic elections in the country's history. Nicaraguan leaders were generally amenable to American advice and rarely opposed what American officials thought was best for Nicaragua. At several key moments when the United States could have transitioned to even stronger political control of Nicaragua, public opinion and congressional opposition seem to have been decisive in restraining the Coolidge and Hoover administrations. First, Coolidge decided to send Stimson to find a peaceful solution to the civil war between Liberals and Conservatives rather than pacify the Liberals through force after congressional and public opinion turned against the intervention. Second, following the 1928 election the Coolidge administration ignored General McCoy's advice for a long-term reconstruction of Nicaraguan politics and economics, again largely because they knew it would be unpopular. Third, when the military solution failed to fully suppress the Sandinista rebellion the Hoover administration chose to quicken the withdrawal rather than intensifying the military campaign. And finally, when Americans in Nicaragua implored Stimson to guarantee their safety by deploying more marines after 1931, he refused and continued with the withdrawal plans. At each of these points public and congressional pressure restrained the president from implementing policies that would increase either the length or intensity of American political control in Nicaragua. Congress finally sent an unambiguous message that further occupation would be opposed through prohibiting further military expenditures in Nicaragua.

In 1926 Coolidge responded to disorder in a Caribbean Basin country as many of his predecessors had at one time or another: he sent in the US military. Why were American presidents so willing to commit US soldiers, sailors, and marines to intervention in Nicaragua? Historian William Kammen identifies several causes of America interest in peace and stability in Nicaragua. First, the United States was consistently interested in the potential for a canal in Nicaragua. In previous years there were worries that a foreign country could build a canal; in the 1920s and 1930s there was serious discussion of the United States building a Nicaraguan canal. Protection of this potential route was deemed vital. Second, there was a continuing concern about Mexican influence in Nicaragua, which was considered antithetical to US interests largely because Nicaragua was so close to the Panama Canal. Third, specific Nicaraguan policy legacies were important, as this was the second major military intervention in that country. Fourth, policy followed the pattern of mission creep. One author argues, "What had begun as a relatively simple, seemingly normal response became a matter of national prestige."[132] Fifth, economic concerns played only a small role (if any) in encouraging intervention. US investment was small and clearly not worth deploying a 5,000-man military force to fight a small guerilla movement in the forests and mountains.[133]

Nicaragua was a formative moment for both Coolidge and Hoover because it illustrated the need for a new policy in an era where there was "no desire for conquest and no need for defense."[134] The experience demonstrated that political education through military intervention and supervision of elections was not a particularly effective way of increasing stability, supporting American interests, or protecting American property.[135] First, it was impossible to gain full compliance of the occupied people. Nicaraguan leaders had their own interests that were not always consistent with the American vision of free and fair elections.[136] Second, Sandino's guerilla war against the US Marines in Nicaragua demonstrated that elections did not automatically bring about peace.[137] Third, it became clear that it was too difficult to attempt to protect all American property in Nicaragua, which led to a change in policy that saw protection of American property as a discretionary rather than a compulsory aspect of the national interests.[138] The second intervention was roundly condemned in Latin America and put pressure on the United States to avoid further interventions.

The US withdrawal of military forces from Nicaragua in 1933 was an act of foreign policy restraint in the form of a retrenchment of previous political–military expansion. The United States pulled out its occupation forces even though—as subsequent events would demonstrate—Nicaragua was not fully stable and it retained high geopolitical value. The cause of restraint was a combination of Coolidge's and Hoover's personal ambivalence or distaste for territorial expansion and the constant pressure from anti-imperialist lobbying groups, journalists, and members of Congress. Furthermore, both presidents felt highly constrained by public opinion and the incentives of electoral politics. There were no strong security-related reasons for restraint, and economic interests were of minor importance.

Conclusion

Unlike in the previous two decades of American foreign policy, in the 1920s there were few advocates of political–military expansion. During this period the politics of American foreign policy was shifting: normative and institutional restraints were becoming less important as strategic restraint became the taken-for-granted policy of the United States. In previous decades advocates of expansionism held the highest political offices in the United States but were stymied in their attempts to fully implement their preferred policy by normative and institutional restraints. After 1920 there were fewer and fewer attempts at expansion, and therefore fewer and fewer strong challenges for domestic restraint. (Though by no means do normative and institutional restraints fade from view.) The slow demise of political–military expansion as a foreign policy option for the United States demonstrates the ultimate triumph of strategic restraint. Domestic political structures dissipated the waves of political–military expansionism and prevented the United States from becoming a revisionist rising power. As expansionism fell by the wayside, dashed upon the rocks of institutional and normative restraints, what remained was the commitment to nonintervention.

The most visible mechanism for the shift in strategic ideas in the 1920s was public opinion. As the previous chapters demonstrate, American public opinion never favored expansionism, but instead supported some discrete instances of expansion as long as they were not too costly and the normative dissonance between anti-imperialism and expansionism was not too great. The generally negative view of political–military expansion is demonstrated by the fact that no presidential candidate or officeholder ever embraced imperialism. The main shift in public opinion that occurred after World War I was from passive to active opposition to political–military expansionism.[139] However, the shift in public opinion was itself a result of the institutional–normative structure of American politics that prevented the full articulation and implementation of political–military expansionism. In short, for better or worse, political–military expansion did not work for the United States, and therefore other policy tools had to be used.

Other factors besides normative and institutional restraint also play a role in explaining US foreign policy in the 1920s. Most historians note the importance of a change in the security environment—a factor that would be considered most important by defensive realists. The argument is that the level of threat decreased following World War I, and therefore military intervention was not required in service of American national security.[140] Thus by 1920 the threat of European intervention in the Western Hemisphere could no longer be invoked as a reason or justification for political–military intervention by the United States. Threat perception certainly played a role; however, as one historian explains, "ihe demotion of national defense as a necessary justification was not in itself important enough . . . either to make the employment of the Marine Corps inappropriate, or to make it essential immediately to reappraise policy toward Latin America."[141] Furthermore, the emergence of the Red Scare after 1919 provided a strong justification for intervention.[142] As discussed above, the fear that Mexico was attempting to spread communism in Central America was a major reason for the American confrontation with Mexico in 1927 and the continued occupation of Nicaragua in the late 1920s.[143] There were still strong security concerns in the Western Hemisphere, but American officials no longer saw political–military expansion as the solution. And the belief in the inadequacy of expansion emerged from the knowledge that American domestic political structure limited the possibilities of expansion and undermined the efficacy of expansion. The expansionist arguments of previous decades no longer had much resonance: "rationalizations for the use of force, which had formerly been socially acceptable either as substitutes or reinforcements for the national security argument, lost much of their former persuasiveness among important sectors of public opinion in the United States, if not in the Department of State."[144]

Another popular explanation for Republican interwar foreign policy cites the shifting interests of American business. Businesses in the United States sought investment opportunities and raw materials in Latin America, and were supportive of a more friendly policy toward US neighbors. Many Republicans, such as Charles Evans Hughes, secretary of state under Harding and Coolidge, envisioned a foreign policy based on expanding the investment opportunities for American business. And since war was bad for trade and investment, they favored cooperation and arbitration.[145] But these goals had been part of American grand strategy since the nineteenth century.[146] The three Republican administrations maintained generally the same goal, but sought to use a new means of achieving that goal.[147] Economic interests did not change—policy changed, and it changed because military intervention was shown to be unsustainable in light of normative and institutional restraints.

The Republican era of the 1920s and early 1930s marked a distinct shift in foreign policy toward the Western Hemisphere. Most historians of the era agree that the administrations of Harding, Coolidge, and Hoover viewed American interests in the hemisphere differently than their predecessors. However, there is very little discussion about why this change in the perception of American national interests occurred. As this chapter demonstrates, the main driver of the shift in regional foreign policy was the perception that political–military intervention was no longer an appropriate tool of strategy, except in extreme circumstances. Strong, overt opposition to intervention by Congress, the American public, and among Latin American countries made an expansionist foreign policy extremely costly to American political leaders.

By the 1920s it had become clear that expansionism had failed as a grand strategy of the United States. It was proven unsuccessful because American norms and institutions could not bear the weight of the concerted, long-term exercise of state power that was necessary for a revisionist foreign policy to be implemented successfully. Political–military interventions were limited by separation of powers (through the mechanism of congressional opposition) and norms (through the mechanisms of public opinion and electoral incentives). Small experiments in governing foreign territory were consistently undermined by the inability of the executive branch to maintain sufficient support from Congress and the public to devote the necessary resources. Support was undermined by the normative dissonance between the American anti-imperialist strategic culture and the subjugation of foreign peoples required for effective political–military control of foreign territory. These restraints became even more prominent under the presidency of Franklin D. Roosevelt and his Good Neighbor policy, the subject of the next chapter.

Notes

1. Herring 2008, 472; Rhodes 2001, 43–44.
2. Though as the previous chapter suggests, Wilson himself had learned the limits of military force by the end of his presidency.
3. Trani and Wilson 1977, 25, 28.
4. Grieb 1976, 1–2, 6; Ferrell 1998, 140.
5. Grieb 1976, 8.
6. Ninkovich 1999, 83; Trani and Wilson 1977, 135; Curry 1979, 33.
7. Grieb 1969, 425.
8. Under the direction of Secretary of State Kellogg, Undersecretary of State J. Reuben Clark and aide Anna O'Neill reinterpreted the Monroe Doctrine to show that it did not provide a basis for the Roosevelt Corollary. This was a necessary step to show that US policy did not contradict the tenets of the Kellogg-Briand Pact. Kellogg issued a memorandum to American embassies in Latin America announcing a revocation of the Roosevelt Corollary, but the memo was withheld waiting for approval from the incoming Hoover administration. Hoover ordered that the memo remain secret to avoid appearing too conciliatory at a time when the United States was negotiating arms control agreements. In 1930 the memo was published without fanfare or publicity; Schoultz 1998, 291–292. Curry is skeptical of the impact of the Clark memo. Curry 1979, 105.
9. FRUS 1917, 877.
10. Rosenberg 1985, 196.
11. FRUS 1917, 878–882. See also Rosenberg 1985, 196–197.
12. FRUS 1917, 895–896. Rosenberg 1999, 86–87; Buell 1928, 811.

13. Starr 1925, 115.

14. *FRUS 1920*, 61.

15. Buell 1928, 813.

16. Rosenberg 1985, 199.

17. Rosenberg 1985, 199–201.

18. Buell 1928, 816.

19. *FRUS 1922*, 632; Buell 1928, 813–816; Starr 1925, 117. See also Chalk 1967, 18; Rosenberg 1999, 120.

20. Rosenberg 1985, 200–201; Buell 1928, 816.

21. Chalk 1967, 19.

22. Buell 1928, 817. See also Starr 1925, 118–122.

23. Starr 1925, 111.

24. Hughes quoted in Starr 1925, 112.

25. Pérez 1986, 193–201; Langley 1980, 112; Munro 1974, 25–26; Grieb 1976, 112–113. For a description of the corruption common in Cuba at the time see Chapman 1927, 425–430, 433–434.

26. Pérez 1986, 201–207; Chapman 1927, 425–426; Munro 1974, 23–24, 26–28.

27. Pérez 1986, 206. See also Langley 1980, 112.

28. Munro 1974, 27–28; Grieb 1976, 118.

29. Crowder quoted in Pérez 1986, 207.

30. Pérez 1986, 200–213; Chapman 1927, 427–428, 432–441; Munro 1974, 28–33; Grieb 1976, 113–115. See also Schoultz 1998, 298–299.

31. Hughes quoted in note 13, Munro 1974, 29. See also Grieb 1976, 114; *FRUS 1922*, V. I, 1022–1024.

32. Grieb 1976, 114–115.

33. Chapman 1927, 413–414, 441–450; Munro 1974, 33–34; Grieb 1976, 115–116, 122–123. See also Schoultz 1998, 298–299; Pérez 1986, 214–256.

34. Grieb 1976, 111.

35. Chapman 1927, 448.

36. The Senate investigation in the Dominican Republic went nowhere and seemed biased in favor of the military occupation. Calder 1984, 215–216.

37. Calder 1984, 68.

38. Calder 1984, 68–69.

39. Calder 1984, 69–72; Curry 1979, 47–48.

40. Calder 1984, 218–221.

41. Grieb 1976, 71–73. See also Curry 1979, 49–51; Calder 1984, 221–223; Grieb 1969, 432–433.

42. Calder 1984, 223–224.

43. Grieb 1969, 432.

44. Quoted in Grieb 1976, 68.

45. Calder 1984, 226.

46. Calder 1984, 225–228; Grieb 1969, 433–434; Grieb 1976, 73–78.

47. Grieb 1976, 74–78; Calder 1984, 229; Grieb 1969, 434–437.

48. Calder 1984, 229–231, 237; Grieb 1969, 437–439; Grieb 1976, 76–78.

49. Curry 1979, 52–75.

50. Calder 1984, 247.

51. Schoultz 1998, 260.

52. Diego Chamorro died in office in October 1923; his vice president Bartolomé Martínez succeeded him. Emiliano Chamorro was Diego's nephew. The split occurred in the Conservative Party because both Emiliano Chamorro and Martínez wanted the Conservative nomination. When Martínez lost he decided to do what he could to prevent Chamorro from becoming president.

53. Kamman 1968, 20–32; Schoultz 1998, 261–262; Walker 2003, 21; Bermann 1986, 183–184.

54. Bermann 1986, 183–184; Kamman 1968, 32–35; Musicant 1990, 288.

55. This argument is made in Bermann (1986, 183–184); if correct, then US nonrecognition of the regime that replaced Solórzano-Sacasa makes no sense.

56. Schoultz 1998, 262. See also McCoy 1967, 351.

57. Bermann 1986, 183.

58. Musicant 1990, 285–286.

59. Trani and Wilson 1977, 127–132; Schoultz 1998, 275–277; Grieb 1976, 129–148; Smith 1972, 194–227; Kane 1975, 299–311.

60. Smith 1972, 232. See also Ferrell 1998, 124–126; Horn 1973, 454–471; Horn 1975, 31–45; Salisbury 1986, 319–339.

61. Quoted in Schoultz 1998, 280; Ferrell 1998, 125.

62. Smith 1972, 235.

63. Cohen 1998, 235. On Mexican intervention in Nicaragua see Kamman 1968, chapters 4 and 5; Wood 1962, 18–23; Salisbury 1986, 319–339.

64. Ferrell 1998, 127–128.

65. Ferrell 1998, 128.

66. Herring 2008, 476.

67. Quoted in Schoultz 1998, 280. Herring 2008, 476; Ferrell 1998, 128. On the issue of communist influence in Mexico see also Horn 1973, 455; Horn 1975, 31–45.

68. Ferrell 1998, 128; Horn 1973, 458.

69. McCoy 1967, 353; Horn 1973, 455–458.

70. Schoultz 1998, 280.

71. Smith 1972, 235, 238.

72. Horn 1973, 455–458, 464–466.

73. Schoultz 1998, 280–282; Smith 1972, 236–241; Cohen 1998, 235–236; McCoy 1967, 353; Wood 1962, 20–21.

74. Coolidge quoted in Ferrell 1998, 129.

75. Schoultz 1998, 281.

76. Schoultz 1998, 282.

77. Schoultz 1998, 280–282; Smith 1972, 244–259; Cohen 1998, 236–237; Ferrell 1998, 129–131; McCoy 1967, 355–356.

78. The most consistent advocates of using coercion against Mexico were oil interests and Catholic interest groups. See Horn 1973, 454–471.

79. Cohen 1998, 236.

80. Walker 2003, 20.

81. Kamman 1968, 42–51; Musicant 1990, 289–290.

82. Kamman 1968, 50–54; Bermann 1986, 184–185; Ferrell 1998, 133.

83. Kamman 1968, 58–59; Bermann 1986, 185.

84. Kamman 1968, 59–62. On Mexican support for the Liberal revolution see Salisbury 1986, 319–339.

85. Kamman 1968, 62–68; Bermann 1986, 186; Musicant 1990, 292.

86. Wood 1962, 15. On the fear of Mexican influence see also Horn 1973, 454–471; Horn 1975, 31–45; Salisbury 1986, 319–339.

87. Kamman 1968, 69–84, 90; Ferrell 1998, 134–135; McCoy 1967, 351–352; Musicant 1990, 292–293.

88. Kamman 1968, 83–92; Bermann 1986, 186–187; Musicant 1990, 293–294.

89. Kamman 1968, 92–95; Musicant 1990, 294–296. Eberhardt returned to Nicaragua around the time of Díaz's inauguration; Ferrell 1998, 134.

90. Kamman 1968, 95.

91. Bermann 1986, 191.

92. In the 1920s dollar diplomacy had a very negative connotation.

93. Kamman 1968, 92–96; Bermann 1986, 190–191, 193–194; Ferrell 1998, 135; Musicant 1990, 296–297.

94. Kamman 1968, 97.

95. Wood 1962, 18.

96. McCoy 1967, 352–353; Wood 1962, 17–18, 22–24; DeConde 1951, 8; Kamman 1968, 83.

97. Bermann 1986, 190.

98. Cabot quoted in MacMichael 1964, 638.

99. Curry 1979, 109–132; MacMichael 1964, 630–643; Atkins and Wilson 1998, 60–61; Peguero 2004, 64–65, 69.

100. Curry 1979, 132–135; MacMichael 1964, 645–646.

101. Curry 1979, 137–141; MacMichael 1964, 642–643; Atkins and Wilson 1998, 60.

102. Curry 1979, 142–143.

103. Curry 1979, 144–154; MacMichael 1964, 647–650; Atkins and Wilson 1998, 61–62.

104. Curry 1979, 165. See also Atkins and Wilson 1998, 63–64.

105. Atkins and Wilson 1998, 64.

106. Curry 1979, 158–167; MacMichael 1964, 644, 650–653; Atkins and Wilson 1998, 62–63; Peguero 2004, 67–68.

107. Schoultz 1998, 263.

108. Wheeler quoted in Bermann 1986, 188.

109. Bermann 1986, 187–188.

110. Bermann 1986, 188–190; McCoy 1967, 352–353. On Mexican involvement see Salisbury 1986, 319–339. On the fear of communist influence in Mexico see Horn 1975, 31–45.

111. Kamman 1968, 92–96; Bermann 1986, 193–194.

112. Cohen 1998, 236.

113. Bermann 1986, 194.

114. Kamman 1968, 97–117; Schoultz 1998, 263–264; Bermann 1986, 194–196; Ferrell 1998, 135; McCoy 1967, 354.

115. Bermann 1986, 205.

116. For a detailed account of the battle see Musicant 1990, 311–315.

117. Schoultz 1998, 264–265; Kamman 1968, 120–134; Bermann 1986, 196–199. For a detailed discussion of conflict see Musicant 1990, 308–361; Bickel 2001, 155–178.

118. Stamp quoted in Bermann 1986, 204.

119. Schoultz 1998, 265–267; Kamman 1968, 136–137, 139–140; Bermann 1986, 199–200, 203–204; Musicant 1990, 327–328.

120. Schoultz 1998, 267–269; Kamman 1968, 134–136, 170; Musicant 1990, 328; Walker 2003, 23; Cohen 1998, 236.

121. Kamman 1968, 154.

122. Schoultz 1998, 269–270; Kamman 1968, 144–167; Musicant 1990, 347–349; Ferrell 1998, 136–138. For a skeptical view of American neutrality see Bermann 1986, 208–209.

123. Ferrell 1998, 139.

124. Kamman 1968, 169–191; Bermann 1986, 210, 214–215; Musicant 1990, 349–352.

125. The Great Depression also ensured that Hoover was too distracted by other considerations to spend much time on Latin American policy: thus Stimson was left as the primary policymaker. Curry 1979, 104.

126. Ferrell 1998, 139.

127. Kamman 1968, 196.

128. Kamman 1968, 193–198; Bermann 1986, 213; Musicant 1990, 353–354.

129. Bermann 1986, 214.

130. Kamman 1968, 198–208; Musicant 1990, 355–356.

131. Schoultz 1998, 269–270; Kamman 1968, 208–218.

132. Kamman 1968, 233.

133. Kamman 1968, 142, 220–227, 226–234.

134. Wood 1962, 6.

135. Wood 1962, 25–47.

136. Wood 1962, 30–35.

137. Wood 1962, 35–41.

138. Wood 1962, 41–46.

139. Ironically, it may have been Wilson's sharp articulation of liberal norms that laid bare the hypocrisy of spreading constitutional government through force and the connection he made between spreading democracy and World War I that fostered American fatigue with political–military intervention.

140. Braeman 1982, 358–360; Herring 2008, 470; Grieb 1976, 8; Ferrell 1998, 121–122.

141. Wood 1962, 4.

142. On the Red Scare see Trani and Wilson 1977, 14–15.

143. Horn 1975, 31–45; Horn 1973, 454–471; Salisbury 1986, 319–339.

144. Wood 1962, 4.

145. Miller 1999, 99–100.

146. See, for example, Pletcher 2001, 1998.

147. Herring 2008, 471.

7

★

FROM NONINTERVENTION
TO NONINTERFERENCE

1933–1941

" F WE HAVE TO GO in there again we will never be able to come out and we
will have on our hands the trouble of thirty years ago." This quotation from
Secretary of State Cordell Hull during the Cuban crisis of 1933 conveys the
change in the perception of US national interests by foreign policy leaders in
the United States between the presidency of Theodore Roosevelt and the inauguration of Franklin D. Roosevelt as president of the United States. The United
States shifted from looking for justifications to "go in there" and stay as long as
possible, to looking for justifications to stay out. This shift was the culmination
of the trend in post-Wilson foreign policy toward nonintervention and noninterference. Under President Franklin Roosevelt the United States renounced its
right to intervene and interfere in the affairs of foreign countries in order to
prove itself a good neighbor in the Western Hemisphere. Attempts at big-stick
diplomacy were eliminated, and so too were attempts to exercise moral influence;
even informal advice regarding the domestic affairs of foreign countries by American diplomats was prohibited.

The Good Neighbor policy of Franklin Roosevelt marked the resolution of an
ongoing contradiction between the political structure of the United States and
the ambitions of individuals and organizations in the executive branch (and for
a time the Republican Party, business, and religious communities). The international and domestic pressures and opportunities generated by America's rise in
relative power between the 1890s and the 1920s led some individuals and organizations within American society to advocate a shift in American grand strategy
away from strategic restraint and toward the strategic expansionism and revisionism of a normal rising power. This shift was prevented by an American political
structure that fragmented and checked the use of state power and a strategic

culture that fostered distaste for expansionist policy. Thus while strategic ideas changed within the executive branch bureaucracy and military establishment, the fundamental institutional and normative structure of the United States did not change. The institutions created to restrain the use of state power—separation of powers, federalism, and democratic elections—combined with the entrenched anti-imperialist strategic culture of the United States to limit the influence of those advocating for a US role in world politics commensurate with its material power.

Unlike previous chapters, this chapter focuses less on the conflict between incentives for expansion and restraint and instead focuses on the reasons for the emergence of the Good Neighbor policy and its implementation in the Caribbean Basin. The reason for this change in emphasis is that military intervention ceases to be an option in American foreign policy after 1933. Once the Good Neighbor policy fully takes hold, it is taken for granted that the United States will not intervene and thus there is nothing to be restrained. In other words, restraint is taken for granted. Advocates of the use of military intervention to expand American political control over territory outside US borders are marginalized and without much influence in American politics. In short, American foreign policy after 1933 is explained by the implementation of the Good Neighbor policy, and therefore a central goal of this chapter is to explain the origins of the policy and demonstrate its implementation.

This chapter is organized as follows. The next section analyzes the causes of the Good Neighbor policy. The subsequent sections examine the cases of withdrawal from Haiti, nonintervention in Cuba, nonintervention in Mexico, and nonintervention in Nicaragua and in El Salvador. This chapter concludes with an overview of several episodes of American foreign policy between 1936 and the attack on Pearl Harbor to demonstrate the consistent application of nonintervention and noninterference even as threats emerged in Europe, East Asia, and to a lesser degree Latin America.

Explaining the Emergence of the Good Neighbor Policy

The one sentence on foreign policy in Roosevelt's inaugural address was directed toward relations within the Western Hemisphere: "In the field of world policy I would dedicate this Nation to the policy of the good neighbor—the neighbor who resolutely respects himself and, because he does so, respects the rights of others—the neighbor who respects his obligations and respects the sanctity of his agreements in and with a world of neighbors."[1] This brief statement suggests the reciprocal logic of the Good Neighbor policy: If the United States demonstrated greater respect for its neighbors by renouncing intervention and interference in domestic affairs, its neighbors would reciprocate by respecting American interests. In 1933 Good Neighborism was a germ of an idea rather than a well-thought-out, fully formulated program of action. It took several years for the idea to become a working policy that convincingly demonstrated to Latin America that the United States truly was committed to nonintervention and noninterference. The Good Neighbor policy evolved between 1933 and 1936. In 1933, at the Seventh International Conference of American States at Montevideo, Secretary of State Cordell Hull declared that "the United States government is as much opposed as any other government to interference with the freedom, the sovereignty, or other internal affairs or processes of the governments of other nations . . . no government need fear any intervention on the part of the United States under the Roosevelt administration."[2] However, Hull also noted a reservation to the policy of nonintervention: the United States maintained the right to intervene to protect the lives of its nationals living abroad. By the time of the 1936 Buenos Aires Conference, the commitment to nonintervention had strengthened. The United States approved, without reservation, article 1 of the Additional Protocol Relative to Non-Intervention, which declared all forms of intervention to be "inadmissible" regardless of the reason.[3] The culmination of these efforts by the United States was the high level of cooperation it received from Latin American countries during World War II.[4]

Throughout the 1930s, the Good Neighbor policy was strengthened by US actions. Implementation of the doctrine would show that Roosevelt was committed to a policy that "terminated existing military occupations and disavowed the US right of military intervention without relinquishing its preeminent position in the hemisphere and dominant role in Central America and the Caribbean."[5] Existing scholarship identifies several causes of the Good Neighbor doctrine. Each is summarized and evaluated below. Since the roots of the doctrine stretch back to the 1920s, some discussion of the policies of Harding, Coolidge, and Hoover is included.[6]

Level of Threat

One potential cause of the emergence of Good Neighborism was the decrease in threat to American interests in the Western Hemisphere. A prominent argument among historians of the 1920s and 1930s is that after World War I the probability of European expansion into the Western Hemisphere decreased to almost zero, which allowed for a shift in emphasis from hard to soft power. Since Germany was considered the main threat to the independence of Latin American countries, its defeat in the war freed the United States from the imperatives of defensive expansion or "preemptive imperialism."[7] Without a European threat, there was little reason for the United States to care about the internal affairs of its neighbors. Thus, after World War I American security was consistent with Latin American sovereignty and a policy of nonintervention.[8]

The problem with level of threat as an explanation is that absent a clear and direct danger to the homeland, threats are ambiguous and the responses are indeterminate. For example, it is not obvious why the United States would react to the German threat in the early 1900s by exercising more political control over its neighbors, but then react to the German threat of the late 1930s by strengthening its Good Neighbor policy. After 1938 and especially 1939, fear of German influence in Latin America increased. There were significant German and Italian populations in Latin America, and Germany was on a trade offensive in the Western Hemisphere. The start of war in Europe made these factors seem more sinister and fears of fascist influence in Latin America were high. However, American policymakers believed that this threat called for a more conciliatory approach rather than increased interventionism.[9] For example, a crisis over Mexican nationalization of foreign-owned oil companies between 1938 and 1941 was settled through negotiation favorable to Mexico. The United States did take aggressive action to remove German influences in its neighborhood, but focused on cooperation and solidarity with other countries in the hemisphere.[10] This approach was very different from the approach to the German threat prior to World War I, which US officials believed called for increased US political control over its neighbors. In sum, it is not clear why both the absence of threat in the early 1930s and then the emergence of threat in the late 1930s would lead to the same policy.

Great Depression

The effect of the Great Depression on all aspects of American policy and politics cannot be overstated. The massive economic downturn had three specific effects on American foreign policy. First, the US government became stingier and sought to eliminate financial obligations abroad, including military operations.[11] The economic downturn also affected US willingness to spend money on the military in general. For example, in 1934 the United States had 100 fewer ships than they were allowed under the treaties signed at the Washington Conference of 1921.[12] Second, increasing trade with Latin America was considered a means for ending the economic downturn. Increasing trade required negotiating lower tariffs, which required better relations with Latin American countries. Third, the Great Depression led to a more insular and less self-confident attitude in American foreign relations: "As they lost faith in their own exceptionalism, North Americans were less inclined to impose their will and values on others."[13]

The economic side to Roosevelt's policy is exemplified by the 1934 Reciprocal Trade Agreements Act "that gave the executive broad authority to negotiate with other nations a lowering of tariffs by up to 50 percent."[14] This legislation helped distance Congress from the process of international trade agreements and reduced the politicization of the tariff issue. The Act also "helped triple US trade with Latin America between 1931 and 1941" and reinforced the economic dependence of Latin America on the United States.[15] The Good Neighbor policy was also about treating the people of the Caribbean and Latin America with respect, something Roosevelt did naturally.

Much like level of threat, an economic downturn does not "come with an instruction sheet."[16] All things being equal, there is no obvious reason that the United States would necessarily choose a strategy of conciliation and trade reciprocity. Other countries turned to autarky, fascism, and military expansionism in response to the Great Depression. Also, in the 1890s and early 1900s the need for new markets was one of the primary arguments offered by American advocates of expansionism. Why in the early 1900s did economic expansionism require political–military expansion, but in the 1930s require the total renunciation of political–military intervention?

Lessons Learned

A third reason given for the emergence of the Good Neighbor doctrine is the argument that after 30 years of attempts, the United States learned that military intervention was counterproductive to American interests. For example, Dana Munro, a State Department official from 1919 to 1932 and Princeton professor, stated:

> After 1920 the United States tried to reduce its interference in the internal affairs of the Caribbean republics. The officers who dealt with Latin American matters at Washington still hoped for the development of stable republican institutions in the Caribbean, but *they realized that the effort to impose peace and progress by force had been unprofitable*. At best the interventions in Nicaragua, Haiti, and the Dominican Republic had only partly achieved their objectives, and they *had aroused hostile criticism which was politically embarrassing at home and harmful to our relations with the other American republics* (emphasis added).[17]

In other words, the game was not worth the candle. It is important to note that Munro identifies the costs as negative domestic and international public opinion, not as a degradation of the strategic position of the United States vis-à-vis other great powers.

Similarly, Wood argues that "questioning of the old policy arose from practical experience and personal disenchantment seems to have been more important than intellectual analysis as a source of new policies."[18] Furthermore, "employment of force in the Caribbean was not only disproportionately expensive in protecting citizens and property abroad and ineffective in promoting democracy; it was also positively disadvantageous to their evolving conception of the national interest of the United States."[19]

These quotations point to a more fundamental cause of the Good Neighbor policy: the costs imposed on an expansionist strategy by American norms and institutions. The costs and disenchantment referenced by Munro and Wood were not simply a result of policy learning.[20] Or perhaps it is better to say that what occurred was a particular type of policy learning. The costs existed primarily because imperialism ran counter to American norms, and the exercise of state power required to implement an imperial strategy was prevented by American institutions of division and balance. Expansion of American political–military control over foreign territory threatened the popularity and electoral success of American political leaders and political parties. Separation of powers gave the opposition party plenty of tools to use to delay, limit, and prevent the implementation of expansionist policy, while imposing increased political costs on the ruling party. Furthermore, as Paul Drake argues, the United States had a particularly difficult time with expansionist policy because it almost always attempted to impose democratic-constitutional government rather than authoritarian rule in the areas it occupied. Because it was more difficult to establish a functioning democracy than to simply implement military control, the United States turned away from interfering with the domestic politics of other countries.[21]

Thus, the lesson learned by American politicians and civil servants was that the American political system could not support an expansionist strategy.

Electoral Incentives

Finally, Robert David Johnson argues that domestic electoral pressures were behind the Good Neighbor policy. By the early 1930s the peace progressives were a large enough block to be a potent force in American politics. Franklin Roosevelt therefore conceded to the peace progressive position on Latin America to gain their votes on domestic issues and prevent them from forming a splinter party. By 1934 the anti-imperialist wing of the peace progressives was fully behind the Good Neighbor policy.[22] The peace progressives were important, because their critique of American foreign policy resonated within wide swaths of American society. There was widespread sentiment that the United States had been too active abroad and should return to a more restrained foreign policy focusing on good relations within the Western Hemisphere and noninvolvement vis-à-vis Europe, a policy similar to the pre-1898 foreign policy.[23] In addition, Roosevelt learned when he was campaigning for the presidency that "informed domestic opinion now seemed strongly against military adventures of any kind."[24]

The agenda of the peace progressives in some ways overlapped with the agenda of the isolationists. Mostly elected from western states, isolationists from both parties distrusted almost any form of engagement with the rest of the world and wanted to focus on domestic reforms and homeland defense. Unlike peace activists, isolationists were against the League of Nations and World Court. They were also strong watchdogs on presidential power, sponsoring neutrality legislation and the Ludlow amendment that would have required a popular vote before declaring war.[25]

Like the other arguments summarized above, the electoral explanation is valid, but incomplete. Territorial expansion has always run the risk of backlash from the American public. This risk may have been higher in the 1930s than the 1910s, but this is not the only reason for Roosevelt's Good Neighbor policy.

A Domestic Structure Synthesis

The limits of any one explanation for Good Neighborism would seem to suggest throwing all the explanations together to produce a multivariate solution. However, a simple additive explanation (absence of threat plus the need to expand trade plus electoral incentives plus . . .) is not as satisfying as an explanation that can identify the underlying reason that the United States reacted the way it did to the Great Depression and the level of threat, and why American officials learned the lesson that military intervention does not pay. The underlying explanation that ties these factors together is the role of the American political structure in preventing expansionism from being fully and successfully implemented. The United States weathered two strong waves for expansionism. Both times domestic institutions and norms slowly degraded the power of these waves until their energy was dissipated.

By 1933, it had become clear that American norms and institutions would not support a grand strategy based on political–military expansionism. Changes in strategic ideas were never translated into wholesale change of American strategic culture with its strong element of anti-imperialism. The normative structure of American politics created significant drag on expansionists' efforts to successfully initiate and effectively implement policies that increased American political control over foreign territory. American institutions provided the political space and organizational capacity for anti-imperialist norms to impose costs on expansionist politicians. American political leaders consistently worried about the electoral effects of American anti-imperialism; while anti-imperialism was never the dominant issue in American politics, it was important enough to a large enough group of voters to shape elections and foreign policy decision making. The decentralized nature of American government allowed a minority of elected representatives to delay and prevent expansionist policies from being successfully implemented. And in many cases, anti-imperialist politicians could impose costs on expansionists simply by publically criticizing expansionist policies and thereby drawing public attention and media scrutiny. Institutions also had a more autonomous effect on American foreign policy. Even without anti-imperialist norms, American institutions provide a strong incentive for the different branches of government to check and balance one another and for the opposition party to oppose the policies of the party in power.

To say that domestic structure was most important is not the same as saying other factors were irrelevant in explaining US foreign policy in the 1930s. Perception of threat is part of the reason that there were strong pressures for a more expansionist foreign policy in the early 1900s and a weaker pressure for expansionism in the 1920s and early 1930s. It is also likely that the low threat level of the 1920s facilitated the emergence of Good Neighbor policy, but a far more important factor was the reality that US experiments in expansionism never gained the popular support required for full implementation of the expansionist program. American officials learned that advocates of expansion could not mobilize sufficient support to implement their preferred policies. The lesson was that expansionism could not work for the United States, and so some other alternative had to be implemented. Stronger political–military control of the Western Hemisphere was a plausible reaction to outside threat, but in practice it could not be implemented systematically because of normative and institutional restraints. The Great Depression reinforced the cost sensitivity of the American public, but did not fundamentally shift American thinking about the utility of political–military control over foreign territory. The renewed emphasis on soft power and trade with Latin America was an acknowledgment that hard power, gunboat diplomacy was ineffective at achieving US interests in the hemisphere. All of these points are supported by the previous chapter and the case studies presented below.

The next section is the first case study of the Good Neighbor era. It spans both the Hoover and Roosevelt administrations, and therefore serves as a bridge between retrenchment of the 1920s and the formalization of nonintervention in the 1930s. It analyzes the end of the American occupation of Haiti as a process that took five years to achieve. Important initial decisions by Hoover to reduce American influence on Haitian politics were completed by Roosevelt's decisive action to eliminate American interference in Hispaniola.

Withdrawal from Haiti (1933)

The United States had occupied Haiti since 1915 and controlled its government through the client president Borno. Like other US occupations during this period, the material and normative difficulties resulting from the military administration of a foreign territory slowly undermined public support. Hoover came to office with a strong desire to withdraw from Haiti, but strong opposition from the State Department and navy officials, especially those on the ground in Haiti, delayed withdrawal.[26] Racial paternalism played a strong role in perpetuating the belief that Haitians were unable to govern themselves and perpetually needed just a few more years of tutelage. The occupation was consistently unpopular among Haitians, but it took the widespread political unrest of 1929 for the level of opposition to reach the American consciousness. Beginning in 1930 the US press and members of Congress began to advocate for an end to the American occupation. Hoover sent the Forbes Commission to study the situation in Haiti and develop an exit plan for the United States. However, Hoover's State Department delayed the implementation of the plan and US forces did not withdraw until Franklin Roosevelt took office in 1933.

The 1929 Uprising and Emergence of Popular Opposition to Occupation in the United States

By 1929 Herbert Hoover had taken office as president of the United States with a clear intention to revise American foreign policy in the Western Hemisphere. However, before any significant change could be implemented, the "latent hatred" of the occupation by the Haitian people exploded into widespread political unrest.[27] The conjuncture of an economic downturn, the cancelation of the 1930 election, fear that President Borno would be given another term in office, and increased taxes led Haitians to the edge of revolt. The spark that turned latent hatred into public protest was a student strike in October 1929 at the Service Technique school caused by a decrease in scholarships for city students. Medical and law students showed support by striking and were followed by all students throughout the country. By December, the student strike had become a general uprising.[28] The Garde d'Harde proved ineffective at controlling the protests without marine leadership. American High Commissioner John Russell declared martial law, shut down the opposition press, reincorporated the Garde under marine control, and sent reinforcements throughout the country to put down uprisings. The Hoover administration urged restraint and criticized the instatement of martial law. Secretary of State Stimson advised Russell to revoke his declaration of martial law and reduce the visibility of marine patrols. Then on December 6 at the town of Aux Cayes, a confrontation between a mob of 1,500 Haitians and 20 marines led to the deaths of at least a dozen Haitians with twice that number wounded; one marine was also injured.[29] There were conflicting accounts as to who started the violence, but the end result was marines firing on Haitians armed with stones, machetes, and clubs. Russell claimed that restraint on the part of the marines prevented hundreds of casualties, and the commanding officer at Aux Cayes was awarded the Navy Cross.[30]

The Cayes massacre energized American and international opposition to the occupation of Haiti. Protests were held in Washington, DC, and New York.

Members of Congress began to attack US policy, even comparing the US occupation to Britain in India and Japan in Korea. Hoover administration policy was also critiqued as contradicting American ideals and undermining American democracy—denial of self-government by the United States undermined American commitment to democratic principles. One member of the US Congress argued that "an imperialism abroad can not remain a democracy at home."[31] The Haitian issue also became embroiled with the controversy over the rights of black Americans. Overall interest in Haiti significantly increased after the 1929 uprisings as news coverage increased.[32] Previously, censorship by the occupation authority and the fact that the Associated Press (AP) and United Press International (UPI) were represented in Haiti by Marine officers led to the suppression of news from Haiti. In 1929 AP and UPI sent additional reporters, and other outlets sent their own reporters. European reaction was critical, often pointing out American hypocrisy in its criticisms of European imperialism. Hostility in the Latin American press was also high. The events of 1929 revealed that there would be no easy way for the United States to leave Haiti.[33]

The Election of 1930 and Hoover's Haitianization

The second half of 1930 marked a major departure in Haitian politics signaled by successful legislative and presidential elections and the end of the American military regime. Following Louis Eugène Roy's inauguration as interim president in May, sporadic unrest continued. The legislative elections occurred on October 15, 1930. The State Department ordered all US personnel to remain neutral and avoid influencing the election; US Marines were confined to barracks. The result was a victory for Haitian nationalists. Pro-American candidates and moderates were soundly defeated by anti-American Haitian nationalists. The legislature then elected antioccupation intellectual Sténio Vincent as the president of Haiti and he was inaugurated on November 18, 1930.[34] Russell resigned and was replaced by State Department Latin American expert Dr. Dana Munro, who was appointed as the new American Minister to Haiti. Colonel Louis McCarty Little was brought in to command the marines. The election of Vincent and transition in personnel ended the era of American military rule of Haiti. The orders of Munro and Little were to interfere as little as possible with the functioning of the new government and maintain an accommodating stance generally.[35] At the same time, both Munro and Stimson agreed that Haitians were not ready for independence and did what they could to delay American withdrawal.[36]

Some progress toward independence was made under the efforts of Munro and Little, but the American strategy of gradual Haitianization of government administration quickly fell apart. The American-led treaty services began to collapse as American officials resigned, unhappy with how their service had been portrayed in the Forbes Report.[37] Munro found the Vincent government unwilling to follow along with State Department plans for slowly ending the occupation. Vincent demanded that the treaty services and Garde be rapidly shifted to Haitian control. Stimson ordered Munro to accede to Haitian demands as necessary, because US public opinion would not support the remilitarization of the occupation in order to have its way on the pace of Haitianization. Stimson noted that "taking a stand . . . would result in virtual military occupancy of Haiti," something that would be difficult to justify in terms of public opinion.[38] As the American position became increasingly untenable President Hoover pushed for a more rapid withdrawal. A Haitianization agreement was formalized in August 1931.[39]

The End of Occupation

The Hoover administration made significant progress toward ending the occupation of Haiti, but the final step was taken only after inauguration of Roosevelt. The final and most difficult problem of withdrawal was Haiti's financial situation. The United States made a commitment in to maintain a customs receivership until the 1922 bond issue was repaid, which went against the Hoover policy to reduce American responsibility for Haiti as much as possible, as soon as possible. American policy was to avoid any action that would "extend in any way the period of its financial stewardship," but Hoover was also committed to fulfilling the US government's responsibility to Haitian creditors.[40] As Munro later argued, "Neither Haiti nor the United States, in fact, was free to terminate American supervision of Haiti's finances, even after the treaty expired, because the protocol of 1919 provided that an official nominated by the president of the United States should control the collection and allocation of the Republic's revenues during the life of the loan which the protocol authorized."[41] Of course the Haitian debt was a result of the US decision in 1922 to procure a $16 million loan on behalf of Haiti, and therefore was never approved by a truly independent Haitian government.

It was only after the election of Franklin Roosevelt that the State Department and the Haitian government signed an executive agreement (on August 7, 1933) specifying that an American representative would remain as a financial advisor to the Haitian government, but with much more limited powers than under the occupation—it was an attempt to please both Haitians and American bondholders. The US "fiscal representative would control customs, inspect the Internal Revenue Service, set limitations on the Haitian government budget, and be able to set up and control reserve funds. The Haitian government was forbidden to increase its indebtedness, change tariffs and taxes, or dispose of investments without his consent. This financial supervision was to continue until all the outstanding bonds, scheduled to expire in 1952, were liquidated. The United

States, in turn, agreed to withdraw American troops by October, 1934, one and one half years before the 1936 date stipulated in the 1915 treaty, and to limit the number of Americans employed by the fiscal representative."[42] The deal was very similar to the unpopular Treaty of Friendship signed on December 31, 1934, but rejected by the Haitian legislature. The Haitian legislature was dominated by nationalists who favored the immediate end of any and all American influence over Haiti. The agreement was also attacked by anti-imperialists in the United States as more of the same old policy where the US government collected loan payments on behalf of private interests. The United States attempted to shift the responsibility of financial supervision to the Banque Nationale, but was stymied by opposition from American bondholders until 1941 when Banque Nationale took over receivership responsibilities.[43]

The United States remained saddled with its financial responsibilities in Haiti, but the withdrawal of all other personnel proceeded according to the 1933 agreement. As an extra symbol of goodwill, President Roosevelt visited Cap-Haïtien in July 1934. Roosevelt celebrated that he was visiting "at a time when the relationship between the Republic of Haiti and the Republic of the United States will be restored to a basis of complete independence."[44] The trip led to better relations—he was the first foreign head of state to visit Haiti in its entire history, and he announced that the occupation would end a few months earlier than had been agreed upon. Roosevelt left a good impression on the Haitian people that had a long-term effect on US-Haitian relations. Upon withdrawing the last American forces on August 15, 1934, the United States donated $120,000 in matériel and buildings.[45]

American occupation of Haiti was marked by significant material achievement, but failed to fundamentally change Haitian politics or society. The United States proved once again that it could not easily maintain a long-term occupation of foreign territory. Excluding the possessions gained in 1898, Haiti was the longest occupation of foreign territory during the period covered in this study. It lasted longer than other occupations for several reasons. The Haitian independence movement received less support from Latin American countries and from within the United States than the Dominican or Nicaraguan independence movements. Schoultz argues that support was lacking because Haitians are predominantly black and not Spanish speakers. It is also true that the Dominican Republic gained independence sooner than Haiti because the Haitian nationalist movement gained strength later in the occupation, and in Haiti some elites cooperated to form a government that put a Haitian face on the occupation. It is all the more striking because the abuses by occupation forces in Haiti were worse than in the Dominican Republic. Haiti was also less important economically, and so its status was irrelevant to the business community.[46]

Historian Donald Cooper does a good job identifying the most important factors that led to the end of the American occupation of Haiti—all of the factors are consistent with explanations for the emergence of the Good Neighbor policy surveyed above. First, the perceived threat to the Panama Canal receded after World War I. Second, it appeared that some American goals, such as financial reform and the establishment of a US-trained Haitian National Guard, had succeeded. Third, it was unlikely that extending the occupation would yield much additional gain. Fourth, the American public had come to view "foreign commitments . . . as threats from which we should disengage ourselves as rapidly as possible. The occupation of Haiti, on these terms, became a 'horrible example'orather than a fertile field for altruistic experiments."[47] For example, the occupation of Haiti was used by Japan as justification for its territorial aggrandizement in East Asia. Fifth, Haitian opposition to occupation fostered American withdrawal. Cooper also cites a 1958 personal letter from Dana Munro where the former ambassador to Haiti gives his own explanation for the end of the occupation:

> I think that the most important factor in the decision to withdraw from Haiti was President Hoover's dislike of military interventions. "Anti-imperialist" criticism of our Caribbean policy in the United States had of course been influencing the policies of the State Department ever since 1921, but I don't believe that it had so much effect on Mr. Hoover as did his own personal convictions. . . . I doubt whether European criticism had much effect, and the State Department was rather insensitive before 1933 to Latin American criticism.[48]

The perceived benefits of occupying Haiti were decreasing as the domestic political cost of occupation was increasing. The Hoover administration prepared the foundation for withdrawal, but it took Roosevelt's election to finally end the occupation. Roosevelt made the final decision to reduce US financial control in Haiti, but more importantly he signaled a new era of American respect for the smaller republics of the Western Hemisphere. Both Hoover and Roosevelt were personally anti-imperialist, and both recognized the political costs of extending the occupation. Therefore, this case of rollback is best explained by strategic culture and institutional structure through the mechanisms of public opinion and congressional opposition.

Nonintervention in Cuba (1933)

One of Franklin D. Roosevelt's first foreign policy problems was renewed internal conflict in Cuba. President Roosevelt was inaugurated on March 4, 1933, and in May he sent his top Latin American advisor, Sumner Welles, to Cuba as the new ambassador. Welles's mission was to mediate between President Gerardo Machado and his opponents and put in place the conditions for a fair election.

Like his immediate predecessor, Roosevelt had no interest in military intervention and Welles's diplomacy was meant to prevent the conditions that would necessitate intervention (i.e., total chaos in Cuba). However, Welles was much more of an active participant in Cuban politics than Roosevelt expected, and came close to drawing the United States into yet another military intervention in Cuba. Roosevelt generally supported Welles, but made it clear that military intervention was not an option because of fear of public opposition in the United States and in Latin America and because of personal values. The Seventh International Conference of American States in Montevideo, Uruguay, was approaching, and Roosevelt wanted to take the opportunity to promote better relations with other countries in the hemisphere. Despite Roosevelt's strong opposition to military intervention, Welles's actions in Cuba came close to creating the conditions for another US military occupation of Cuba. Roosevelt learned that allowing any interference in the domestic politics of another country increased the likelihood of military intervention.

A Cuban Plan, Agreed Upon by Cubans

When Roosevelt was inaugurated, Gerardo Machado was president of Cuba after being reelected in a fraudulent election in 1928. At the time of Machado's reelection the Coolidge administration made it known that the United States would not interfere in Cuban domestic politics. Machado was seen as a good friend to the United States, but by 1929 he was rapidly losing support in Cuba in part due to economic collapse and his policies of repression. In 1929 Secretary of State Stimson was being pressured by American and Cuban groups to intervene under the rights set forth in the Platt Amendment, but he declined, stating that intervention was unnecessary because Machado was maintaining stability. The United States did try to moderate Machado's oppressive policies, but was generally unsuccessful. Even the attempted revolution in 1931 was insufficient to cause US intervention.[49] By 1933, revolution seemed imminent.

A general strike in August of 1933 convinced Welles that the political unrest would only get worse if Machado remained in office. He gave the Cuban president an ultimatum to resign or be deposed by the United States—a bluff that had no support in Washington, but officials were too busy for close oversight of Welles's actions in Havana.[50]

As the political crisis in Cuba intensified in August, Hull and Roosevelt did provide Welles with support by communicating to Cuban Ambassador Oscar Cintas that Welles was acting with the full knowledge and confidence of the president, and Roosevelt continued to voice support for the resignation of Machado.[51] However, Welles was instructed "not to press him [Machado] further at the moment" and was reminded that he was there to "persuade" not "coerce," and that it was not his job to develop a plan to end the crisis; instead he was to support the development of "a Cuban plan, agreed upon by Cubans."[52] President Roosevelt and Secretary Hull did not endorse Welles's threat of intervention to remove Machado, and stated that intervention would only occur to prevent "starvation and chaos" in Cuba.[53] Military intervention in Cuba would undermine Roosevelt's plan to increase trade between the United States and Latin America and would make Roosevelt vulnerable to "a storm of criticism from pacifists at home and Latins abroad and distract energy and attention from pressing domestic needs."[54]

Welles took a much more invasive approach than what his superiors intended. The Ambassador to Cuba recommended that the United States withdraw support for President Machado and send two naval vessels to maintain stability. When this proposal didn't get anywhere, Welles helped orchestrate Machado's resignation with the collaboration of Cuban Secretary of War, General Alberto Herrera. Once the president understood that he no longer had the support of the army, he agreed to step down. Carlos Manuel de Céspedes was installed as interim president, but political unrest continued and he was quickly replaced by Ramón Grau San Martín in a September 4 coup led by Sergeant Fulgencio Batista and other noncommissioned officers. Batista named himself commander of the army and was the real leader of the government. Welles did not approve of the new government of "extreme radicals" and repeatedly called for the United States to intervene militarily to install a new government and prevent increased influence by communist leaders.[55] He argued that it would be a police action and not an armed intervention, and warned Washington about the imminent danger of drunken communists.[56]

Despite Welles's repeated requests, Secretary of State Cordell Hull and President Roosevelt were unmoved. US Ambassador to Mexico Josephus Daniels urged caution, and his position carried weight with Hull because of Daniels's eight years as Secretary of the Navy under President Wilson and personal relationship with Franklin Roosevelt. On September 6 Hull observed, "If we have to go in there again we will never be able to come out and we will have on our hands the trouble of thirty years ago."[57] This quote demonstrates two fundamental aspects to Roosevelt's Good Neighbor policy: first, the general aversion to the military intervention in other countries and, second, the belief that long-term political control of foreign territory had no utility and instead was "trouble."

Roosevelt was also highly concerned with Latin American opinion. For the first time in American history, Roosevelt consulted with Latin American leaders (from Argentina, Brazil, Chile, and Mexico) before making a foreign policy decision.[58] It was clear that Latin American countries would not approve of an American military intervention in Cuba—Argentina and Mexico said as much—and good relations with Latin America was a top priority for Roosevelt. Hull later wrote that he was influenced by "the disastrous reaction that would follow throughout Latin America if we agreed to his [Welles's] request."[59] The

Seventh International Conference of American States at Montevideo was rapidly approaching and Roosevelt hoped to lay the groundwork for better economic relations with Latin American countries including tariff reductions. The United States was also afraid that Mexico might seek support for a debt moratorium at the conference, which would put the United States in a difficult position of being the only country to support the bankers. There was even talk among Latin American countries that the conference would be postponed if the United States intervened in Cuba.[60]

On May 29, 1934 the special relationship between Cuba and the United States ended when the United States foreswore any right to intervene in Cuban affairs. The treaty agreement abrogated the Platt Amendment, lowered tariffs on bilateral trade, and allowed the United States to maintain its naval base at Guantánamo Bay. It was a symbolically important action, but nonintervention was well entrenched as American policy by 1934. In fact, "by 1933 the Platt Amendment . . . had become for the United States a burdensome responsibility involving duties to maintain order which appeared not only incompatible with the Good Neighbor policy but also expensive and troublesome."[61] The revocation of the Platt Amendment paid immediate dividends throughout Latin America. It was a clear renunciation of interventionism and raised the moral standing of the United States in the Western Hemisphere.[62]

Nonintervention

Roosevelt refused calls for military intervention, but allowed Welles to use political influence and intimidation to help shape the outcome of Cuba's fluid political situation. On Welles's advice Roosevelt refused to recognize the Grau government and deployed as many as 30 naval ships around the coast to restrain revolutionary excess and prevent any action that might endanger American nationals. Since danger to lives of American citizens was the only reason that the United States would deploy military forces to Cuba, the mission of the navy was to prevent intervention. At the same time, nonrecognition made it extremely difficult for the Grau regime to establish stability, as Welles clearly understood. The main criterion for recognition was the ability of the government to maintain order. After two months US policy came under criticism from Latin American leaders and the US press; the Roosevelt administration continued to claim that Grau could not be recognized because he could not establish order in Cuba. But Roosevelt continued to support Welles's position and refused to recognize Grau.[63]

The policy of nonrecognition continued after Welles was replaced by Jefferson Caffery as ambassador to Cuba in late 1933, probably because Welles was getting too personally involved in Cuban politics and overly favorable to the Céspedes Government. His insistence on the removal of Grau seemed to go beyond what was necessary for the purposes of US interests. However, when Caffery supported Welles's position, Batista concluded that the Grau regime would not be recognized by the United States. In January of 1934 Batista convinced Grau to resign from office to be replaced provisionally by Carlos Mendieta, a popular politician from the Nationalist party. President Roosevelt quickly recognized the Mendieta government.[64]

Of the three cases presented in this chapter, this is the only one where military intervention was suggested by a high-ranking US official. Roosevelt's experience with Cuba reinforced his commitment to nonintervention, demonstrated by the subsequent revocation of the Platt Amendment.[65] While concern about the Montevideo conference was probably the most proximate factor in President Roosevelt's mind, broader factors also came into play. Many US officials understood the strong underlying resentment in Latin America and were worried about the impact intervention would have on relations in the region, and the Great Depression made increasing trade a national priority.[66] The most important underlying reason was that Roosevelt had committed himself to a course of action—nonintervention—for reasons stated above, and he stuck to that commitment.

Lars Schoultz makes the important point that Roosevelt's Cuban policy was considered a successful implementation of Good Neighborism only because intervention was so narrowly defined.[67] Partly in response to Welles's interference in Cuban politics in 1933, the Good Neighbor policy was subsequently expanded to prohibit any interference in the domestic politics of other countries. The experience with Cuba in 1933 was instructive for the Roosevelt administration. The lesson was that once interference in the domestic politics commences it is difficult to control and may lead to intervention. Better to renounce interference and intervention, except in very specific circumstances.[68]

The Cuban crisis of 1933 did not result in any political–military expansion. The deployment of gunboats was certainly a coercive measure but not an expansionist measure. Therefore this is a case of restraint caused by the personal beliefs of Franklin Roosevelt, the fear of opposition from Latin American countries, and public opposition in the United States.

Nonintervention in Mexico (1938–1940)

War with Mexico again became plausible in 1938 when President Lázaro Cárdenas nationalized several foreign-owned oil operations. Rumors circulated that the Axis Powers were behind the policy, and FBI director J. Edgar Hoover claimed that Mexican President Cárdenas was a supporter of Germany *and* tied to communists. The United States initially chose a coercive strategy, but voices of moderation won the day with Ambassador to Mexico Josephus Daniels and President

Roosevelt supporting a conciliatory approach. As the war in Europe intensified, the United States sought to settle its problems with Mexico. The United States declared that Mexico had the right to nationalize foreign holdings if the owners received just compensation, and a bilateral commission was set up to determine the amount of compensation. The US oil companies involved in the issue were not satisfied with the outcome, but Secretary Hull made the deal anyway. The United States wanted to dissuade Mexico from selling oil to Germany, Italy, and Japan, and developed a new emphasis on hemispheric security.[69] The personal commitment to the core principles of Good Neighborism by Ambassador Daniels and Secretary of the Treasury Morgenthau was also a decisive factor, because they were in a position to soften US policy and because President Roosevelt supported their preference for a more conciliatory policy.

Initial US Reaction to Nationalization

On March 18, 1938, President Lázaro Cárdenas partially nationalized the oil industry in Mexico, expropriating approximately $500 million worth of land and equipment from American, British, and Dutch oil companies. Cárdenas pledged to pay compensation for the expropriated property, but when and how this would be done was unclear. American companies estimated that they lost $260 million—an estimate later found to be wildly inflated. Nationalization was the culmination of decades of conflict between the Mexican government and foreign oil companies. Successive Mexican governments attempted to gain more control over their oil industry, while foreign companies remained intransigent to any changes in Mexican law that might degrade their property rights.[70]

Up until the moment of expropriation, the US State Department was content to let the Mexican government and the oil companies resolve their own dispute. In Mexico the US ambassador, Josephus Daniels, sought to foster cooperation and compromise between the American oil companies and the Mexican government. The expropriation announcement caught US officials off guard, but the State Department quickly settled on the general understanding that Mexico had a right to expropriate private property, but must pay adequate compensation for the taking, and the United States should support oil company claims for compensation.[71] But reaching an agreement that would satisfy Mexico and the oil companies took years to achieve and required considerable trial and error by the State Department. At times US-Mexican relations were quite troubled, but at no time was military action considered by US officials.[72]

The first action of the State Department was a sharply worded protest to the Mexican government demanding to know "what specific action with respect to payment for the properties in question is contemplated by the Mexican government, what assurances will be given that payment will be made, and when such payment may be expected."[73] To emphasize the seriousness of the inquiry the

United States also announced a suspension of silver purchases from Mexico, which created the potential for significant economic loss for Mexico. Daniels convinced Hull to soften the US approach and used his own personal diplomacy to informally retract Hull's memo. Mexican officials were offended that Hull's note did not mention Cárdenas's pledge to compensate the oil companies and the inference that the word of the Mexican president was not sufficient to reassure the US government. A confused situation emerged where the Mexican government assumed Hull's note had been retracted while Hull still expected a formal response. In the short run both countries made conciliatory statements, but the situation required additional diplomacy by Daniels before the matter was fully settled. Without the interference of Daniels the US-Mexico relationship could have worsened considerable. However, there was never any danger that the United States would try to interfere in Mexican domestic politics through military force or otherwise. Suggestions from private citizens that the United States take a harder line were quickly dismissed by Roosevelt administration officials and the president himself.[74]

Economic Pressure

While the United States was unwilling to use military coercion or support regime change, the Roosevelt administration was willing to use economic pressure to convince Mexico to quickly and fully compensate American companies for the expropriation of their property. One form of economic leverage with Mexico was the standing agreement that the United States would buy 5 million ounces of silver every month at a price slightly above market value. Silver exports were almost as important to the Mexican economy as oil because it was a major source of government revenue through export taxes and was Mexico's most valuable export commodity. In response to Mexican expropriation, Secretary Hull wanted to use this leverage from the silver purchasing agreement to encourage Mexico to move forward with compensation. Hull pressured Secretary of the Treasury Henry Morgenthau to put a moratorium on silver purchases from Mexico. But the most that Morgenthau would agree to was to purchase silver at the market price instead of the slightly elevated price, without preference to or discrimination of Mexican silver. In sum, the special agreement ended in March of 1938, but US purchase of Mexican silver continued. The move disappointed the Mexican government, but since the harm to Mexico was relatively minor no formal protest was issued. The only other measure by the United States that bordered on coercion was the suggestion to the American private sector and to foreign allies that it was risky to purchase oil from Mexico until compensation was made. As a result, Mexican oil sales dropped significantly and forced Mexico to increase its oil sales to the Axis powers.[75]

Overall the State Department, including Hull, wanted to take a harder line with Mexico, but other administration officials like Daniels and Morgenthau disagreed and received support from President Roosevelt for a more conciliatory posture.[76]

Toward Accommodation

The main barrier to settlement of the claims of foreign oil companies was disagreement over the forum used to adjudicate the dispute. The British, Dutch, and US governments, along with the oil companies (except Sinclair Oil, which was negotiating with Mexico independently) wanted arbitration by an international tribunal. Mexico was adamant that decisions involving compensation for expropriated property should be made by two-man commissions, with one member from each country party to the dispute. The American position was that the Good Neighbor Policy required adherence to international law, and international law required arbitration by an international tribunal. By November of 1938 the United States was coming around to the Mexican position, and agreed that a bilateral commission would settle claims for compensation due to the expropriation of land by the Mexican government. A similar capitulation over oil expropriation compensation claims occurred in November of 1941, though the Mexican position was accepted in principle in 1940. Woods argues that the United States continued to advocate for arbitration between 1938 and 1941 in order to demonstrate to oil companies and their supporters in the government that every effort had been made to convince Mexico accept arbitration. Ultimately, "the national interest was . . . seen by the Department of State as being different from that of the oil companies and as superior to it."[77] The United States was anxious to gain Mexican cooperation for hemispheric defense projects, particularly the use of Mexican airfields. Woods argues that the developing military crisis in Europe and East Asia shaped the timing but not substance of the agreement, because there was no deep attachment to arbitration by the Roosevelt administration. Oil companies protested, especially Standard Oil, but to no avail.[78]

In this case the level of systemic threat was high due to the war in Europe, but ambiguous in the Western Hemisphere. Some figures within the US government believed there was a link or a potential link between Mexico nationalization and the objectives of the Axis powers. Others saw a need to remain on good terms with the Mexico to prevent any link from forming between Mexico and the Axis powers. Therefore the threat from Mexico was ambiguous in the sense that US leaders could either emphasize the potential threat from Mexico or the opportunity for cooperation. So threat perception is indeterminate in this case, favoring neither expansion nor restraint. Whether or not Mexico was viewed as a threat was strongly shaped by the personal values of men like Ambassador Daniels and

Secretary Morgenthau as well as the ubiquitous belief within the US government that military intervention and coercion were not appropriate responses to disputes with foreign nations. The final agreement on compensation for Mexican expropriation of American property was contrary to American business interests, which demonstrates that the US decision was not determined by private interests.[79] While this is considered a case of restraint, it is a relatively weak case because the push for expansion was much weaker than in the other cases.

Noninterference in Central America 1936–1941

As in previous decades, the 1930s presented the United States with opportunities for expanding their political–military control over foreign territory. The United States repeatedly passed up these opportunities in favor of a policy of nonintervention and noninterference. In addition to the cases presented above, the United States also altered its treaty with Panama to more equitably distribute canal revenues and revoke the right of the United States to intervene in Panamanian domestic affairs, and declined to intervene after the 1936 coup in Nicaragua by Somoza and other instances of unconstitutional actions by Central American leaders.[80]

Despite requests for intervention from the Sacasa government in Nicaragua, the United States took no action to prevent Somoza from taking power in the summer of 1936. The United States also refused to exercise its influence in El Salvador when President Maximiliano Martínez changed the constitution to allow for his own reelection. The State Department learned the lesson that even the most benign influence on the domestic affairs of foreign countries gave the perception that the United States was responsible for subsequent events in that country. The dominant perspective was that the United States should eliminate its influence on domestic affairs outside its borders in order to eliminate its responsibility for the domestic politics of foreign countries. Noninterference was widely popular in Latin America.[81] One potential black mark on the policy of nonintervention and noninterference was Panama in 1941. President Arnulfo Arias was overthrown in a military coup in 1941 after the United States had shown strong disapproval of his reluctance to grant the United States rights to ten one-acre bases for the purposes of air defense. The United States supported the end of Arias's presidency, but it is unclear what influence the United States had on the coup.[82]

Some historians criticize the Good Neighbor policy because Roosevelt did nothing to prevent the rise of military dictators in Latin America, and even hold him responsible for the subsequent atrocities committed by these dictators. For example, LaFeber argues that Roosevelt met the military coups in Central America and the Caribbean with open arms: "As long as the regimes maintained order and protected private property, they were perfectly acceptable. They accomplished for less cost what the Marines had been trying to do for more than thirty years. Deals were easily struck."[83] Lars Schoultz also seems to blame the United States for being "unwilling to grant complete freedom to the people of the Caribbean region."[84] Both quotes suggest that the United States somehow encouraged the emergence of dictators such as Somoza and Trujillo. However, neither scholar suggests what the United States could have done except send in the Marines—a practice that both consistently criticize. This attitude also assumes that the State Department knew from the moment of Somoza's coup that he would provide stability and be amenable to US interests. It is far more likely that the United States had simply given up on interventions regardless of the domestic political situation that developed in Central America and the Caribbean. For example, the United States accepted a nationalist government in Mexico that was not exactly supportive of American interests. LaFeber and other critics of US policy seem to suffer from the fallacy of spurious correlation. At a more lucid moment Schoultz observes, "as the pre-Depression era was coming to an end, leaders in Washington did not know what would occur in places like Nicaragua, and they therefore remained uncertain about an appropriate policy to follow."[85]

Conclusion

Throughout the 1930s the United States had plenty of reasons to impose its will on its weaker neighbors. Disorder continued to be a problem, and few if any of the countries in Latin America were willing the follow the lead of the giant to the north.[86] The level of threat in the international system increased throughout the late 1930s, and while the United States did take measures like blacklisting Latin American companies thought to have German connections, it did not increase its political–military interventionism in the Western Hemisphere.[87] The incentives created by the domestic political structure of the United States are the main reason that nonintervention became the taken-for-granted policy of the United States. In the decades between the War of 1898 and World War II the increase in the material power of the United States interacted with new ideas about the role of the United States in world politics to push the United States toward a more expansionist grand strategy. However, even during the times of strongest internal and external pressure for expansion, the political institutions and strategic culture of the United States delayed, limited, undermined, and prevented political–military expansion. American political structure dissipated the pressure for expansion until the emergence of the Good Neighbor policy marked the end of expansionism as a legitimate political position in the United States. The negative feedback generated by domestic structural restraints imposed costs and dissipated the momentum of expansionist policies, causing American political leaders to learn that expansionism was incompatible with the political structure of the United States. Most presidents throughout this period did attempt some form of territorial expansion, and each of them learned through experience that these policies were not sustainable.

Notes

1. Peters and Woolley 2009–2014.
2. Hull quoted in Wood 1962, 118–119.
3. Wood 1962, 120.
4. Wood 1962, 7–10, 159–161; Pike 1995, 164–166.
5. Herring 2008, 497.
6. For a discussion of who deserves credit for Good Neighborism see Wood 1962, 123–135; Curry 1979.
7. The phrase is from Ninkovich 2001, 91.
8. On the disappearance of national security as a justification or reason for military intervention see Wood 1962, 3–5.
9. Cf. Friedman 2003.
10. Herring 2008, 527–529; Dallek 1979, 175–176.
11. See Atkins and Wilson 1998, 64.
12. Rhodes 2001, 43.
13. Herring 2008, 498. See also Pike 1995, 13, 32–33, 39.
14. Herring 2008, 500.
15. Herring 2008, 501.
16. This phrase is taken from Blyth 2003, 695–706.
17. Munro 1969, 1.
18. Wood 1962, 6.
19. Wood 1962, 7.
20. For the classic survey of learning and foreign policy see Levy 1994, 279–312.
21. Drake 1991, 3–40.
22. Johnson 1995, 285–287. For a discussion of the different factions within the peace movement see Accinelli 1980, 19–38.
23. Pike 1995, 31.
24. Dallek 1979, 18.
25. McJimsey 2000, 186–187. See also Accinelli 1980, 19–38.
26. Schoultz 1998, 293; Shannon 1976, 53–54.
27. Schmidt 1995, 196. See also Cooper 1963, 88–89.
28. Schmidt 1995, 197.
29. Now called Le Cayes.
30. Schmidt 1995, 196–200; Shannon 1976, 54–55; Shannon 1996, 81–85; Cooper 1963, 90–92.
31. Representative George Huddleson quoted in Schmidt 1995, 203. See also Douglas 1927b, 396.
32. Critiques of American policy in Haiti were published prior to 1929. For a particularly sophisticated example see, Douglas 1927a, 228–258; Douglas 1927b, 368–396.

33. Schmidt 1995, 203–207; Shannon 1996, 87–89. See also Cooper 1963, 91. It is important to note that Haiti received much less attention than the Dominican Republic and Central American countries, largely because the population of Haiti was black and seen as particularly lacking in the capacity to govern themselves; Schoultz 1998, 293.

34. For more on Vincent and the emergence of Haitian nationalism see Smith 2009, 9–10, chapter 1.

35. Schmidt 1995, 218–220; Shannon 1996, 95–99; Shannon 1976, 65–66, 69; Cooper 1963, 94; Munro 1969, 7–8.

36. Schoultz 1998, 294–295; Fausold 1984, 184–185. In an article written decades later Munro continued to argue that the American-led treaty services were making progress and "seemed to offer the best hope for the country's future"; Munro 1969, 3.

37. In 1929 Hoover created the Commission for the Study and Review of Conditions in Haiti (Forbes Commission) to conduct an independent investigation into the US occupation. See Shannon 1976; Schoultz 1998, 294; Cooper 1963, 208.

38. *FRUS 1931*, V. II, 484.

39. Schmidt 1995, 220–222; Munro 1969, 9–18. See also Cooper 1963, 95.

40. State Department memo quoted in Schmidt 1995, 223.

41. Munro 1969, 8.

42. Schmidt 1995, 226.

43. Schmidt 1995, 222–229; Shannon 1996, 123–126; Shannon 1976, 69–71; Cooper 1963, 97–98; Munro 1969, 21–25.

44. Speech accessed at Peters and Woolley 2009–2014.

45. Schmidt 1995, 222–230; Langley 2002, 215–216.

46. Schoultz 1998, 293; Calder 1984, 249.

47. Cooper 1963, 100.

48. Cooper 1963, 101.

49. Schoultz 1998, 299; Wood 1962, 51–59; Pérez 1986, 275–300; Dallek 1979, 60.

50. Wood 1962, 59–65; Schoultz 1998, 299–300; Pérez 1986, 304–311; Cronon 1959, 538–540; Dallek 1979, 60–62.

51. *FRUS 1933*, 348.

52. *FRUS 1933*, 348, 354.

53. *FRUS 1933*, 348.

54. Dallek 1979, 62.

55. Welles quoted in Schoultz 1998, 300.

56. Schoultz 1998, 300; Wood 1962, 65–75; Pérez 1986, 312–325; Cronon 1959, 544–548.

57. Hull quoted in Dallek 1979, 63.

58. Dallek 1979, 63.

59. Hull quoted in Wood 1962, 73.

60. Schoultz 1998, 301–302; Herring 2008, 497–499; Wood 1962, 75–76; Cronon 1959, 542–543, 547–552, 557–558; Pérez 1986, 325.

61. Wood 1962, 112.

62. Wood 1962, 112; Dallek 1979, 86–87.

63. Wood 1962, 76–98; Schoultz 1998, 302; Pérez 1986, 325–332; Cronon 1959, 449–460; Dallek 1979, 63–65.

64. Wood 1962, 98–106; Schoultz 1998, 302; Pérez 1986, 332; Cronon 1959, 460–463.

65. See Cronon 1959, 564.
66. Schoultz 1998, 303.
67. Schoultz 1998, 303.
68. Wood 1962, 137–138.
69. Schoultz 1998, 306–307; Herring 2008, 527–528.
70. Wood 1962, 203–204; Koppes 1982, 64–66. See also the previous discussion of Mexican-American relations, especially the 1925–1927 war scare.
71. Britain took the position that the expropriation was illegal and consistently demanded the return of property to the oil companies.
72. Wood 1962, 204–208.
73. Secretary of State Cordell Hull, quoted in Wood 1962, 210.
74. Wood 1962, 209–223; Koppes 1982, 70–71.
75. Wood 1962, 223–233.; Koppes 1982, 69–70.
76. Dallek 1979, 176.
77. Wood 1962, 249.
78. Wood 1962, 234–259; cf. Koppes 1982, 72–74.
79. For more on this issue see Krasner 1978, 155–188.
80. Herring 2008, 500.
81. Wood 1962, 140–155.
82. Schoultz 1998, 311.
83. LaFeber 1993b, 83.
84. Schoultz 1998, 271.
85. Schoultz 1998, 271. See also Kamman 1968, 235.
86. Wood 1962, 7.
87. Friedman 2003.

CONCLUSION

THE ANALYSIS IN THIS BOOK suggests that domestic structural restraint played a central role in limiting American political–military expansion during the rise of the United States to the status of great power and then potential hegemon. As is clear from the cases discussed, domestic restraints did not always prevent expansion; in fact, in many cases domestic structure did not prevent expansion. Instead, the effect of institutional and normative restraint was to reduce the overall trajectory of American expansion by delaying, limiting, undermining, and preventing political–military expansion. Structural restraint also fostered backlash against expansionism and retrenchment of most expansionist projects. Specifically, institutional and normative restraints limited the territorial gains from the Spanish-American War, fostered retrenchment in the Philippines, prevented a Liberian protectorate, prevented formal protectorates throughout Central America and the Caribbean, delayed the annexation of Hawaii and the creation of an isthmus canal, and played a major role in the liquidation of American occupations and the emergence of the Good Neighbor policy in the 1930s.

The basic logic of my argument is that between 1898 and 1941 the US domestic political structure presented policymakers with strong incentives to oppose territorial expansion.[1] For the period from 1898 to 1913 the Republican Party (which had a more favorable view of expansion) held the presidency while the Democratic Party maintained a strong enough presence in Congress to delay, limit, and prevent expansionist attempts from the executive branch.[2] And, of course, Democratic presidential candidates consistently attempted to impose electoral costs on Republican candidates for their support for territorial expansionism. Thus during this period the clearest restraint on expansion was separation of powers and electoral costs. Democrats in Congress were motivated by both principles and partisanship, but they could influence foreign policy only because of the institutional checks and balances of the American political structure. At the same time, the impact of anti-imperialist norms should not be overlooked. Anti-imperialist arguments consistently resonated with many American leaders and large portions of the American electorate, creating a major resource for those opposing expansionist policies. Importantly, several prominent Republicans were anti-imperialists, which often led to bipartisan opposition to the expansionist policies of Republican presidents. The combined effect of institutions and norms provided for high levels of redundancy, facilitating robust and reliable restraint. Throughout this first wave of expansionism, institutions and norms reinforced one another in imposing costs and creating inertia that slowed the momentum of expansionist surge.

The Wilson presidency marked a significant departure from the previous pattern: the opposition Republicans generally supported expansionist policies, and Wilson's Democratic colleagues were generally unwilling to oppose a Democratic president. When Wilson wanted to implement expansionist policies there was little institutional opposition. Normative restraints acting through public opinion and Wilson's personal values were more important than institutional restraints during this period. Norms also had a second effect. In an attempt to maintain consistency with American norms, the Wilson administration emphasized the duty of the United States to bring good government to Latin America. However, the focus on constitutional government seemed to make American expansionism more difficult. As Paul W. Drake argues, "The degree of interventionism required to foment democratic behavior . . . eventually became too costly to US public opinion, to peaceful economic expansion, and to good relations with Latin America, so the Wilson Doctrine was discarded."[3] Thus norms about appropriate US grand strategy had the effect of both limiting the scope and the effectiveness of Wilsonian intervention. The Wilsonian period highlights the importance of redundancy, showing that even when the powerful restraint of separation of powers was absent, restraint still occurred.

By the 1920s it was becoming clear that the institutional and normative drag on foreign policymaking prevented the mobilization of sufficient public support to successfully implement an expansionist grand strategy. Two decades of negative feedback significantly decreased the enthusiasm for territorial expansion. Actions that would increase American political control over foreign territory were rarely attempted during this period, and their occurrence decreased to almost zero by the time Franklin D. Roosevelt took office in 1933. After flirting with intervention in Cuba in 1933, the Roosevelt administration's foreign policy was one of nonintervention and noninterference, even in the face of multiple usurpations of constitutional government in the Caribbean Basin. However, rather than signifying a transformation in foreign policy, Roosevelt's Good Neighborism was a rearticulation of the dominant pre-1900 American foreign policy strategy of restraint. The American political system had weathered the storm of expansionist impulses without a strategic transformation taking place. Restraint proved to be highly resilient and endured beyond the drive for expansion that began in 1898. American presidents learned by doing—territorial expansionism was incompatible with American institutions and strategic culture.

It would be inaccurate, however, to claim that there was no change in American foreign policy between 1898 and 1941. High-ranking politicians, bureaucrats, and military officials advocated for expansionist policies up through the 1930s and clearly had an effect on American foreign policy. The Republican Party was home to the most ardent expansionists of this period and held the presidency for most of the years covered in this study (though the party platform never embraced straightforward imperialism, and several prominent Republicans were antiexpansionist). Republicans McKinley, Roosevelt, and Taft were among the most expansionist American presidents. Democrat Woodrow Wilson also favored expansionist policies, though his actions were framed as anti-imperialist expansionism. American diplomats and military officers abroad were generally the strongest advocates for increasing US political control over the foreign territories they were stationed in. Within the State Department and military services, the sailors, troops, and diplomats on the ground almost always argued in favor of increased and prolonged American influence over foreign countries. Public intellectuals, business leaders, and senators were also influential expansionists. In many cases expansionists were successful in their advocacy. But in almost all cases their success was highly circumscribed, prevented, or caused counterproductive backlash.

Mechanisms of Restraint

The central mechanisms of restraint highlighted in this book are congressional opposition to executive proposals for expansionist measures, public opposition to expansion, fear of electoral costs of expansion, personal anti-imperialist values of various leaders, and leaders' perception of American anti-imperialistic national values. Other important mechanisms include executive opposition to congressional proposals for expansionist measures, congressional failure to fund imperial policies, public backlash over imperial failures, and public backlash over oppressive and antidemocratic colonial policies. Political leaders opposed expansionist foreign policies for economic, ideological, racial, partisan, and institutional reasons. The motivation for restraint is less important than the political structure that enables actors to access veto points in the policymaking process and the reinforcing nature of institutional and normative restraints. The redundancy of structural restraint in the United States produced robust and resilient restraint that outlasted the expansions attempts made between 1898 and 1941. Restraint was crucial because it prevented the shift to a new path of strategic expansionism through the mechanism of negative feedback. Advocates of expansion were worn down by the costs imposed by opponents of expansion that capitalized on the many avenues of obstruction provided for in the American political structure. The brute force of structural inertia reinforced the opponents of expansion by forcing advocates of expansion to gain the approval of multiple veto players and garner high levels of public support.

The most common instruments used by Congress to check the executive branch were its formal treaty and investigative powers as well as its informal power to shape press coverage and public opinion through public statements, nonbinding resolutions, and by simply introducing legislation. The treaty power was especially important because annexation and other forms of political control over foreign countries required bilateral treaties that had to be approved by a supermajority in the US Senate. As long as opponents of expansion could muster enough votes to prevent a two-thirds majority, they could prevent the extension of formal US control over foreign territory. Opposition members of Congress could also shape public opinion through public statements and through investigations. For example, during the 1927 war scare with Mexico, the Senate passed a unanimous resolution in favor of arbitration and conducted multiple investigations of US-Mexico relations, putting pressure on the Coolidge administration to take a more conciliatory approach toward Mexico.

The main reasons for executive restraint were presidents' personal values and their perceptions of American interests and values. For example, McKinley held off a belligerent Congress for months in 1898 because he did not think the risk of war with Spain was worth the potential gains, and he was also personally opposed to the war. In 1919 Wilson put an end to a Congress–State Department push for a hard line against Mexico because he viewed aggression as inconsistent with American interests and values. Earlier, during the occupation of Veracruz, Mexico, and the Punitive Expedition into Northern Mexico, Wilson exercised self-restraint because of his own values of self-determination and his understanding of the ideals of America.

The final set of restraints arises from the long-standing American tradition of anti-imperialism. The importance of anti-imperialism comes from the rhetorical resources it provided individuals and groups that opposed American expansionism and its manifestation in the personal values of American leaders. Because anti-imperialism is a strong element of American strategic culture it ensured that a significant portion of the American public would oppose expansionist policies and that an even larger portion of the American public would only support expansion that was cheap, easy, and could be construed as somehow consistent with anti-imperialism or other strongly held values. Public opinion and elections are the central mechanisms that connect norms with political outcomes. The restraining effect of norms is clear throughout the case studies in this book. For example, after the War of 1898 nationalism and a sense of confidence in American power swept the country, creating a permissive context for imperialism. However, normative dissonance and the cost in blood and treasure from the Philippine-American War irrevocably soured American public opinion toward colonialism. A similar dynamic occurred after the 1929 Haitian uprising.

Strikes and public demonstrations by Haitians revealed to the American people that the US occupation was unpopular and antidemocratic, which decisively shifted public opinion and led to a policy of withdrawal.

Implications for Theory and Practice

The argument of this book has several important implications for theory, policy, and our understanding of history. First, it is clear that international relations theories of rising power grand strategy are incomplete. Some rising powers expand more than others, and some expand in different ways than others, which can have significant implications for the dynamics of world politics. This book offers an explanation for this variance: rising powers with high levels of domestic structural restraint tend to enact relatively restrained grand strategies. These internal restraints can overcome international structural expansionist incentives and significantly reduce political–military expansion. This theoretical insight has implications for current US policy toward rising powers like China, India, and Brazil. The framework developed in this book suggests new variables that can serve as indicators that help us determine the trajectory of current rising powers' grand strategies. For example, instead of focusing on Chinese military doctrine and spending, we should be seeking to understand the number and strength of internal institutional and normative restraints on the use of state power in China.

Second, in crafting a new interpretation of America's rise and a new way of understanding rising power behavior, this book also contributes to international relations theory by elaborating a unique understanding of domestic structure that brings together scholarship from international relations, comparative politics, and American politics literatures to develop a more systematic account of the influence of domestic structure on foreign policy. The key theoretical insight that emerges from this domestic structural approach is the importance of structural redundancy and negative feedback. When institutions and norms are congruent, they reinforce one another to produce a multiplicative effect. You cannot simply add up the cultural and institutional restraints because one type of institutional restraint may strengthen certain restraining norms, and vice versa. This restraint produces negative feedback in the form of costs and inertia. Advocates of expansion are subject to political costs and find themselves constantly delayed and subverted through their opponents' use of political structure. For example, separation of powers allows for a minority of the citizenry to have a significant effect on policymaking. Because of this political space opened up by separation of powers, diversity of political thought is encouraged and opposition parties are empowered. Also, the resonance of anti-imperialism gave Congress a weapon to use against the executive branch and incentivized opposition to the president.

Anti-imperialist ideas also provided a justification for limiting both territorial expansion and the power of the executive branch—it was widely believed that imperialism abroad would lead to tyranny at home. Focusing only on institutions or on culture can lead scholars and practitioners to underestimate the influence of domestic structure on foreign policy. From institutionalists we gain an understanding of how the political rules of the game create incentives for political actors. From culturalists we gain an understanding of the pervasiveness and importance of the logic of appropriateness. Institutions tell political actors what they can do; norms tell them what they should do. Scholars who try to isolate institutions or norms overestimate the autonomous effect of each factor and understate the holistic effect of both factors together. When institutions and norms are mutually reinforcing, they are at their most powerful.[4]

Third, since at least the 1990s analysts of various perspectives and pedigrees have been calling for an American grand strategy of restraint; however, most of these strategists simply make an argument for why restraint is better for the United States without providing a realistic approach for actually achieving restraint.[5] The argument of this book implies that a durable shift in American strategy toward restraint will be much more likely if there is a rebalancing of foreign affairs powers and rebalancing of political rhetoric in the United States.[6] Institutional rebalancing requires stronger controls on the use of force by the legislative and judicial branches of government—that is, a strengthening of checks on executive power. As various scholars of American politics have noted, there are strong incentives for Congress and the judiciary to delegate foreign affairs authority to the executive branch; therefore, advocates of a more restrained US grand strategy should also be advocates for revisions in existing law that modify those incentives.[7] Normative rebalancing is emphasized far less than its institutional counterpart, but is also crucial for those interested in fostering a strategy of restraint. It requires a concerted strategy of rhetorical persuasion and coercion by political leaders and advocacy groups.[8] If one views restraint as normatively good, then this book suggests that domestic norms and institutions play a role in producing optimal grand strategy.

Fourth, this book provides a unique explanation for the evolution of world politics during the first half of the twentieth century by encouraging an increased emphasis on a counterfactual: What if the United States had behaved like the other rising powers of the nineteenth and twentieth centuries? The world would be a very different place if the United States had gone down the path of revisionism and expansionism instead of the path of restraint. For example, American strategic restraint was a necessary condition for rapprochement between the United States and Great Britain and helped prevent the United States from becoming embroiled in an imperial war with European powers in Africa or Southeast Asia. The history of US restraint may also have been a necessary condition for the institutionalization of the western alliance after World War II.[9]

Understanding Rising Power Grand Strategy

Moving forward, it is important to pursue a more complete understanding of the causes of expansion and restraint in terms of international and domestic structural incentives and pressures and the extent to which they reinforce one another. A brief application of the domestic structural approach to Chinese grand strategy provides some guidance to how we might gain a more normal understanding of rising power behavior.

The Future of Chinese Grand Strategy

With respect to twenty-first-century rising powers, there is considerable concern about the direction Chinese grand strategy will take as China steadily increases in national power.[10] The basis of this concern are the assumptions that (1) rising powers are especially aggressive and (2) countries that are approximately equal in material power are likely to compete over international influence (see chapter 1). The possibility for ideological conflict exacerbates the existing propensity for conflict between the United States and China. However, the findings of this study raise questions about the assumption that conflict is inevitable or even likely between a rising power and existing status quo powers. The structure of the Chinese political system will have a major effect on whether China becomes a revisionist or status quo power. The level of domestic institutional and normative restraint on the use of state power—whatever form it takes—is an important factor in shaping the external ambitions of a rising power.

The main policy-relevant lesson of this book is that when attempting to determine if rising powers will implement aggressive, expansionist foreign policies it is important to gain an understanding of their domestic political structures. We should ask: Is power centralized, or are there institutionalized checks and balances? Are there informal restraints on power? Does public opinion play a role in foreign policy decision making? If so, how? What is the dominant strategic culture? When is it considered permissible to use force? Is it morally acceptable to exercise political control over foreign territory?

Looking at China today, there are some domestic political factors that point toward restraint, and some that point toward potential expansionism. First, in terms of Chinese political culture it is difficult to talk about any unified sense of political values or beliefs except regarding economic development. There is a widespread belief in China that the core purpose of the state is to foster continued economic growth. Therefore, one could speak of a normative commitment to economic growth; a central role of government is to produce prosperity. This aspect of Chinese political culture would seem to work in favor of restraint, because upsetting the status quo would likely create economic problems for China.

When it comes to norms regarding the use of state power internationally, the main debate is between those that argue that China has a parabellum (peace through strength) strategic culture that fosters a preference for offensive strategies and those that argue that China has a Confucian strategic culture, or preference for an accommodationist strategy and avoidance of violence unless threatened.[11] For our purposes it is not important if one or the other is the dominant culture; as long as Confucian norms are well entrenched and widely accepted, they will serve as a powerful resource for Chinese that oppose aggressive, revisionist policies.

The characteristics of Chinese political institutions also provide some evidence of Chinese restraint. The Chinese Communist Party (CCP) currently refers to the Chinese political system as an intraparty or interparty democracy.[12] After Mao's death, Chinese political elites took steps to prevent one person from gaining absolute power. This process had evolved to include a variety of power sharing mechanisms. First, intraparty elections are held for membership in the Central Committee and for positions in provincial and city government, and consensus-based decision making is widely practiced. Second, major decisions within the government are made through voting by Party committee or executive committee rather than made unilaterally by the Party secretary. Third, term limits and mandatory retirement also limit the aggregation of personal power. Fourth, factional competition between populist and elitist factions within the CCP helps preserve a balanced approach to public policy. Fifth, the policy of decentralization gives provinces considerable power—all provinces get two seats on the CCP Central Committee. There are also signs of increased transparency for regular Party members.[13]

There are also signs that China could transition to an aggressive, revisionist grand strategy.[14] First, China lacks a free press and is nondemocratic. This eliminates any independent basis for information for the Chinese people and means that there is no electoral incentive for elites to pay attention to the opinion of the people.[15] Second, the governing elite do seem to pay attention to public opinion, but it is hard to measure and may overemphasize nationalist sentiment.[16] Third, and most importantly, there is no formal separation and balance of power within the domestic political system. The majority of important decisions are made by a small group of the most powerful political elites—the Politburo Standing Committee—vulnerable to groupthink and other pathologies of small-group decision making.[17] None of these factors inherently promote aggressive or belligerent foreign policy, but to the extent that international structural incentives encourage rising powers to implement expansionist, revisionist policies, the absence of domestic restraints is important.

Conclusion: American Exceptionalism?

The preceding chapters of this book attempt to demonstrate in detail that the United States was a highly restrained rising power when compared to other rising powers of the twentieth century. The purpose of this demonstration is to question the widespread assumption that all rising powers are highly expansionist, belligerent, revisionist states. However, even if one is convinced that the United States did practice strategic restraint in its rise to world power, it does not necessarily follow that that finding is transferable. It could be argued that the United States is exceptional in terms of its institutional and normative political structure as well as its size and geopolitical isolation from the core of the international system.[18] There is something to this idea: for over a century and a half, the United States had the highest levels of institutional and normative restraints on state power in the world. However, while the United States was born exceptional and continued to be exceptional well into its second century of existence, today it is considerably less exceptional.[19] Many other states, including the reformed revisionist powers German and Japan, have high levels of domestic institutional and normative restraint.[20] It also seems that two of today's rising powers—Brazil and India—have institutionalized restraint in their political systems. However, a comparative study of current rising powers using the framework of domestic political structural theory is the subject for another project.

Notes

1. For a discussion of this logic in the post–World War II context see Howell and Pevehouse 2005, 2007a, 2007b.

2. The Republican Party had unified control of the federal government except from 1911 to 1913, when the Democratic Party had a majority in the House of Representatives. See Table 1.1.

3. Drake 1991, 35.

4. In the American politics and comparative politics subfields it has long been known that dissonant norms and institutions produce friction that often leads to significant political change. There is every reason to believe that the opposite—mutually reinforcing norms and institutions—will have the opposite effect of structural stability.

5. See Gholz, Press, and Sapolsky 1997; Walt 2005; Posen 2007; Mearsheimer 2014.

6. A few analysts do see the need for a rebalancing of political power domestically. See Preble 2009, 135–163.

7. On the shift of power to the executive branch see Schlesinger 1973; Rudalevige 2006; Crenson and Ginsberg 2007.

8. On the difference between rhetorical persuasion and coercion see Krebs and Jackson 2007, 35–48.

9. See Ikenberry 1998/99, 2001.

10. For a recent expression of concern see Mearsheimer 2010. And to a lesser extent there is concern about other rising powers such as Russia, India, and Brazil.

11. See Johnston 1998, chapter 3; Feng 2007, chapter 2. Shambaugh (2011, 8) uses the term "identity" rather than culture, but also suggests that the underlying assumptions and beliefs of Chinese leaders and people regarding foreign policy are very much in flux.

12. Li 2005, 388, 2009, 2; Fewsmith 2010, 1.

13. Li 2009, 7–11; Roy 2009, 27.

14. For a brief discussion of aggressive tendencies in Chinese foreign policy see Roy 2009, 32–38.

15. However, several scholars note that the press has become commercialized and has more freedom than in the past. See Roy 2009, 27; Nathan 2003, 12.

16. Shambaugh 2011, 22; cf. Roy 2009, 27–30.

17. On the pathologies of small-group decision making see George 1972; George and Stern 2002.

18. The best work on this issue continues to be de Tocqueville (1988). For an updated analysis of the geopolitics of the American founding and early political development see Deudney1995; Deudney and Meiser 2008, 29–30.

19. See Nau 2002, 14; Deudney and Meiser 2008. Clearly all states are exceptional in their own ways in terms of folkways and customs that have developed over the centuries. However, here we are concerned primarily with the question of whether the United States is exceptional in terms of institutional and normative restraints on state power.

20. Berger 1996, 1998; Duffield 1998.

BIBLIOGRAPHY

Abdelal, Rawi, Yoshiko M. Herrera, Alastair Iain Johnston, and Rose McDermott. 2006. "Identity as a Variable." *Perspectives on Politics* 4, no. 4: 695–711.

Abernethy, David B. 2000. *The Dynamics of Global Dominance: European Overseas Empires, 1415-1980.* New Haven, CT: Yale University Press.

Accinelli, Robert D. 1980. "Militant Internationalists: The League of Nations Association, the Peace Movement, and U.S. Foreign Policy, 1934–38." *Diplomatic History* 4, no. 1 (January): 19–38.

Aldrich, John H., Christopher Gelpi, Peter Feaver, Jason Reifler, and Kristin Thomas Sharp. 2006. "Foreign Policy and the Electoral Connection." *Annual Review of Political Science* 9: 477–502.

Arrow, Kenneth J. 1962. "The Economic Implications of Learning by Doing." *Review of Economic Studies* 29, no. 3: 155–173.

Atkins, G. Pope, and Larman C. Wilson. 1998. *The Dominican Republic and the United States: From Imperialism to Transnationalism.* Athens: University of Georgia Press.

Auxier, George W. 1939. "The Propaganda Activities of the Cuban Junta in Precipitating the Spanish-American War, 1895–1898." *Hispanic American Historical Review* 19, no. 3: 286–305.

Axelrod, Alan. 2007. *Political History of America's Wars.* Washington, DC: CQ Press.

Bailey, Thomas A. (1931) 1969. "United States and Hawaii during the Spanish-American War." In *Essays Diplomatic and Undiplomatic of Thomas A. Bailey,* eds. Alexander Deconde and Armin Rappaport, 89–103. New York: Appleton-Century-Crofts.

———. 1937. "Was the Presidential Election of 1900 a Mandate on Imperialism?" *Mississippi Valley Historical Review* 24, no. 1: 43–52.

Bairoch, Paul. 1993. *Economics and World History: Myths and Paradoxes.* New York: Harvester Wheatsheaf.

Baker, George William. 1961. "The Caribbean Policy of Woodrow Wilson, 1913–1917." PhD diss., University of Colorado.

Baum, Matthew A. 2004. "How Public Opinion Constrains the Use of Force: The Case of Operation Restore Hope." *Presidential Studies Quarterly* 34, no. 2: 187–226.

Baum, Matthew A., and Philip B. K. Potter. 2008. "The Relationships between Mass Media, Public Opinion, and Foreign Policy: Toward a Theoretical Synthesis." *Annual Review of Political Science* 11: 39–65.

Beisner, Robert L. 1968. *Twelve against Empire.* New York: McGraw-Hill.

———. 1986. *From the Old Diplomacy to the New, 1865–1900,* 2nd ed. Wheeling, IL: Harlan Davidson.

Bender, Thomas. 2006. A Nation among Nations: America's Place in World History. New York: Hill and Wang.

Bennett, Andrew, and Colin Elman. 2006. "Complex Causal Relations and Case Study Methods: The Example of Path Dependence." Political Analysis 14, no. 3: 250–267.

Berger, Thomas U. 1996. "Norms, Identity, and National Security in German and Japan." In The Culture of National Security: Norms and Identity in World Politics, ed. Peter J. Katzenstein, 317–356. New York: Columbia University Press.

———. 1998. Cultures of Antimilitarism: National Security in Germany and Japan Baltimore, MD: Johns Hopkins University Press.

Bermann, Karl. 1986. Under the Big Stick: Nicaragua and the United States since 1848. Boston: South End Press.

Beveridge, Albert J. 1907. "The Development of a Colonial Policy for the United States." Annals of the American Academy of Political and Social Science 30, no. 1: 3–15.

Bickel, Keith B. 2001. Mars Learning: The Marine Corps Development of Small Wars Doctrine, 1915–1940. Boulder, CO: Westview Press.

Biddle, Stephen. 2007. "Strategy in War." PS: Political Science & Politics 40, no. 3: 461–466.

Blassingame, John W. 1969. "The Press and American Intervention in Haiti and the Dominican Republic, 1904–1920." Caribbean Studies 9, no. 2: 27–43.

Blodgett, Geoffrey T. 1962. "The Mind of the Boston Mugwump." Mississippi Valley Historical Review 48, no. 4: 614–634.

Blount, James H. 1912. The American Occupation of the Philippines, 1898–1912. New York: G. P. Putnam's Sons.

Blyth, Mark. 2002. Great Transformations: Economic Ideas and Institutional Change in the Twentieth Century. New York: Cambridge University Press.

———. 2003. "Structures Do Not Come with an Instruction Sheet: Interests, Ideas, and Progress in Political Science." Perspectives on Politics 1, no. 4 (December): 695–706.

Bolton, Grania. 1972. "Military Diplomacy and National Liberation: Insurgent-American Relations after the Fall of Manila." Military Affairs 36, no. 3: 99–104.

Braeman, John. 1982. "Power and Diplomacy: The 1920s Reappraised." Review of Politics 44, no. 3: 342–369.

Braisted, William R. 1957. "The United States Navy's Dilemma in the Pacific, 1906–1909." Pacific Historical Review 26, no. 3: 235–244.

Brands, H. W. 1992. Bound to Empire: The United States and the Philippines. New York: Oxford University Press.

Brands, H. W. 1995. The Reckless Decade: America in the 1890s. New York: St. Martin's.

———. 1997. T. R.: The Last Romantic. New York: Basic Books.

Buell, Raymond Leslie. 1928. The Native Problem in Africa. Vol. II. New York: Macmillan.

Bueno de Mesquita, Bruce, James D. Morrow, Randolph M. Siverson, and Alastair Smith. 1999. "An Institutional Explanation of the Democratic Peace." American Political Science Review 93, no. 4: 791–807.

Burton, David H. 1961. "Theodore Roosevelt: Confident Imperialist." Review of Politics 23, no. 3, 356–377.

———. 1965. "Theodore Roosevelt's Social Darwinism and Views on Imperialism." Journal of the History of Ideas 26, no. 1: 103–118.

———. 1968. Theodore Roosevelt: Confident Imperialist. Philadelphia: University of Pennsylvania Press.

Cable, James. 1994. *Gunboat Diplomacy, 1919–1991*. 3rd ed. New York: St. Martin's.

Calder, Bruce J. 1984. *The Impact of Intervention: The Dominican Republic during the U.S. Occupation of 1916–1924*. 1st ed. Austin: University of Texas Press.

Calhoun, Frederick S. 1986. *Power and Principle: Armed Intervention in Wilsonian Foreign Policy*. Kent, OH: Kent State University Press.

———. 1993. *Uses of Force and Wilsonian Foreign Policy*. Kent, OH: Kent State University Press.

Capoccia, Giovanni, and R. Daniel Kelemen. 2007. "The Study of Critical Junctures: Theory, Narrative, and Counterfactuals in Historical Institutionalism." *World Politics* 59, no. 3 (April): 341–369.

Carr, E. H. (1946) 1964. *The Twenty Years' Crisis, 1919–1939: An Introduction to the Study of International Relations*, 2nd ed. New York: Harper and Row.

Chalk, Frank. 1967. "The Anatomy of an Investment: Firestone's 1927 Loan to Liberia." *Canadian Journal of African Studies* 1, no. 1: 12–32.

Challener, Richard D. 1973. *Admirals, Generals,and American Foreign Policy, 1898–1914*. Princeton, NJ: Princeton University Press.

Chapman, Charles E. 1927. *A History of the Cuban Republic: A Study in Hispanic American Politics*. New York: Macmillan.

Choi, Seung-Whan. 2010. "Legislative Constraints: A Path to Peace?" *Journal of Conflict Resolution* 54, no. 3: 438–470.

Choucri, Nazli, and Robert C. North. 1975. *Nations in Conflict: National Growth and International Violence*. San Francisco: W. H. Freeman.

Choucri, Nazli, Robert C. North, and Susumu Yamakage. 1992. *The Challenge of Japan before World War II and After: A Study of National Growth and Expansion*. London: Routledge.

Cizel, Annick. 2008. "Nation-Building in the Philippines: Rooseveltian Statecraft for Imperial Modernization in an Emergent Transatlantic World Order." *Diplomacy and Statecraft* 19, no. 4: 690–711.

Clausewitz, Carl von. 1976. *On War*. Edited and translated by Michael Howard and Peter Paret. Princeton, NJ: Princeton University Press.

Clegg, Claude A. 1996. "'A Splendid Type of Colored American': Charles Young and the Reorganization of the Liberian Frontier Force." *International Journal of African Historical Studies* 29, no. 1: 51–60.

Clements, Kendrick A. 1980. "Woodrow Wilson's Mexican Policy, 1913–15." *Diplomatic History* 4, no. 2: 113–136.

———. 1987. *Woodrow Wilson: World Statesman*. Boston: Twayne.

———. 1992. *The Presidency of Woodrow Wilson*. Lawrence: University Press of Kansas.

Clendenen, Clarence C. 1961. *The United States and Pancho Villa: A Study in Unconventional Diplomacy*. Ithaca, NY: Cornell University Press.

Cohen, Warren I. 1998. "America and the World in the 1920s." In *Calvin Coolidge and the Coolidge Era: Essays on the History of the 1920s*, ed. John Earl Haynes, 233–243. Washington, DC: Library of Congress.

Coletta, Paolo E. 1957. "Bryan, McKinley, and the Treaty of Paris." *Pacific Historical Review* 26, no. 2: 131–146.

Coletta, Paolo E. 1961. "McKinley, the Peace Negotiations, and the Acquisition of the Philippines." *Pacific Historical Review* 30, no. 4: 341–350.

Collin, Richard H. 1990. *Theodore Roosevelt's Caribbean: The Panama Canal, the Monroe Doctrine, and the Latin American Context*. Baton Rouge: Louisiana State University Press.

Collin, Richard H. 1995. "Symbiosis versus Hegemony: New Directions in the Foreign Relations Historiography of Theodore Roosevelt and William Howard Taft." *Diplomatic History* 19, no. 3: 491–492.

Commager, Henry Steele. 1949. *Documents of American History*. 5th ed. New York: Appleton-Century-Crofts.

Congressional Quarterly. 1991. *Congressional Quarterly's Guide to Congress*. 4th ed. Washington, DC: Congressional Quarterly.

Cooper, Donald B. 1963. "The Withdrawal of the United States from Haiti, 1928–1934." *Journal of Inter-American Studies* 5, no. 1 (January): 83–101.

Cooper, John Milton Jr., 2009. *Woodrow Wilson: A Biography*. New York: Knopf.

Crenson, Matthew, and Benjamin Ginsberg. 2007. *Presidential Power: Unchecked & Unbalanced*. New York: Norton.

Cronon, E. David. 1959. "Interpreting the New Good Neighbor Policy: The Cuban Crisis of 1933." *Hispanic American Historical Review* 39, no. 4 (November): 538–567.

Cummins, Lejeune. 1967. "The Formulation of the 'Platt' Amendment." *The Americas* 23, no. 4: 370–389.

Curry, Earl R. 1979. *Hoover's Dominican Diplomacy and the Origins of the Good Neighbor Policy*. New York: Garland Publishing.

Curry, Richard O. 1972. "Copperheadism and Continuity: The Anatomy of a Stereotype." *Journal of Negro History* 57, no. 1: 29–36.

Dallek, Robert. 1979. *Franklin D. Roosevelt and American Foreign Policy, 1932–1945*. New York: Oxford University Press.

Dalton, Kathleen. 2002. *Theodore Roosevelt: A Strenuous Life*. New York: Knopf.

Davidson, Jason. 2006. *The Origins of Revisionist and Status-Quo States*. New York: Palgrave Macmillan.

De la Torriente, Cosme. 1930. "The Platt Amendment." *Foreign Affairs* 8, no. 3: 364–378.

De Tocqueville, Alexis. 1988. *Democracy in America*. Translated by George Lawrence. 1st Perennial Library ed. New York: Perennial Library, Harper & Row.

DeConde, Alexander. 1951. *Herbert Hoover's Latin-American Policy*. Redwood City, CA: Stanford University Press.

DeRoche, Andrew. 2003. "Relations with Africa since 1900." In *A Companion to American Foreign Relations*, ed. Robert D. Schulzinger, 103–120. Malden, MA: Blackwell.

Desch, Michael C. 1993. *When the Third World Matters: Latin America and United States Grand Strategy*. Baltimore, MD: Johns Hopkins University Press.

Deudney, Daniel H. 1995. "The Philadelphian System: Sovereignty, Arms Control, and Balance of Power in the American States-Union, Circa 1787–1861." *International Organization* 49, no. 2: 191–228.

———. 2004. "Publius before Kant: Federal—Republican Security and Democratic Peace." *European Journal of International Relations* 10, no. 3: 315–356.

———. 2007. *Bounding Power: Republican Security Theory from the Polis to the Global Village*. Princeton, NJ: Princeton University Press.

Deudney, Daniel, and Jeffrey W. Meiser. 2008. "American Exceptionalism." In *US Foreign Policy*, eds. Michael Cox and Doug Stokes. Oxford: Oxford University Press.

Dickson, Peter R., Paul W. Farris, and Willem J. M. I. Verbeke. 2001. "Dynamic Strategic Thinking." *Journal of the Academy of Marketing Science* 29, no. 3: 216–237.

Domínguez, Jorge I. 1978. *Cuba: Order and Revolution*. Cambridge, MA: Belknap Press.

Doran, Charles F. 1991. *Systems in Crisis: New Imperatives of High Politics at Century's End.* Cambridge: Cambridge University Press.

Doran, Charles F., and Wes Parson. 1980. "War and the Cycle of Relative Power." *American Political Science Review* 74, no. 4 (December): 947–965.

Douglas, Paul H. 1927a. "The American Occupation of Haiti I." *Political Science Quarterly* 42, no. 2 (June): 228–258.

———. 1927b. "The American Occupation of Haiti II." *Political Science Quarterly* 42, no. 3 (September): 368–396.

Drake, Paul W. 1991. "From Good Men to Good Neighbors: 1912–1932." In *Exporting Democracy: The United States and Latin America,* ed. Abraham Lowenthal, 3–40. Baltimore, MD: Johns Hopkins University Press.

Dueck, Colin. 2001. "The Sources of American Expansion." *Security Studies* 11, no. 1: 171–190.

———. 2006. *Reluctant Crusaders: Power, Culture, and Change in American Grand Strategy.* Princeton, NJ: Princeton University Press.

Duffield, John S. 1998. *World Power Forsaken: Political Culture, International Institutions, and German Security Policy After Unification.* Redwood City, CA: Stanford University Press.

Duignan, Peter, and Lewis H. Gann. 1984. *The United States and Africa: A History.* Cambridge: Cambridge University Press.

Edelstein, David M. 2002. "Managing Uncertainty: Beliefs about Intentions and the Rise of Great Powers." *Security Studies* 12, no. 1 (Autumn): 1–40.

Eisinger, Robert M. 2000. "Gauging Public Opinion in the Hoover White House: Understanding the Roots of Presidential Polling." *Presidential Studies Quarterly* 30, no. 4: 643–661.

Elliott, Jane E. 2002. *Some Did It for Civilisation, Some Did It for Their Country: A Revised View of the Boxer War.* Hong Kong: The Chinese University Press.

Ellis, Elmer. 1932. "The Silver Republicans in the Election of 1896." *Mississippi Valley Historical Review* 18, no. 4: 519–534.

Elman, Miriam Fendius. 1995. "The Foreign Policies of Small States: Challenging Realism in Its Own Backyard." *British Journal of Political Science* 25, no. 2: 171–215.

Engel, Jeffrey A. 2008. "The Democratic Language of American Imperialism: Race, Order, and Theodore Roosevelt's Personifications of Foreign Policy Evil." *Diplomacy and Statecraft* 19, no. 4: 671–689.

Erhagbe, Edward O. 1996. "African-Americans and the Defense of African States against European Imperial Conquest: Booker T. Washington's Diplomatic Efforts to Guarantee Liberia's Independence 1907–1911." *African Studies Review* 39, no. 1: 55–65.

Esherick, Joseph. 1987. *The Origins of the Boxer Uprising.* Berkeley: University of California Press.

Esthus, Raymond A. 1967. *Theodore Roosevelt and Japan.* Seattle: University of Washington Press.

Fausold, Martin L. 1984. *The Presidency of Herbert C. Hoover.* Lawrence: University Press of Kansas.

Fazal, Tanisha M. 2007. *State Death: The Politics and Geography of Conquest, Occupation, and Annexation.* Princeton, NJ: Princeton University Press.

Fearon, James D. 1991. "Counterfactuals and Hypothesis Testing in Political Science." *World Politics* 43, no. 2 (January): 169–195.

————. 1994. "Domestic Political Audiences and the Escalation of International Disputes." *American Political Science Review* 88, no. 3: 577–592.

Feldman, Stanley. 1988. "Structure and Consistency in Public Opinion: The Role of Core Beliefs and Values." *American Journal of Political Science* 32, no. 2: 416–440.

Feng, Huiyun. 2007. *Chinese Strategic Culture and Foreign Policy Decision-Making: Confucianism, Leadership and War.* New York: Routledge.

Ferguson, Niall. 2004. *Colossus: The Price of America's Empire.* New York: Penguin.

Ferrell, Robert H. 1998. *The Presidency of Calvin Coolidge.* Lawrence: University Press of Kansas.

Fewsmith, Joseph. 2010. "Inner-Party Democracy: Development and Limitations." *China Leadership Monitor* 31: 1–11.

Finnemore, Martha, and Kathryn Sikkink. 1998. "International Norm Dynamics and Political Change." *International Organization* 52, no. 4: 887–91.

Fioretos, Orfeo. 2011. "Historical Institutionalism in International Relations." *International Organization* 65, no. 2: 367–399.

Fiorina, Morris P., and Samuel J. Abrams. 2008. "Political Polarization in the American Public." *Annual Review of Political Science* 11: 563–588.

Foreign Relations of the United States (FRUS), 1909. Washington, DC: US Government Printing Office, 1914. http://digital.library.wisc.edu/1711.dl/FRUS.FRUS1909.

Foreign Relations of the United States, 1910. Washington, DC: US Government Printing Office, 1916. http://digital.library.wisc.edu/1711.dl/FRUS.FRUS1910.

Foreign Relations of the United States, 1911. Washington, DC: US Government Printing Office, 1918. http://digital.library.wisc.edu/1711.dl/FRUS.FRUS1911.

Foreign Relations of the United States, 1912. Washington, DC: US Government Printing Office, 1919. http://digital.library.wisc.edu/1711.dl/FRUS.FRUS1912.

Foreign Relations of the United States, 1914. Washington, DC: US Government Printing Office, 1922. http://digital.library.wisc.edu/1711.dl/FRUS.FRUS1914.

Foreign Relations of the United States, 1915. Washington, DC: US Government Printing Office, 1924. http://digital.library.wisc.edu/1711.dl/FRUS.FRUS1915.

Foreign Relations of the United States, 1916. Washington, DC: US Government Printing Office, 1925. http://digital.library.wisc.edu/1711.dl/FRUS.FRUS1916.

Foreign Relations of the United States, 1917. Washington, DC: US Government Printing Office, 1926. http://digital.library.wisc.edu/1711.dl/FRUS.FRUS1917.

Foreign Relations of the United States, 1920, Vol. II. Washington, DC: US Government Printing Office, 1936. http://digital.library.wisc.edu/1711.dl/FRUS.FRUS1920v02.

Foreign Relations of the United States, 1922, Vol. I. Washington, DC: US Government Printing Office, 1938. http://digital.library.wisc.edu/1711.dl/FRUS.FRUS1921v01.

Foreign Relations of the United States, 1922, Vol. II. Washington, DC: US Government Printing Office, 1938. http://digital.library.wisc.edu/1711.dl/FRUS.FRUS1922v02.

Foreign Relations of the United States, 1931, Vol. II. Washington, DC: US Government Printing Office, 1946. http://digital.library.wisc.edu/1711.dl/FRUS.FRUS1931v02.

Foreign Relations of the United States, 1933, Vol. V. The American Republics. Washington, DC: US Government Printing Office, 1952. http://digital.library.wisc.edu/1711.dl/FRUS.FRUS1933v05.

Friedberg, Aaron L. 2000. *In the Shadow of the Garrison State: America's Anti-Statism and its Cold War Grand Strategy.* Princeton, NJ: Princeton University Press.

Freidel, Frank. 1969. "Dissent in the Spanish-American War and the Philippine Insurrection." *Proceedings of the Massachusetts Historical Society* 81: 167–184.

Friedman, Max Paul. 2003. "There Goes the Neighborhood: Blacklisting Germans in Latin America and the Evanescence of the Good Neighbor Policy." *Diplomatic History* 27, no. 4 (September): 569–597.

Fry, Joseph A. 2002. *Dixie Looks Abroad: The South and U.S. Foreign Relations, 1789–1973.* Baton Rouge: Louisiana State University Press.

Gardner, Lloyd C. 1982. "Woodrow Wilson and the Mexican Revolution." In *Woodrow Wilson and a Revolutionary World, 1913–1921,* ed. Arthur S. Link, 3–48. Chapel Hill: University of North Carolina Press.

Gates, John M. 1977. "Philippine Guerrillas, American Anti-Imperialists, and the Election of 1900." *Pacific Historical Review* 46, no. 1: 51–64.

George, Alexander L. 1969. "The 'Operational Code': A Neglected Approach to the Study of Political Leaders and Decision-Making." *International Studies Quarterly* 13, no. 2: 190–222.

———. 1972. "The Case for Multiple Advocacy in Making Foreign Policy." *American Political Science Review* 66, no. 3: 751–785.

George, Alexander L., and Andrew Bennett. 2005. *Case Studies and Theory Development in the Social Sciences.* Cambridge, MA: The MIT Press.

George, Alexander L., and Eric K. Stern. 2002. "Harnessing Conflict in Foreign Policy Making: From Devil's to Multiple Advocacy." *Presidential Studies Quarterly* 32, no. 3: 484–508.

Gholz, Eugene, Daryl G. Press, and Harvey M. Sapolsky. 1997. "Come Home America: The Strategy of Restraint in the Face of Temptation." *International Security* 24, no. 4 (Spring): 5–48.

Gilpin, Robert. 1983. *War and Change in World Politics.* Cambridge: Cambridge University Press.

Glaser, Charles L. 1997. "The Security Dilemma Revisited." *World Politics* 50, no. 1: 171–201.

Goertz, Gary. 2006. *Social Science Concepts: A User's Guide.* Princeton, NJ: Princeton University Press.

Golay, Frank H. 1998. *Face of Empire: United States-Philippine Relations, 1898–1946.* Madison: University of Wisconsin-Madison.

Goldenberg, Bonnie. 2000. "Imperial Culture and National Conscience: The Role of the Press in the United States and Spain during the Crisis of 1898." *Bulletin of Spanish Studies* 77, no. 3: 171–181.

Gould, Lewis L. 1980. *The Presidency of William McKinley.* Lawrence: University of Kansas Press.

———. 1982. *Spanish-American War and President McKinley.* Lawrence: University Press of Kansas.

———. 1991. *The Presidency of Theodore Roosevelt.* Lawrence: University Press of Kansas.

Graebner, Norman A. 1980. "The Mexican War: A Study in Causation." *Pacific Historical Review* 49, no. 3 (August): 405–426.

Grenville, John A. S. 1968. "American Naval Preparations for War with Spain, 1896–1898." *Journal of American Studies* 2, no. 1: 33–47.

Grenville, John A. S., and George Berkeley Young. 1966. *Politics, Strategy, and American Diplomacy: Studies in Foreign Policy, 1873–1917.* New Haven, CT: Yale University Press.

Grieb, Kenneth J. 1969. "Warren G. Harding and the Dominican Republic U.S. Withdrawal, 1921–1923." *Journal of Inter-American Studies* 11, no. 3: 425–440.

———. 1976. *The Latin American Policy of Warren G. Harding*. Fort Worth: Texas Christian University Press.

Grieco, Joseph M. 1996. "State Interests and Institutional Rule Trajectories: A Neorealist Interpretation of the Maastricht Treaty and European Economic and Monetary Union." *Security Studies* 5, no. 3: 261–306.

Haley, P. Edward. 1970. *Revolution and Intervention: The Diplomacy of Taft and Wilson with Mexico, 1910–1917*. Cambridge, MA: The MIT Press.

Hall, Linda B., and Don M. Coerver. 1997. "Woodrow Wilson, Public Opinion, and the Punitive Expedition: A Re-Assessment." *New Mexico Historical Review* 72, no. 2 (April): 171–194.

Hall, Peter A., and Rosemary C. R. Taylor. 1996. "Political Science and the Three New Institutionalisms." *Political Studies* 44, no. 5: 936–957.

Halle, Louis Joseph. 1985. *The United States Acquires the Philippines: Consensus vs. Reality*. Lanham, MD: University Press of America.

Hamilton, Richard F. 2006. *President McKinley, War and Empire, Volume 1: President McKinley and the Coming of War, 1898*. New Brunswick, NJ: Transaction Publishers.

———. 2007. *President McKinley, War and Empire, Volume 2: President McKinley and America's "New Empire."* New Brunswick, NJ: Transaction Publishers.

Harlan, Louis R. 1966. "Booker T. Washington and the White Man's Burden." *American Historical Review* 71, no. 2: 441–467.

Harrington, Fred H. 1935. "The Anti-Imperialist Movement in the United States, 1898–1900." *Mississippi Valley Historical Review* 22, no. 2: 211–230.

Harris, Charles H., III, and Louis R. Sadler. 1978. "The Plan of San Diego and the Mexican-United States War Crisis of 1916: A Reexamination." *Hispanic American Historical Review* 58, no. 3: 381–408.

Hart, B. H. Liddell. 1991. *Strategy*. 2nd rev. ed. London: Meridian.

Hattam, Victoria, and Joseph Lowndes. 2013. "From Birmingham to Baghdad: The Micro Politics of Partisan Identification." In *Political Creativity: Reconfiguring Institutional Order and Change*, eds. Gerald Berk, Dennis Galvan, and Victoria Hattam, 211–236. Philadelphia: University of Pennsylvania Press.

Healy, David. 1963. *The United States in Cuba, 1898–1902: Generals, Politicians, and the Search for Policy*. Madison: University of Wisconsin Press.

———. 1976. *Gunboat Diplomacy in the Wilson Era: The U.S. Navy in Haiti, 1915–1916*. Madison: University of Wisconsin Press.

———. 1988. *Drive to Hegemony: The United States in the Caribbean, 1898–1917*. Madison: University of Wisconsin Press.

Henisz, Witold J. 2000. "The Institutional Environment for Economic Growth." *Economics and Politics* 12, no. 1: 1–31.

Hensel, Paul R. 2000. "Territory: Theory and Evidence on Geography and Conflict." In *What Do We Know about War?*, ed. John A. Vasquez, 60. Lanham, MD: Rowman and Littlefield.

Herman, Robert G. 1996. "Identity, Norms, and National Security: The Soviet Foreign Policy Revolution and the End of the Cold War." In *The Culture of National Security: Norms and Identity in World Politics*, ed. Peter J. Katzenstein, 271–316. New York: Columbia University Press.

Hernández, José M. 1993. *Cuba and the United States: Intervention and Militarism, 1868–1933*. Austin: University of Texas Press.

Herring, George C. 2008. *From Colony to Superpower: U.S. Foreign Relations since 1776.* Oxford: Oxford University Press.

Hilderbrand, Robert C. 1981. *Power and the People: Executive Management of Public Opinion in Foreign Affairs, 1897–1921.* Chapel Hill: University of North Carolina Press.

Hill, Howard C. (1927) 1965. *Roosevelt and the Caribbean.* New York: Russell & Russell.

Hirschman, Albert O. 1970. *Exit, Voice, and Loyalty: Responses to Declines in Firms, Organizations, and States.* Cambridge, MA: Harvard University Press.

Hitchman, James H. 1967. "The Platt Amendment Revisited: A Bibliographical Survey." *The Americas* 23, no. 4: 356–369.

Hitchman, James H. 1968. "The American Touch in Imperial Administration: Leonard Wood in Cuba, 1898-1902." *The Americas* 24, no. 4: 394–403.

Hobson, J. A. 1965. *Imperialism: A Study.* Ann Arbor: University of Michigan Press.

Hodge, Carl Cavanagh. 2008. "A Whiff of Cordite: Theodore Roosevelt and the Transoceanic Naval Arms Race, 1897–1909." *Diplomacy and Statecraft* 19, no. 4: 712–731.

Hofstadter, Richard. (1952) 1965. "Cuba, the Philippines, and Manifest Destiny." In *The Paranoid Style in American Politics and Other Essays,* ed. Richard Hofstadter, 145–187. New York: Knopf.

Hogan, J. Michael. 1986. *The Panama Canal in American Politics: Domestic Advocacy and the Evolution of Policy.* Carbondale: Southern Illinois University Press.

Holbo, Paul S. 1967. "Presidential Leadership in Foreign Affairs: William McKinley and the Turpie-Foraker Amendment." *American Historical Review* 72, no. 4: 1321–1335.

Hollander, Jacob H. 1907. "The Convention of 1907 between the United States and the Dominican Republic." *American Journal of International Law* 1, no. 2: 287–296.

Holsti, Ole. 1992. "Public Opinion and Foreign Policy: Challenges to the Almond-Lippman Consensus." *International Studies Quarterly* 36, no. 4: 446–455.

Holt, Michael F. 1999. *The Rise and Fall of the American Whig Party: Jacksonian Politics and the Onset of the Civil War.* New York: Oxford University Press.

Holt, W. Stull. 1933. *Treaties Defeated by the Senate: A Study of the Struggle between President and Senate over the Conduct of Foreign Relations.* Baltimore, MD: Johns Hopkins Press.

Hooley, Richard. 2005. "American Economic Policy in the Philippines, 1902–1940: Exploring a Dark Age in Colonial Statistics." *Journal of Asian Economics* 16, no. 3: 464–488.

Horn, James J. 1973. "Did the United States Plan an Invasion of Mexico in 1927?" *Journal of Interamerican Studies and World Affairs* 15, no. 4: 454–471.

———. 1975. "U. S. Diplomacy and 'the Specter of Bolshevism' in Mexico (1924–1927)." *The Americas* 32, no. 1: 31–45.

Hornblower, Simon, and Charles Stewart. 2005. "No History without Culture." *Anthropological Quarterly* 78, no. 1: 269–277.

Howard, Michael. 2001. "Grand Strategy in the 20th Century." *Defence Studies* 1 (Spring): 1–10.

Howe, Daniel Walker. 2007. *What Hath God Wrought: The Transformation of America, 1815–1848.* New York: Oxford University Press.

Howell, William G., and Jon C. Pevehouse. 2005. "Presidents, Congress, and the Use of Force." *International Organization* 59, no. 1: 209–232.

Howell, William G., and Jon C. Pevehouse. 2007a. "When Congress Stops Wars." *Foreign Affairs* 96, no. 5: 95–107.

———. 2007b. *While Dangers Gather: Congressional Checks on Presidential War Powers.* Princeton, NJ: Princeton University Press.

Hunt, Michael H. 1979. "The Forgotten Occupation: Peking, 1900–1901." *Pacific Historical Review* 48, no. 4: 501–529.

———. 1987. *Ideology and U.S. Foreign Policy.* New Haven, CT: Yale University Press.

———. 1998. "1898: The Onset of America's Troubled Asian Century." *Magazine of History* 12, no. 3: 30–36.

Hurst, James E. 2008. *Pancho Villa and Black Jack Pershing.* Westport, CT: Praeger.

Huth, Paul K. 2000. "Territory: Why Are Territorial Disputes between States a Central Cause of International Conflict?" In *What Do We Know about War?*, ed. John A. Vasquez, 87–94. Lantham, MD: Rowman and Littlefield.

Ikenberry, G. John. 1998/99. "Institutions, Strategic Restraint, and the Persistence of the American Postwar Order." *International Security* 23, no. 3 (Winter): 43–78.

———. 2001. *After Victory: Institutions, Strategic Restraint, and the Rebuilding of Order after Major Wars.* Princeton, NJ: Princeton University Press.

Immergut, Ellen M. 1990. "Institutions, Veto Points, and Policy Results: A Comparative Analysis of Health Care." *Journal of Public Policy* 10, no. 4 (Oct.–Dec.): 391–416.

Inglehard, Ronald. 1988. "The Renaissance of Political Culture." *American Political Science Review* 82, no. 4: 1203–1330.

———. 1990. *Culture Shift in Advanced Industrial Society.* Princeton, NJ: Princeton University Press.

Johnson, Robert David. 1995. *The Peace Progressives and American Foreign Relations.* Cambridge, MA: Harvard University Press.

Johnston, Alastair Iain. 1998. *Cultural Realism: Strategic Culture and Grand Strategy in Chinese History* Princeton, NJ: Princeton University Press.

———. 2003. "Is China a Status Quo Power?" *International Security* 27, no. 4: 5–56.

Jones, David R. 2001. "Party Polarization and Legislative Gridlock." *Political Research Quarterly* 54, no. 1: 125–141.

Jones, Gregg. 2012. *Honor in the Dust: Theodore Roosevelt, War in the Philippines, and the Rise and Fall of America's Imperial Dream.* New York: New American Library.

Kamman, William. 1968. *A Search for Stability: United States Diplomacy toward Nicaragua, 1925–1933.* Notre Dame, IN: University of Notre Dame Press.

Kane, N. Stephen. 1975. "American Businessmen and Foreign Policy: The Recognition of Mexico, 1920-1923." *Political Science Quarterly* 90, no. 2: 293–313.

Katz, Friedrich. 1978. "Pancho Villa and the Attack on Columbus, New Mexico." *American Historian Review* 83, no. 1: 101–130.

Katzenstein, Peter J. 1996. *The Culture of National Security: Norms and Identity in World Politics.* New York: Columbia University Press.

———. 1998. *Cultural Norms and National Security Policy: Police and Military Power in Postwar Japan.* Ithaca, NY: Cornell University Press.

Kaufman, Robert G. 1992. "To Balance or to Bandwagon? Alignment Decisions in 1930s Europe." *Security Studies* 1, no. 3: 417–447.

Kelly, Sean Q. 1993a. "Divided We Govern? A Reassessment." *Polity* 25, no. 3: 475–484.

———. 1993b. "Let's Stick with the Larger Question." *Polity* 25, no. 3: 489–490.

Kennedy, Paul M. 1987. *The Rise and Fall of the Great Powers: Economic Change and Military Conflict from 1500 to 2000.* 1st ed. New York: Random House.

Kilroy, David. 2003. *For Race and Country: The Life and Career of Colonel Charles Young.* Westport, CT: Greenwood Publishing Group.

Kim, Woosang, and James D. Morrow. 1992. "When Do Power Shifts Lead to War?" *American Journal of Political Science* 36, no. 4 (November): 896–922.

Kirshner, Jonathan. 2007. *Appeasing Bankers: Financial Caution on the Road to War.* Princeton, NJ: Princeton University Press.

Knight, Franklin W. 1990. *The Caribbean: The Genesis of a Fragmented Nationalism.* 2nd ed. New York: Oxford University Press.

Kramer, Paul A. 2006. "Race-Making and Colonial Violence in the U.S. Empire: The Philippine-American War as Race War." *Diplomatic History* 30, no. 2: 169–210.

Koppes, Clayton R. 1982. "The Good Neighbor Policy and the Nationalization of Mexican Oil: A Reinterpretation." *Journal of American History* 69, no. 1 (June): 62–81.

Krasner, Stephen D. 1978. *Defending the National Interest: Raw Materials Investments and U.S. Foreign Policy.* Princeton, NJ: Princeton University Press.

Krebs, Ronald R., and Patrick Thaddeus Jackson. 2007. "Twisting Tongues and Twisting Arms: The Power of Political Rhetoric." *European Journal of International Relations* 13, no. 1: 35–66.

Kupchan, Charles. 1994. *The Vulnerability of Empire.* Ithaca, NY: Cornell University Press.

Labs, Eric J. 1997. "Beyond Victory: Offensive Realism and the Expansion of War Aims." *Security Studies* 6, no. 4: 1–49.

LaFeber, Walter. 1963. *The New Empire: An Interpretation of American Expansion, 1860–1898.* Ithaca, NY: Cornell University Press.

———. 1989. *The Panama Canal: The Crisis in Historical Perspective.* Updated ed. New York: Oxford University Press.

———. 1993a. *The American Search for Opportunity, 1865–1913.* Vol. 2 in The Cambridge History of American Foreign Relations. Cambridge: Cambridge University Press.

———. 1993b. *Inevitable Revolutions: The United States in Central America.* 2nd ed. New York: Norton.

Langley, Lester D. 1980. *The United States and the Caribbean, 1900–1970.* Athens: University of Georgia Press.

———. 2002. *The Banana Wars: United States Intervention in the Caribbean, 1898–1934.* Wilmington, DE: Scholarly Resources Books.

Lantis, Jeffrey. 2006. "Strategic Culture: From Clausewitz to Constructivism." In *Comparative Strategic Culture: Assessing Strategic Culture as a Methodological Approach to Understanding WMD Decision-Making by States and Non-State Actors,* ed. Jeffrey A. Larson, 3–31. Fort Belvoir, VA: Defense Threat Reduction Agency, 2006. www.dtic.mil/cgi-bin/GetTRDoc?AD = ADA521640&Location = U2&doc = GetTRDoc.pdf.

Larson, Deborah Welch, and Alexei Shevchenko. 2010. "Status Seekers: Chinese and Russian Responses to U.S. Primacy." *International Security* 34, no. 4: 68–76.

Layman, Geoffrey C., Thomas M. Carsey, and Juliana Menasce Horowitz. 2006. "Party Polarization in American Politics: Characteristics, Causes, and Consequences." *Annual Review of Political Science* 9: 83–110.

Layne, Christopher. 2002/2003. "The 'Poster Child for Offensive Realism': America as a Global Hegemon." *Security Studies* 12, no. 2: 120–164.

Lebow, Richard Ned. 2010. *Why Nations Fight: Past and Future Motives for War.* New York: Cambridge University Press.

Leech, Margaret. 1959. *In the Days of McKinley.* New York: Harper.

Legro, Jeffrey. 1996. "Cultural Preferences and the International Cooperation Two-Step." *American Political Science Review* 90, no. 1: 118–137.

———. 2000. "The Transformation of Policy Ideas." *American Journal of Political Science* 44, no. 3: 419–432.

———. 2005. *Rethinking the World: Great Power Strategies and International Order*. Ithaca, NY: Cornell University Press.

———. 2007. "What China Will Want: The Future Intentions of a Rising Power." *Perspectives on Politics* 5, no. 3: 515–534.

———. 2009. "The Plasticity of Identity under Anarchy." *European Journal of International Relations* 15, no. 1: 37–65.

Levy, Jack S. 1994. "Learning and Foreign Policy: Sweeping a Conceptual Minefield." *International Organization* 48, no. 2 (Spring): 279–312.

Li, Cheng. 2005. "The New Bipartisanship within the Chinese Communist Party." *Orbis* 49, no. 3: 387–400.

———. 2009. "Intra-Party Democracy in China: Should We Take It Seriously?" *China Leadership Monitor* 30 (Fall): 1–14.

Liberman, Peter. 1993. "The Spoils of Conquest," *International Security* 18, no. 2 (Autumn): 125–153.

Lieberman, Robert C. 2002. "Ideas, Institutions, and Political Order." *American Political Science Review* 96, no. 4: 697–712.

Link, Arthur S. 1956. *Wilson: The New Freedom*. Vol. 2. Princeton, NJ: Princeton University Press.

———. 1964. *Wilson: Confusions and Crises, 1915–1916*. Vol. 4. Princeton, NJ: Princeton University Press.

———. (ed.). 1982. *Papers of Woodrow Wilson, May 9–August 7, 1916*, V. 37. Princeton, NJ: Princeton University Press.

Linn, Brian McAllister. 2000. *The Philippine War, 1899–1902*. Lawrence: University Press of Kansas.

Lipset Seymour Martin. 1997. *American Exceptionalism: A Double Edged Sword*. New York: Norton.

Loomis, Albertine. 1976. *For Whom Are the Stars?* Honolulu: University Press of Hawaii.

Loveman, Brian. 2010. *No Higher Law: American Foreign Policy and the Western Hemisphere since 1776*. Chapel Hill: University of North Carolina Press.

Lynn-Jones, Sean M. 1998. "Realism and America's Rise: A Review Essay." *International Security* 23, no. 2: 157–182.

Lyon, Judson M. 1981. "Informal Imperialism: The United States in Liberia, 1897–1912." *Diplomatic History* 5, no. 3: 221–43.

Machado, Manuel A., Jr., and James T. Judge. 1970. "Tempest in a Teapot? the Mexican-United States Intervention Crisis of 1919." *Southwestern Historical Quarterly* 74, no. 1: 1–23.

MacMichael, David C. 1964. "The United States and the Dominican Republic, 1871–1940: A Cycle in Caribbean Diplomacy." PhD diss., University of Oregon.

Maddison, Angus. 1995. *Monitoring the World Economy, 1820–1992*. Paris: OECD Development Centre.

———. 2001. *The World Economy: A Millennial Perspective*. Paris: OECD Development Centre.

Madison, James. 1788. Federalist 47, 48, 49, 50, and 51. http://avalon.law.yale.edu/18th_century/fed47.asp.

Mahoney, James E. 2000. "Path Dependence in Historical Sociology." *Theory and Society* 29, no. 4: 507–548.

Mahoney, James E., and Gary Goertz. 2004. "The Possibility Principle: Choosing Negative Cases in Comparative Research." *American Political Science Review* 98, no. 4 (November): 653–669.

Major, John. 1984. "Who Wrote the Hay-Bunau-Varilla Convention?" *Diplomatic History* 8, no. 2: 115–124.

Manicas, Peter T. 2006. *A Realist Philosophy of Social Science: Explanation and Understanding*. Cambridge: Cambridge University Press.

Mann, Michael. 1984. "The Autonomous Power of the State: Its Origins, Mechanisms and Results." *European Journal of Sociology* 25, no. 2: 185–213.

Mansfield, Edward D., Helen V. Milner, and Jon C. Pevehouse. 2007. "Vetoing Co-Operation: The Impact of Veto Players on Preferential Trading Agreements." *British Journal of Political Science* 37, no. 3: 403–432.

Mansfield, Edward D., Helen V. Milner, and Jon C. Pevehouse. 2008. "Democracy, Veto Players and the Depth of Regional Integration." *World Economy* 31, no. 1: 67–96.

Mansfield, Edward D., and Jack Snyder. 2005. *Electing to Fight: Why Emerging Democracies Go to War*. Cambridge, MA: MIT Press.

Maoz, Zeev, and Bruce Russett. 1993. "Normative and Structural Causes of Democratic Peace, 1946-1986." *American Political Science Review* 87, no. 3: 624–638.

March, James G., and Johan P. Olsen. 1984. "The New Institutionalism: Organizational Factors in Political Life." *American Political Science Review* 78, no. 3: 734–749.

Markey, Daniel. 1999. "Prestige and the Origins of War: Returning to Realism's Roots." *Security Studies* 8, no. 4: 126–173.

May, Ernest R. 1961. *Imperial Democracy: The Emergence of America as a Great Power*. New York: Harcourt, Brace & World.

May, Glenn Anthony. 1991. *Battle for Batangas: A Philippine Province at War*. New Haven, CT: Yale University Press.

———. 1996. "The Unfathomable Other: Historical Studies of U.S.-Philippine Relations." In *Pacific Passage: The Study of American-East Asian Relations on the Eve of the Twenty-First Century*, ed. Warren I. Cohen, 279–312. New York: Columbia University Press.

Mayhew, David R. 1991. *Divided We Govern: Party Control, Lawmaking, and Investigations, 1946-1990*. New Haven, CT: Yale University Press.

———. 1993. "Let's Stick with the Longer List." *Polity* 25, no. 3: 485–488.

McCormick, Thomas J. 1967. *China Market: America's Quest for Informal Empire, 1893–1901*. Chicago: Quadrangle Books.

———. 1990. *China Market: America's Quest for Informal Empire, 1893–1901*. Chicago: Ivan Dee.

McCoy, Donald R. 1967. *Calvin Coolidge: The Quiet President*. New York: Macmillan.

McDonald, Paul K. 2009. "Is Imperial Rule Obsolete? Assessing the Barriers to Overseas Adventurism." *Security Studies* 18, no. 1: 79–114.

McJimsey, George T. 2000. *The Presidency of Franklin Delano Roosevelt*. Lawrence: University Press of Kansas.

McWilliams, Tennant S. 1988. "James H. Blount, the South, and Hawaiian Annexation." *Pacific Historical Review* 57, no. 1: 25–46.

Mearsheimer, John J. 2001. *The Tragedy of Great Power Politics*. New York: W. W. Norton.

———. 2009. "Reckless States and Realism." *International Relations* 23, no. 2: 241–256.

———. 2010. "The Gathering Storm: China's Challenge to US Power in Asia." *Chinese Journal of International Politics* 3, no. 4: 381–396.

———. 2014. "America Unhinged." *The National Interest* (January–February). http:// nationalinterest.org/article/america-unhinged-9639.

Menon, Rajan, and John R. Oneal. 1986. "Explaining Imperialism: The State of the Art as Reflected in Three Theories." *Polity* 19, no. 2: 185–191.

Meyer, Leo J. 1930. "The United States and the Cuban Revolution of 1917." *Hispanic American Historical Review* 10, no. 2: 138–166.

Miller, Karen A. J. 1999. *Populist Nationalism: Republican Insurgency and American Foreign Policy Making, 1918–1925*. Vol. 69. Westport, CT: Greenwood Press.

Minger, Ralph Eldin. 1961. "William H. Taft and the United States Intervention in Cuba in 1906." *Hispanic American Historical Review* 41, no. 1: 75–89.

———. 1975. *William Howard Taft and United States Foreign Policy: The Apprenticeship Years, 1900–1908*. Urbana: University of Illinois Press.

Mintzberg, Henry. 1994. *Rise and Fall of Strategic Planning*. New York: Free Press.

Monten, Jonathan. 2005. "The Roots of the Bush Doctrine." *International Security* 29, no. 4: 112–156.

Montesquieu, Charles de Secondat. 1989. *The Spirit of the Laws*. Cambridge: Cambridge University Press.

Moravcsik, Andrew. 1997. "Taking Preferences Seriously: A Liberal Theory of International Politics." *International Organization* 51, no. 4: 513–553.

Morgan, H. Wayne. 2003. *William McKinley and His America*. Rev ed. Kent, OH: Kent State University Press.

Morgenthau, Hans J. 1950. "The Mainsprings of American Foreign Policy: The National Interest vs. Moral Abstractions." *American Political Science Review* 44, no. 4: 833–854.

Munro, Dana Gardner. 1964. *Intervention and Dollar Diplomacy in the Caribbean, 1900–1921*. Princeton, NJ: Princeton University Press.

———. 1969. "The American Withdrawal from Haiti, 1929–1934." *Hispanic American Historical Review* 49, no. 1: 1–26.

———. 1974. *The United States and the Caribbean Republics, 1921–1933*. Princeton, NJ: Princeton University Press.

Musicant, Ivan. 1990. *The Banana Wars: A History of United States Military Intervention in Latin America from the Spanish-American War to the Invasion of Panama*. New York: Macmillan.

Naeem, Shahid. 1998. "Species Redundancy and Ecosystem Reliability." *Conservation Biology* 12, no. 1: 39–45.

Narizny, Kevin. 2001. "The New Debate: International Relations Theory and American Strategic Adjustment in the 1890s." *Security Studies* 11, no. 1: 151–170.

———. 2003. "Rational Idealism: The Political Economy of Internationalism in the United States and Great Britain, 1870–1945." *Security Studies* 12, no. 3: 1–39.

———. 2007. *The Political Economy of Grand Strategy*. Ithaca, NY: Cornell University Press.

Nathan, Andrew J. 2003. "Authoritarian Resilience." *Journal of Democracy* 14, no. 1: 6–17.

Nau, Henry R. 2002. *At Home Abroad: Identity and Power in American Foreign Policy*. Ithaca, NY: Cornell University Press.

New York Times. 1898a. "Ultimatum to Spain." April 20.

———. 1898b. "The War has Come." April 22.

———. 1898c. "Hawaii in the Senate." June 21.

————. 1898d. "Objections to Hawaii." June 22.

————. 1898e. "Speeches Against Hawaii." June 28.

————. 1898f. "The Hawaiian Question." June 20.

————. 1898g. "Hawaii almost Ours." July 7.

————. 1898h. "Annexation of Hawaii." May 15.

————. 1898i. "House Debates Hawaii." June 12.

Ninkovich, Frank A. 1986. "Theodore Roosevelt: Civilization as Ideology." *Diplomatic History* 10, no. 3: 221–245.

————. 1999. *The Wilsonian Century: U.S. Foreign Policy since 1900*. Chicago: University of Chicago Press.

————. 2001. *The United States and Imperialism* Malden, MA: Blackwell.

Nordholt, Jan Willem Schulte. 1991. *Woodrow Wilson: A Life for World Peace*. Berkeley: University of California Press.

North, Douglass C. 1990. *Institutions, Institutional Change, and Economic Performance*. Cambridge: Cambridge University Press.

North, Robert C. 1977. "Toward a Framework for the Analysis of Scarcity and Conflict." *International Studies Quarterly* 21, no. 4 (December): 569–591.

Nowak, Martin A., Maarten C. Boerlijst, Jonathan Cooke, and John Maynard Smith. 1997. "Evolution of Genetic Redundancy." *Nature* (Letters to Nature) 388 (July 10): 167–171.

Offner, John L. 1992. *An Unwanted War: The Diplomacy of the United States and Spain over Cuba, 1895–1898*. Chapel Hill: University of North Carolina Press.

————. 2004. "McKinley and the Spanish-American War." *Presidential Studies Quarterly* 34, no. 1: 50–61.

Organski, A.F.K. 1968. *World Politics*. 2nd ed. New York: Knopf.

Orren, Karen, and Stephen Skowronek. 1994. "Beyond the Iconography of Order: Notes for a 'New Institutionalism.'" In *The Dynamics of American Politics: Approaches and Interpretations*, eds. Lawrence C. Dodd and Calvin Jillson, 311–330. Boulder, CO: Westview Press.

Osborne, Thomas J. 1981. *"Empire can Wait": American Opposition to Hawaiian Annexation, 1893–1898*. Kent, OH: Kent State University Press.

Ouellet, Eric. 2009. "Multinational Counterinsurgency: The Western Intervention in the Boxer Rebellion 1900-1901." *Small Wars & Insurgencies* 20, no. 3–4: 507–527.

Owen, John M. 1997. *Liberal Peace, Liberal War: American Politics and International Security*. Ithaca, NY: Cornell University Press.

Owens, Mackubin Thomas. 2007. "Strategy and the Strategic Way of Thinking." *Naval War College Review* 60, no. 4: 111–124.

Oyos, Matthew M. 1996. "Theodore Roosevelt and the Implements of War." *Journal of Military History* 60, no. 4: 631–655.

Page, Scott E. 2006. "Path Dependence." *Quarterly Journal of Political Science* 1, no. 1: 87–115.

Peguero, Valentina. 2004. *The Militarization of Culture in the Dominican Republic, from the Captains General to General Trujillo*. Lincoln: University of Nebraska Press.

Pérez, Louis A. Jr. 1973. "The Military and Electoral Politics: The Cuban Election of 1920." *Military Affairs* 37, no. 1: 5-8.

————. 1983. *Cuba between Empires, 1878–1902*. Pittsburgh: University of Pittsburgh Press.

―――. 1986. *Cuba under the Platt Amendment, 1902–1934.* Pittsburgh: University of Pittsburgh Press.

―――. 1989. "The Meaning of the Maine: Causation and the Historiography of the Spanish-American War." *Pacific Historical Review* 58, no. 3: 293–322.

―――. 1997. *Cuba and the United States: Ties of Singular Intimacy.* Athens: University of Georgia Press.

―――. 1998. *The War of 1898: The United States and Cuba in History and Historiography.* Chapel Hill: University of North Carolina Press.

Perkins, Whitney T. 1981. *Constraint of Empire: The United States and Caribbean Interventions.* Westport, CT: Greenwood Press.

Peters, Gerhard, and John T. Woolley. 2009–2014. "Theodore Roosevelt: 'Fourth Annual Message,' December 6, 1904." *The American Presidency Project.* www.presidency .ucsb.edu/ws/?pid=29545.

Pierson, Paul. 2004. *Politics in Time: History, Institutions, and Social Analysis.* Princeton, NJ: Princeton University Press.

―――. 2006. "Public Policy as Institutions." In *Rethinking Political Institutions: The Art of the State,* eds. Ian Shapiro, Stephen Skowronek, and Daniel Galvin, 114–131. New York: New York University Press.

Pike, Fredrick B. 1995. *FDR's Good Neighbor Policy: Sixty Years of Generally Gentle Chaos.* Austin: University of Texas Press.

Pletcher, David M. 1998. *The Diplomacy of Trade and Investment: American Economic Expansion in the Hemisphere, 1865–1900.* Columbia: University of Missouri Press.

Pletcher, David M. 2001. *The Diplomacy of Involvement: American Economic Expansion across the Pacific, 1784–1900.* Columbia: University of Missouri Press.

Posen, Barry R. 1984. *The Sources of Military Doctrine: France, Britain, and Germany between the World Wars.* Ithaca, NY: Cornell University Press.

―――. 2007. "The Case for Restraint." *The American Interest* (November/December). www.the-american-interest.com/article.cfm?piece=331.

Pratt, Julius William. 1950. *America's Colonial Experiment: How the United States Gained, Governed, and in Part Gave Away a Colonial Empire.* New York: Prentice Hall.

―――. 1951. *Expansionists of 1898: The Acquisition of Hawaii and the Spanish Islands.* New York: P. Smith.

―――. 1967. *Challenge and Rejection: The United States and World Leadership, 1900–1921.* New York: Macmillan.

Preble, Christopher A. 2009. *The Power Problem: How American Military Dominance Makes Us Less Safe, Less Prosperous, and Less Free.* Ithaca, NY: Cornell University Press.

Pringle, Henry F. 1939. *The Life and Times of William Howard Taft: A Biography, Volume Two.* New York: Farrar & Rinehart.

Puente, Faustino Guerra. 1906. "Causes of the Cuban Insurrection." *North American Review* 183, no. 599: 538–540.

Purcell, Victor. 1963. *The Boxer Uprising: A Background Study.* Cambridge: Cambridge University Press.

Quirk, Robert E. 1962. *An Affair of Honor: Woodrow Wilson and the Occupation of Vera Cruz.* New York: Norton.

Rathbun, Brian C. 2010. "Is Anybody Not an (International Relations) Liberal?" *Security Studies* 19, no. 1: 2–25.

Remini, Robert V. 2006. *The House: The History of the House of Representatives*. New York: Smithsonian Books/HarperCollins.

Rhodes, Benjamin D. 2001. *United States Foreign Policy in the Interwar Period, 1918–1941: The Golden Age of American Diplomatic and Military Complacency*. Westport, CT: Praeger.

Rhodes, Edward. 1999. "Constructing Power: Cultural Transformation and Strategic Adjustment in the 1890s." In *The Politics of Strategic Adjustment: Ideas, Institutions, and Interests*, eds. Peter Trubowitz, Emily O. Goldman, and Edward Rhodes, 29–78. New York: Columbia University Press.

Ricard, Serge. 2008. "Theodore Roosevelt: Imperialist or Global Strategist in the New Expansionist Age?" *Diplomacy and Statecraft* 19, no. 4: 639–657.

Riker, William H. 1964. *Federalism: Origin, Operation, Maintenance*. Boston: Little, Brown and Company.

Risse-Kappen, Thomas. 1991. "Public Opinion, Domestic Structure, and Foreign Policy in Liberal Democracies." *World Politics* 43, no. 4: 479–512.

Robinson, Ronald, and John Gallagher. 1968. *Africa and the Victorians: The Climax of Imperialism*. Garden City, NY: Anchor Books.

Roosevelt, Theodore. 1894. *The Winning of the West, Volume 3: The Founding of the Trans-Alleghany Commonwealths, 1784–1790*. New York: G. P. Putnam's Sons.

———. 1902. *The Strenuous Life: Essays and Addresses*. New York: The Century Company.

———. 1910. *African and European Addresses*. New York: G. P. Putnam's Sons.

———. 1915a. *Letter from Theodore Roosevelt to W. Cameron Forbes*, 1915-04-06, Theodore Roosevelt Collection, bMS Am 1364 (6), Houghton Library, Harvard University. http://theodorerooseveltcenter.org/Research/Digital-Library/Record .aspx?libID=o283207, Theodore Roosevelt Digital Library, Dickinson State University.

———. 1915b. *Letter from Theodore Roosevelt to W. Cameron Forbes*, 1915-10-25, Theodore Roosevelt Collection, bMS Am 1364 (7), Houghton Library, Harvard University. http://theodorerooseveltcenter.org/Research/Digital-Library/Record .aspx?libID=o283208, Theodore Roosevelt Digital Library, Dickinson State University.

———. 1946. *Letters to Kermit from Theodore Roosevelt*, ed. Will Irwin. New York: Charles Scriber's Sons.

Rosecrance, Richard N., and Arthur A. Stein (eds.). 1993. *The Domestic Bases of Grand Strategy*. Ithaca, NY: Cornell University Press.

Rosenberg, Emily S. 1975. "Economic Pressures in Anglo-American Diplomacy in Mexico, 1917–1918." *Journal of Interamerican Studies and World Affairs* 17, no. 2: 123–152.

———. 1982. *Spreading the American Dream: American Economic and Cultural Expansion, 1890–1945*. New York: Hill and Wang.

———. 1985. "The Invisible Protectorate: The United States, Liberia, and the Evolution of Neocolonialism, 1909–40." *Diplomatic History* 9, no. 3: 191–214.

———. 1999. *Financial Missionaries to the World: The Politics and Culture of Dollar Diplomacy, 1900–1930*. Cambridge, MA: Harvard University Press.

Rosenberg, Emily S., and Norman L. Rosenberg. 1987. "From Colonialism to Professionalism: The Public-Private Dynamic in United States Foreign Financial Advising, 1898–1929." *Journal of American History* 74, no. 1: 59–82.

Rossiter, Clinton (ed.). 1961. *The Federalist Papers*. New York: New American Library.

Roy, Denny. 2009. "China's Democratized Foreign Policy." *Survival* 51, no. 2: 25–40.

Rudalevige, Andrew. 2006. *The New Imperial Presidency: Renewing Presidential Power after Watergate*. Ann Arbor: University of Michigan Press.

Rynning, Sten, and Jens Ringsmose. 2008. "Why Are Revisionist States Revisionist? Reviving Classical Realism as an Approach to Understanding International Change." *International Relations* 45, no. 1: 32–33.

Rystad, Göran. 1975. *Ambiguous Imperialism: American Foreign Policy and Domestic Politics at the Turn of the Century*. Stockholm: Lund.

Salisbury, Richard V. 1986. "Mexico, the United States, and the 1926–1927 Nicaraguan Crisis." *Hispanic American Historical Review* 66, no. 2: 319–339.

Sandos, James A. 1970. "German Involvement in Northern Mexico, 1915–1916: A New Look at the Columbus Raid." *Hispanic American Historical Review* 50, no. 1: 70–88.

———. 1981. "Pancho Villa and American Security: Woodrow Wilson's Mexican Diplomacy Reconsidered." *Journal of Latin American Studies* 13, no. 2 (November): 293–311.

Schirmer, Daniel B. 1972. *Republic or Empire: American Resistance to the Philippine War*. Cambridge, MA: Schenkman Publishing.

Schlesinger, Arthur M. Jr. 1973. *The Imperial Presidency*. Boston: Houghton Mifflin Company.

Schmidt, Hans. 1995. *The United States Occupation of Haiti, 1915–1934*. New Brunswick, NJ: Rutgers University Press.

Schoultz, Lars. 1998. *Beneath the United States: A History of U.S. Policy toward Latin America*. Cambridge, MA: Harvard University Press.

Schoultz, Lars. 2002. "Blessings of Liberty: The United States and the Promotion of Democracy in Cuba." *Journal of Latin American Studies* 34, no. 2: 397–425.

Schultz, Kenneth A. 1998. "Domestic Opposition and Signaling in International Crises." *American Political Science Review* 92, no. 4: 829–844.

Schwartz, Shalom H., Gian Vittorio Caprara, and Michele Vecchione. 2010. "Basic Personal Values, Core Political Values, and Voting: A Longitudinal Analysis." *Political Psychology* 31, no. 3: 421–452.

Schweller, Randall L. 1992. "Domestic Structure and Preventive War: Are Democracies More Pacific?" *World Politics* 44, no. 2: 235–269.

———. 1998. *Deadly Imbalances: Tripolarity and Hitler's Strategy of World Conquest*. New York: Columbia University Press.

———. 1999. "Managing the Rise of Great Powers: History and Theory." In *Engaging China: The Management of an Emerging Power*, eds. Alastair Iain Johnston and Robert S. Ross, 1–31. London: Routledge.

———. 2009. "Neoclassical Realism and State Mobilization: Expansionist Ideology in the Age of Mass Politics." In *Neoclassical Realism, the State, and Foreign Policy*, ed. Steven E. Lobell, Norrin M. Ripsman, and Jeffrey W. Taliaferro, 227–250. Cambridge: Cambridge University Press.

Scott-Smith, Giles. 2008. "Introduction: The Name Looms Large: The Legacies of Theodore Roosevelt." *Diplomacy & Statecraft* 19, no. 4: 635–638.

Sewell Jr., William H. 1992. "A Theory of Structure: Duality, Agency, and Transformation." *American Journal of Sociology* 98, no. 1: 1–29.

Shambaugh, David. 2011. "Coping with a Conflicted China," *Washington Quarterly* 34, no. 1: 7–27.

Shannon, Magdaline W. 1976. "The U. S. Commission for the Study and Review of Conditions in Haiti and Its Relationship to President Hoover's Latin American Policy." *Caribbean Studies* 15, no. 4: 53–71.

———. 1996. *Jean Price-Mars, the Haitian Elite and the American Occupation, 1915–1935.* New York: St. Martin's, 1996.

Shulman, Mark. 1999. "Institutionalizing a Political Idea: Navalism and the Emergence of American Sea Power." In *The Politics of Strategic Adjustment: Ideas, Institutions, and Interests,* eds. Peter Trubowitz, Emily O. Goldman, and Edward Rhodes, 79–101. New York: Columbia University Press.

Sibley, David. 2012. *The Boxer Rebellion and the Great Game in China.* New York: Hill and Wang.

Silverstone, Scott A. 2004. *Divided Union: The Politics of War in the Early American Republic.* Ithaca, NY: Cornell University Press.

Small, Melvin. 1995. *Democracy & Diplomacy: The Impact of Domestic Politics on U.S. Foreign Policy, 1789–1994.* Baltimore, MD: Johns Hopkins University Press.

Smith, Ephraim K. 1985. "'A Question from Which We Could Not Escape:' William McKinley and the Decision to Acquire the Philippine Islands." *Diplomatic History* 9, no. 4: 369–370.

———. 1993. "William McKinley's Enduring Legacy: The Historiographical Debate on the Taking of the Philippine Islands." In *Crucible of Empire: The Spanish-American War and Its Aftermath,* ed. James C. Bradford, 205–249. Annapolis, MD: Naval Institute Press.

Smith, Matthew J. 2009. *Red & Black in Haiti: Radicalism, Conflict, and Political Change, 1934–1957.* Chapel Hill: University of North Carolina Press.

Smith, Robert Freeman. 1972. *The United States and Revolutionary Nationalism in Mexico, 1916–1932.* Chicago: University of Chicago Press.

Snyder, Jack L. 1991. *Myths of Empire: Domestic Politics and International Ambition.* Ithaca, NY: Cornell University Press.

Sobel, Richard. 2001. *The Impact of Public Opinion on U.S. Foreign Policy since Vietnam: Constraining the Colossus.* New York: Oxford University Press.

Starr, Frederick. 1925. "Liberia after the World War." *Journal of Negro History* 10, no. 2: 113–130.

Steele, Brent J. 2007. "Making Words Matter: The Asian Tsunami, Darfur, and 'Reflexive Discourse' in International Politics." *International Studies Quarterly* 51, no. 4: 901–925.

Steinmo, Sven, Kathleen Thelen, and Frank Longstreth (eds.). 1992. *Structuring Politics: Historical Institutionalism in Comparative Analysis.* Cambridge: Cambridge University Press.

Stevens, Sylvester Kirby. 1945. *American Expansion in Hawaii, 1842–1898.* Harrisburg: Archives Publishing Company.

Stillson, Albert C. 1961. "Military Policy without Political Guidance: Theodore Roosevelt's Navy." *Military Affairs* 25, no. 1: 18–31.

Straus, Scott. 2011. "Retreating from the Brink: Theorizing Mass Violence and the Dynamics of Restraint." *Perspectives on Politics* 10, no. 2 (June): 343–362.

Swidler, Ann. 1986. "Culture in Action: Symbols and Strategies." *American Sociological Review* 51 (April): 273–286.

Taliaferro, Jeffrey W. 2000/2001. "Security Seeking under Anarchy: Defensive Realism Revisited." *International Security* 25, no. 3: 128–161.

Tannenwald, Nina. 1999. "The Nuclear Taboo: The United States and the Normative Basis of Nuclear Non-use." *International Organization* 53, no. 3: 433–468.
———. 2007. *The Nuclear Taboo: The United States and the Non-use of Nuclear Weapons Since 1945*. Cambridge: Cambridge University Press.
Tate, Merze. 1965. *The United States and the Hawaiian Kingdom: A Political History*. New Haven, CT: Yale University Press.
———. 1968. *Hawaii: Reciprocity or Annexation*. East Lansing: Michigan State University Press.
Taylor, Wayne Chatfield. 1956. *The Firestone Operations in Liberia*. Washington, DC: National Planning Association.
Tessman, Brock. 2009. "The Evolution of Chinese Foreign Policy: New Incentives with Slowing." *Asian Security* 5, no. 3: 296–318.
Tetlock, Philip E., and Aaron Belkin. 1996. "Counterfactual Thought Experiments in World Politics: Logical, Methodological, and Psychological Perspectives." In *Counterfactual Thought Experiments in World Politics: Logical, Methodological, and Psychological Perspectives*, eds. Philip E. Tetlock and Aaron Belkin, 1–38. Princeton, NJ: Princeton University Press.
Thelen, Kathleen. 1999. "Historical Institutionalism in Comparative Politics." *Annual Review of Political Science* 2: 369–404.
———. 2004. *How Institutions Evolve: The Political Economy of Skills in Germany, Britain, the United States, and Japan*. Cambridge: Cambridge University Press.
Tilchin, William N. 2008. "For the Present and the Future: The Well-Conceived, Successful, and Farsighted Statecraft of President Theodore Roosevelt." *Diplomacy & Statecraft* 19, no. 4: 658–670.
Tompkins, E. Berkeley. 1970. *Anti-Imperialism in the United States: The Great Debate, 1890–1920*. Philadelphia: University of Pennsylvania Press.
Trani, Eugene P., and David L. Wilson. 1977. *The Presidency of Warren G. Harding*. Lawrence: Regents Press of Kansas.
Trask, David F. 1996. *The War with Spain in 1898*. Lincoln: University of Nebraska Press.
Trow, Clifford W. 1971. "Woodrow Wilson and the Mexican Interventionist Movement of 1919." *Journal of American History* 58, no. 1: 46–72.
Trubowitz, Peter. 1998. *Defining the National Interest: Conflict and Change in American Foreign Policy*. Chicago: University of Chicago Press.
Trubowitz, Peter, Emily O. Goldman, and Edward Joseph Rhodes (eds.) 1999. *The Politics of Strategic Adjustment: Ideas, Institutions, and Interests*. New York: Columbia University Press.
Tsebelis, George. 1995. "Decision Making in Political Systems: Veto Players in Presidentialism, Parliamentarianism, Multicameralism, and Multipartyism." *British Journal of Political Science* 25, no. 3: 289–325.
———. 2002. *Veto Players: How Political Institutions Work*. Princeton, NJ: Princeton University Press, 2002.
Tyler, Tom R. 2006. *Why People Obey the Law*. Princeton, NJ: Princeton University Press.
Valeriano, Brandon, and John Van Benthuysen. 2012. "When States Die: Geographic and Territorial Pathways to State Death." *Third World Quarterly* 33, no. 7: 1165–1189.
Van Evera, Stephen. 1997. *Guide to Methods for Students of Political Science*. Ithaca, NY: Cornell University Press.
———. 1999. *Causes of War: Power and the Roots of Conflict*. Ithaca, NY: Cornell University Press.

Vasquez, John A. 2000. "What Do We Know about War?" In *What Do We Know about War?*, ed. John A. Vasquez, 335–370. Lantham, MD: Rowman and Littlefield.

Veeser, Cyrus. 2002. *A World Safe for Capitalism: Dollar Diplomacy and America's Rise to Global Power.* New York: Columbia University Press.

———. 2003. "Inventing Dollar Diplomacy: The Gilded-Age Origins of the Roosevelt Corollary to the Monroe Doctrine." *Diplomatic History* 27, no. 3: 301–326.

Vivian, James F. 1980. "The 'Taking' of the Panama Canal Zone: Myth and Reality." *Diplomatic History* 4, no. 1 (January): 95–100.

Walker, Brian H. 1992. "Biodiversity and Ecological Redundancy." *Conservation Biology* 6, no. 1: 18–23.

Walker, Thomas W. 2003. *Nicaragua: Living in the Shadow of the Eagle.* 4th ed. Boulder, CO: Westview Press.

Walt, Stephen M. 1987. *The Origins of Alliances.* Ithaca, NY: Cornell University Press.

———. 2005. *Taming American Power: The Global Response to U.S. Primacy.* New York: Norton.

Waltz, Kenneth N. 1979. *Theory of International Politics.* Reading, MA: Addison-Wesley Pub. Co.

Weaver, Judith L. 1985. "Edith Bolling Wilson as First Lady: A Study in the Power of Personality, 1919–1920." *Presidential Studies Quarterly* 15, no. 1: 51–76.

Weinberg, Albert K. 1963. *Manifest Destiny: A Study of Nationalist Expansionism in American History.* Chicago: Quadrangle Books.

Welch, Richard E., Jr. 1964. "Senator George Frisbie Hoar and the Defeat of Anti-Imperialism, 1898-1900." *Historian* 26, no. 3 (May): 362–380.

———. 1974. "American Atrocities in the Philippines: The Indictment and the Response." *Pacific Historical Review* 43, no. 2: 233–253.

———. 1979. *Response to Imperialism: The United States and the Philippine-American War, 1899–1902.* Chapel Hill: University of North Carolina Press.

Wellborn, Fred. 1928. "The Influence of the Silver-Republican Senators, 1889–1891." *Mississippi Valley Historical Review* 14, no. 4: 462–480.

Wertheim, Stephen. 2009. "Reluctant Liberator: Theodore Roosevelt's Philosophy of Self-Government and Preparation for Philippine Independence." *Presidential Studies Quarterly* 39, no. 3: 494–518.

Wilkerson, Marcus M. (1932) 1967. *Public Opinion and the Spanish-American War: A Study in War Propaganda.* New York: Russell & Russell.

Williams, William Appleman. 1962. *The Tragedy of American Diplomacy.* Revised and enlarged edition. New York: Dell Publishing.

Wilson, Charles Morrow. 1947. *Liberia.* New York: W. Sloane Associates.

Wilson, Huntington. 1916. "The Relation of Government to Foreign Investment." *Annals of the American Academy of Political and Social Science* 68: 298–311.

Wilson, James Q. 1991. *Bureaucracy: What Government Agencies Do And Why They Do It.* New York: Basic Books.

Wohlfers, Arnold. 1965. *Discord and Collaboration: Essays on International Politics.* Baltimore, MD: Johns Hopkins University Press.

Wohlforth, William C. 2009. "Unipolarity, Status Competition, and Great Power War." *World Politics* 61, no. 1: 28–57.

Wood, Bryce. 1962. *The Making of the Good Neighbor Policy.* New York: Columbia University Press.

Woodworth, Steven E. 2010. *Manifest Destinies: America's Westward Expansion and the Road to the Civil War.* New York: Knopf.

Xiang, Lanxin. 2003. *The Origins of the Boxer War: A Multinational Study.* London: Routledge.

Young, Marilyn Blatt. 1968. *The Rhetoric of Empire: American China Policy, 1895–1901.* Cambridge, MA: Harvard University Press.

Zakaria, Fareed. 1999. *From Wealth to Power: The Unusual Origins of America's World Role.* Princeton, NJ: Princeton University Press.

INDEX